GIRLS' CHRISTIAN NAMES

GIRLS' CHRISTIAN NAMES

THEIR HISTORY, MEANING AND ASSOCIATION

BY

HELENA SWAN

TYNRON PRESS
DUMFRIESSHIRE

First published in 1900

This edition first published in 1989 by
Tynron Press
Dumfriesshire DG3 4LD
Scotland

ISBN 1-871948-07-X

Cover design by K. H. Teo
Printed in Singapore
by Jin Jin Printing Industry Pte Ltd

PUBLISHER'S FOREWORD

The more than 1,000 girls' Christian names featured in this book range from the common to the unusual, the plain to the exotic. The names originate from sources as diverse as the Bible, Church history, Greek mythology and ancient Anglo-Saxon and Teutonic history, among others. The various forms, as well as the meanings and origins of the names are given, together with examples and illustrations from history and literature — for example, the use of 'Abigail' by Beaumont and Fletcher and of 'Adah' by Lord Byron. Sketches of historical characters are also included, such as the story of Grace Darling, the heroine who rescued nine men from a wreck during a violent sea storm. In fact, the entire book itself, compiled at the end of the last century, is a unique historical record.

For all women and girls (and others) who are interested in finding out more about their own names, or about girls' Christian names in general, it is hoped that this little volume will provide many hours of enjoyable reading.

PREFACE

In offering this little volume to the public, I lay no claim to original research. Having myself been struck by the various eccentricities in the development of personal names, it has occurred to me that others too might find some interest in knowing whence and how their names originated. I have, therefore, tried to state the results of my own reading, in a purely popular form, in which all may discover at a glance the salient points about their names: whether they owe their existence to some personal beauty or defect of one who lived long centuries ago, to some quality that especially appealed to our ancestors, or to some passing event. The recently christened Modderina Belmontina Methuena Jones, Baden Harry Herbert Mafeking Francis, or that fifth son of pious parents who was called Acts Apostles, will find little difficulty in tracing the origins of their names; but succeeding generations may well be puzzled by them.

The key to the meaning of some names has been lost; but in the case of most of those now in use some clue to their history, at any rate, remains.

Only such names are treated of here as have a fair chance of being met with in everyday life amongst English-speaking peoples, except in such cases as where, in the growth of a name, some form, once popular, has fallen out of use: it is then given to show how the present form was evolved.

In a few instances, where the names seemed to have a claim to be admitted, yet could not be said to be in general use, they have been inserted in the Index, together with their supposed meanings, but they will not be found in the body of the book.

I have gleaned my information wherever I have been able, limiting myself, however, to really authoritative writers. The chief of these have been Miss Yonge (*History of Christian Names*) and Dr G. Michaelis (*Wörterbuch der gebräuchlichsten Taufnamen*), whilst for legendary and historical illustrations I have drawn freely upon a large number of such works as Dr Alban Butler's *Lives of the Saints*, Dr Wägner's *Asgard and the Gods* and *Epics and Romances of the Middle Ages*, the Rev. S. B. Gould's *Curious Myths of the Middle Ages*, Kennedy's *Legendary Lore of the Irish Celts*, and the Rev. Hilderic Friend's *Flowers and Flower-lore*.

H. S.

INDEX

INDEX

INDEX

INDEX

INDEX

INDEX

INDEX

INDEX

INDEX

GIRLS' CHRISTIAN NAMES

ABIGAIL is a name that has, for some people, become perverted in its meaning: originally Hebrew, signifying "a father's joy", from *abi* = father, and *giyl* = to dance, it has now become almost synonymous with "a lady's-maid". This is, of course, due to the fact that the Abigail of Scripture, the wife, first of Nabal and then of David, constantly applies the epithet "hand-maid" to herself. The Puritans in their religious fervour loved to think that their little one should grow to be "a hand-maid of the Lord", and popular dramatists carried on the idea by giving the name "Abigail" to the "maids" in their plays, as witness Beaumont and Fletcher in *The Scornful Ladie*, and Vanbrugh in *The Relapse; or Virtue in Danger*. Thus "an Abigail" simply now means a lady's maid; and, the beautiful original signification of the word being lost sight of, the name has fallen into disuse.

I saw them all—four sweet-faced girls—grow up to womanhood;
I felt that they were beautiful—I knew that they were good.
The first that left us, Abigail, passed off one summer morn,
When all the air was filled with life, the fields with ripening corn.

She had been failing many months, but hope held to the last;
We could not think our darling gone until the hour was past.
It was the first great chastening blow that fell upon my head,
When Abigail, my first-born child, was numbered with the dead.

The Outcast (J. W. Watson.)

ADA: a contraction of Edith (which see).

ADAH. The Hebrew name Adah (meaning "ornament") occurs in the Old Testament as the name of one of the daughters of Adam and Eve, and the wife of Cain; Lord Byron in his so-called mystery-play of *Cain* introduces Adah in the capacity of Cain's wife.

Cain: The loveliest thing I know is loveliest nearest.
Lucifer: Then there must be delusion—what is that,
Which being nearest to thine eyes is still
More beautiful than beauteous things remote?
Cain: My sister Adah.—All the stars of heaven,
The deep blue noon of night, lit by an orb
Which looks a spirit, or a spirit's world—
The hues of twilight—the Sun's gorgeous coming—
His setting indescribable, which fills
My eyes with pleasant tears as I behold
Him sink, and feel my heart float softly with him
Along the western paradise of clouds—
The forest shade — the green bough — the bird's voice—
The vesper bird's, which seems to sing of love,
And mingles with the song of cherubim,
As the day closes over Eden's walls;—
All these are nothing, to my eyes and heart,
Like Adah's face: I turn from earth and heaven
To gaze on it.

ADELAIDE, Adela, etc.: derivatives of Ethel (which see).

ADOLFINA, Adolfine, or Adolphina, is the feminine of Adolf or Adolphus, which is itself derived from the Teutonic Athaulf, meaning "noble wolf", the original English form of which is Aethelwulf. As a woman's name it is scarcely known, except in Germany, and there the diminutives Fienchen and Dofine are far more usual than Adolfine.

AFRA, or Aphra, signifying "peaceful ruler", is a name hardly ever met with, but known as that of a female novelist, dramatist, and poetess of some repute in the seventeenth century, Mrs. Aphra Behn; and also as that of a Saint Afra, who suffered martyrdom in the Diocletian persecutions.

AGATHA, Agathias, Agathoina, Gytha; Spanish and Italian, Agata; Russian, Agafia; Lettish, Apka. The name of Agatha, which, especially in the North of England, used to be much more frequently met with than it is now, is derived from the Greek ἀγαθός = good, the masculine name being Agathon.

As is so often the case, the popularity of the name has been due more to the misfortunes than to the prosperity of those who have borne it. The Teutonic form is Gytha, which was the name of the mother of our Saxon king, Harold II. The name is still occasionally met with in England.

She who probably contributed most to the repute of the name Agatha, and spread its use throughout Christian lands, was St. Agatha, the Martyr, a Sicilian woman by birth; but whether a native of Palermo or Catana is not known.

Both towns claim the honour of her birth. Catana was the scene of her martyrdom, which took place in the year 251, during the third consulship of Decius.

The daughter of an illustrious and wealthy house, she attracted the attention of Quintianus, Consul of Sicily, and, under cover of Decius' edict against the Christians, Quintianus caused Agatha to be apprehended and brought before him, hoping that in her terror she would throw herself under his protection. Enraged when he found his hopes futile, Quintianus cast her into prison, and subjected her for weeks to trial and bodily torture, which included the rack, accompanied by stripes and the tearing and burning of her sides. Agatha remained firm in virtue and in faith; and, on being finally rolled naked over live coals, died proclaiming her unshaken trust in God.

In the year 500 A.D., Pope Symmachus built a church on the Aurelian Way in Rome and dedicated it to St. Agatha; a second was built in her honour in 726 by Pope Gregory II.; and since then many churches have been dedicated to her. St. Agatha is one of the Patron Saints of Sicily, and also of Malta, where it was claimed for her in 1551 that it was through her intercession that that island was preserved from the Turks.

A second, but less well known, Saint, is Agatha Hildegardes (A.D. 1024), the wife of Count Palatine Paul. Being of a jealous temperament and fancying he had cause of complaint against his wife, he locked her up in the dungeon of his castle for many days; then, feigning remorse for his harshness towards her, invited her one day to walk with him on the Castle keep, and pushed her over the battlements into the moat below. Never doubting but that the fall from such a height must have killed her, he began uttering false cries of despair and summoned his servants to aid him in her rescue. To his amazement the Count found Agatha quite uninjured by her terrible fall, and, seeing that such a marvellous escape could be due only to divine intervention on her behalf, confessed his crime and endeavoured to atone for it by years of penitence.

Though never canonized, Gytha, too, led a life of tribulation, and bore it, as far as we can tell, with a brave and dauntless spirit. She was the daughter of Earl Ulf, the wife of Earl Godwine and the mother of King Harold II., and of Edith the forlorn Queen of Edward the Confessor.

One of her first troubles must have been when her first-born, Sweyn, was outlawed; and not long afterwards, in 1051, when Earl Godwine aroused the anger and suspicion of Edward the Confessor by declining to harry the town of Dover for resisting some unlawful acts of some foreign friends of the king, Godwine had to flee the land, and with him fled his wife Gytha and several of their children. They escaped to Bosham (in Chichester harbour), and thence made good their flight into Flanders.

Within a year Gytha and her husband were back in England again and reinstated in their Earldom of Wessex; but fresh and worse troubles soon came to vex poor Gytha's spirits, for in 1053 "the great Earl Godwine" died, and she was left alone to make benefactions to Winchester and several other churches, for the repose of her husband's soul.

Thirteen years later her son Harold ascended the throne of England, but the next we hear of his mother is in the guise of a petitioner, vainly sueing William the Conqueror for Harold's body. William of Normandy would have no tomb for Harold that might in future years come to be looked upon, by the conquered people, as a martyr's shrine; so Gytha pleaded in vain, though she offered its weight in gold for the body of her slain son.

After the battle of Hastings Gytha made her home in Exeter, where the neighbouring Thegns gathered round her, and where the House of Godwine had influence and possessions. Here, too, probably some of her children and grandchildren lived with her, and she may have enjoyed some peaceful days; but in 1068 William I. laid seige to Exeter, and, though upon the city's submission William made no reprisals, Gytha with her following left the town and made a home on one of the islands in the Bristol Channel, finally making her way to Flanders once more, and ending her days at St. Omer.

Agatha, the niece of Queen Gisela of Hungary, and sister of the Emperor Henry II., became the wife of Eadward Atheling (1057). Upon the advent in England of William the Conqueror, she, unable to endure his presence here, retired with her son, Eadgar Atheling, and her daughters Margaret and Christina to the Scottish court.

William the Conqueror himself had a daughter Agatha, who was betrothed to the unfortunate Earl Edwin, whom, however, she did not marry.

In fiction the name of Agatha has not found much favour ; but Sir Walter Scott introduces an Agatha into his *Count Robert of Paris*, and Southey has one in his *Doctor;* an Agatha, moreover, is the heroine in Weber's opera *Der Freischütz.* There is an Agatha, too, in Massinger's play *The Old Law.* From George Eliot's delicately drawn portrait of the old peasant-woman Agatha we quote a few lines :

Within the prettiest hollow of these hills,
Just as you enter it, upon the slope
Stands a low cottage neighboured cheerily
By running water . . . . .
That cottage on the slope, whose garden gate
Has caught the rose-tree boughs and stands ajar ;
So does the door, to let the sunbeams in ;
For in the slanting sunbeams angels come
And visit Agatha who dwells within,—
Old Agatha, whose cousins Kate and Nell
Are housed by her in Love and Duty's name,
They being feeble, with small withered wits,
And she believing that the higher gift
Was given to be shared.
. . . . Agatha
Sat at her knitting, aged, upright, slim,
And spoke her welcome with mild dignity
She kept the company of kings and queens
And mitred saints who sat below the feet
Of Francis with the ragged frock and wounds
And rank for her meant Duty, various,
Yet equal in its worth, done worthily.

. . . . "I take it much to heart
That other people are worse off than I,—
I ease my soul with praying for them all.
. . . . . Nay, I cannot sing:
My voice is hoarse, and oft I think my prayers
Are foolish, feeble things; for Christ is good
Whether I pray or not,—the Virgin's heart
So kinder far than mine; and then I stop
And feel I can do nought towards helping men,
Till out it comes, like tears that will not hold,
And I must pray again for all the world.
. . . . So I try
All ways that I know of to be cleansed and pure.
. . . . Nay, I have none,—
Never had better clothes than these you see.
Good clothes are pretty, but one sees them best
When others wear them, and I somehow thought
'Twas not worth while, I had so many things
More than my neighbours, I was partly shy
Of wearing better clothes than they, and now
I am so old and custom is so strong
'Twould hurt me sore to put on finery."
. . . .
I stayed among those hills; and oft heard more
Of Agatha. I liked to hear her name,
As that of one half grandame and half saint,
Uttered with reverent playfulness.

AGNES, Agneta, Nessa, Inez, etc. Ageno = chaste is, according to one theory, the origin of the name Agnes; but the generally received opinion is in this case probably the right one: the name is most likely derived from *agnus*, the Latin for lamb. The Greek adjective ἅγνος, meaning sacred or pure, was the origin of the Latin word, and the lamb stands allegorically for the triumph of innocence. The first St. Agnes, to whose memory Constantine the Great built a church only a few years after her death (she is said to have cured Constantine's daughter of a serious illness), is always represented in sacred art with a lamb by her side, emblematic of her purity. Constantine built his church over the spot where the Saint suffered martyrdom, and another church, dedicated to her, was built by Pope Innocent X. over the place of her burial. Her name became popular throughout Christendom wherever the history of her sufferings was known, and one legend after another was added to lend pathos to the story.

St. Agnes, in the Roman Catholic Church, shares with the Virgin Mary and St. Thecla the honour of being the special Patroness of Purity. She was the daughter of noble and wealthy Romans, and suffered martyrdom not long after the beginning of the persecutions under Diocletian: that Emperor's cruel edicts were issued in A.D. 303. Agnes was only thirteen years of age when she met her death. Extremely beautiful and very rich, her hand was sought in marriage by many of the young nobles of Rome, and especially by the son of Sempronius the Roman Governor; but Agnes had the same answer for all her suitors. She was wedded, she said, to Christ, and should never take an earthly spouse. Hoping to terrify her into compliance, some of her suitors denounced her to the Governor as a Christian, thinking that fear of torture might succeed in overcoming her resolve, where their solicitations had failed.

The Judge himself, touched by her youth, and influenced by her position, did all he could by gentle means to induce her to change her mind. Agnes remained firm; she would not marry, nor would she renounce her faith; and, when actually confronted with fire and instruments of torture, she viewed them all without a visible tremor.

Her tormentors then dragged her before their idols, and commanded her to offer incense; but she "could by no means be compelled to move her hand, except to make the sign of the Cross".

Other vile threats were then used against her, but St. Agnes remained firm; until at last one young profligate, Procopius, the son of a Roman Prefect, attempted to insult her, whereupon he was struck blind by a sudden flash of lightning, and fell to the ground; but St. Agnes, who was at the time singing hymns, prayed that his sight might be restored to him, and her prayer was heard, and Procopius returned to his own home a chastened and a better man.

The Governor, exasperated at the failure of all his efforts at persuasion, condemned St. Agnes to be beheaded. She heard her sentence with transports of joy, and according to St. Ambrose "went to the place of execution more cheerfully than others go to their wedding". The spectators wept to see one so young and beautiful "loaded with fetters, and to behold her fearless under the very sword of the executioner".

Her body was buried at some little distance from Rome, near the Nomantan Road. She is said to have appeared to her mother eight days after death, surrounded by a band of angelic virgins, and clothed in a robe of golden cloth studded with precious stones, a garland of pearls and diamonds on her head, and in her arms a snow-white lamb, and to have said, "Weep not for me, dear mother, as for the dead; but rather rejoice with exceeding joy that I reign with Christ in the Kingdom of Heaven".

St. Agnes' Eve—Ah, bitter chill it was!
The owl, for all his feathers, was a-cold;
The hare limp'd trembling through the frozen grass,
And silent was the flock in woolly fold:
Numb were the Beadsman's fingers while he told
His rosary, and while his frosted breath,
Like pious incense from a censer old,
Seem'd taking flight for heaven without a death,
Past the sweet Virgin's picture, while his prayer he
saith.
St. Agnes' Eve (KEATS.)

A thousand or more years later there lived a second saint of the name, known as Saint Agnes of Monte Pulciano. She, like her predecessor, dedicated herself to a religious life at a very early age, and when only nine years old was placed by her parents in a convent of Sackins of the Order of St. Francis. At the age of fifteen she was appointed Abbess to a convent at Orvieto, at that time a new foundation of the Order of St. Dominic. She always slept on the ground, with a stone for a pillow; and for fifteen years imposed upon herself a life of the greatest hardship, until obliged by illness to relax her austerities. Eventually she returned to her native town of Pulciano, her fellow-townsmen having built a nunnery there, which they bestowed upon her; here she remained until her death in 1317, at the age of 43.

Many miracles are attributed to her, one being that, on one occasion when the Convent over which she presided was wholly without food for three days, Agnes prayed that at least five loaves of bread might be sent them that they might not starve, and one of the sisters chancing just then to enter the cell where Agnes prayed, Agnes said to her, "Go into the tower and bring out the bread which Christ has just sent", and when the bread was set upon the table the loaves multiplied so fast that the convent was supplied for many days.

A third Agnes noted in Church History was Agnes de Jésus, who was much favoured by visions.

Agnes, Aggie, and Agneta are the English forms of the name, Nessie is the Manx, Nessa the Scotch, and Nest or Nesta the Welsh; but we have also adopted of late years the Spanish Ines and the Portuguese Inez.

The Agnes best known to us in England, apart from the Saints, is Black Agnes, the Countess of March, who defended Dunbar so vigorously against the English. In Germany and France it has been a Royal name; and in Portugal there is the romantic history of Inez de Castro, the "beauty of Castile", who is said to have been privately married in 1345 to Don Pedro, the son of Alfonso IV. of Portugal.

The King, discovering the marriage, was so indignant that in 1355 he caused Inez to be put to death. Two years afterwards King Alfonso himself died, and Don Pedro succeeded to the crown; and it is said that in 1361 he had the body of Inez exhumed and crowned as Queen of Portugal.

In literature there is Inesella de Cantarilla in *Gil Blas*, by Lesage; Inez of Cadiz in *Childe Harold*, by Lord Byron; Donna Inez, the mother of Don Juan, in Lord Byron's poem of that name; *Inez de Castro, or the Bride of Portugal*, by Ross Neil; Agneia in *The Purple Island*, by Phineas Fletcher; Agnes Wickfield in *David Copperfield*, by Charles Dickens; Inez in *The Dark Lady of Doona*, by W. H. Maxwell; Agnès, in *L'Ecole des Femmes*, by Molière, who pretends to be an unsophisticated ingénue, and who gave rise to the French phrase "elle fait l'Agnès"; Inez in *Calderon the Courtier*, by Lord Lytton; a curious, mystical story by Dante G. Rossetti, called *Saint Agnes of Intercession*, in prose; Anne Brontë's novel, *Agnes Grey*; and some sad verses by Elizabeth Barrett Browning, called *Where's Agnes?*

She wore her hair away
  From her forehead—like a cloud
Which a little wind in May
  Peels off finely: disallowed,
Though bright enough to stay.

For the heavens must have place
  To themselves, to use and shine in,
As her soul would have her face
  To press through upon mine, in
That orb of angel grace.

. . . . . .

Her sweetness strained the sense
  Of common life and duty;
And every day's expense
  Of moving in such beauty
Required, almost, defence.

. . . .

She, my white rose, dropping off
  The high rose-tree branch! and not
That the night-wind blew too rough,
  Or the noon-sun burnt too hot,
But, that being a rose—'twas enough!

Then henceforth, may earth grow trees!
  No more roses!—hard straight lines
To score lies out! none of these
  Fluctuant curves, but firs and pines,
Poplars, cedars, cypresses!

Everyone probably knows Tennyson's *St. Agnes Eve:*

Deep on the convent roof the snows
  Are sparkling to the moon:
My breath to heaven like vapour goes:
  May my soul follow soon!
The shadows of the convent towers
  Slant down the snowy sward,
Still creeping with the creeping hours
  That lead me to my Lord:
Make Thou my spirit pure and clear
  As are the frosty skies,
That in my bosom lies.

Tom Hood's *Fair Ines* is less familiar:

O saw ye not fair Ines,
She's gone into the west,
To dazzle when the sun is down,
And rob the world of rest:
She took our daylight with her,
The smiles that we love best,
With morning blushes on her cheek,
And pearls upon her breast.

O turn again, fair Ines,
Before the fall of night,
For fear the moon should shine alone,
And stars unrivall'd bright;

And blessed will the lover be
That walks beneath their light,
And breathes the love against thy cheek
I dare not even write!

Would I had been, fair Ines,
That gallant cavalier,
Who rode so gaily by thy side,
And whisper'd thee so near!
Were there no bonny dames at home,
Or no true lovers here,
That he should cross the seas to win
The dearest of the dear?

I saw thee, lovely Ines,
Descend along the shore,
With bands of noble gentlemen,
And banners waved before;
And gentle youth and maidens gay,
And snowy plumes they wore;
It would have been a beauteous dream,—
If it had been no more!

Alas, alas, fair Ines,
She went away with song,
With music waiting on her steps.
And shoutings of the throng;
But some were sad and felt no mirth
But only music's wrong,
In sounds that sang "Farewell, Farewell,
To her you've loved so long".

Farewell, Farewell, fair Ines,
That vessel never bore
So fair a lady on its deck,
Nor danced so light before,—
Alas, for pleasure on the sea,
And sorrow on the shore!
The smile that blest one lover's heart
Has broken many more.

In conclusion we will quote from what Thomas Moore pronounced to be "some of the dreariest touches of sadness that ever Byron's pen let fall":

TO INEZ.

Nay, smile not at my sullen brow;
 Alas! I cannot smile again:
Yet Heaven avert that ever thou
 Shouldst weep and haply weep in vain.

And dost thou ask, what secret woe
 I bear, corroding joy and youth?
And wilt thou vainly seek to know
 A pang, ev'n thou must fail to soothe?

It is not love, it is not hate,
 Nor low Ambition's honours lost,
That bids me loathe my present state,
 And fly from all I prized the most.

It is that weariness which springs
 From all I meet, or hear, or see;
To me no pleasure Beauty brings;
 Thine eyes have scarce a charm for me.

It is that settled, ceaseless gloom
 The fabled Hebrew wanderer bore;
That will not look beyond the tomb,
 But cannot hope for rest before.

. . . . . .

Through many a clime 'tis mine to go
 With many a retrospection curst;
And all my solace is to know,
 Whate'er betides, I've known the worst.

What is that worst? Nay, do not ask—
 In pity from the search forbear;
Smile on—nor venture to unmask
 Man's heart, and view the Hell that's there.

AILEEN: see HELEN.

ALBERTA, ALBERTINE. This name means

"noble", "bright", or "glorious". In its original form it is a true English name, and, as Aethelbryht or Ethelbert, was that of the first Christian king of Kent, who for the sake of his wife Bertha welcomed St. Augustine and his fellow-workers to England. Two hundred years later a second Ethelbert reigned as king in England. From this country the name travelled to Germany, where it assumed the contracted forms of Albrecht and Albert, and thence was brought back again to this country by "Albert the Good", the Consort of Queen Victoria. During the present reign the name has again become a national one.

ALEXANDRA, Alexandrina, and Alexia are the feminine forms of the Greek name Alexander, which means strong man, or brave defender and helper, being derived from *alexis* (ἄλεξις) = help or defence, and *andreios* (ἀνδρεῖος) = bold, courageous.

Besides these feminine forms, Alexander has many other derivatives, especially in Scotland, where Alexander has come to be an almost national name: amongst these are found Alick, Alison, M'Alister, Hallack, Alasdair, Adair, Sanderson, Sandy, Sands, Sandys, and Scanderberg. In Russia, too, the name is very popular in both masculine and feminine forms, three Emperors and many Princesses having been bearers of it. Dante Gabriel Rosetti wrote a sonnet to the memory of Alexander II., ending—

He stayed the knout's red-ravening fangs; and first
Of Russian traitors, his own murderers go
White to the tomb. While he,—laid foully low

With limbs red-rent, with festering brain which erst
Willed kingly freedom,—'gainst the deed accurst
  To God bears witness of his people's woe.

March 13th, 1881

His daughter, Marie Alexandrovna, married the Duke of Edinburgh, now the Duke of Saxe Coburg-Gotha; and Lord Tennyson, as Poet Laureat, wrote an ode for the occasion containing the following lines:

The Son of him with whom we strove for power—
  Whose will is lord thro' all his world-domain—
  Who made the serf a man, and burst his chain—
Has given our Prince his own imperial Flower,
  Alexandrovna.

. . . .

So now thy fuller life is in the west,
  Whose hand at home was gracious to thy poor:
  Thy name was blest within the narrow door;
Here also, Marie, shall thy name be blest,
  Marie Alexandrovna!

March 7th, 1874

The popularity of the name in Scotland probably began in the days of the two Scottish Kings of that name; but the great Macedonian conqueror is doubtless the true progenitor of the race: as he led his victorious soldiers from land to land his name spread far and wide, and admiration for his prowess was shown by those he conquered in their naming after him the children born to them.

Amongst the ancient Greeks, Alexandra and Cassandra seem to have been interchangeable names, and Cassandra, the fairest of Priam's daughters, on whom, in exchange for the promise of her love, Apollo conferred the gift of prophecy, was, in several places, worshipped with Apollo under the name of Alexandra.

As Cassandra broke her word to Apollo, he punished her by letting her retain the gift of prophecy, but deprived her of the power of making her hearers believe her; hence her prophecies were laughed to scorn as the ravings of a lunatic: her doleful prophecies passed unregarded, and hence our modern phrase, "Cassandra-like".

Rend, rend thine hair, Cassandra: he will go.
  Yea, rend thy garments, wring thine hands, and cry
  From Troy still towered to the unreddened sky.
See, all but she that bore thee mock thy woe.

D. G. Rossetti.

W. Mackworth Praed has a poem on *Cassandra*.

The *cass* in this name is supposed to be derived from the Sanscrit verb *kash* = to shine, so that it would really mean shining or glorious man, not like Alexander, strong or bold man.

The name Alexander won increase of honour, as the years advanced, in the persons of two pious men, Alexander, Bishop of Jerusalem in the third century, and Alexander, Patriarch of Constantinople in the fourth century; whilst, under the form of Alexis or Alexius, St. Alexius shed honour on it in the fifth century.

The first of these was a fellow-student of Origen's at the great Christian school at Alexandria, when St. Pantenus, and subsequently St. Clement, were teachers there; and, after leaving the school, Alexander was appointed Bishop of some Capadocian city. During the persecutions of Severus [204] he staunchly upheld the faith, and for seven years or more suffered imprisonment. Shortly after his release he was appointed Bishop of Jerusalem, jointly with St. Narcissus, who was growing old and feeble.

Alexander collected together a large and valuable library of manuscripts at Jerusalem, which was still in existence in the days of Eusebius, who mentions it. In about the year A.D. 251 Alexander was seized for the second time by the enemies of the Christian Church, and under the persecutions of Decius died in chains at Cæsarea and was canonized. St. Alexander of Jerusalem was chiefly noted amongst his contemporaries for the gentleness and sweetness of his nature.

The Patriarch of Alexandria was appointed to that see in 313. Though a man of an irreproachable life, he incurred the enmity of Arius, a Deacon in the Church. He was founder of the sect called Arians, and denied the divinity of Christ. Arius's ruling motive in his opposition to the Patriarch is said to have been jealousy; whatever the motive, there seems to be little doubt of the fact, and as Arius could find no vulnerable point in Alexander's life, he was fain to attack him on points of doctrine. The Patriarch, a man of a peaceable disposition, tried all persuasive measures to bring Arius back to the Church's fold; but, finding him obdurate, summoned him before an assembly of his clergy, and finally excommunicated him at a Council held in Alexandria in A.D. 320.

The questions in dispute were at last submitted o the Pope, St. Sylvester, and the Emperor Constantine was also appealed to, and he invited all the Bishops to a gathering at Nice, in Bithynia, offering to pay their expenses himself: 318 Bishops accordingly assembled in that town on June 19th, 325. The results of their debates are embodied in what has since been known as the Nicene Creed. After the Council was dispersed, Alexander returned to Egypt, but died in the following year on February 26th, and was succeeded in the Patriarchate by St. Athanasius.

St. Alexius, or Alexis, was a man of very different calibre from the others, but Butler, in his *Lives of the Saints*, says he "may be taken as a model of generous contempt of the world". The son of a Roman senator, he was reared in the midst of pomp and luxury; but his parents were pious people, and he early learnt from them the luxury and pleasure of doing good. Whilst still young, he entertained thoughts of renouncing the world and its vanities, but in compliance with the wishes of his parents married a wealthy Roman lady. Almost immediately after the wedding ceremony, however, on the self-same day, he deserted her—a proceeding which according to our modern ideas was of doubtful virtue; and travelling into a distant part of the country remained concealed there until his place of retreat was discovered. He then disguised himself, and, returning to his father's house, served there as a menial, unrecognised, until, shortly before his death, he revealed his identity by letter.

Thus those who are attracted by the qualities of gentleness, piety, and humility have named their children after one or other of these three

Saints, whilst those who more admire a martial spirit and a soldier's genius have tried to call down these gifts on their little ones by naming them after Alexander the Great.

Warrior of God, whose strong right arm debased
The throne of Persia, when her Satrap bled
At Issus by the Syrian gates, or fled
Beyond the Memmian naptha-pits, disgraced
For ever.

Alexander (TENNYSON.)

In England, in spite of the name being one of those borne by the Queen, who was christened Victoria Alexandrina, and by our much-loved Princess of Wales, the name has never in its feminine form become really a popular one: perhaps it is too high-sounding to attract people in the humbler walks of life.

Sea-king's daughter from over the sea,
Alexandra!
Saxon and Norman and Dane are we,
But all of us Danes in our welcome of thee,
Alexandra!
Welcome her, thunders of fort and of fleet!
Welcome her, thundering cheers of the street!
Welcome her, all things youthful and sweet,
Scatter the blossom under her feet!
Break, happy land, into earlier flowers!
Make music, O bird, in the new-budded bowers!
Blazon your mottoes of blessing and prayer!
Welcome her, welcome her, all that is ours!

. . . .

The sea-kings' daughter as happy as fair,
Blissful bride of a blissful heir,
Bride of the heir of the kings of the sea—
O joy to the people and joy to the throne,
Come to us, love us and make us your own:

ALEXANDRA

For Saxon or Dane or Norman we,
Teuton or Celt, or whatever we be,
We are each all Dane in our welcome of thee,
Alexandra!

A Welcome to Alexandra, March 7, 1863.
(TENNYSON.)

The name *Alexandrine* has been given to the 12-syllable metre since a French poem on the life of Alexander was written in it; and an umbelliferous plant which is found upon rocks by the sea-shore, and which flowers during May and June is called *Alexander* after the place whence it is supposed to have been introduced. One of William Drummond of Hawthornden's sonnets is addressed to Sir William Alexander, whom he called Alexis. But we will close this chapter by quoting a few verses of J. Greenleaf Whittier's poem on Cassandra Southwick, the young New-England Quakeress condemned, on account of her faith, to be transported and sold as a slave.

To the God of all sure mercies let my blessing rise to-day,
From the scoffer and the cruel He hath plucked the spoil away,—
Yea, He who cooled the furnace around the faithful three,
And tamed the Chaldean lions, hath set His handmaid free!

Last night I saw the sunset melt through my prison bars,
Last night across my damp earth-floor fell the pale gleam of stars;
In the coldness and the darkness all through the long night-time,
My grated casement whitened with Autumn's early rime.

. . . .

O, the weakness of the flesh was there—the shrinking and the shame;
And the low voice of the Tempter like whispers to me came:
"Why sit'st thou thus forlornly"? the wicked murmur said,
"Damp walls thy bower of beauty, cold earth thy maiden bed?

"Where be the smiling faces, and voices soft and sweet,
Seen in thy father's dwelling, heard in the pleasant street?
Where be the youths whose glances, the summer Sabbath through,
Turned tenderly and timidly unto thy father's pew?

"Why sit'st thou here, Cassandra?—Bethink thee with what mirth
Thy happy schoolmates gather around the warm bright hearth;
How the crimson shadows tremble on foreheads white and fair,
On eyes of merry girlhood, half hid in golden hair.

. . . .

"And what a fate awaits thee!—a sadly toiling slave,
Dragging the slowly lengthening chain of bondage to the grave!
Think of thy woman's nature, subdued in hopeless thrall,
The easy prey of any, the scoff and scorn of all"!

. . . . .

I thought of Paul and Silas, within Philippi's cell,
And how from Peter's sleeping limbs the prison-shackles fell,
Till I seemed to hear the trailing of an angel's robe of white,
And to feel a blessed presence invisible to sight.

. . . . .

At length the heavy bolts fell back, my door was open cast,
And slowly at the Sheriff's side, up the long street I passed;
I heard the murmur round me, and felt, but dared not see,
How, from every door and window, the people gazed on me.

And doubt and fear fell on me, shame burned upon my cheek,
Swam earth and sky around me, my trembling limbs grew weak:
"O Lord! support thy handmaid; and from her soul cast out
The fear of man, which brings a snare,—and weakness and the doubt".

. . . . .

We paused at length, where at my feet the sunlit waters broke
On glaring reach of shining beach, and shingly wall of rock;
The merchant-ships lay idly there, in hard clear lines on high,
Tracing with rope and slender spar their network on the sky.

And there were ancient citizens, cloak-wrapped and grave and cold
And grim and stout sea-captains with faces bronzed and old,
And on his horse, with Rawson, his cruel clerk at hand,
Sat dark and haughty Endicott, the ruler of the land.

. . . . .

Dark lowered the brows of Endicott, and with a deeper red
O'er Rawson's wine-empurpled cheek the flush of anger spread;
"Good people", quoth the white-lipped priest, "heed not her words so wild,
Her Master speaks within her,—the Devil owns his child"!

. . . . . .

Then to the stout sea-captains the Sheriff, turning, said,—
"Which of ye, worthy seamen, will take this Quaker maid?
In the Isle of fair Barbadoes, or on Virginia's shore,
You may hold her at a higher price than Indian girl or Moor".

Grim and silent stood the captains; and when again he cried,
"Speak out, my worthy seamen"!—no voice, no sign replied;
But I felt a hard hand press my own, and kind words met my ear,—
"God bless thee, and preserve thee, my gentle girl and dear"!

. . . . .

"Pile my ship with bars of silver,—pack with coins of Spanish gold,
From keel-piece up to deck plank, the roomage of her hold,
By the living God who made me!—I would sooner in your bay
Sink ship and crew and cargo, than bear this child away"!

. . . . . .

Loud was the cheer which, full and clear, swept round the silent bay,
As, with kind words and kinder looks, he bade me go my way;
For He who turns the courses of the streamlet of the glen,
And the river of great waters, had turned the hearts of men.

ALICE, Alix: a derivative of Ethel (which see).

ALISON: see Louisa.

ALMA is to be classed amongst the Christian names derived from place-names; it first came into vogue with us after the Battle of Alma, where the French and English achieved their first victory over the Russians in the Crimean War. The name Alma, however, existed before amongst the Kelts, and meant "all good"; and there is an ancient Jewish word *almah*, which signifies "maiden".

ALMIRA, ALMERIA, ALMEIRA means a woman of Almeira, in Andalusia, Spain. Vanbrugh in *A Very Woman* introduces the name, and Congreve's heroine in *The Mourning Bride* is Almeria.

ALTHEA, ALETHIA. It must not be supposed that the names Alethea and Althea are one and the same. The first, Alethea, is derived from the Greek *aletheia* (ἀλήθεια) = truth, and was the Greek name for the symbol of truth, a sapphire ornament worn by the Egyptian high-priest, and referred to by more than one Greek writer.

Althea, on the other hand, is the name of a marsh-mallow, ἀλθαία, noted for its healing properties, and the word is used in Homer's *Iliad* as a proper name. It is derived from ἀλθαίνω = I heal.

> But when wrath darkened Meleazer's life,
> Wrath, which in hearts of even the wise is rife,
> He angry with Althaea, who him bare,
> Lay housed with Cleopatra, his dear wife,
> Child of Evenus' child, Marpessa fair,
> And Idas, flower of knights that on the earth then were.
>
> *Iliad* of HOMER, Book IX.

Lovelace's celebrated lines were addressed *To Althea from Prison*:—

When love with unconfined wings
  Hovers within my gates,
And my divine Althea brings
  To whisper at my grates;
When I lye tangled in her haire,
  And fetter'd with her eye,
The birds that wanton in the aire,
  Know no such libertye.

Wycherley has chosen Alithea as the name of one of his characters in his play *The Country Wife*.

AMABEL: see Amy.

AMARANTHA signifies "unfading flower".

Amarantha sweet and faire,
  Ah brade no more that shining haire!
    As my curious hand or eye,
Hovering round thee, let it flye.
(Lovelace.)

AMARYLLIS means "refreshing stream"; and is the name of a rustic beauty in Virgil's *Eclogues*; in Theocritus's *Idylls*; in Spenser's *Colin Clout's Come Home Again*; in Milton's *Arcades*; in Dryden's poems, and in some of Wither's poems.

AMELIA: a derivative of Emily (which see).

AMINTA, Amynta. This name is perhaps derived from the Greek ἀμύνω (amūno) I protect; but it is possibly a variant of Amanda (see Amy). It was much favoured in the past by English pastoral poets and dramatists of the classical period. It occurs in *Æsop* by Vanbrugh; in some lines by Drummond of Hawthornden; and *Amynta* is also the title of an old pastoral song by Sir Gilbert Elliott, and by Sir Charles Sedley :—

Fair Amynta, art thou mad,
To let the world in me
Envy joys I never had,
And censure them in thee?

AMY, Amabel, Amanda, etc. Of all the names derived direct from the Latin or Romance tongues, perhaps none are prettier than those having their root in the verb *amare* = "to love". Amongst the masculine names we find Amadeus, Amand, Amabilis, Amadeo, and in England pretty and old-fashioned Amyot and Amyas, whilst Amy, Amice, Amabel and Amabella are still in use for women, though Amanta, Amicia, Amoret and Amata have become obsolete. During what is called the Classical period of English literature, namely the eighteenth century, poets were very fond of addressing their verses to Amandas and Amorets, as for example Congreve in his little lyric beginning :

Fair Amoret is gone astray,
Pursue and seek her, every lover;
I'll tell the signs by which you may
The wandering shepherdess discover.

and James Thomson :

Unless with my Amanda blest,
In vain I twine the woodbine bower;
Unless I deck her sweeter breast,
In vain I rear the breathing flower.

Awakened by the genial year,
In vain the birds around me sing,
In vain the freshening fields appear,
Without my love there is no spring.

Vanbrugh introduces Amanda into his play *The Relapse*, and an Amanda inspired much of James Thomson's verse.

Saint Amatus or Amandus or Amé was a hermit of the seventh century to whom St. Peter is said to have appeared whilst he was shut up in a cell on the ramparts of Bourges waiting for a "call". St. Peter said to him, "God desires you to go to the Gauls, and has promised you a great harvest of souls". So great were St. Amand's merits that it was reported that the blind would be restored to sight if they only bathed their eyes in the same water in which he had washed his hands; and several other miracles are reported of him. Saint Amata or Aimée of St. Angelo was the wife of one Compagnone, a wealthy but childless pair, who so besought Saint Nicholas for a son that in due time a child was born to them. Of Saint Amable, or Amabilis, of Riom, it is recorded that he hung a cloak on a sunbeam. These three are the only Saints bearing any of these names in old Church history. St. Amatus or Amandus became Bishop of Sion and the Patron Saint of Savoy, where his name under the form of Amé was at one time common.

In more modern days, the tragic history of the Earl of Leicester's first wife has been familiarized to us by Sir Walter Scott in his novel *Kenilworth*, so that "Amy Robsart" has become a household name. There is an old ballad in Evans's *Ancient Ballads* relating to the story, and Scott himself has written one as a kind of introduction to his novel:

"Leicester," she cried, "is this thy love
That thou so oft has shown to me,
To leave me in this lonely grove,
Immured in shameful privity?
. . . . . .

If that my beauty is but small,
Among court ladies all despised,
Why didst thou rend it from that hall,
Where, scornful Earl, it was well prized?

And when you first to me made suit,
How fair I was you oft would say!
And, proud of conquest, pluck'd the fruit,
Then left the blossom to decay.

Yes, now neglected and despised,
The rose is pale, the lily's dead;
But he that once their charms so prized,
Is sure the cause those charms are fled.

Then, Earl, why didst thou leave the beds
Where roses and where lilies vie,
To seek a primrose, whose pale shades
Must sicken when those gauds are by?
. . . . . .

My spirits flag—my hopes decay—
Still that dread death-bell smites my ear;
And many a boding seems to say,
'Countess, prepare, thy end is near!'"
. . . . . .

And ere the dawn of day appear'd,
In Cumnor Hall, so lone and drear,
Full many a piercing scream was heard,
And many a cry of mortal fear.

The death-bell thrice was heard to ring,
An aerial voice was heard to call,
And thrice the raven flapp'd his wing
Around the towers of Cumnor Hall.

There is a *chanson de geste*, of Oriental origin, called *Amis and Amiles*, the English version of which is entitled *Amis and Amiloun*. Herrick indited a charming poem

To Mrs Amy Potter.

Ah me! I love; give him your hand to kiss
Who both your wooer and your poet is.
Nature hath precompos'd us both to love:
Your part's to grant; my scene must be to move.

Dear, can you like, and liking, love your poet?
If you say "Aye," blush-guiltiness will show it.
Mine eyes must woo you, though I sigh the while:

True love is tongueless as a crocodile.
And you may find in love these differing parts—
Wooers have tongues of ice, but burning hearts.

John Greenleaf Whittier has a pretty ballad called *Amy Wentworth*, of which the two first verses are:

Her fingers shame the ivory keys,
They dance so light along,
The bloom upon her parted lips
Is sweeter than the song.

O perfumed suitor, spare thy smiles!
Her thoughts are not of thee;
She better loves the salted wind,
The voices of the sea.

We conclude with Elizabeth Barrett Browning's poem entitled:

Amy's Cruelty.

Fair Amy of the terraced house,
Assist me to discover
Why you who would not hurt a mouse
Can torture so your lover.

AMY

You give your coffee to the cat,
  You stroke the dog for coming,
And all your face grows kinder at
  The little brown bee's humming.

But when *he* haunts your door . . . the town
  Marks coming and marks going . . .
You seem to have stitched your eyelids down
  To that long piece of sewing!

You never give a look, not you,
  Nor drop him a "Good morning",
To keep his long day warm and blue,
  So fretted by your scorning.

She shook her head—"The mouse and bee
  For crumb or flower will linger:
The dog is happy at my knee,
  The cat purrs at my finger.

"But *he* . . . to *him*, the least thing given
  Means great things at a distance;
He wants my world, my sun, my heaven,
  Soul, body, whole existence.

"They say love gives as well as takes;
  But I'm a simple maiden,—
My mother's first smile when she wakes
  I still have smiled and prayed in.

"I only know my mother's love
  Which gives all and asks nothing;
And this new loving sets the groove
  Too much the way of loathing.

"Unless he gives me all in change,
  I forfeit all things by him:
The risk is terrible and strange—
  I tremble, doubt . . . deny him.

"He's sweetest friend or hardest foe,
  Best angel or worst devil;
I either hate or . . . love him so,
  I can't be merely civil!

"You trust a woman who puts forth
Her blossoms thick as summer's?
You think she dreams what love is worth,
Who casts it to new-comers?

"Such love's a cowslip-ball to fling,
A moment's pretty pastime;
I give . . . all me, if anything,
The first time and the last time.

"Dear neighbour of the trellised house,
A man should murmur never,
Though treated worse than dog or mouse,
Till doated on for ever"!

ANASTASIA and ANSTACE are the British feminines of Anastasius, which has contracted into the surnames of Anstey and Stacey. The meaning is "rising again", a "resurrection", and the name is often given to babies who happen to be born at Easter.

In these Islands the feminine forms of the name always found more favour than the masculine, and in Ireland it is especially popular, where it has the pet diminutive "Anty".

Two virgin martyrs have added dignity to the name, and there have been four St. Anastasiuses. The anniversary of no less than three of these is celebrated on April 21st, whilst the fourth falls on April 27th.

ANGELICA, ANGELA, ANGELOT, and ANGELINA are from the Greek, and mean "Messenger from God".

Turn, Angelina, ever dear!
My charmer, turn to see
Thy own, thy long-lost Edwin here,
Restor'd to love and thee.

The Hermit (GOLDSMITH.)

Examples of this name occur frequently in mediæval history, and occasionally even as far back as the Byzantine Empire. In Italy it has been more popular than in any other European country, though in England and Ireland it was at one time in high favour, and was patronised by poets and dramatists of the seventeenth and eighteenth centuries. George Farquhar introduced the name into two of his plays—*The Constant Couple; or, a Trip to the Jubilee*, and *Sir Harry Wildair*; and Richard Congreve so christened his heroine in *Love for Love*. In *Parismus, the Renowned Prince of Bohemia*, by Edward Ford (1598), Angelica is the name of the Princess, the "Lady of the Golden Tower", beloved by the hero; and Angelica is the heroine of Ariosto's *Orlando Furioso*, whilst we all know Oliver Goldsmith's *Edwin and Angelina*, Longfellow's Angelica in *The Spanish Student*, and Thackeray's Angelica in *The Rose and the Ring*.

The brightest living example in England was Angelica Kaufmann, the lady artist, who achieved the unique distinction of being elected a member of the Royal Academy, and who, though not of English birth, passed the best years of her life here; and was the subject of Miss Thackeray's story, *Miss Angel*. Living in our midst, too, is an Angela, who, by her munificence to suffering humanity, may well have appeared at times to those whom she has relieved as a veritable "messenger from God"—we mean the Baroness Burdett Coutts.

ANN(E), Annette, Nancy, Hannah,

ANNABEL, etc. The Hebrew word *chaanach*, meaning "favour", "mercy", or "grace", is the root of the name Hannah = favour, mercy, or grace, whence Hanan = merciful, Hannethon = free-gift, Hananiah or Ananias = grace of Jehovah, Anne, Anna, Ann, Annie = gracious, with the diminutives Annette, Nancy, Nannie, Nan, and Nina. Another variant of the name is Anaïs. The same name was current amongst the Phœnicians, but we seem to have taken ours from the Greeks and Romans. Dido had a sister Anna, who was no doubt really Hannah, but, according to Miss Yonge, she got, in the popular mind, mixed up with Anna Perena, who was the deity of the revolving years (*annus* = year). Annabella or Annabel, which so many think means simply beautiful Anne, has probably a quite different derivation: the name occurs too early for it to have come from Anne, and may either be a descendant of Ainè = joy, or of the Teutonic Arnhilda, but as Hannibal and Hannyball are still common boys' names in Cornwall, Annabel may possibly come from them, or, it may be, as Miss Yonge suggests, the old Scottish name of Annaple. The Greeks changed Hannah into Anna, just as they changed Hananiah into Ananias, and England is almost the only place in Europe where the Hebrew Hannah is still in use; even in England it is nothing like so common as it used to be, and is daily losing ground.

Hannah, the wife of Elkanah, the mother of Samuel, she whom her husband "loved", and who tried to console her for the absence of children, asking if he were not "better than ten sons" to her, is the first Hannah that we know of; and the beautiful old Bible story, telling of Hannah's outburst of gratitude and joy, when a child is given her, have made her name beloved throughout the Christian world.

According to the apocryphal gospels, Anna was the name of the Virgin Mary's mother; and, though it is not known whence the tradition arose, the Roman Catholic Church has canonized her as a Saint, and appointed the 26th of July as her festival. St. Jerome says that Joachim and Anna, though married for twenty years, were still childless, and that Anna in her distress journeyed to the temple of Jerusalem, and there offered up a vow, that, should a child be granted to her in answer to her prayers, she would dedicate it to the service of God. "God heard her prayer, and granted her a daughter". In 550 the Emperor Justinian I. built a church at Constantinople which he dedicated to Saint Anna, and a second was built in her honour in 705 by Justinian II., and Saint Anne is the patron Saint of Prague in Bohemia.

An Order of St. Anne was instituted in 1738, in Schleswig-Holstein, by Charles VI. of Russia, which was in 1762 transferred to Russia by Peter III.

The chamomile plant is dedicated to Saint Anne. The botanical name for the Common or Dog Chamomile is Matricaria, and the flower seems to have been dedicated to Saint Anne from an imagined derivation of this word from *mater* and *cara*—beloved mother.

In the gospel of St. Luke we read that "there

was one Anna, a prophetess, the daughter of Phanuel, of the tribe of Aser"; and ever since those dim far-away days, down to the present, the name of Hannah, Anna, or Anne has steadily held its ground as one of the best beloved of Christian names.

Though really a woman's name, it was adopted by the men even of the house of De Montmorency, the Premier Baron of Christendom; the great Constable of France was Anne de Montmorency, the name having been first introduced into that family by Anne of Bretagne, who gave it to her godson.

In the seventh century we, too, had an instance of the name being borne by a man in the person of Anna, King of the East Angles, who was slain in battle, fighting against Pendia, King of Mercia, somewhere about A.D. 645.

Thus it may be seen that from the first Anne was adopted as a Royal name. In England and France there have been many Queens Anne. The first in this country was Anne of Bohemia, who as wife to our Richard II. won for herself the title of "Good Queen Anne". She was a daughter of the Emperor Charles IV., and sister to Wenceslaus, Emperor of Germany. She died long before her unfortunate husband lost his crown, having been his first wife, for the King was only sixteen years of age at the time of his first marriage.

Our second Anne was the Queen of Richard III., that Anne Neville, daughter of Warwick "the King-Maker" and widow of Edward, Prince of Wales, of whose murder Richard III.

was suspected, and whose weak character Shakespeare has drawn for us. She is said to have been poisoned by Richard in order to make way for Elizabeth of York, whom Richard was anxious to wed:

Gloucester. "I never su'd to friend, nor enemy;
My tongue could never learn sweet soothing word,
But now thy beauty is propos'd my fee,
My proud heart sues, and prompts my tongue to speak.
Teach not thy lip such scorn; for it was made
For kissing, lady, not for such contempt.
If thy revengeful heart cannot forgive,
Lo! here I lend thee this sharp-pointed sword;
Which if thou please to hide in this true breast,
And let the soul forth that adoreth thee,
I lay it naked to the deadly stroke,
And humbly beg the death upon my knee,
Nay, do not pause; for I did kill King Henry;—
But 'twas thy beauty that provoked me.
Nay; now despatch; 'twas I that stabb'd young Edward;—
But 'twas thy heavenly face that set me on.
Take up the sword again, or take up me".

. . .

"Was ever woman in this humour woo'd?
Was ever woman in this humour won?
I'll have her—but I will not keep her long".

King Richard III. (SHAKESPEARE.)

Next in order came Anne Boleyn, who lived to rue the day whereon her beauty caught the eye of Henry VIII., and she forgot her duty to poor Queen Katharine.

Anne of Cleves followed next— the sister of William, Duke of Cleves, with whose portrait by Holbein Henry VIII. fell in love, only to be disenchanted the moment he beheld the original.

Poor Anne proved to be dull and apathetic, and not at all beautiful after all; so in a few months Henry had divorced her, and her brief reign was over.

James I. of Scotland and VI. of England married Anne of Denmark, and her son, afterwards James II., married Ann Hyde, daughter of the Earl of Clarendon. She died before her husband succeeded to the throne; but both her daughters were crowned Queens of England, Mary reigning in conjunction with her husband William III., and Anne, who in spite of her crown and the fact of her reign having been one of the most glorious in English history, presents rather a pathetic figure: for splendid victories, under Marlborough abroad, and a brilliant literature at home, could not reconcile Anne's kindly and yielding disposition to political strife at home, nor make the imperious and jealous temper of her friend, Sarah, Duchess of Marlborough, less harassing—still less could they console her for the loss in early youth of all her seventeen children. She is said to have had the power of curing the "King's Evil" by touch, and Dr. Johnson as an infant was touched by her.

The French Royal Annes have been many from Anne of Russia (1051), the Queen of Henri I., Anne Beaujeu (1462), Regent of France during the minority of Charles VIII. (introduced by Sir Walter Scott in his novel *Quentin Durward*), and Anne de Bretagne (1476) the daughter of Francis II., and wife, first of Maximilian of Austria, then of Charles of France, and finally of Louis XII., to Anne of Austria, the eldest daughter of Philip III. of Spain and Queen of Louis XIII. of France. She acted as Regent during the long minority of Louis XIV., having the three great cardinals, Mazarin, de Retz, and Richelieu as her chief ministers. Upon her son assuming the reins of Government, Anne retired into private life.

Russia has had an Empress of the name, who succeeded to the throne in 1730, and there was a Princess Anna Commena, who was of a literary turn, for she wrote a Greek history relating to her father Alexis, Emperor of the East, which is, however, of no great merit.

The name of Marianne is probably a combination of the names of the Virgin Mary and of her mother Saint Anne.

Turning our thoughts towards those who have moved in a less exalted social sphere, we find that this name is well represented there also—Anne Hathaway, (Shakespeare's love) and the names of Hannah More, Ann Brontë, Anne Isabella Thackeray, Anna Buckland, Annie Thomas, Anaïs Ségalas (the French poetess) occur to us at once.

In literature, too, the name is represented in every branch, and especially so in ballad and lyrical poetry; even in the borderland between history and romance there is Anne, sister to King Arthur, daughter of Uther and Ygerna, and wife of Lot, King of Norway. Amongst our old nursery-tales, too, who does not know "Sister Anne", the sister of Fatima, Bluebeard's seventh and last wife, that "Sister Anne" who ascends to the tower to watch for and announce the deliverers of the trembling victim below?

We have in DRAMA: Annette in *The Polish Jew* . . . by J. E. Ware; Anne Boleyn in *Henry VIII.* by Wm. Shakespeare; and "Sweet Anne Page" in *The Merry Wives of Windsor*, by Wm. Shakespeare; Annabel in *The Little French Lawyer*, by Beaumont and Fletcher. In FICTION: Hannah in *Redgauntlet*, by Sir Walter Scott; Annie Winnie in *The Bride of Lammermoor*, by Sir Walter Scott; *Anne of Geierstein*, by Sir Walter Scott; *Anne Hereford*, by Mrs. Henry Wood; Hannah in *Nature and Art*, by Mrs. Inchbald; Annaple Bailzon in *The Heart of Midlothian*, and Annaple in *The Black Dwarf*, both by Sir Walter Scott. In OPERA: Anna in *Don Giovanni* by Johann W. von Mozart. In POETRY: *Fair Annie*, an old ballad, of which there are also versions in Old-French, Swedish, Danish, Dutch and German; *Fair Annie of Lochroyan.*

"O it's Annie of Lochroyan,
    Your love, come o'er the sea,
Bearing your young son in her arms;
    So open the door to me".

. . . .

Lord Gregory started out o' his sleep,
    And to his mother did say,
"O I hae dreamt a dream, mother,
    That mak's my heart right wae.

I dreamt that Annie of Lochroyan,
    The flower o' a' her kin,
E'en now was standing at my door,
    But none would let her in".

. . . .

O quickly, quickly raise he up,
And fast ran to the strand;
And there he saw her, fair Annie,
A-sailing frae the land.

. . . .

And "hey, Annie!" and "how, Annie!"
"O Annie, speak to me!"
But aye the louder that he cried "Annie"
The louder rair'd the sea.

High blew the blast, the waves ran fast,
The boat was overthrown,
And soon he saw his fair Annie
Come floating in the foam.

Burns has a poem entitled *Bonnie Ann*:

Youth, grace, and love, attendant move
And pleasure leads the van;
In a' their charms, and conquering arms,
They wait on bonnie Ann.
The captive bands may chain the hands,
But love enslaves the man:
Ye gallants braw, I rede you a',
Beware o' bonnie Ann.

Then there is the well-known song by William Douglas of Fingland called *Annie Laurie*, after the eldest daughter of Sir Robert Laurie of Maxwelton. Everyone knows the song, but everyone does not know that Annie Laurie was a real person. There are also a touching ballad entitled *Robin an' Nanny* by James Hogg; *Ma Nannie's awa*, *Bonnie Ann*, *The Gowden Locks of Anna*, and *Lady Mary-Ann*, all songs by Robert Burns; *To the most fair and lovely mistress Anne Soame, now Lady Abdie*, by Robert Herrick; two short poems *To Anne* by Lord Byron;

Anna and Harland by S. T. Coleridge; *For Annie* by Edgar Allan Poe; an epitaph to *Anne Powel* by William Shenstone, and two poems by the same author, one called *Slender's Ghost*, having "O sweet! O sweet Anne Page"! for its refrain, and a pretty ballad entitled *Nancy of the Vale*, which runs

> Her shape was like the reed so sleek,
> So taper, strait, and fair;
> Her dimpled smile, her blushing cheek,
> How charming sweet they were!

as well as Allan Cunningham's *My Nanie, O!*; *Nancy, the Pride of the West* by A. P. Graves; Annabel in *Absalom and Achitophel* by John Dryden [this Annabel was really Anne Scott, Countess of Buccleuch, who became Duchess of Monmouth]; and *Annabel Lee*, a poem by Edgar Allan Poe. We will close by quoting from Bishop Percy:

> O Nancy, wilt thou go with me,
> Nor sigh to leave the flaunting town?
> Can silent glens have charms for thee,
> The lowly cot and russet gown?
> No longer dressed in silken sheen,
> No longer decked with jewels rare,
> Say, canst thou quit each courtly scene
> Where thou wert fairest of the fair?
>
> O Nancy, when thou'rt far away,
> Wilt thou not cast a wish behind?
> Say, canst thou face the parching ray,
> Nor shrink before the wintry wind?
> O can that soft and gentle mien
> Extremes of hardship learn to bear,
> Nor, sad, regret each courtly scene,
> Where thou wert fairest of the fair?

O Nancy, canst thou love so true?
Through perils keen with me to go?
Or, when thy swain mishap shall rue,
To share with him the pang of woe?
Say, should disease or pain befall,
Wilt thou assume the nurse's care,
Nor, wistful, those gay scenes recall,
Where thou wert fairest of the fair?

And when at last thy love shall die,
Wilt thou receive his parting breath?
Wilt thou repress each struggling sigh,
And cheer with smiles the bed of death?
And wilt thou o'er his breathless clay
Strew flowers, and drop the tender tear,
Nor then regret those scenes so gay,
Where thou wert fairest of the fair?

ANTHEA means "a lady of flowers", and is derived from the Greek ἄνθος (*anthos*) = a flower. Both Herrick and Drummond of Hawthornden wrote verses to Antheas.

Sick is Anthea, sickly is the spring,
The primrose sick, and sickly everything;
The while my dear Anthea does but droop,
The tulips, lilies, daffodils do stoop:
But when again she's got her healthful hour,
Each bending then will rise a proper flower.

(HERRICK.)

ANTONIA, ANTONINA, ANTOINETTE, the feminine of Antonius, Antonio, Antony, or Anthony, means "strength". It is derived from Antius, of the race of Hercules.

This name is so little used in these Islands that it would hardly claim attention here were it not that now and again admirers of Mark Anthony, "great Cæsar's friend", and devout Roman Catholics, followers of St. Anthony the

Great, who, withdrawing from the world went to dwell alone in the desert and ultimately became the founder of the Monastic system, have bestowed the name on their children; whilst sympathy for the unhappy fate of Marie Antoinette of France has given her a few English namesakes.

Antonio was a favourite name with Shakespeare, who introduced it into at least five of his plays.

ARABELLA. The meaning of the Scottish name Arabella is not very clear. The prefix may be derived from *ari* (eyrie) meaning "eagle" or it may come from *arin* meaning "hearth", which would make the name mean either "eagle-heroine" or "hearth-heroine".

Many Scottish women of note have adorned the name, the best known of whom is perhaps the luckless Arabella Stuart, generally known as the Lady Arabella. Her misfortunes have surrounded her name with a halo of romance, for her being in the direct line of succession to the English throne aroused the jealousy of King James I. who caused her to be imprisoned in the Tower, where her mind became unhinged by her misfortunes, and where she died. Mrs. Hemans has a long poem founded on her history, entitled *Arabella Stuart*.

Arabella Allen is Emily Wardle's schoolfellow in *The Pickwick Papers*, by Chas. Dickens.

On Mrs. Arabella Hunt, singing.

Let all be hushed, each softest motion cease,
Be ev'ry loud tumultuous thought at peace,
And ev'ry ruder gasp of breath
Be calm, as in the arms of death:
And thou, most fickle, most uneasy part,
Thou restless wanderer, my heart,
Be still; gently, ah! gently, leave,
Thou busy, idle thing, to heave:
Stir not a pulse; and let my blood,
That turbulent unruly flood,
Be softly staid:
Let me be all, but my attention dead.
Go, rest, unnecessary springs of life
Leave your officious toil and strife;
For I would hear her voice, and try
If it be possible to die.

(Congreve.)

AUDRY, Awdry: a derivative of Ethel (which see).

AUGUSTA, Augustine, Gussie are the feminine forms of Augustus, and its diminutives, Augustine and Gussy; and its derivatives, chiefly met with as surnames, are August, Austin, and Austen. Some derive the name from *augeo* = I increase; others derive it from *augur* = a prophet. In Rome, after the death of Diocletian, in the early part of the fourth century, the Roman Emperors were all called *Augustus*, and their Empresses *Augusta*; and it was out of compliment to Augustus Cæsar that the month of August was so named. It is from the Roman Emperors, too, that we have obtained our adjective august = awful, sublime, or grand.

During the Middle Ages the name became acclimatized in Germany amongst the reigning families of its numerous petty states; and, when once owned by the sundry Margraves, Dukes, and Princes, it followed as a matter of course that in due time the Margravines, Duchesses, and Princesses would bear the feminine forms. With the House of Hanover the names came over to these shores, and soon became common in England. George II.'s name was George Augustus; so also was that of George IV.; whilst the Duke of Sussex was named Augustus Frederick. George IV.'s Queen was Caroline Amelia Augusta, and the Princess, on whom the hopes of England were centred during the unhappy reign of her father George IV., was called Charlotte Augusta. That the name has held its own through succeeding generations is evidenced by the number of representatives it has had in the near past, and still has in the present. The names occur to us at once of Lord Byron's sister—the Hon. Mrs. Leigh, of Mr. Augustine Birrell, of Mr. Austin Chamberlain, of the Rev. Augustus Jessopp, of Mrs. Augusta Webster, Augustus Hare, etc.

Epistle to Augusta.

My sister! my sweet sister! if a name
Dearer and purer were, it should be thine.
Mountains and seas divide us, but I claim
No tears, but tenderness to answer mine:
Go where I will, to me thou art the same—
A loved regret which I would not resign.
There yet are two things in my destiny,—
A world to roam through, and a home with thee.

Lord Byron addressed three different poems

to his sister. From one of these we have quoted the first stanza above. Those beginning

> When all around grew drear and dark,
>   And reason half withheld her ray—
> And hope but shed a dying spark
>   Which more misled my lonely way!

were the last verses, it is believed, ever written by Lord Byron in England; but the following have achieved a world-wide reputation for their beauty:

> Though the day of my destiny's over,
>   And the star of my fate hath declined,
> Thy soft heart refused to discover
>   The faults which so many could find;
> Though thy soul with my grief was acquainted,
>   It shrunk not to share it with me,
> And the love which my spirit hath painted
>   It never hath found but in *thee*.
>
> . . . .
>
> Though the rock of my last hope is shiver'd,
>   And its fragments are sunk in the wave,
> Though I feel that my soul is deliver'd
>   To pain—it shall not be its slave.
> There is many a pang to pursue me:
>   They may crush, but they shall not contemn—
> They may torture, but shall not subdue me—
>   'Tis of *thee* that I think—not of them.
>
> Though human, thou didst not deceive me,
>   Though woman, thou didst not forsake,
> Though loved, thou forborest to grieve me,
>   Though slander'd, thou never couldst shake,—
> Though trusted, thou didst not disclaim me,
>   Though parted, it was not to fly,
> Though watchful, 'twas not to defame me,
>   Nor, mute, that the world might belie.
>
> . . . . . .

AUGUSTA

From the wreck of the past, which hath perish'd,
  Thus much I at least may recall,
It hath taught me that what I most cherish'd
  Deserved to be dearest of all:
In the desert a fountain is springing,
  In the wide waste there still is a tree,
And a bird in the solitude singing,
  Which speaks to my spirit of *thee*.

In the annals of the Church the name first appears as that of St. Augustine, or St. Austin as he is often called, Bishop of Hippo, and one of the most persuasive orators the Church has ever produced.

St. Augustine was born in Tagaste, a small town in Numidia, on November 13th, 354, of parents who, though not wealthy, were in comfortable circumstances.

According to his own account, given in his *Confessions*, he seems to have been a wayward child, though he early gave promise of great intelligence: it was, however, long before he took any pleasure in the study of Greek; yet he, from his youth up, delighted in the Latin poets, filling his head, as he afterwards lamented, with the wanderings of Æneas, whilst he forgot his own spiritual wanderings, and shedding tears over the death of Dido "when he beheld himself with dry eyes perishing from God". Patricius, his father, was a heathen; his mother, Santa Monica, a devout Christian; and she spared no pains in the effort to train up her child in the path of truth and duty. But the gifted though self-willed boy broke from her guidance, and during a year of idleness which occurred between leaving school and going to Carthage to prosecute his higher studies, St. Augustine led a dissolute and wild life. When at Carthage, whither he went at the age of seventeen, he at once distinguished himself by his intellectual attainments; but broke away, in questions of religion, from the associations of his youth, and joined the sect of the Manichees, endeavouring to try everything "by the test of reason". "I sought", he says, "with pride what only humility could make me find. Fool that I was, I left the nest, imagining myself able to fly, and I fell to the ground". In his twentieth year St. Augustine left Carthage, and, to relieve his mother from the cost of his maintenance (for his father was now dead), he opened a school in Tagaste. The loss of his dearest friend soon, however, made Tagaste unbearable to him, so that he removed once more to Carthage, and there opened a school of rhetoric. St. Augustine carried off the chief prizes in the theatre for poetry and oratory, and his reputation grew daily greater; but he tired of these empty glories after a time, and determined on a visit to Rome. Here, too, he professed rhetoric with great success; but again wearied of his surroundings and proceeded to Milan, where he fell under the influence of the great Bishop, St. Ambrose.

This proved a turning-point in St. Augustine's religious development. The good work once begun, it went steadily forward in the young man's soul; and, though he often hesitated and hovered on the brink of doubt and unbelief, he never really turned back. St. Augustine's final conversion took place in 386, when he was thirty-two years of age.

For two years he lived in retirement with his mother and friends, and then was ordained priest; in 395 he was made Bishop of Hippo Regius. In this capacity he exercised a wide influence for good, until he died in A.D. 430, one of the best-loved and most revered of all the Church's teachers.

Two of his greatest works are his *Confessions* and his *Retractations*; in the first he confesses his errors of conduct, in the second his errors of judgment. One of his maxims was, that one could make a ladder to heaven by treading on one's sins, and on this Longfellow has founded his poem called *The Ladder of St. Augustine*:

Saint Augustine! well hast thou said,
That of our vices we can frame
A ladder, if we will but tread
Beneath our feet each deed of shame!

All common things, each day's events,
That with the hour begin and end,
Our pleasures and our discontents,
Are rounds by which we may ascend.

. . . . .

The longing for ignoble things;
The strife for triumph more than truth;
The hardening of the heart, that brings
Irreverence for the dreams of youth;

All thoughts of ill; all evil deeds,
That have their root in thoughts of ill;
Whatever hinders or impedes
The action of the nobler will;—

All these must first be trampled down
Beneath our feet, if we would gain
In the bright fields of fair renown
The right of eminent domain.

. . . .

AUGUSTA

The second St. Augustine is sometimes called the "Apostle of England".

Pope Gregory the Great, being much troubled by the idolatrous condition of the British Isles, sought for someone whom he could trust to preach the Gospel to the neglected people, and finally selected Augustine, Priar of the Monastery of St. Andrew's in Rome, for the work. Accordingly Augustine, accompanied by a chosen band of assistants, numbering some forty people in all, set sail for England, and in 596 landed on the Isle of Thanet. St. Augustine at once addressed himself to Ethelbert, King of Kent, who, though not himself a Christian, afforded the small army of Christian workers every protection for the sake of his wife, Queen Bertha, who was herself an ardent member of the Church. Before 597 Ethelbert himself had been baptised, as well as great numbers of his people—some accounts say over 10,000. In 597-8 Augustine returned to Rome, seeking advice on many points; but was soon back in England again, having, in the interim, been created a Bishop. St. Augustine's activity was untiring; he sent to Rome for more workers, he consecrated churches, destroyed idols, and encouraged the people to abandon their heathen rites and festivals, and to lead lives of self-restraint.

The Cathedral at Canterbury was built by him, and he also founded the Abbey of SS. Peter and Paul without the walls of that City; in the porch of the Church his own remains were afterwards laid.

Amongst his Converts were, not only King

Ethelbert of Kent, but Sebert, King of the East Saxons, and Redwald, King of the East Angles.

In 600 St. Augustine was created Archbishop of Canterbury with power to ordain twelve bishops.

In 607 A.D. St. Augustine died, and over his remains was placed the following epitaph :—

"Here rests Lord Augustine, first Archbishop of Canterbury, who being sent hither, by the blessed Gregory, Bishop of Rome, and by God upheld by the working of miracles, brought King Ethelbert and his nation from idolatry to the faith of Christ; and having completed the days of his office in peace, died on the seventh day before the Calends of June, in the reign of the same King".—CAMDEN's *Remains*.

Of places that derive their names from Augustus we may instance Augsburg = City of Augustus, and Austin Friars, a street in the ancient part of the City of London. The Romans called the City of London Augusta, and the poet William Shenstone, following their example, addresses it as "Augusta", too,

For rural virtues, and for native skies,
I bade Augusta's venal sons farewell;
Now 'mid the trees I see my smoke arise,
Now hear the fountains bubbling round my cell.

Falconer, in *The Shipwreck*, also refers to the great city in the same way :

Where full in view Augusta's spires are seen,
With flowery lawns and waving woods between,
A humble habitation rose, beside
Where Thames meandering rolls his ample tide.

Modern examples of this name are the wife of

the Emperor William I. of Germany, grandmother of the present Emperor; and the present Empress of Germany, who was a Princess of Schleswig-Holstein, and whose name is Augusta Victoria.

AURORA, from the Latin *aurum* = gold, signifies the "beauty of the morning", the "rosy-fingered morn", the "dawn".

This name, common in France, is rarely met with in England, though, since the publication of Mrs. Browning's poem *Aurora Leigh*, from which we quote a few lines below, it has had a few votaries.

> "You have the stars", he murmured,—"it is well:
> Be like them! shine, Aurora, on my dark,
> Though high and cold and only like a star,
> And for this short night only,—you, who keep
> The same Aurora of the bright June day
> That withered up the flowers before my face,
> And turned me from the garden evermore
> Because I was not worthy".

Byron, in *Don Juan*, introduces a noble English orphan girl,

> Aurora Baby, a young star who shone
> O'er life, too sweet an image for such glass,
> A lovely being, scarcely form'd or moulded,
> A rose with all its sweetest leaves yet folded.

Aurora Floyd is the title of one of Miss Braddon's best known novels.

AVICE, Avis, etc. Hawisa, Havoise, Hawoyse, Havoisia, Avicia, Avice, and Avis, come from the German Haduwig, or Heldewig, which signify "War-refuge", or "Lady of Defence". The name in all its developments was at one time common with us, but except as Avice and Avis has now become almost extinct; and when it does occur is generally given in the form of Avis under the impression that it means "a bird".

BARBARA, Bab, Babie, Babet(te). The meaning of this name Barbara is simply "a stranger", being the feminine of the Greek word Βάρβαρος.

The English have three forms of the name. The original form is Barbary, though this is now rarely met with even in rural districts. The second form, Bab, is still often found as a pet abbreviation, but seldom as a full name; whilst Barbara, from having grown almost obsolete, in the modern love of resuscitating old favourites bids fair to again become fashionable. The Scottish national form is Babie, whilst in Italy and Germany the name is exactly the same as in England—Barbara—and in France it is Barbe.

St. Barbary, who is supposed to be the representative of artistic devotion, is one of the most popular of all the Saints in the Church Calendar; and this though the details of her life are shrouded in mystery even more than usual, and obscured by a number of undoubtedly false "acts", those recorded by Metaphrastes and Mombretius being apparently the best authenticated.

Barbara, according to these authorities, was the daughter of one Dioscorus, a nobleman of Nicomedia. Her father had caused a bath of white marble to be constructed for her use; in this bath-room Barbara insisted that there should be three windows, in honour, as it afterwards transpired, of the Holy Trinity. Upon the first occasion of her using it, the young girl made the mark of the Cross on it with her finger, and this mark proving indelible betrayed the fact that she had become a Christian. Upon discovering this, her father was furious, and in his rage at once denounced his daughter and handed her over to the authorities, to be dealt with as the law directed. She was imprisoned, stripped, beaten, branded, and otherwise tortured; but to no purpose: through all her trials Barbara remained firm in the Christian faith. Whereupon her body was mutilated, and she, a forerunner of Godiva, was led naked through the streets, and moreover scourged as she passed along. Her faith still remaining unshaken, the Governor of Nicomedia, one Marrianus, ordered that her head should be cut off; and her father, in his relentless anger, begged that the execution of that decree might fall to him.

So Barbara was led to the place of execution beyond the City walls, and there her own father cut off her head; but hardly had he performed this unnatural act when his own head was struck off by a thunderbolt. Metaphrastes adds that, whilst angels descended and bore off the head of the martyred girl to Paradise, devils at once appeared, who carried off her father's head to the bottomless abyss. According to this version of the story, St. Barbara suffered martyrdom in 235; but other accounts affirm that her martyrdom took place at Heliopolis, in Egypt, in 306.

Amongst the "acts" attributed to this Saint is one said to have been performed in the middle of the sixteenth century, when Stanislaus Kostka was preparing to enter the Society of Jesus. Kostka was lying desperately ill at the house of a "heretic", where he could get no spiritual aid, and, though he did not fear death, he lay in great terror lest he should die without having first partaken of the Eucharist. As he lay awake one night lamenting his evil plight, St. Barbara appeared by his bed-side attended by two angels bearing the Holy Elements of bread and wine, and from St. Barbary the suffering man received the Sacrament.

Miss Yonge points out that in St. Barbara "was symbolized the consecration of architecture and the fine arts, to express religious ideas", and that thus she "became the patroness of architects and thence of engineers, and the protectress from thunder and its mimic—artillery". A thunderbolt having been the divine instrument of revenge for the cruel manner of her death probably caused her to be regarded as the protectress from thunder, and on French ships the powder-room is still called after her "la Sainte Barbe".

Whittier tells us of a second Barbara, willing to lay down her life, too, if need be, in the cause of right—old *Barbara Frietchie*.

Up from the meadows rich with corn,
Clear in the cool September morn,
The clustered spires of Frederick stand
Green-walled by the hills of Maryland.

Round about them orchards sweep,
Apple and peach tree fruited deep,
Fair as a garden of the Lord
To the eyes of the famished rebel horde.

BARBARA

On that pleasant morn of the early fall
When Lee marched over the mountain wall,—
Over the mountains winding down,
Horse and foot into Frederick town.

Forty flags with their silver stars,
Forty flags with their crimson bars,
Flapped in the morning wind: the sun
Of noon looked down and saw not one.

Up rose old Barbara Frietchie then,
Bowed with her fourscore years and ten;
Bravest of all in Frederick town,
She took up the flag the men hauled down;

In her attic window the staff she set,
To show that one heart was loyal yet.
Up the street came the rebel tread,
Stonewall Jackson riding ahead.

Under his slouched hat left and right
He glanced; the old flag met his sight.
"Halt"!—the dust-brown ranks stood fast.
"Fire"!—out blazed the rifle-blast.

It shivered the window, pane and sash;
It rent the banner with seam and gash.
Quick, as it fell, from the broken staff
Dame Barbara snatched the silken scarf;

She leaned far out on the window-sill,
And shook it forth with a royal will.
"Shoot, if you must, this old grey head,
But spare your country's flag", she said.

A shade of sadness, a blush of shame,
Over the face of the leader came;
The nobler nature within him stirred
To life at that woman's deed and word:

"Who touches a hair of yon grey head
Dies like a dog! March on"! he said.
All day long through Frederick street
Sounded the tread of marching feet:

All day long that free flag tost
Over the heads of the rebel host.
Ever its torn folds rose and fell
On the loyal winds that loved it well;

And through the hill-gaps sunset light
Shone over it with a warm good night.
Barbara Frietchie's work is o'er,
And the rebel rides on his raids no more.

Honour to her! and let a tear
Fall, for her sake, on Stonewall's bier.
Over Barbara Frietchie's grave
Flag of Freedom and Union wave!

Peace and order and beauty draw
Round thy symbol of light and law;
And ever the stars above look down
On thy stars below in Frederick town.

There is a second version—a Scottish one—of the ballad of Barbara Allen, entitled *Sir John Grehme and Barbara Allen*, which, in January 1665-6 Samuel Pepys heard Mrs. Knipp, the actress, sing at Lord Brouncker's house, "her little Scotch song of Barbery Allen"; it was "perfect pleasure to hear her sing". We here append the first two verses.

Barbara Allen's Cruelty.

In Scarlet towne, where I was borne,
   There was a faire maid dwellin,
Made every youth crye, Wel-awaye!
   Her name was Barbara Allen.

All in the merrye month of May,
   When greene buds they were swellin,
Yong Jemmye Grove on his death-bed lay,
   For love of Barbara Allen.

In Wordsworth's lyric, *'Tis said, that some have died for love*, the lover mourns a "pretty Barbara".

Barbary was the name of Richard II.'s favourite roan mare; and a Barbary mare has come to be a name for a certain class of small mares.

> "O, how it yearn'd my heart when it beheld
> In London streets, that coronation day,
> When Bolingbroke rode on roan Barbary,
> That horse that thou so often hast bestrid,
> That horse that I so carefully have dress'd"!
> (A groom.)
>
> "Rode he on Barbary"? (King Richard.)
> SHAKESPEARE, *Richard II.*, Act V. Sc. v.

BEATRICE, BEATRIX, BEATA, BENEDICTA, VENETIA, &c. The names mean "happy" or "blessed", and are derived from the early Latin verb *beo*, which forms the root of several names, both masculine and feminine. Of these the English feminine ones are Beatrice = blesser, or joy-giver, Beatrix meaning the same, and Beata = blessed, with their diminutives Trixy, Trix, and Beatie--very rare are Benedicta = blessed, Venetia = blessed, and Bonté = blessing. The masculine names of Benedict, Bennet, both meaning blessed, and Boniface, from Bonifacius = good worker, though not now in use as Christian names, are not uncommon as surnames. Beata is not so common now as it used to be, but it still lingers on in some country districts; Beatrix and Beatrice, on the other hand, grow in favour daily, the second and less correct form of the name being perhaps the favourite on account of its softer and more musical final syllable. In Italy Beatrice is common, but Germany, France, Russia, and Portugal have remained true to Beatrix.

The first Beatrix recognised in historical records seems to have been a Christian girl who lived in the reign of the Emperor Diocletian, and whose brothers suffered martyrdom, their bodies being cast into the Tiber. Beatrix is said to have rescued their bodies, and to have buried them. She afterwards herself suffered martyrdom. This happened about the year A.D. 300.

The story is that Lucretius, Diocletian's deputy, coveted a vineyard which belonged to St. Beatrix: he wanted to join it to his own lands to which it was adjacent. Lucretius accordingly summoned Beatrix to appear before him, and charged her with being a Christian, and upon her acknowledging her faith, he ordered her to prison, where she was secretly strangled during the night.

Lucretius then immediately took possession of the vineyard, and celebrated the event by giving a great feast; when lo, just as the merriment was at its height, a woman appeared before Lucretius bearing a young child in her arms, and the child in a loud voice, which could be heard by all present, cried, "Lucretius, thou hast put Beatrix to death, and taken possession of her vineyard sinfully; therefore the devil shall take possession of thee". Immediately these words had been spoken, Lucretius began to roll his eyes and make most hideous faces. For three hours he writhed in an agony, and then expired.

Miracles are recorded in relation to a sister Benedicta, who lived A.D. 1643-1718.

Amongst the several Saints bearing the name of Benedict or Boniface, two have been of English birth. None of these have been more honoured by posterity than St. Benedict Biscop, commonly known as St. Bennet. A member of a noble English family, and an officer high in favour at the Court of Good King Oswi of Northumbria, he was English to the core. At the age of twenty-five, fearing the attractions of the Court and the allurements of riches and power, he made a journey of devotion to Rome, and upon his return to England gave himself up to study and religious exercises. Making a second pilgrimage to Rome, he went thence to the monastery of Lerins, and there assumed the monastic habit, not returning to England for two or three years, and not until after he had made yet a third journey to the Papal City.

He was created Abbot of the monastery of SS. Peter and Paul, near Canterbury, upon his return; but in two years resigned the office, and again went to Rome. After his return from this fourth journey, he, through the munificence of King Egfrid, who had succeeded his father Oswi as King of Northumbria, founded and built the monastery of Weremouth, bringing skilled masons over from France for the building of the monastery Church, stone buildings being at that time almost unknown in England, wood being usually employed. He also brought glaziers from France.

King Egfrid was so edified with St. Bennet's labours, that he endowed him with yet more land, and thus enabled the saint to build a second monastery at Jarrow on the Tyne, six miles distant from Weremouth. St. Bennet endowed his monastaries with books and paintings, and governed them both himself with the aid of two abbots, who laboured under his direction.

After a fifth journey to Rome, St. Bennet was struck down with a palsy, whereby he lost the use of his lower limbs; and for the last three years of his life lay helpless and unable to move. When taking his last leave of his monks, and exhorting them to observe the rules which he had laid down for their guidance, he, anxious not to take undue credit to himself, said to them, "You must not think that the constitutions which you have received from me were my own invention; for having in my frequent journeys visited seventeen well-ordered monasteries, I informed myself of all their laws and rules, and picking out the best among them, these I have recommended to you". St. Bennet died on January 12th, 690.

Another English Saint, whose name should be mentioned here, was Saint Boniface, who, born at Kirton in Devonshire and educated at Exeter, ultimately became Archbishop of Mentz, retaining his love for and interest in his native country to the end.

St. Boniface, or Saint Bruno, St. Boniface of Rome, St. Benedict, Patriarch of the Western

Monks, and St. Benedict of Anian, though not English, may also be named.

Occasionally we meet with a Beatrice in history, but not very often.

There was the Beatrice who first married Boniface II., Duke of Tuscany, in 1036, and who upon her husband's death acted as regent to her son, and who then (1052) married Godfrey IV., Duke of Lorraine. She was captured by the Emperor Henry III., and carried off to Germany, but regained her liberty in the following year, and returned with Godfrey to Tuscany, where she reigned as guardian to her daughter Matilda. She died in 1076.

Beatrice of Este was a daughter of one of the most ancient and illustrious families of Italy, which traces back its origin to the days of the Carlovingian Kings, when the Estes were petty princes and governed Tuscany. Beatrice in 1491 married Ludovico Maria Sforza, called *Il Moro* (the Moor), Duke of Milan. The origin of his nickname may have been his dark complexion, but is more likely to have been owing to his device, a mulberry-tree, which in Italian is *El Moro*. She was canonized at Rome.

Dante's idol, too, Beatrice Portinari, was a real woman of flesh and blood, and not a creature of his imagination only. When Dante was about ten years of age, he met Beatrice in her father's, Folco Portinari's, house. Her beauty and goodness inspired the poet with a very passion of admiring love, which afterwards became a powerful element in his life and the source of some of his sublimest thoughts. Beatrice Portinari died in

1290, and her memory became to Dante a glorified ideal, and in his *Divina Commedia* he makes her his guide through Paradise.

The following poems are addressed to her:

Last All Saints' holy-day, even now gone by,
  I met a gathering of damozels:
  She that came first, as one doth who excels,
Had Love with her, bearing her company:
A flame burned forward through her steadfast eye,
  As when in living fire a spirit dwells:
  So, gazing with the boldness which prevails
O'er doubt, I knew an angel visibly.
  (Dante, *Canzoniere*, transl. by D. G. Rossetti.)

HE WILL GAZE UPON BEATRICE.

Even as an angel, up at his great height
Standing amid the light,
Becometh blessed by only seeing God:—
So, though I be a simple earthly wight,
Yet none the less I might,
Beholding her who is my heart's dear load,
Be blessed, and in the spirit soar abroad.
  (Dante, *Canzoniere*, transl. by D. G. Rossetti.)

There was also Beatrice, the daughter of King Ferdinando of Naples, who married Mathias Corvinus of Hungary; and Beatrice Cenci, the "beautiful parricide", who took part in the murder of her brutal father, in 1598, and who was beheaded at Rome just a year and a week afterwards for the crime. On her miserable story Shelley has founded his play of *The Cenci*.

  Beatrice:—"Do you know
I thought I was that wretched Beatrice
Men speak of whom her father sometimes hales
From hall to hall by the entangled hair;
At others, pens up naked in damp cells
Where scaly reptiles crawl, and starves her there,
Till she will eat strange flesh".

After she is accused of the crime, she defends herself thus:

"Oh, thou who tremblest on the giddy verge
Of life and death, pause ere thou answerest me;
So mayest thou answer God with less dismay:
What evil have we done thee? I, alas!
Have lived but on this earth a few sad years
And so my lot was ordered that a father
First turned the moments of awakening life
To drops, each poisoning youth's sweet hope; and
then
Stabbed with one blow my everlasting soul;
And my untainted fame; and even that peace
Which sleeps within the core of the heart's heart.
But the wound was not mortal; so my hate
Became the only worship I could lift
To our great Father, who in pity and love,
Armed thee, as thou dost say, to cut him off;
And thus his wrong becomes my accusation.
. . . . Think
What 'tis to blot with infamy and blood
All that which shows like innocence, and is.
Hear me, great God! I swear, most innocent,
So that the world lose all discrimination
Between the sly, fierce, wild regard of guilt,
And that which now compels thee to reply
To what I ask: Am I, or am I not
A parricide"?

Two literary examples of the Spanish form of the name—Beatriz—will be found in Lord Lytton's novel, *Calderon the Courtier*, where Beatriz Coello is the heroine, and Mary Beatriz Sandalen a minor character.

Beatrix is not the heroine, but she is, nevertheless, one of the most predominant characters in Thackeray's great novel, *Esmond*, and we meet her again in *The Virginians*, when the *quondam* beauty has grown into anything but a loveable old woman.

Longfellow has translated from Dante's *Purgatorio* xxx., xxxi., a poem which he calls *Beatrice*, and finally, to close with something brighter, we have witty, high-spirited, affectionate Beatrice, our "Dear Lady Disdain", in Shakespeare's *Much Ado about Nothing*, one of the great dramatist's happiest creations in his crowd of noble women.

> Leonardo: "There's little of the melancholy element in her, my lord: she is never sad but when she sleeps; and not ever sad then; for I have heard my daughter say, she hath often dreamed of unhappiness, and waked herself with laughing".

An asteroid discovered by De Gasparis in 1865 was named by him Beatrix.

> I sing the just and uncontroll'd descent
> Of dame Venetia Digby, styled the fair;
> For mind and body the most excellent
> That ever nature, or the later air,
> Gave two such houses as Northumberland
> And Stanley, to the which she was co-heir.
> *The Lady Venetia Digby*, in *Underwoods*
> (Ben Jonson.)

Venetia is the Keltic form of Benedicta, and means "blessed". The Russians in Venedict have much the same development of the word. *Venetia* is the name of one of Lord Beaconfield's novels.

BEGA, or Begga, is a Keltic name meaning "life". There was an Irish Saint Begga in the seventh century.

BELINDA means "beautiful snake", and was at one time a fashionable name in England. It is the name of one of Maria Edgworth's novels and was also that of Pope's heroine in *The Rape of the Lock*, though Mrs. Fermor for whom the Belinda of the poem was intended, was really called Arabella, to whom Pope addressed the famous lines:

> If to her share some female errors fall,
> Look on her face, and you'll forget them all.

There is a Belinda in Congreve's play *The Old Bachelor*, and a Belina in Vanbrugh's *Provoked Wife*.

BERTHA. PERAHTA or BERTHA is a Teutonic name, and comes from *perchten* = shining. *Perchten tac*, or *perchten naht* is really synonymous in meaning with Epiphany day, or Epiphany night, commemorating the appearance of Christ to the magi or philosophers of the East who went to adore Him on the twelfth day after his birth, namely, January 6th.

Just as Epiphanus, Theophania or Tiphaina and Tiffane became personal names derived from Epiphany, so Perchten, signifying bright, became a woman's name, first changing into Perchta, then Berchta, then Bertha or Berthe.

The name of Bertha therefore signifies bright or shining one, and is often given to those who happen to be born on the 6th of January.

Gradually the idea of the Epiphany got crystalized, in the minds of the old Germans, into a concrete form, and became personified in the shape of Berchta, the mild, who sometimes watched over deserted or uncared for children, at others punished naughty ones, and again on other occasions manifested anger towards those who failed to accomplish their allotted task of spinning by the time the last day of the year had drawn to its close.

Almost identical with Holda the Earth-Goddess, she was worshipped by many Germanic tribes under the name of Berchta.

You are the beautiful Bertha the Spinner, the queen of Helvetia,
Who as she rode on her palfrey o'er valley, and meadow, and mountain,
Ever was spinning her thread from the distaff fixed to her saddle.
She was so thrifty and good that her name passed into a proverb.
So shall it be with your own, when the spinning wheel shall no longer
Hum in the house of the farmer, and fill its chambers with music.

(H. W. Longfellow.)

Sometimes her almost heathen followers fancied she rode at the head of the Raging Host in the midst of a terrific storm, but generally she dwelt in the hollow mountains where (at any rate in Thuringia) she watched over the "Heimchen", or souls of children yet unborn or of those who had died in infancy. She busied herself moreover by ploughing up the soil under the earth, whilst the babes she shielded watered the fields; but if offended she left the country-side, and then the fields lost their fruitfulness.

In many legends, Berchta appears as an enchantress, or again as an enchanted maiden, who is ready to provide untold riches for him who is so fortunate as to free her from the spell that binds her.

We recognize her, too, as the "Ahnfrau" or ancestress of some noble families, dwelling as a guardian spirit in their castles, and ever ready to warn them against some impending misfortune.

She appears in the story told of Kunigunda or Orlamünd, who fell in love with Albrecht of Hohenzollern.

Albrecht told her that four eyes stood between them to prevent their union, thereby meaning his parents, who objected to the match; but Kunigunda thought he meant her two children, so she had them secretly murdered.

Albrecht abhorred her for her sin and broke off all association with her. Kunigunda afterwards made a pilgrimage to Rome, and then entered a nunnery, where, in severe penance, she atoned for her crime.

After her death she was buried at Plassenburg and thenceforth as "Ahnfrau" forewarned Albrecht's family of any approaching evil: later on she removed to Berlin, and amongst other events warned the people there of their King's approaching death.

Clad in a long trailing white garment, with a long white veil thrown over her head, "below which her long flaxen hair hung twisted with strings of pearls", and with her face of a deathly pallor, she passed slowly down the corridor, holding in her right hand a bunch of keys, in her left a bunch of cowslips.

"It is the White Lady; the King is about to

die", whispered the officers of the guard, and "The White Lady has appeared", was passed from mouth to mouth through the crowd outside, for all knew what this meant. By mid-day the the King's death was known to all.

With her keys Berchta, or the White Lady, opens the doors of life and happiness, and he to whom she gives a cowslip will succeed in all he undertakes.

She is said to have appeared in 1806 before the overwheming misfortunes of that year, and again on the eve of the battle of Belle-Alliance.

Another account of Berchta connects her with the Swan-Knight, so often mentioned among the old heroes of the Middle Ages: in these she is represented as web-footed.

Yet another version of Berchta's story refers us to a Bohemian Countess Bertha of Rosenberg, who never laid aside the white garments of her widowhood as long as life lasted, and who has ever since appeared in them from time to time, in spirit form, prophesying to the families of Rosenberg, Neuhaus and Berlin, any coming event, either good or ill.

The Germanic races carried the worship of Berchta the Earth-Goddess to Gaul and Italy, and at last, in the long course of ages, real people got mixed up with the mythical, so that around the names of King Pepin's Queen Bertha, who became the mother of Charlemagne, and about his daughter Bertha too, wonderful legends got woven, until the great Emperor's mother at last became confused with the web-footed lady connected with the Swan-Knight, whose webbed feet become transformed into nothing more startling than very big ones : *Bertha aux grands pieds* came to be her usual soubriquet.

Herrings and oat-bread are placed, by her devotees, outside Berchta's door on her festival night [January 6th], and in some parts of Alsace, bells are rung and whistles blown in her honour.

Some French legends give a mythical Bertha, who is no doubt the same as Holda : this Bertha shed such bitter tears for her lost spouse that the very stones were penetrated by them, and she also meted out rewards and punishments to spinners, according to their deserts.

Many students of the subject consider that Holda and Berchta are identical with the Freya of the North, who wept golden tears for her husband.

There is a French proverb which refers to Berchta's underground kingdom, intended to recall that time of innocence and peace : *au temps que Berthe filait.*

The name of Bertha is common in France and Germany and only a little less so in England, where the name is first met with as owned by one Bertha, the daughter of Chilperic, King of Paris, who became the wife of King Ethelbert of Kent, to whom, according to Dr. Creighton, Bishop of London, the introduction of Christianity into England is largely due : according to this authority it was "her tact with her husband, and seizing on the right opportunity for the work of St. Augustine which had largely conduced to the conversion of England". [Speech delivered at Sion College, 26th of May, 1898.]

Bertha was then a name new in England and it did not become acclimatized until after the the Norman Conquest. At the time of the Conquest both Bertha and Tiffane were introduced, but though Tiffane had some vogue here, as may be proved by the following rhyme, it gradually died out and finally vanished in the seventeenth century, whilst Bertha has grown in popularity.

William de Coningsby
Came out of Brittany
With his wife Tiffany.

Saint Bertha was probably related to Queen Bertha, but it is rather doubtful how. She had, however, some connection with Kent, where Bertha was Queen.

She ranks in the Roman Church Calendar as a Saint, and her festival is celebrated on July 4th.

She was the daughter of Count Rigobert and Ursana, and married one Sigefroi by whom she had five daughters, of whom two were canonized: one of these was St. Gertrude, the other St. Deotila.

During her husband's lifetime Bertha had built a nunnery at Blangy in Artois. Of this nunnery she became Abbess when her husband died, and her daughters Gertrude and Deotila entered it as nuns. After establishing a regular observance in her community, she retired from its management, leaving her daughter Deotila as Abbess there in her stead. She herself withdrew to a cell where she spent her days in prayer.

She built three churches: one she dedicated

to St. Omer, one to St. Vaast, and the third to St. Martin of Tours.

To this Saint is attributed the miracle of supplying the town of Avenay with water, the monks of the Abbey of Val d'Or having implored her to aid them in obtaining a better supply. Whilst she was praying for this object, St. Peter appeared to her holding in his hands two golden keys. He told her to buy a little plot of land near the Abbey, where she would find a fountain of water which she might utilize for the benefit of the town.

Saint Bertha bought this land for a livre of silver [£2 present value of money], and tracing on the earth with a stick a line from the fountain to the town, the water flowed along this track, and never after deviated from it, gradually working a deep channel for itself. This river is still called the "Livre" from the price originally paid for it by Saint Bertha.

In literature Bertha is not met with often, but there are a few instances; among them in Beaumont and Fletcher's play, *The Beggar's Bush*, there is Bertha, the supposed daughter of the Burgomaster of Bruges, really the daughter of the Duke of Brabant; Bertha, a minor character, in *The Golden Legend*, by Henry W. Longfellow; Bertha, the blind daughter of Caleb Plummer, in *The Cricket on the Hearth*, by Charles Dickens; Bertha, the betrothed of Hereward, in *Count Robert of Paris*, by Sir Walter Scott; Bertha, in *The Courtship of Miles Standish*, by Henry W. Longfellow; and *Bertha in the Lane*, a lyric in thirty-four stanzas, by Elizabeth Barrett Browning, describing the transfer of a lover's affections from one sister to another: from this we quote a few lines.

> Put the broidery-frame away,
> For my sewing is all done:
> The last thread is used to-day,
> And I need not join it on.
> Though the clock stands at the noon
> I am weary. I have sewn
> Sweet, for thee, a wedding-gown.
>
> Lean thy face down; drop it in
> These two hands, that I may hold
> 'Twixt their palms thy cheek and chin,
> Stroking back the curls of gold;
> 'Tis a fair, fair face in sooth—
> Larger eyes and redder mouth
> Than mine were in my first youth
>
> Mother, mother, up in heaven,
> Stand up on the jasper sea,
> And be witness I have given
> All the gifts required of me,—
> Hope that blessed me, bliss that crowned,
> Love that left me with a wound,
> Life itself that turneth round!
>
> And, dear Bertha, let me keep
> On my hand this little ring,
> Which at nights, when others sleep,
> I can still see glittering.
> Let me wear it out of sight,
> In the grave,—where it will light
> All the dark up, day and night.

BETH, Bethia, Bethiah, meaning "daughter of Jehovah"—a name met with in old English families in rural districts.

Mrs. Gaskell has introduced a Bethia into her novel, *Wives and Daughters*.

BERENGARIA, Berenguela. Berenguela, altered by us into Berengaria, and known as the name of the Queen of Richard Cœur de Lion, is another "bear" name, signifying "bear-spear". Sir Walter Scott introduces Queen Berengaria in *The Talisman.*

BERNARDINE, Bernarda, and Bernardina. Though there are not a great many names which take their origin from the bear, he had many admirers in Scandinavia, in the Pyrenees, and in Switzerland; and to this are due such names as Bernadotte, Bernier, and Berenger. The best loved is Biornhard = firm bear or bear's heart. This has got changed now into Bernhard or Bernard, and has grown famous as the name of the great Abbot of Clairvaux, who flourished in the twelfth century. One hundred and fifty years earlier there had been a devout Bernard de Menthou, who founded the monasteries of the Great and Little St. Bernard in the passage of the Alps, and another of the same name, a religious enthusiast of Thuringia, who predicted that the end of the world was at hand, spreading terror around him amongst his ignorant and superstitious countrymen and followers. No wonder, then, that, thus "fathered", Bernard soon grew to be a favourite name, of which the feminines Bernardina, Bernarda, and Bernardine were formed, though the last was given to men as well as to women, and glorified in the fourteenth century by St. Bernardine of Siena, who founded some three hundred monasteries, and commanded the admiration of the devout by his life of self-devotion.

BERYL = soothsayer, is a jewel-name: the beryl stone is not often used now, but, by our ancestors, this green or bluish green mineral, with its six-sided prism, not unlike the emerald, though not so rich in its colouring, was supposed to possess occult properties, and was much consulted by fortune-tellers, who used to gaze into its depths before uttering their prophecies.

> Fire-spirits of dread desire,
> We whose home is the Beryl.
>
> *Beryl Song* (ROSSETTI.)

According to Aubrey in his *Miscellanies*, "certain formulas of prayer are to be used before they make the inspection, which they term a 'call'. James Harrington told me that the Earl of Denbigh, then ambassador at Venice, did tell him that one did show him three several times in a glass things past and to come".

It was believed that the power of reading its hidden mysteries was confined to the absolutely pure in thought and deed, and that even should the power of reading the future in the stone be given to anyone who afterwards wandered from the paths of rectitude, the gift would be lost.

Rossetti's poem *Rose Mary* is partly based on this superstition:—

> Did you read my heart in the Beryl-stone?
>
> The lady answered her mournfully:—
> "The Beryl-stone has no voice for me:
> But where you charged its power to show
> The truth which none but the pure may know,
> Did naught speak once of a coming woe"?

Beryl Molozane is the name of the heroine of Mrs. Riddell's novel *George Geith*.

BETTY, Bessie, etc.: see Elizabeth.

BLANCHE, Blanch, Bianca. According to our best authority in these matters, Miss Yonge, this is one of the few Teutonic names which have had their origin in some personal peculiarity.

The meaning of the name is white, pale, or very fair.

In Anglo-Saxon the word *bloecan* means to bleach or whiten, and the Anglo-Saxon *bloeco* is the same word as that still in everyday use in Germany, *bleich* = pale. *Bloec* seems to denote a certain negative quality, that is, it means absence of all colour rather than the presence of "whiteness".

Our "black" and the French *blanc* are actually the same words philologically, and denote merely an absence of colour, which happens in this case to be employed only to point out opposite effects of the same conditions.

A few surnames, such as Lablanche, Blanchard, etc., have come from the word *blanc*; but as first or Christian names the only common ones are the feminines Blanche, Blanch, and, in Italy, Bianca.

The first historical use of the name is that of Blanche, the Queen of Sancho IV. of Castille, and the mother of our "Good Queen Eleanor".

This Eleanor in her turn had a daughter named Blanche, who, if there be any such things as "lucky names", certainly had one, for Herrera the Spanish historian, himself tells us how Louis VIII. of France, surnamed Cœur de Lion, desiring to take a Spanish Princess for his bride, sent Ambassadors to the Court of Madrid to secure one for him.

Now the eldest and loveliest of King Alfonso's daughters had always, in the opinion of her own family, been the destined bride of France; but unhappily for her, this unfortunate Princess had at her birth received the name, unattractive in both sound and meaning, of Urraca, which in Spanish meant magpie.

To take back with them to France, as their royal master's bride, a Princess burdened with such a name as this, appeared to the French Ambassadors nothing short of impossible, so, rejecting the lovely Urraca (= Council of War) on account of her ugly name, they chose her far less beautiful younger sister Blanche the Fair as future Queen of France. Blanche accordingly became the much-honoured wife of Louis VIII. of the Lion Heart, and the mother of Saint Louis.

May the worldly-wise take warning, and pause before they give their little girls ugly names!

> If zealous love should go in search of virtue
> Where should he find it purer than in Blanch?
> (SHAKESPEARE.)

Blanche of Castille was married A.D. 1200, and crowned with her husband in 1223. Three years later she was left a widow, and was named Regent of France during the minority of her son Louis IX. She displayed great energy and address as a ruler. Upon her son going to the

Crusades, an act which she strongly opposed, she accompanied him on this journey as far as Cluni, and then acted as regent for him during his absence from the land.

His long sojourn in the Holy Land, and the rumour that he contemplated settling there for life, caused her such distress that good Queen Blanche was taken ill, and died in 1252.

Shakespeare introduces her into his play of *King John*, rather distorting historical sequences for the sake of dramatic effects. Blanche was King John's niece, and that wily King tried to use her as a lever for detaching Philip of France from the cause of the luckless Prince Arthur of Brittany. It had been arranged by treaty that the Dauphin of France should wed a daughter of Alphonso of Spain, but it had not been specified which daughter. Through her mother, however, Blanche had English blood in her veins, and the Pope used this fact as a motive in urging Blanche's husband, the Dauphin, to espouse the cause of Arthur, and to oppose the designs of John.

Citizen. That daughter there of Spain, the Lady Blanche,
Is niece to England. Look upon the years
Of Lewis the Dauphin, and that lovely maid.
If lusty love should go in quest of beauty,
Where should he find it fairer than in Blanch?
If zealous love should go in search of virtue,
Where should he find it purer than in Blanch?
If love ambitious sought a match of birth,
Whose veins bound richer blood than Lady Blanch?

King John. Speak, then, Prince Dauphin: can you love this lady?
Lewis. Nay, ask me if I can refrain from love;
For I do love her most unfeignedly.

In the House of Lancaster the name of Blanche occurs more than once. Edmund, Earl of Lancaster, for instance, married Blanche, the Dowager-Queen of Navarre; and John of Gaunt, Duke of Lancaster, and Earl of Derby, the fourth son of Edward III., married as his first wife Blanche, the daughter of Henry, Duke of Lancaster, and had by her a son who afterwards ascended the English throne as Henry IV.

The name of Blanche was beloved by the writers of early romance, and thus we have, in the Arthurian Cycle, *Blanchardine* and *Eglantine*, as well as *Florice* and *Blancheflour*.

The second of these romances was probably composed in French in the thirteenth century, and was rendered into English in the early part of the fourteenth: a copy of about a half of the English version is still extant in manuscript.

The Spanish poem, *Flores y Blancaflor*, which was long supposed to be the original, is probably nothing more than a translation from French of the plot of which we herewith give a short abstract.

Prince Perse, the heir presumptive of the Emperor of the West, married Topase, the beautiful daughter of the Duke of Ferrara. Grateful for the promise of a child, they went on a pilgrimage to offer up thanks at the shrine of St. James of Compostella.

Upon entering Galicia, faint and weary with

their long journey, they lay down to rest at the entrance of a forest, ignorant of the fact that the Kings of Galicia and Portugal were at war with the Saracens.

Hardly had they lain down to take their much-needed repose, when Saracen soldiers rushed upon them and slew Prince Perse, Topase only awaking to find herself covered with his blood. Struck by her beauty, the soldiers, instead of slaying Topase also, led her into the presence of their commander and Prince, Felix.

Felix took pity on her distress, and at once sent her on to the Queen of Murcia for protection.

The Queen and Topase became such close friends that when, upon the same day, their children were born, they were, by the Queen's express desire, called Florice and Blancheflour. Topase just lived long enough to embrace her little daughter and to baptise her, and then died; but the good Queen, faithful to her promise to Topase, treated Blancheflour just as if she were her own child, so that Florice and Blancheflour grew up side by side, and were trained in all courtly graces; the only difference was that, whilst Florice was trained up in the heathen faith of his fathers, Blanchflour remained a Christian.

Florice could not, however, be persuaded to look with disrespect upon the religion professed by one who seemed so perfect in every way, so that, fearful lest he might be converted to her faith, his father was persuaded to banish his son from his court, aud sent him to dwell with his uncle, the King of Algarva, at Monterio.

At their parting Blancheflour gave Florice a ring in pledge of their mutual love, saying that he was to look at it every day, and that, should the jewel in it remain clear and bright, he might know that all was well with her; but that, should its brilliancy become tarnished, he was to know that then her liberty was endangered.

One day, during his long exile, Florice looked at his talisman, and was horrified to see that its surface had become black and opaque.

He shuddered, turned pale, and, rushing from the presence of his friends, sprang on to his horse and was instantly gone.

Riding all day and night, he reached the gates of Murcia by daybreak of the following morning, and entered the town unperceived, when the gates were opened.

Hardly had he entered, before he met a string of carts passing out, in one of which lay a woman veiled and heavily laden with chains. Florice lowered his vizor, rode up to the waggon and asked, "Who are you"? "Ah"! answered the woman, "I call to witness my God and my Redeemer that Blancheflour is not guilty".

The voice pierced his very soul! He straightway drew his sword, and, threatening instant death to the first who should dispute his will, sent a messenger at once to Felix with the news that an unknown knight had appeared who was prepared to defend Blancheflour against all her accusers.

It appeared that Blancheflour had been charged

with an attempt to kill her benefactor, Felix, through the medium of some chickens she had amused herself with breeding.

The lists were at once prepared, and Florice came out of the ordeal as victor. Blancheflour's innocence was established, and the true poisoner discovered; but Florice, mindful of the danger he ran, should his presence be discovered in the city, dared not remain. Kissing the hands of the King and Queen and Blancheflour, he immediately vanished, and returned to his uncle's court.

Of course their enemies were not satisfied with this, and many more trials awaited the lovers, to test their constancy, until the crowning one of all resulted in poor Blancheflour being sold into slavery. She was carried to Carthagena, to Egypt, and to Babylon, and at last found herself in the harem of the "Amiral of Babylon".

Florice traced her, following her from port to port, and at last got himself conveyed into the harem in a hamper of flowers. He arrived half smothered, but, through the kindness of Clarice, one of Blancheflour's fellow-captives, at last found himself in the presence of his beloved mistress. Blancheflour, speechless with joy and astonishment, sank into his arms; and whilst Florice pressed her to his heart in silent rapture,

Clarice beheld all this,
Their countenance, and their bless,
And laughing said to Blancheflour,
"Fellow, knowest thou ought this flower?
Little ere, he wouldest thou it see;
And now, thou ne might let it fro thee"!

BLANCHE

In the romance of *Tristram and Isolde*, Blancheflour is Tristram's mother, and the wife of Rivalin.

A Blanchefleur is also the heroine of Boccaccio's prose romance called *Il Filocopo.* Her lover Flores is Boccaccio himself, and Blanchefleur represented the daughter of King Robert.

Other literary Blanches are: — Blanche in *The Betrothed*, by Sir Walter Scott; and Blanche in *Old Maids*, by Sheridan Knowles.

Bianca has never become naturalised in England, but a Bianca will be found in Beaumont and Fletcher's play *The Women's Prize*, in *The Taming of the Shrew*, by William Shakespeare, and in *Othello*, by William Shakespeare. Robert Herrick, too, has two little poems, one entitled *Being once blind, His Request to Biancha*, and the other *Kissing Usury.*

Biancha, let
Me pay the debt
I owe thee for a kiss
Thou lent'st to me,
And I to thee
Will render ten for this.

If thou wilt say
Ten will not pay
For that so rich a one;
I'll clear the sum,
If it will come
Unto a million.

By this, I guess
Of happiness
Who has a little measure,
He must of right
To th'utmost mite
Make payment of his pleasure.

BOADICEA, meaning "Victory" was the name of a British heroine who headed an insurrection against the Romans and reduced London to ashes, but was at last defeated by Suetonius Paulinus, and then, according to tradition, poisoned herself, A.D. 61.

When the British warrior queen,
  Bleeding from the Roman rods,
Sought, with an indignant mien,
  Counsel of her country's gods.

Sage beneath a spreading oak
  Sat the Druid hoary chief,
Ev'ry burning word he spoke,
  Full of rage and full of grief.

Boadicea (Cowper.)

Upon her story two tragedies have been based, one by Richard Glover, the other by John Fletcher, besides the well-known Ode by Cowper and Tennyson's poem beginning,

While about the shore of Mona those Neronian legionaries
Burnt and broke the grove and altar of the Druid and Druidess,
Far in the East Boädicéa, standing loftily charloted,
Mad and maddening all that heard her in her fierce volubility,
Girt by half the tribes of Britain, near the colony Cámulodúne
Yell'd and shriek'd between her daughters o'er a wild confederacy.

BRENDA, signifying "a sword", has, in the modern craving for unhackneyed names, steadily gained ground with the English public.

A Zetland name, Sir Walter Scott in *The Pirate* chose it for one of the daughters of Magnus Troil, the Zetland *udaller*, or landholder.

BRIDGET, Bride, or Biddy means *strength*, some deriving it from the word *brygge* = bridge, symbolic of succour, others, and amongst these Miss Yonge, who is perhaps our most trustworthy authority on this name, considering that it comes from *brîgh* = strength, and that the first Brighid, or Bridget, was "probably the daughter of the [Keltic] fire-god and the goddess of Wisdom and Song".

The English contraction of the name is Bride, the Irish Biddy: the Scotch have only Bride, the French and German, Brigitta, the Italian Brigida and Brigita, whilst the Swedes have many modifications, including Brita, Beret, and Begga.

> These three rest in one tomb in Down—
> Brigid, Patrick, and pious Columba.

In Ireland Bridget has always been a very favourite name, and is one example, among only a few, of a Keltic name obtaining European popularity. Like so many honoured names, it owes its vogue, not to its musical sound, but to its association in the minds of a grateful peasantry with one of the best-loved Saints of the Western Church.

St. Bridget, St. Bridgit, St. Brigid, St. Bride, for she is known by all these names, was born at Fochard, in Ulster, and was the daughter of a converted Druid, named Dubhshach: she was from her childhood remarkable for an intensely religious spirit, and received the religious veil in her youth, at the hands of St. Niel, the nephew of St. Patrick. She built herself a cell under a large oak tree, which came to be known as

Kill-dara, signifying cell of the oak, whence her title of St. Bridget of Kildare. Living there, she devoted herself to deeds of mercy, and benefited the whole countryside by her good works and spotless life. After a time, the beauty of Bridget's life attracted other women to her side, and they formed themselves into a sisterhood, which gradually extended its branches over all Ireland.

St. Bridget lived in the sixth century; but, though no less than five "lives" have been written of her, none of them gives any real account of the Saint herself, but all are mainly devoted to describing wonderful miracles performed by her.

It is told of her that on one occasion, when listening to St. Patrick preaching, Bridget fell asleep. Those sitting near her made signs to the preacher to rouse her, but the Saint took no notice until he had closed his address, and then he begged Bridget to tell him her dream. "Alas! Father", she answered, "I am sad from the vision vouchsafed me while I slept. I was standing on a height with all Ireland in view, and from all parts there issued flames that rose up and joined, and filled the air around. I looked a second time, and lo! the mountains and hills were still burning, but the flames were not so widespread as before; and then, when I looked a third time, only small flames of candles met my sight. And when I looked a fourth time the whole island was covered with ashes, except for a half-hidden torch here and there. I closed my eyes and wept, but on opening them yet a fifth time I beheld a bright flame burning in the north, which gradually spread until the whole island was again illuminated". This vision is supposed to have been a forecast of the general decay of religion which beset Ireland during the Danish invasions, and its revival after the advent of St. Malachy.

Another legend connected with her depicts her in a truly business light. We are told that the then King of Leinster had a nature which erred on the side of frugality, and was rather annoyed by St. Bridget's frequent applications for aid towards her numerous charities, so that, when she appealed to him for a grant of land, he answered her in rather a grudging spirit. Finding her petition was likely to be met with a rebuff, the Saint asked him whether he would not at least grant her so much of the land on which they then stood, as could be covered by her cloak. To this, the King, glad to be rid of her importunity, readily assented. At the time of their interview they were standing on the highest point of the Curragh, but what was the King's horror when he saw that, upon St. Bridget directing four of her Sisters to spread out her cloak, they at once took up the garment, standing back to back, and then, still holding firmly to the cloth, began running as fast as they could in four directions, the cloak stretching as they ran, until they had covered at least a mile square of ground. The King exclaimed in consternation as he watched; but St. Bridget calmly said, "My cloak will cover your whole province to punish you for your meanness to the poor". Whereupon the

King promised amendment, provided the Saint would call her maidens back.

Upon another occasion, the legend goes that, when St. Bridget and some of her sisterhood were upon a journey, they sought shelter at the court of a petty king, who, with his chief officers, happened to be from home. It remained for his younger sons to act as hosts to their saintly guests. After St. Bridget had joined in a simple meal, she asked for music ; but her hosts were fain to confess that, alas! there were no musicians to be had, although they would have been willing to have gratified St. Bridget had they been able. Whereupon St. Bridget touched their fingers with her own and uttered a prayer over them, and straightway the young men played on harps, as though inspired.

Amongst many other acts accredited to her, St. Bridget of Kildare is said to have, in at least one case, restored sight to the blind, to have healed lepers, to have caused useless cows to yield milk, to have hung her cloak on a sunbeam, and to have rendered a whole company of horsemen immovable when in pursuit of a fugitive, until their victim had had time to escape.

This Saint is one of the patron Saints of Ireland.

The second St. Bridgit, Brigit, or Birget, who has conferred, indirectly, her name on as many Scandinavian babies as her Irish sister has on children of the Emerald Isle, was of Royal blood, and the daughter of Birger, legislator of Upland, and of Ingeburgis, a lady descended from the Gothic kings.

Both her parents were devout Christians, but her mother died whilst the future Saint was still in her infancy, and the child was therefore brought up by an aunt. Bridgit early gave signs of intense piety, and by the age of ten years began to feel a call to the religious life: at the age of sixteen, however, in obedience to her father's wish, she married Ulpho, Prince of Nericia in Sweden, who was himself only eighteen years of age. They soon enrolled themselves in the third Order of St. Francis, and, withdrawing themselves from the gaieties of a court life, led noble, self-sacrificing lives, and brought up their eight children to be good men and women. Ulpho died in 1344 in the Monastery of Aloastre, and after her husband's death Bridgit, having divided her property equally between her children, withdrew from worldly affairs altogether, leading a life of self-renunciation and privation. She built a large monastery at Wastein in Lincopen, Sweden, and for some years retired thither herself. This monastery contained two absolutely distinct convents, one for men and the other for women: it was, like so many others, destroyed upon the change in the national religion.

St. Bridgit made a pilgrimage to Rome, was the subject of many "revelations", and finally died, at the age of seventy-one, on July 23rd, 1373, at Rome, and was buried in the Church of St. Laurence in Panis Perna, her body being subsequently removed to her monastery of Wastein at the request of some of her children. She was canonized in 1415.

Many churches have from time to time been

dedicated to one or other of these Saints, the best known of which is St. Bride's Church, Fleet Street, London. Bridewell Prison was originally, as a palace, named after St. Bride; and an island of the Hebrides was called after her, Brigidiani, from a famous monastery built there in her honour.

> Sweet Bridget blush'd, and therewithal
> Fresh blossoms from her cheeks did fall;
> I thought at first 'twas but a dream,
> Till after I had handled them
> And smelt them, then they smelt to me
> As blossoms of the almond tree.
>
> *Upon his Kinswoman, Mistress Bridget Herrick*
> (ROBERT HERRICK.)

Bridget is not a name which occurs very frequently in literature; but there are a few instances — for example, Bridget, the mother of Tom Jones, in Fielding's novel of that name; Mistress Bridget, who figures in Sterne's great novel, *The Life and Opinions of Tristram Shandy*; Mother Bridget, the aunt of Catherine Seyton and Abbess of St. Catherine, in Sir Walter Scott's *Abbot*; and Bridget, the milk-woman at Falkland Castle, in his *Fair Maid of Perth*. As a modern example, we may instance Bride, the heroine in George Cardella's novel, *For the Life of Others*.

In drama there is Bridget, in Ben Jonson's play, entitled *Every Man in his Humour*; whilst in verse we have Tom Moore's humorous letters of *The Fudge Family in Paris*, in which he immortalises the Irish abbreviation of the name— Biddy; and Mr. Alfred Percival Graves, in his little lyric *Loobeen*, gives us a Bridgid. Herrick, besides the verse quoted above, wrote the following lines :

THE MEADOW-VERSE ; OR, ANNIVERSARY TO MISTRESS BRIDGET LOWMAN.

Come with the spring-time forth, fair maid, and be
This year again the meadow's deity.
Yet ere ye enter give us leave to set
Upon your head this flowery coronet ;
To make this neat distinction from the rest,
You are the prince and princess of the feast ;
To which with silver feet lead you the way,
While sweet-breath nymphs attend you on this day.
This is your hour, and best you may command,
Since you are lady of this fairy land.
Full Mirth wait on you, and such mirth as shall
Cherish the cheek, but make none blush at all.

BRITOMART, or Britomartis, comes from the Greek Βριτόμαρτις, and means "sweet maiden", a Cretan epithet for Diana, whence Spenser introduces her into his *Faëry Queene* to personify Chastity, where she is armed with

A mighty spear
Which Bladud made by magick art of yore
And used the same in batteill aye to beare.

Sir Walter Scott wrote—

She charmed at once, and tamed the heart
Incomparable Britomart.

BRUNHILDA, BRYNHILD, BRUNILLA, or BRUNEHAUT are all the same name really, and mean breast-plate battle-maid, an old Teutonic name still in use, and now in England becoming more generally used than it has been for very many years.

The original Brunhilda was a Walkyrie of human extraction, who, like some of her companions, used to take a keen interest in human concerns, and to hover over her favourite heroes when they were engaged in battle. If these Walkyries married mortals, they lost their Walkyrie power.

Brunhilda was Queen of Isenland, renowned for her stately beauty and strength. Of wooers she had many, and with all of them she entered into personal combat, and almost invariably she slew them.

When Siegfried, the son of Sigmund, started on his adventures, he determined to try his luck as a suitor to Brunhilda. She met him graciously, but clad in full armour ; and as he saw her in her majestic beauty towering above all the women of her court, he said, " I could never love her ; she is too like a man ", and therewith he left her.

After a time Siegfried's friend Gunther, King of Burgundy, asked him to go with him to Isenland, as he was reolved to win and wed the queen. Accordingly they went, and met with a courteous reception from Brunhilda. In the inevitable contest which ensued, Gunther was victorious, but only because he was aided by Siegfried in his cap of darkness, which rendered him invisible. Brunhild, when defeated, calmly accepted her fate, and, summoning her nobles, caused them to take the oath of allegiance to Gunther, and then travelled with him and

Siegfried to Worms, and became his bride. The thought, however, that she, a Walkyrie, had been overcome by a mortal in single combat always rankled in her breast, and hearing, through unadvised words that fell from the lips of Siegfried's wife Criemhilda that Siegfried had given his aid to Gunther, Brunhilda waited for an opportunity of revenge, and found it one day when Siegfried and Criemhilda were on a visit to the Burgundian Court. Siegfried went out hunting, and as he stooped to drink water at a spring, he was stabbed in the back by Hagan, a tool of Brunhilda's.

Time passed, Criemhilda mourned for Siegfried, and Brunhilda sat embroidering tapestry by her mother-in-law Ute's side, and as she tried to depict on her canvas, the death of Baldur, she said to Ute, "is it not strange that do what I will, the face I am working will resemble Siegfried and not Baldur, Siegfried as he looked that last time we saw him as he rode off to the hunt. I must get Hagan to give me Siegfried's sword Baldung". Accordingly, Brunhilda obtained the sword Baldung, and went with it to Siegfried's grave and laid it on his coffin, and lay down beside the coffin and died.

Sir Walter Scott introduces a Brenhilda in *Count Robert of Paris*.

CALISTA, probably from the Greek καλλίστη (*kalliste*), meaning "most beautiful", with the Latin feminine termination "a". The masculine form of the name occurs in an old "tragicomedy" entitled *Calisto and Melibæa*, and

Massinger introduces a Calista into his play *The Guard*.

CAMILLA is supposed to be a name of Etruscan origin, and signifies "freeborn servant of the Temple". The Camilli and Camillæ were the children of both sexes who attended on the priests and priestesses during the performance of their religious duties. It was necessary that they should be the children of freeborn parents, and that both parents should still be living: they were especially attached to the Flamen Dialis and his wife the Flaminica, and also to the Curiones. The priests generally selected their own children for the office, so that they might teach them their duties and secure them succession to the priestly office.

Camilla, the virgin Queen of the Volscians, whom Virgil celebrates in the *Æneid*, was a votaress of Diana and thus received the name. She is said to have been so swift and light of foot that she could run over a field of corn without bending a single blade, and could even cross the ocean waves without wetting her feet. Pope refers to her exploits in his *Essay on Criticism*, ll. 372-3, thus:—

Not so when swift Camilla scours the plain,
Flies o'er the unbending corn and skims along the main.

(POPE.)

Camilla goes
To meet her death amidst her fatal foes—
The nymph I loved of all my mortal train,
Invested with Diana's arms, in vain.
Nor is my kindness for the virgin new:
'Twas born with her; and with her years it grew.

CAMILLA

Her father Metabus, when forced away
From old Privernum for tyrannic sway,
Snatch'd up, and saved from his prevailing foes,
This tender babe, companion of his woes.
Casmilla was her mother: but he drown'd
One hissing letter in a softer sound,
And call'd Camilla. . . .

—*Æneid*, Bk. XI. ll. 809-21 (VIRGIL.)

Last from the Volscians fair Camilla came,
And led her war-like troops, a warrior dame:
Unbred to spinning, in the loom unskill'd,
She chose the nobler Pallas of the field.
Mix'd with the first, the fierce virago fought,
Sustain'd the toils of arms, the danger sought,
Outstripp'd the winds in speed upon the plain,
Flew o'er the field, nor hurt the bearded grain:
She swept the seas, and as she skimm'd along,
Her flying feet unbathed on billows hung.
Men, boys, and women, stupid with surprise,
Where'er she passes, fix their wond'ring eyes:

. . . .

Her purple habit sits with such a grace
On her smooth shoulders, and so suits her face;
Her head with ringlets of her hair is crown'd;
And in a golden caul the curls are bound.
She shakes her myrtle jav'lin: and, behind,
Her Lycian quiver dances in the wind.

—*Æneid*, Bk. VII. ll. 1094-1113.

Camillus was one of the names of the *gens* of Furius, and was borne by the Roman who, after having five times served his Country as Dictator, was then falsely accused of embezzlement, and went into voluntary exile; but returned when his country was in danger, and delivered it from the Gauls.

Camille is a popular name in France now, and has been since the middle of the seventeenth century. Camilla became popular in England during the classical period of her literature when all things classic were in favour, and it still survives amongst us though it is not common.

In Italy the name has long been a favourite, and a Neapolitan of the sixteenth century has been canonised. Born in 1550, he was left fatherless and motherless when only six years of age. He entered the army when still a mere boy, and there contracted a great love of gambling and all games of hazard. He at last, to pay his gambling debts, had to part even with necessities, so that when the army was disbanded in 1574 his circumstances were so reduced that he had to take to the occupation of a driver of asses, and to work as a bricklayer.

Working at the Capuchin Monastery, he fell under the influence of some of the friars, who induced him to reconsider his position and reflect upon the follies of his past life. So earnestly did they exhort him, that he became converted; and, going to Rome, devoted himself to tending the sick in St. James's Hospital there. He introduced so many improvements for the comfort and welfare of the sufferers and in the methods of nursing, that he was after a time appointed director of the Hospital, and from that time onwards his life was one continual effort to lessen the sufferings of mankind. St. Camillus afterwards founded religious houses in many parts of Italy, including Bologna, Milan, Genoa, Florence, Mantua and elsewhere, and, though a great sufferer himself, went on with his good work until his death in 1614, in his sixty-sixth year.

In Literature Camilla is the name of the wife of Anselmo of Florence in *Don Quixote;* a Camille occurs in Corneille's tragedy of *Les Horaces;* there is a Camillo in Shakespeare's *Winter's Tale;* and a Camilla in *The Mistake* by Congreve, whilst Drummond of Hawthornden has an epigram upon a Camilla; and, perhaps best known of all, Mme. D'Arblay has a novel entitled *Camilla.* In Dryden, Pope, Thomson, and Drummond innumerable references will be found to Virgil's heroine.

> Ye loveless bards! intent with artful pains
> To form a sigh, or to contrive a tear!
> Forego your Pindus, and on —— plains
> Survey Camilla's charms, and grow sincere.
>
> *Elegy No. I.* (William Shenstone.)

CAROLINE: see Charlotte.

CASSANDRA: see Alexandra.

CATHERINE, etc.: see Katherine, etc.

CELIA: see Lilian.

CHARITY: see Faith.

CHARLOTTE, Caroline, Carrie, and Lottie are names of Teutonic origin, the original form being, amongst the Franks, Karl, changed in Latin to Carolus, and in Anglo-Saxon England recognizable in Ceorl. Karl means simply "man" and was the family name of a whole line of Frankish Kings whose greatest member is known to us as Charlemagne, or Charles the great.

An old wives' tale would have us believe that Charlemagne got his name in this wise. He had been put out to nurse, as an infant, as the custom was, and when the nurse returned him to his mother he was so much grown that the

Queen exclaimed "what great carle is this"? and that henceforth he was known as Charlemagne instead of as David, which was his true name.

There is no evidence whatever of the truth of this story, or that his name was David, and it is certainly only one of the many fables which have gathered round the now half-mythical figure of the great Carlovingian King.

All we know with any certainty about him is, that he was the eldest son of King Pepin the Short, and grandson of Charles Martel, and that he was born at Salsburg in 742.

He and his brother Carloman together succeeded their father on the throne in 768, and upon Carloman dying three years later Charlemagne became sole King. He spent the first thirty years of his reign in almost continual warfare against the Saxons, whom he sought to convert to Christianity as well as to conquer, alternatively using the arguments of great mildness and great cruelty to strengthen those of ordered reason (on one occasion alone, he is said to have ordered 4000 people to be beheaded).

Charlemagne also conquered Lombardy and part of Spain, and was, in the year 800 crowned Emperor of the West, at Rome, by Pope Leo III., receiving the title of Augustus.

He encouraged science and letters, himself studying under the direction of the great English scholar Alcuin, and as a great legislator as well as a successful soldier deserved the surname bestowed upon him of "the Great". Charlemagne died at Aix-la-Chapelle in 814.

The Karlings and their descendants intermarried with all the royal houses of Europe, so that in Spain, Germany, Austria, Hungary, France, and Italy the name of Charles was thenceforth recognised as a royal one. France alone has had nine Kings of the name, Hungary three, Germany seven, Sweden no less than fifteen, and Spain, if we include Navarre, seven, whilst even in England we have had two.

An immense proportion of these derived their names directly from Charles I. of Spain and V. of Germany and of the Holy Roman Empire.

The fate of those who sat on the English throne was not so happy, nor their influence on the nation so beneficent as to encourage their successors to revive the name, and for other obvious reasons it has not been adopted by the members of the House of Hanover. The pathos and romance, however, which have clung round the memory of Charles I., and of the young Pretender "bonnie Prince Charlie," have, in spite of their faults, served to popularize their name in the British Isles, until now it is one of the commonest we have.

> Name to thy loved Elysian groves,
> That o'er enchanted spirits twine,
> A fairer form than cherub loves,
> And let the name be Caroline.
>
> (THOMAS CAMPBELL.)

The feminine forms are Charlotte and Caroline with the diminutives Lolotte, Lotty, Carlina, Chatty, Lottie and Carrie. As a woman's name it is nothing like as old as the masculine form, and does not probably date back further than the beginning of the fifteenth century. Louis XI.

of France married Charlotte of Savoy, and thus introduced the name into France, and the name Caroline, which originated in Italy, became popular in England through its being the name of George II.'s Queen, whilst Charlotte became fashionable upon the advent of the Queen of George III., the mother of his fifteen children. She was very popular, being a woman full of homely, household virtues which touched the people's hearts, though politically she was a nonentity.

Both names were, however, known in England before the accession of the House of Hanover, though not in common use, and when Sir Walter Raleigh discovered the first great American colony in 1585 he called it Carolina, and the name of its capital became Charles' town or Charleston.

The misfortunes of our second Queen Caroline, and the early death of the people's favourite, the Princess Charlotte of Wales, put the finishing touches to the popularity of both names in England and Scotland, and ever since then Charlottes and Carolines, Lotties and Carries have multiplied in every nook and corner of the British Isles.

Queen Caroline Wilhelmina married George II. of England whilst he was still only Prince George of Hanover, and she was crowned in Westminster Abbey in 1727. She died ten years afterwards. She was the grand-mother of the unhappy Queen Caroline Amelia Elizabeth who in 1795 married her cousin, the Prince of Wales, who afterwards ascended the English throne as George IV.

Almost immediately after the birth of her first and only child, the Princess Charlotte, her husband abandoned her. The unhappy princess retired to Blackheath, and there, devoting most of her hours to the arts and sciences, lived a life of benevolence. Her husband sought a divorce which he failed to obtain, the King, George III., strongly taking the part of his daughter-in-law.

Caroline afterwards left England, and, assuming the title of Countess of Wolfenbüttel, travelled on the continent and in the East. Whilst at Jerusalem she founded a new Order of Knighthood—the Order of St. Caroline.

During her absence from England her chief protector—George III.—had died, as well as the Duke of Kent, who was also her friend, besides her brother, the Duke of Brunswick, and her daughter, the much loved Princess Charlotte. When she returned therefore, she found herself without friends at Court and George IV. advanced fresh charges against her.

These charges, with the help of Mr., afterwards Lord, Brougham, the Queen refuted, and demanded the right to be crowned with her husband in Westminster Abbey.

She was, however, denied even admission into the building, and crushed by this last insult her health at last broke down, and on August 7th, 1821 this unhappy Caroline died.

Her daughter, the Princess Charlotte, born on 7th January 1796, and married in 1816 to Prince Leopold of Coburg (afterwards Leopold I. of Belgium), had from her early childhood given signs, not only of great mental endowments, but also of great nobility of character, and as she grew into womanhood she commanded the love as well as the deep respect of those by whom she was surrounded.

Her marriage, too, was known to have been one of true affection, and not of policy, and the nation, wearied by the domestic broils and the dissolute habits of George IV., looked forward with ardent hope and confidence to the time when the English throne should be filled by one in every way worthy of the high position she would fill. All the nation's hopes, however, were crushed by the Princess Charlotte's sudden death in November 1817.

The following extracts from verses by Thomas Campbell, and by Mrs. Hemans, upon the sad occasion, will give some idea of the national feelings when the blow fell.

Daughter of England! for a nation's sighs,
A nation's heart went with thine obsequies!—
And oft shall time revert a look of grief
On thine existence, beautiful and brief.
Fair spirit! send thy blessing from above
On realms where thou art canonised by love!
Give to a father's, husband's bleeding mind,
The peace that angels lend to human kind;
To us who in thy loved remembrance feel
A sorrowing, but a soul-ennobling zeal—
A loyalty that touches all the best
And loftiest principles of England's breast!
Still may thy name speak concord from the tomb—
Still in the Muse's breath thy memory bloom!
They shall describe thy life, thy form pourtray;
But all the love that mourns thee swept away,
'Tis not in language or expressive arts
To paint; ye feel it, Britons, in your hearts!

(THOMAS CAMPBELL.)

And she is gone!—the royal and the young,
In soul commanding, and in heart benign!
Who, from a race of kings and heroes sprung,
Glow'd with a spirit lofty as her line.

. . . .

Oh, many a bright existence we have seen
Quench'd in the glow and fullness of its prime;
And many a cherish'd flower, ere now, hath been
Cropt ere its leaves were breathed upon by time.
We have lost heroes in their noon of pride,
Whose fields of triumph gave them but a bier;
And we have wept when soaring genius died,
Check'd in the glory of his mid career!
But here our hopes were centred—all is o'er:
All thought in this absorb'd,—she was—and is no more!

We watch'd her childhood from its earliest hour,
From every word and look blest omens caught;
While that young mind developed all its power,
And rose to energies of loftiest thought.
On her was fix'd the patriot's ardent eye—
One hope still bloom'd, one vista still was fair;
And when the tempest swept the troubled sky,
She was our dayspring—all was cloudless *there*;
And oh! how lovely broke on England's gaze,
E'en through the mist and storm, the light of distant days.

(Mrs. Hemans.)

Another Charlotte of world-wide fame is Charlotte Corday, a native of Normandy, born in 1768, of a decayed but noble family, and a blood-connection of the great poet Corneille. Though brought up in the seclusion of a convent, she yet obtained access to many books, and zealously read the writings of Jean Jacques Rousseau and of Raynal, besides the histories of Greece and Rome; and by the time Charlotte Corday returned to her father's house she had become an ardent republican.

Her father, a moderate royalist, could not sympathise with her revolutionary views: they quarrelled, and in 1792 Charlotte left her home and went to live at Caen, where she became intimate with many of the proscribed Girondists, with whom she sympathised warmly in their detestation of Marat.

Convinced that while Marat lived there could be no hope for her beloved France, Charlotte Corday resolved to give her life in order that she might destroy his.

Her face was beautiful, cultured and refined, but of singularly determined expression, and it was a true index to her mind.

Obtaining an introduction to one of the Deputies, she, in July 1793 started for Paris, leaving behind her a message to her father, praying that he might forgive her.

A few days after her arrival in the capital Charlotte Corday called at Marat's house, but he was ill and she failed to gain admission. A second effort was more successful; she was admitted and found him in his bath. For some time they conversed on public affairs, but before the interview was ended Marat was dead—stabbed in the breast by Charlotte Corday's knife.

She wrote an address to her countrymen justifying her deed, then went to meet her death on the guillotine with a calm, unshaken courage.

She is of stately Norman figure; in her twenty-fifth year; of beautiful still countenance; her name is Charlotte Corday, heretofore styled D'Armans, while nobility still was. . . . " She was a Republican before the Revolution, and never wanted energy ". A completeness, a decision, is in this fair female figure: " by energy she means the spirit that will prompt one to sacrifice himself for his country What if she, this fair young Charlotte, had emerged from her secluded stillness, suddenly like a star; cruel, lovely, with half-angelic, half-demoniac splendour, to gleam for a moment, and in a moment to be extinguished: to be held in memory, so bright, complete, was she, through long centuries ".

(Thomas Carlyle.)

Another very different Charlotte, yet worthy of some mention here, is Charlotte Brontë, only the daughter of a poor Yorkshire rector, but full of genius, and the authoress of some of the most popular novels ever written by a woman. Her life, as pictured to us by her biographers, is one of the most touching and attractive in the annals of English literature.

The number of Charlottes or Carolines occurring in literature is not great, but there are in drama: Charlotte, in *Fatal Curiosity*, by Lillo; Charlotte, in *The Mock Doctor*, by Fielding; Charlotte, in *The Hypocrite*, by Isaac Bickerstaff; Charlotte, in *The Stranger*, by Benjamin Thompson; Charlotte Goodchild, in *Love à-la-Mode*, by Charles Macklin; Charlotte, in *An Honest Man's Fortune*, by Beaumont and Fletcher; Charlotte, in *The Little French Lawyer*, by Beaumont and Fletcher. In fiction: Charlotte, and Caroline, in *The Adventures of Philip*, and Caroline, in *A Shabby Genteel Story*, all by Thackeray; Lady Caroline Campbell, in *The Heart of Midlothian*, and Charlot, in *Quentin Durward*, both by Sir Walter

Scott; Charlotte, in *Oliver Twist*, by Dickens; and Lady Charlotte, in *High Life Below Stairs*, by Rev. J. Townley. In poetry: *Lines to Miss Charlotte Pulteney*, by Ambrose Philips; *Caroline: a poem in Two Parts*, by Thomas Campbell; and three poems by Lord Byron, to *Caroline*.

Oh! when, my adored, in the tomb will they place me,
  Since, in life, love and friendship for ever are fled!
If again in the mansion of death I embrace thee,
  Perhaps they will leave unmolested the dead.
(LORD BYRON.)

O! sacred to the fall of day,
  Queen of propitious stars, appear,
And early rise, and long delay,
  When Caroline herself is here!
(THOS. CAMPBELL.)

CHLOE signifies "blooming", and was a very popular name with pastoral and amatory poets of the Elizabethan and classical periods in English literature. It is now quite out of favour in England, but for some odd reason popular amongst the coloured people in America.

  "Yet Chloe sure was form'd without a spot".—
Nature in her then err'd not, but forgot.
  "With every pleasing, every prudent part,
Say, what can Chloe want"?—She wants a heart,
She speaks, behaves, and acts just as she ought;
But never, never, reach'd one generous thought.
Virtue she finds too painful an endeavour,
Content to dwell in decencies for ever.

CHRISTINE, CHRISTABELLE, etc. The Greek verb χρίω (*chrio*), signifying to touch, rub, or anoint, gave rise to the term *Christos*, the anointed, the Greek translation of the old

Hebrew prophetic word Messiah, whence the title of Jesus of Nazareth; whence also the word Christianoi, used to designate his disciples.

The pagan Roman of Diocletian's time had no dislike to the term Chrestian, that only signifying that those who employed it were the followers of one Chrestus, a philosopher, but they resented the name of Christian, which meant the anointed of God, and it was applied to the followers of Christ as a term of reproach.

> Go now, my little book, to every place
>
> . . . . . .
>
> Call at their door. If any say, who's there?
> Then answer thou, Christina is here.
>
> (John Bunyan.)

> And she came all unattended, her protection in her mien;
> And with somewhat of reluctance bade me call her name Christine.
>
> (T. B. Read.)

The names Christian, Christine, Christina, Christiana, with the diminutives Chrissie and Kirsty, mean a follower of Christ; Christabel = a fair follower of Christ.

Christos is now a common name in Greece, and was so at one time with us, but was discontinued at the period of the Reformation. The surname Christie is doubtless a survival.

Christabel, revived by Coleridge in his poem of the name (1797), had long before his time been popularized in England through the old ballad of *Sir Cauline*, wherein Christabelle is the heroine.

CHRISTINE

In Ireland, ferr over the sea
  There dwelleth a bonnye King;
And with him a young and comlye knighte,
  Men call him syr Cauline.

This king had a "daughter deere", whose name was Christabelle. Christabelle and Sir Cauline fall in love, and though at first she protests that as her father's "onlye heire" she cannot entertain his suit, after Sir Cauline has worked wonders to obtain the lady's love, she yields, and

From that daye forthe that ladye fayre
  Lovde syr Cauline the knighte:
From that daye forthe he only joyde
  Whan shee was in his sight.

Everye white will have its blacke,
  And everye sweete its sowre:
This founde the ladye Christabelle
  In an untimely howre.

For so it befelle, as syr Cauline
  Was with that ladye faire,
The kinge her father walked forthe
  To take the evenyng air.

. . . .

Then forthe sir Cauline he was ledde,
  And throwne in dungeon deepe:
And the ladye into a towre so hye,
  There left to wayle and weepe.

Christabelle became so "woe-begone" that, to rouse her, a tournament is held at which Sir Cauline comes off champion, but he is mortally wounded.

Then giving her one partinge looke,
  He closed his eyes in death,
Ere Christabelle, that ladye milde,
  Begane to drawe her breathe.

CHRISTINE

. . . . . .

Then fayntinge in a deadlye swoune,
And with a deepe-fette sighe,
That burst her gentle hearte in twayne
Fayre Christabelle did dye.

The first Christina whose name has come down to us, is one of noble Roman birth, who suffered martyrdom in A.D. 295 or 300. It is asserted that on being condemned to death by drowning she was cast into lake Bolsena with a mill-stone round her neck, in spite of which she floated to the surface supported by angels, so that in order to kill her her persecutors had to shoot her with arrows. During her life and from the early age of ten many miracles are attributed to this Saint.

It is after her that all the numerous Venetian Christinas are called, and amongst them probably Christina Rossetti, the poetess of Italian parentage, though of English birth.

There was also a Saint Christiana, a Christian slave, who was instrumental in converting the King and Queen of Iberia to Christianity, in the third century. From Italy the name travelled to England, Ireland and Scotland, becoming especially popular in the last-named country.

The name is very common in Germany too, and in Sweden, Norway, and Denmark, commonest of all, in both masculine and feminine forms. Christian or Christiern has been the name of no less than nine Kings of Denmark and five of Norway, and of one Queen, Christina of Sweden.

As a modern Swedish representative of the name we at once think of the great singer, Christine Nillson. The daughter of a small farmer, she first earned her living by singing and playing the violin at fairs. She has ended by being one of our greatest operatic and oratorio singers.

In 1872 she was married in Westminster Abbey to M. Auguste Rouzaud, who has since died.

The name Christopher = Christ-bearer, belongs to the same class, and has the English feminine Christophera, which is however now rarely met with.

Neither Queen Christina of Sweden, nor Queen Christina of Spain, can be looked upon as ornaments to their name, unfortunately.

Christina of Sweden, the only child of Gustavus Adolphus, was only a little girl of six years old when she succeeded to the throne in 1632, and was not formally crowned until 1650. For four years she governed her kingdom wisely, and endeavoured to encourage learning and the arts, but she then abdicated in favour of her cousin Charles Gustavus, left Sweden, embraced the Roman religion, and led a life of dissipation. Upon the death of her cousin in 1660 she returned to Sweden, but her change of religion and her evil life combined to make her former subjects decline to reinstate her in the sovereignty. She died in 1689.

Queen Christina of Spain, who was born in 1806 and who died in 1878, was the mother of Queen Isabella, and was appointed queen-regent during her daughter's minority; but she secretly married an officer of the guards, Fernando Munoz, and in 1840 was compelled to abdicate. She so roused the resentment of the Spaniards by her constant support of arbitrary and tyrannical measures, that she was at last driven into exile, and died at Havre.

We all know Christiana, the wife of Christian in the Pilgrim's Progress, by John Bunyan, who sets out to join her husband in the Celestial City, with her four children, and her friend Mercy, under the guidance of Great Heart, and who therefore went in silver slippers along the thorny road.

What Christian left lock'd up, and went his way
Sweet Christiana opens with her key.

Other literary examples of the name are Christina in *Love in a Wood* by Wycherly; *Christine*, "the Maid of the South Seas", a tale written in metre by Mary Russell Mitford, after the manner of Sir Walter Scott; Christina in *Gustavus Vasa* by H. Brooke; Christine in *The Prisoner of State* by Edward Stirling; *The Ballad of Babe Christabel*, by Gerald Massey: this last is an elegy on the death of one of the author's children, and runs

In this dim world of clouding cares,
  We rarely know, till 'wildered eyes
  See white wings lessening up the skies,
The angels with us unawares. . . .

Strange glory streams through life's wild rents,
  And through the open door of death
  We see the heaven that beckoneth
To the beloved going hence.

CHRISTINE

There is also a poem called *Christine* by T. Buchanan Read; also Samuel Taylor Coleridge's *Christabel*

All they who live in the upper sky
Do love you, holy Christabel.

and lastly Robert Browning's poem *Cristina*

She should never have looked at me
  If she meant I should not love her!
There are plenty . . . men, you call such,
  I suppose . . . she may discover
All her soul to, if she pleases,
  And yet leave much as she found them:
But I'm not so, and she knew it
  When she fixed me, glancing round them.

Doubt you if, in some such moment,
  As she fixed me, she felt clearly,
Ages past the soul existed,
  Here an age 'tis resting merely,
And hence fleets again for ages,
  While the true end, sole and single,
It stops here for is, this love-way,
  With some other soul to mingle?

Else it loses what it lived for,
  And eternally must lose it;
Better ends may be in prospect,
  Deeper blisses (if you choose it),
But this life's end and this love-bliss
  Have been lost here. Doubt you whether
This she felt as, looking at me,
  Mine and her souls rushed together?

Such am I: the secret's mine now!
  She has lost me, I have gained her;
Her soul's mine: and thus, grown perfect,
  I shall pass my life's remainder.
Life will just hold out the proving
  Both our powers, alone and blended:
And then, come the next life quickly!
  This world's use will have been ended.

(*Stanzas* 1, 5, 6, 8.)

CICELY, or CECILIA, is one of those names which, like Gladys, must, one would think, have originated in a personal defect. *Coecus* in Latin means "blind", and *caecilia* is the Latin for a slow-worm, which in England also is by country-folk called the blind-worm. The family name of Cecil doubtless comes from this, but some who have studied the subject are of opinion that Cecilia, instead of being the feminine of Cecil, is, together with the name of the large Roman gens or family of the Caecilii, derived from Caiguilius = the son of Caiguil. With such a much simpler and more obvious derivation before us this last suggestion seems perhaps a little far-fetched.

Caecilias occur frequently in ancient history, one of the best-known being Caia Caecilia, the wife of Tarquinius Priscus, and both on the Continent and in England it is popular to this day. The pretty English forms of Cicely and Cecily were at one time discarded as being too common, but are now daily gaining ground again.

Saint Cecilia, or Saint Cicely, is chiefly responsible for the popularity of her name, and, a favourite subject for both painters and poets, has had namesakes wherever music is loved.

She is nearly always represented in art as in the act of playing an organ, and has consequently been credited in the popular imagination with the invention of that instrument.

At last divine Cecilia came,
Inventress of the vocal frame;
The sweet enthusiast, from her sacred store,

Enlarged the former narrow bounds,
And added length to solemn sounds,
With nature's mother-wit, and arts unknown before.
Let old Timotheus yield the prize,
Or both divide the crown;
He raised a mortal to the skies;
She drew an angel down.

Alexander's Feast (JOHN DRYDEN.)

She died about A.D. 230. A native of Rome, and springing from a good family, Saint Cicely, when quite young, consecrated herself to the service of God, and took vows of virginity, vows which she never broke, though forced by her parents into a marriage with a young nobleman named Valerian. After her marriage she converted her husband and his brother Tiburtius to Christianity. Both Valerian and Tiburtius suffered martyrdom for their faith under either Alexander Severus or Marcus Aurelius; and Saint Cecily suffered the same fate shortly afterwards. They were all interred in the cemetery of Calixtus in the part since called St. Cecily's cemetery.

Saint Cecily has been for centuries regarded as the patroness of Church Music, owing to her assiduity in singing the divine praises, in which she frequently joined instrumental music to vocal; and she is said to have actually died singing.

In the fifth century there still stood an ancient church in Rome dedicated to Saint Cecily, but as it had become ruinous, Pope Paschal I. commenced rebuilding it. Whilst the work was in progress, Paschal became distressed to find the whereabouts of the Saint's body, fearing that it might have been removed by the Lombards when they attacked the city. One Sunday whilst assisting, as his habit was, at matins in St. Peter's, Pope Paschal fell asleep, and in his dreams was visited by Saint Cecily herself, and she told him that her body still lay undisturbed in the ancient church.

Thus instructed, the Pope directed search to be made for the holy remains, and in due course the body of Saint Cecily was found, undecayed and clothed in a robe of golden tissue, lying by the side of her husband. The bodies of Tiburtius and other martyrs were also discovered, and were, by direction of the Pope, removed to the Church of Saint Cecily in the City, and a Monastery in honour of the martyrs was founded by Paschal I. near by. This Church was in 1599 rebuilt by Cardinal Paul Sfondrati, a nephew of Pope Gregory XIV., and is known as the Church of St. Cecilia in Trastevere—or beyond the Tiber—to distinguish it from two other Churches in Rome dedicated to that Saint. A Cardinal takes his title from this Church.

Music the fiercest grief can charm,
And fate's severest rage disarm;
Music can soften pain to ease,
And make despair and madness please:
Our joys below it can improve,
And antedate the bliss above.
This the divine Cecilia found,
And to her Maker's praise confined the sound.
When the full organ joins the tuneful choir,
The immortel powers incline their ear;
Borne on the swelling notes our souls aspire,
While solemn airs improve the sacred fire;
And angels lean from heaven to hear.

CICELY

Of Orpheus now no more let poets tell,
  To bright Cecilia greater power is given;
His numbers raised a shade from hell,
  Hers lift the soul to heaven.

Ode on St. Cecilia's Day (ALEXANDER POPE.)

How rich that forehead's calm expanse!
How bright that heaven-directed glance!
—Waft her to glory, winged Powers,
Ere sorrow be renewed,
And intercourse with mortal hours
Bring back a humbler mood!
So looked Cecilia when she drew
An Angel from his station;
So looked; not ceasing to pursue
Her tuneful adoration!
But hand and voice alike are still;
No sound *here* sweeps away the will
That gave it birth: in service meek
One upright arm sustains the cheek,
And one across the bosom lies—
That rose, and now forgets to rise,
Subdued by breathless harmonies
Of meditative feeling;
Mute strains from worlds beyond the skies
Through the pure light of female eyes,
Their sanctity revealing!

On a Picture of St. Cecilia
(WILLIAM WORDSWORTH.)

How can that eye, with inspiration beaming,
  Wear yet so deep a calm? O child of song!
Is not the music-land a world of dreaming,
  Where forms of sad, bewildering beauty throng?

But thou!—the spirit which at eve is filling
  All the hush'd air and reverential sky—
Founts, leaves, and flowers, with solemn thrilling—
  This is the soul of *thy* rich harmony.

This bears up high those breathings of devotion
 Wherein the currents of thy heart gush free;
Therefore no world of sad and vain emotion
 Is the dream-haunted music-land for *thee.*

For a Picture of St. Cecilia attended by Angelo
(Felicia D. Hemans.)

A male Saint of the name, Saint Cecilius, was one of three African friends, the others being Octavius and Marcus Minutius Felix. Octavius and Minutius when converted to Christianity were most anxious that their friend should embrace the faith also, but to bring this about was a work of great difficulty. After much prayer and many arguments, Octavius at last succeeded in overcoming his friend's doubts and scruples, whereupon Cecilius exclaimed, "I congratulate both Octavius and myself exceedingly: we are both conquerors. Octavius triumphs over me, and I triumph over error. But the chief victory and gain are mine, who, by being conquered, find the crown of truth".

It is believed that this Cecilius was the priest who afterwards converted St. Cyprian, A.D. 211.

Geoffrey Chaucer gives the whole legend of Saint Cecily in *The Second Nonnes Tale*, one of *The Canterbury Tales.*

First wol I you the name of Seinte Cecilie
Expoune, as men may in hire storie see;
It is to sayn in English, Hevens lilie,
For pure chastenesse of virginitee,
Or for she whitenesse had of honestee,
And grene of conscience, and of good fame
The swole [sweet] savour, Lelie was hire name

. . . .

CICELY

This maiden bright Cecile, as hire lif saith
Was come of Romaines and of noble kind,
And from her cradle fostred in the faith
Of Crist, and bare his Gospel in hire mind.

. . . .

The palme of martirdome for to receive,
Saint Cecilie, fulfilled of Goddess yeft [geft],
The world and eke hire chambre gan she weive
[waive],
Witnesse Tiburces and Ceciles shrift,
To which God of his bountee wolde shift
Corones two, of floures wel smelling,
And made his angels hem the corones bring.

The various English forms of the name are Cecil, Cecile, Cecilia, Cecilie, Cecily, Cicely, Cicily, Cissie, Sisley, Sis, Sissot and Cis. The pretty Irish forms of Sighile, Sheelah, Sheelagh, or Sheila, are very popular in the Emerald Isle.

Cecile is very common in France, and Cecilia in Germany and Italy.

Our King Richard III.'s mother was Cicely, twelfth daughter of Ralph Neville, Earl of Westmoreland, known as the "Rose of Raby" [1415-1495].

Sir Toby was a portly party;
Sir Toby took his turtle hearty;
Sir Toby lived to dine:
Château Margot was his fort;
Bacchus would have backt his port;
He was an Alderman, in short,
Of the very first Water—and wine.

An Alderman of the first degree,
But neither wife nor son had he:
He had a daughter fair,—
And often said her father, "Cis",
You shall be dubbed 'my Lady', miss,
When I am dubbed Lord Mayor".

CICELY

Oh vision of paternal pride!
Oh, blessed Groom to such a Bride!
    Oh happy Lady Cis!
Yet sparks won't always strike the match,
And miss may chance to lose " her catch ",
    Or he may catch—a *miss!*

Such things do happen, here and there,
When knights are old and nymphs are fair,
    And who can say they don't?
When worldly takes the gilded pill,
And Dives stands and says " I will ",
    And Beauty says " *I won't* "!

Sweet Beauty! Sweeter thus by far—
Young Goddess of the silver star,
    Divinity capricious!—
Who would not barter wealth and wig,
And pomp and pride and *otium dig.*,
For youth—when " plums " weren't worth a fig
    And Venus smiled propitious?

. . . .

That luckless heart! too soon misplaced!—
Why is it that parental taste
On sagest calculation based
    So rarely pleases miss?
Let those who can the riddle read;
For me, I've no idea indeed,
    No more, perhaps, had Cis.

It might have been she found Sir G.
Less tender than a swain should be,—
    Young—sprightly—gay?—
It might have been she thought his hat
Or head too round or square or flat
    Or empty—who can say?

What bard shall dare? Perhaps his nose?—
A shade too pink, or pale, or rose?—
His cut of beard, wig, whisker, hose?—
    A wrinkle?—here—or there?—
Perhaps the *preux chevalier's* chance
Hung on a word or on a glance,
    Or on a single hair.

I know not! But the Parson waited,
The Bridegroom swore, the Groomsman rated,
Till two o'clock or near;—
Then home again in rage and wrath,
Whilst pretty Cis—was rattling north
With Jones the Volunteer!

"*Rejected Addresses*" (CHOLMONDELEY PENNELL.)

CLARA, CLARISSA, CLARE, etc. The name of Clara, with its variants of Clarice, Clarissa, Clare, Clair, Clarinda, Claribel, Esclairmonde, and Clarimond, is derived from the Latin word *clarus* = "clear, bright, shining, brilliant to the sight", from *clareo* = "I am bright, I shine", or figuratively "I am renowned, illustrious", from which we have *claresco* = "I become illustrious, grow famous". Clarus was a Roman name, there having been at least three consuls who bore it, namely, Clarus C. Erucius, (923, A.U.C.) 170 A.D.; Clarus C. Julius Erucius, (946, A.U.C.) 193 A.D.; and Clarus Sextus Erucius, (899, A.U.C.) 146 A.D. As early as the third century the name was rendered famous in France by St. Clarus or Clair, the first Bishop of Nantes, and a second St. Clare died Abbot of Marcel, Vienna, in 660. Three villages in France were called after Saint Clair, and in their turn gave rise to the territorial names of St. Clair, whence the Clares and Sinclairs of Ireland trace their descent. Some of the family came over to Britain with Norman William, and their descendants, settling in Ireland, received grants of land there, and became lords of, and gave their name to, County Clare.

One Gilbert de Clare, generally known as Gilbert Strongbow, was created Earl of Pembroke by King Stephen in 1138, and in 1149 he was succeeded in the title by his son Richard de Clare, also called Strongbow. Richard de Clare invaded Ireland on the pretext of espousing the cause of the Dermots, married a lady of that house, besieged and took Waterford, besieged and took Dublin, and then ravaged Meath, but in 1171 returned to England and submitted himself to Henry II. He was an altogether stormy, restless sort of man, but one of his descendants, Lady Elizabeth Clare, the sister of a second Gilbert de Clare, Earl of Clare, was of a more peaceful disposition than her ancestor, and in 1326 she founded Clare Hall, at Cambridge.

King Edward III.'s son Lionel, who was born in Antwerp in 1338, married a descendant of the first of the family who settled in Ireland, and as her father's heiress brought the Irish lands to her husband, who was thereupon created Duke of Clarence; and this, though at times for years in abeyance, has ever since been held as a royal title. Thomas, Duke of Clarence (1389-1421), was brother to Henry V. of England, George, Duke of Clarence (1449-1474), of Malmsey-butt renown, was brother to King Edward IV., whilst William, Duke of Clarence (1765-1837), a brother of King George IV., himself became King of England as William IV.; and the last holder of the title was the elder son of His Royal Highness the Prince of Wales.

The name has in all countries been more popular in its feminine than in its masculine forms, a fact chiefly due to the admiration felt in the Middle Ages for St. Clara of Assisi in Italy, the daughter of a noble knight, Phavorino Sciffo, who was himself distinguished for his piety. Her mother s name was Hortulana. As a member of the leading family in Assisi, the birthplace of St. Francis, Clara naturally heard much concerning this great man, she herself being from early youth remarkable for her charity and piety. The idea of marriage had always been distasteful to her; and, her parents desiring her marriage, she obtained means to seek the advice of St. Francis as to her future course of life, and had a long interview with him.

At the age of nineteen, she, in company with another young woman, escaped from home and went to Portiuncula, where St. Francis was then living in the midst of his little community; he and his religious brethren met her at the door of his monastery with lighted tapers in their hands, and before the altar of the Virgin, Clara doffed her fine clothes, had her beautiful hair cut off, and assumed a penitential garb handed to her by St. Francis, which consisted of a piece of sackcloth, and a piece of cord to bind it on with. As at that time St. Francis had not yet founded a nunnery of his own, he placed St. Clara temporarily in the Benedictine convent of St. Paul.

Her family and friends did all in their power to withdraw her from her retreat, even resorting to acts of violence to attain their object; but all to no purpose. Ere long St. Francis placed St. Clara in another nunnery of the Benedictine Order, that of St. Angelo of Panso. Thus commenced the foundation of the Order of Poor Clares. At St. Angelo Clara was soon joined by her young sister Agnes, who also assumed the monastic habit, and not long afterwards their mother Hortulana, with many other noble ladies of Florence and other cities of Italy, entered the sisterhood. Within a few years of her first becoming a nun, St. Clare had founded monasteries for women at Perugia, Padua, Rome, Venice, Mantua, Bologna, Milan, Sienna, Pisa, etc., and also in many towns in Germany.

St. Clara and her nuns practised the severest austerities, going about bare-footed, lying on the ground at night, speaking only when absolutely necessary, and eating and drinking little save bread and water. St. Clara herself always wore next her skin a shirt of horsehair or of hog's bristles cut short.

By the hardships and fastings which she imposed upon herself St. Clara so reduced her strength that St. Francis and the Bishop of Assisi had to interfere, and to compel her to somewhat relax her austerities.

St. Clara believed so firmly in the purifying effects of extreme poverty, that when she, upon her father's death, inherited great wealth, she firmly declined to receive a farthing of it for the benefit of either herself or the community over which she presided, but gave the whole away in charity.

Devoting her whole life to the service of others, she found her greatest comfort in prayer, from which she at times arose with her face looking as though glorified.

To her prayers many marvellous answers are said to have been vouchsafed, and one of her recorded sayings, was, "There is nothing insupportable to a heart that loveth God".

After many years of suffering Saint Clara died in 1253. The blind resort to her shrine and solicit her intervention on their behalf, owing to the meaning of her name (just as they do to that of Saint Lucy), and also on account of the success she is credited with in the healing of sickness. The first monastery of Poor Clares in England was founded about the year 1293.

St. Clare, Abbot of St. Ferréol, is also said to have had the power to heal in cases of sickness, and he is further credited with having, in his boyhood, laid a furious tempest at sea by prayer.

One of the Emperor Charlemagne's daughters is supposed to have been named Clara, and the wife of Lorenzo de Medici was named Clarice, the Italian form of our Clarissa, which in French is Clarisse, but these appear to be comparatively modern developments of the name. In Germany the name of Clara is as common as with us. Amongst contemporary celebrities Clara Schumann, the pianiste, may be mentioned.

Surely Nature must have meant you
For a Syren, when she sent you
That sweet voice, and glittering hair
—Was it touch of human passion
Made you woman, in a fashion—
Beauty Clare!

Men of every age and station
Listen to your conversation,
  With a rapt admiring stare;
As though words that from your mouth fall,
Sweet as grapes were, on a south wall,
            Beauty Clare!

All-accomplish'd little creature!
Fatally endow'd by Nature,—
  Were your inward soul laid bare,
What should we discover under
That seductive mask, I wonder,
            Beauty Clare?

Beauty Clare (HAMILTON AIDÉ.)

The name is found in all branches of literature.

In DRAMA:

We have Clara, in *The Cheats of Scapin* by Thomas Otway — the English version of Molière's play *Les Fourberies de Scapin*; Clara in *The Duenna* by Richard B. Sheridan; Donna Clara in *Two Strings to Your Bow* by Robert Jephson; Clarinda in *The Beau's Ideal* by Mrs. Centlivre; Clarissa in *The Suspicious Husband* by Dr. Hoadley; Clarissa in *The Confederacy* by Sir John Vanbrugh; Clarissa in *All in the Wrong* by A. Murphy; Clarona in *The Destruction of Jerusalem* by John Crowne; and Clärchen in *Egmont* by J. W. von Goethe.

In FICTION:

Samuel Richardson's great novel *The History of Clarissa Harlowe* leads the way, and W. Harrison Ainsworth has an Esclairmonde in his novel *Crichton*; whilst

In Poetry:

Clarice, the sister of Huon de Bordeaux is introduced into both Tasso's and Ariosto's romances; Spenser has a Clarin or Clarinda (variously spelt) in his *Faëry Queene;* Sir Walter Scott sings of a Clare in *Marmion*—indeed it is of her that the well-known lines were written:

O, Woman! in our hours of ease,
Uncertain, coy, and hard to please,
And variable as the shade
By the light quivering aspen made;
When pain and anguish wring the brow
A ministering angel thou!

. . . . .

Short space, few words, are mine to spare;
Forgive and listen, gentle Clare!

Robert Burns wrote a poem to *Clarinda,* who was in reality a Mrs. Maclehose, with whom he carried on a long correspondence; and William Shenstone wrote an *Ode* in which he celebrates a Clara—

In Clara's eyes the lightning view;
Her lips with all the rose's hue
  Have all its sweets combined;
Yet vain the blush, and faint the fire,
Till lips at once, and eyes, conspire
  To prove the charmer kind—

W. Harrison Ainsworth has a song called *Esclairmonde,* sung by Henry III. of France, in his novel *Crichton;* whilst everyone knows the three poems by our great modern poet, Lord Tennyson, *Claribel, Lady Clara Vere de Vere,* and *Lady Clare.*

"If I'm a beggar born", she said,
  "I will speak out, for I dare not lie.
Pull off, pull off the brooch of gold,
  And fling the diamond necklace by".
. . . .

She clad herself in a russet gown,
  She was no longer Lady Clare:
She went by dale and she went by down,
  With a single rose in her hair.
. . . . .

O and proudly stood she up!
  Her heart within her did not fail:
She look'd into Lord Ronald's eyes,
  And told him all her nurse's tale.

He laugh'd a laugh of merry scorn:
  He turn'd and kiss'd her where she stood:
"If you are not the heiress born,
  And I", said he, "the next in blood—

"If you are not the heiress born,
  And I", said he, "the lawful heir,
We two will wed to-morrow morn,
  And you shall still be Lady Clare".

CLAUDIA: see GLADYS.

CLEMENTINA, CLEMENTINE, CLEMENTIA, CLEMENTE—with Clemenza in Italy and Clémence in France—are the feminine forms of Clemens, or Clement. The name is a Latin one, and means "clement", "mild", or "merciful". It has been the name of no less than fourteen Bishops or Popes of Rome, one of whom, Clemens Romanus, preached the Gospel in company with St. Paul at Philippi, and wrote a letter to the Corinthians; by some he is supposed to have been the immediate successor of St. Peter, whilst other authorities place him after

St. Linus. He is regarded as the patron of sailors.

Clementia was one of the personified virtues to whom the Romans paid adoration. Neither Clementia nor Clementina are common in England, but the latter is very popular in Germany. The names Menzies, Mence, Mentzel, and Mendelssohn are all derived from Clemens.

In literature we have Lady Clementina in Richardson's *Sir Charles Grandison*, who is in love with the hero; in the drawing of this character Richardson has probably displayed almost as great skill as Shakespeare himself in the delineation of a suffering woman.

CLOTHILDA: see HILDA.

CONSTANCE, CONSTANTIA. This name comes from the Latin word *constans* which means "holding firmly together"—it being a compound of con = together, and stans, the participle of sto = I am, or I stand.

This name compared with many others, is of comparatively modern origin, and instead of dating back to the days of heathen mythology first comes into existence with Flavius Valerius Chlorus Constantius, that Roman general who so distinguished himself at the close of the third century by the conquest of Britain, and who married Helena, supposed to be an English woman, as his first wife, his eldest son being Constantine the Great. Constantius died at York in A.D. 306, and Constantine who was in Britain at the time, was at once proclaimed Emperor by the Roman troops stationed here.

The new Emperor soon became involved in

war with his brother-in-law Maxentius who endeavoured to usurp Constantine's throne, and it was during this war that Constantine is alleged to have seen a luminous cross in the heavens and beneath it the inscription *In hoc signo vinces* (Under this sign thou shalt conquer).

In obedience to this message direct, as he deemed it, from God, Constantine caused a new standard to be made, which had on it a monogram of the name of Christ, and with this borne before his army he marched triumphantly into Rome, where he was forthwith proclaimed Augustus, and pontifex maximus, by the senate. Proclaiming himself a Christian he at once put an end to the persecution of his co-religionists.

In A.D. 325 Constantine became the acknowledged head of the Eastern and Western Empires, which had until that time been divided, and making Byzantium his seat of government, he changed the name of that city to Constantinople.

Many acts of cruelty have been laid to this Emperor's account, and especially brutal was his murder of his own son Crispus, but when we have regard to the manners of the age in which he lived, his firm government, his wise laws, and his protection of the Christians, the general consensus of posterity will proclaim him entitled to the surname of Great.

Upon his death at Nicomedia in May 337 his vast empire was divided between his three sons, Constantine, Constantius, and Constans.

He had a daughter Constance, too, she who was cured of a grievous malady through the intercession of Saint Agnes, to whom she afterwards erected a magnificent church in sign of her gratitude.

From this time forward the name under one form or another occurs frequently in Roman history, and its feminine forms of Constance and Constantia were both common amongst the women of the Imperial families of Rome: the name was even adopted in Greece, an event of rare occurrence with Latin names, the general practice being the reverse.

The popularity of Constantius Chlorus in Britain, the supposed British birth of his first wife, Helena, and the current belief that Constantine the Great had also been born in England, were all points that combined to insure the name considerable popularity in this country, a popularity which in the case of its feminine forms, it has maintained until the present day.

In Wales the Keltic form of the name, *i.e.*, Cystenian, is still occasionally met with, and the Irish name of Conan is probably descended from it. Chaucer spelt the name Custance.

In England, Spain, Germany, and Italy, Constance and Constantia have been royal names. The wife of Robert the Pious was a Constance, and there was Constance, Queen of the Two Sicilies, who married Henry, the son of the Emperor Frederick I., and who was crowned with her husband at Rome in 1190. This Constance became the mother of Ferdinand II. and through him introduced the name into Germany.

CONSTANCE

Here in England we all know Constance of Brittany, the wife of Geoffrey Plantagenet and mother of the poor young Prince whose sole offence was that of being the rightful heir to the English throne, at a time when an unscrupulous uncle wanted to secure it to himself. The offence was, however, great enough to cost him his life.

> Bind up those tresses. O ! what love I note
> In the fair multitude of those her hairs !
> Where but by chance a silver drop hath fallen.
> Even to that drop ten thousand wiry friends
> Do glue themselves in sociable grief ;
> Like true, inseparable, faithful loves,
> Sticking together in calamity.

If we accept Shakespeare's portrait, as he draws it in his play of *King John*, as a faithful one, we cannot but feel that Constance had a shrewish temper, even after making all due allowance for the bitterness of her misfortunes, but perhaps Shakespeare was not quite true in his portraiture, for Constance, after Duke Geoffrey's death, married twice again. Her second husband was Ranulph, Earl of Chester, her third, Guy of Thouars. She died in 1201.

John of Gaunt's second wife was Constance of Castile, the daughter of Pedro the Cruel, and of Constance, the daughter of Manfred, Regent and afterwards King of Sicily. She was a woman of noble character, and greatly added to the popularity of the name of Constance in England. It was by virtue of his marriage with this Constance that "Old John of Gaunt, time-honoured Lancaster", laid claim to the

Castilian crown, and called himself King of Castile. Entering into an alliance with the King of Portugal, John of Gaunt attacked Castile, but ultimately settled the dispute peacefully by marrying his daughter to the son of the reigning king.

Chaucer in *The Man of Lawes Tale*, one of the *Canterbury Tales*, takes this Constance, whom he calls Custance, for the heroine.

> I am your daughter, your Custance, quod she,
> That whilom ye han sent into Surrie;
> It am I, fader, that in the salte see
> Was put alone, and dampned for to die.
> Now, goode fader, I you mercie crie,
> Send me no more into non hethenesse,
> But thonketh my lord here of his kindenesse.

Besides Constance in Shakespeare's *King John*, there is Constance in *The Twin Rivals* of Farquhar; Constance in *The Provost of Bruges*, by Sheridan Knowles; Constance, in *The Love Chase*, by the same author; Lady Constance, in *The Way to keep Him*, by A. Murphy; Constantia, in *The Man of the World*, by Charles Maçklin; Constantia, in *The Chances*, by Beaumont and Fletcher;

> The abstract of all beauty, soul of sweetness!
> . . . . Men say gold
> Does all, engages all, works through all dangers:
> Now, I say beauty can do more.

as well as *Constance de Castile*, a poem by W. Sotheby, in ten cantos, written in the romantic metrical narrative style adopted by Sir Walter Scott. Then in *Marmion* there is Constance

CONSTANCE

Beverley, the unhappy nun, who was walled up for having broken her vows, according to the terrible monastic laws of those days.

There met to doom in secrecy,
Were placed the heads of convents three.
. . . . . .

The Abbess of St. Hilda's there,
Sat for a space with visage bare,
Until, to hide her bosom's swell,
And tear-drops that for pity fell,
She closely drew her veil :
. . . .

Before them stood a guilty pair ;
But though an equal fate they share,
Yet one alone deserves our care.
Her sex a page's dress belied ;
The cloak and doublet, loosely tied,
Obscured her charms, but could not hide.
. . . . . .

But, at the Prioress' command,
A monk undid the silken band,
That tied her tresses fair,
And raised the bonnet from her head,
And down her slender form they spread,
In ringlets rich and rare.
Constance de Beverley they know,
Sister profess'd of Fontevraud,
Whom the Church number'd with the dead,
For broken vows, and convent fled.
. . . . . .

Her look composed, and steady eye
Bespoke a matchless constancy ;
And there she stood so calm and pale,
That, but her breathing did not fail,
And motion slight of eye and head,
And of her bosom, warranted
That neither sense nor pulse she lacks,
You might have thought a form of wax,
Wrought to the very life, was there ;
So still she was, so pale, so fair.
. . . . . .

And when her silence broke at length,
Still as she spoke she gathered strength,
And arm'd herself to bear.
. . . . . .
Now, men of death, work forth your will,
For I can suffer, and be still;
And come he slow or come he fast,
It is but Death who comes at last.

There was a real Constance Beverley, a nun, who in the reign of Henry VIII. got into trouble, but Scott's Constance Beverley is not the same, and he probably only chose the name because of its musical sound.

In conclusion we will quote from Percy Bysshe Shelley's *To Constantia Singing*.

Thus to be lost and thus to sink and die
Perchance were death indeed!—Constantia, turn!
In thy dark eyes a power like light doth lie,
Even though the sounds, which were thy voice, which burn
Between thy lips, are laid to sleep;
Within thy breath, and on thy hair, like odour, it is yet,
And from thy touch like fire doth leap,
Even while I write, my burning cheeks are wet;
Alas, that the torn heart can bleed but not forget!
. . . . . .
Her voice is hovering o'er my soul—it lingers
O'ershadowing it with soft and lulling wings:
The blood and life within those snowy fingers
Teach witchcraft to the instrumental strings.
My brain is wild, my breath comes quick—
The blood is listening in my frame,
And thronging shadows, fast and thick,
Fall on my overflowing eyes;
My heart is quivering like a flame;
As morning dew that in the sunbeam dies,
I am dissolved in these consuming ecstasies.

I have no life, Constantia, now, but thee,
  Whilst, like the world-surrounding air, thy song
Flows on, and fills all things with melody.
  Now is thy voice a tempest swift and strong,
    On which, like one in trance upborne,
      Secure o'er rocks, and waves I sweep,
    Rejoicing like a cloud of morn:
    Now 'tis the breath of summer night,
      Which, when the starry waters sleep,
  Round western isles with incense blossoms bright
Lingering, suspends my soul in its voluptuous flight.

CORDELIA, or CORDULA, is a Kymric or Welsh name, and, according to Mr. Davies, who has made an exhaustive study of the subject, the name was originally Creirdyddlydd; this means "the token of the flowing tide", or "daughter of the sea", her father Lear or Llyr being "the sea". Hence Cordelia was the sister of Branwen.

One of the legends relating to Cordelia is that she was one of the eleven thousand virgins who sailed with St. Ursula on her ill-starred three years' voyage; but in the story of Llyr and his three daughters fact and fable are so inextricably blended, that it is now quite impossible to unravel the tangled thread.

In the *Mabinogion* Creirdyddlydd plays an important part, and is the gentle daughter through good report and through evil report, just as she appears in the old ballad and in Shakespeare's play, which in this particular closely follows the still earlier play upon which it is based, *The true chronicle History of Leir and his three daughters, Gonorill, Ragan, and Cordella.*

CORDELIA

Cordelia, Cordelia! stay a little. Ha!
What is 't thou say'st? Her voice was ever soft,
Gentle, and low, an excellent thing in woman.
King Lear (SHAKESPEARE.)

For poor Cordelia patiently
  Went wandring up and down,
Unhelp'd, unpity'd, gentle maid,
  Through many an English town:

Until at last in famous France
  She gentler fortunes found;
Though poor and bare, yet she was deem'd
  The fairest on the ground:

Where when the King her virtues heard,
  And this fair lady seen,
With full consent of all his Court
  He made his wife and Queen.

From *A lamentable song of the Death of King Leir and his Three Daughters* (an old Ballad.)

One wonders how it is that its own beauty joined to the beautiful tradition connected with it has not made the name of Cordelia more common in England: the Irish with their ready instinct for the choice of musical names have, however, made Cordelia their own, and for every Cordelia to be found in England, Ireland could shew at least a dozen.

Geoffrey of Monmouth, in his *Chronicon, sive Historia Britonum*, a Latin version of the prophecies of Merlin, which the author professed to have translated from a Welsh history of Britain given him by Walter Calemus of Oxford, gives us the history of Cordeilla. But in Monmouth's version poor Cordelia ends her life by her own act, and Spenser in his *Faëry Queene* follows this tradition.

The wretched man gan then avise too late,
That love is not where most it is profest;
Too truly tryde in his extremest state.
At last, resolv'd likewise to prove the rest,
He to Cordelia him selfe addrest,
Who with entyre affection him receav'd,
As for her Syre and King her seemed best;
And after all an army strong she leav'd,
To war on those which him had of his realme bereav'd.

So to his crowne she him restored againe;
In which he dyde, made ripe for death by eld,
And after wild it should to her remaine,
Who peaceably the same long time did weld,
And all mens harts in dew obedience held;
Till that her sister's children, woxen strong
Through proud ambition against her rebeld,
And overcommen kept in prison long,
Till weary of that wretched life her selfe she hong.

Faëry Queene (SPENSER.)

William Wordsworth wrote a sonnet to *Cordelia M—— of Hallsteads, Ullswater*; and Mark Akenside also had his *Cordelia*.

Kordula and Kordel are German names, and according to Miss Yonge, the Germans have the mistaken impression that the name is derived from the Latin *cor* = heart.

From pompous life's dull masquerade,
From Pride's pursuits, and Passion's war,
Far, my Cordelia, very far,
To thee and me may Heaven assign
The silent pleasures of the shade,
The joys of peace, unenvied, though divine!

(AKENSIDE.)

CORNELIA. *Cornu* is the Latin for "a horn", whence the name Cornelius = powerful or kingly, the horn being the symbol of kingship.

In the *Psalms* (cxxxii. 17) we find "I will make the horn of David to bud; I will make his power and glory to flourish and increase. I will cut off the horns of the wicked".

The Cornelian *gens* was the most powerful in Rome, and from it sprang more illustrious men than from any other: hence names connected with it are spread far and wide. Perhaps the most illustrious of the race were Publius Cornelius Scipio Africanus and his daughter Cornelia, who became the mother of the Gracchi. So dignified and self-controlled was she, that, when offered sympathy upon the death of her sons, she answered, "The woman who had the Gracchi for sons cannot be considered unfortunate". Such was the admiration that her countrymen felt for her, that, upon her death, they erected a statue to her memory in Rome bearing the inscription:

"To Cornelia, the Mother of the Gracchi".

With the Irish both Cornelius and Cornelia are favourite names, Cornelius being often contracted into Corny; but the favour they enjoy is not so much in token of admiration for the Roman nation as of love and veneration for that Pope Cornelius, who suffered martyrdom in the third century. Two examples of its use in modern English may be cited: Cornelia in *The Triumph of Love*, by Beaumont and Fletcher, and Cornelia Blimber in Dickens's *Dombey & Son*.

CYNTHIA: see PHŒBE.

DAISY: see MARGARET.

DEBORAH, DEBERAH, or DEBIR, is a Hebrew name meaning "a bee", and also, later, "eloquent" or "oracle".

Since the days of the Puritans the name has been in use in England, especially in rural districts; but it has never been very common. Many of those who have chosen it have been attracted to it as being the name of Rebecca's faithful nurse, who went with her from Padan-aram, and after Rebecca's death remained in Jacob's family until she died at a great age, near Bethel, and was buried under an oak-tree known as the "oak of weeping". Yet more have been attracted to the name by Deborah, the wife of Lappidoth, a Prophetess and Judge in Israel, who "dwelt under the palm-tree of Deborah" between Ramah and Bethel, and was the chief instrument in bringing about the defeat of the Canaanites in a great battle near Tabor. Deborah and the Hebrew general, Barak, after the battle composed a song to commemorate their victory.

In the days of Shamgar the son of Anath,
In the days of Jael, the highways were unoccupied,
And the travellers walked through by-ways.
The rulers ceased in Israel, they ceased,
Until that I Deborah arose,
That I arose a mother in Israel.
They chose new gods;
Then was war in the gates:
Was there a shield or spear seen
Among forty thousand in Israel?
My heart is towards the governors of Israel,
That offered themselves willingly among the people
Bless ye the Lord. *Judges*, v. 6-9.

Michael Drayton, in *The Harmony of the Church*, celebrates this heroine of Israel.

In *Peveril of the Peak* Sir Walter Scott has chosen the name Deborah for that of his heroine's nurse, and there is a Deborah in Colman's play, *The Heir-at-Law*. Last, but not least, Deborah is one of the characters in Mrs. Gaskell's little literary gem *Cranford*.

DIANA: see PHŒBE.

DINAH is a name not infrequently met with in rural England, especially amongst dissenters, and in America. It was the name of the daughter of Jacob and Leah, and she had the reputation of being very beautiful. The meaning of the name is "a judge", "a judgment".

In literature there are many examples of the name: we have Dinah in *The Bashful Man*, by Moncrieff; Dinah in *St. Ronan's Well*, by Sir W. Scott; Aunt Dinah in *Tristram Shandy*, by Laurence Sterne; and perhaps the best known of all, Dinah in *Uncle Tom's Cabin*, by Mrs. Beecher Stowe; and beautiful Dinah Morris in *Adam Bede*, by George Eliot, one of the most perfect characters ever drawn in fiction, after whom any girl might rejoice to be named.

DOLORES, DOLORA, LOLA, signifies "sorrow". This is a Spanish and Italian name, that needs no explanation. It is usually bestowed on children born in times of deep sorrow, and is, to all intents and purposes, synonymous with Mary: indeed it was originally adopted to commemorate the sorrows of the Virgin Mary. Dolores is the Spanish, Dolora the Italian form; Lola the diminutive.

DORCAS, TABITHA. Tabitha is a Syriac word signifying "clear sighted"; Dorcas a Greek, meaning "a gazelle" or female of a roe-buck. Both names belonged to the Christian Widow of Joppa, whom Peter raised from the dead, and who was so noted for her good works that the name Dorcas has become a common epithet applied to modern work-societies. Her charitable deeds have endeared both her names to the English people, and from the days of the Puritans to the present both Dorcas and Tabitha are found scattered here and there in rural England. Shakespeare gives the name Dorcas to one of the Shepherdesses in *The Winter's Tale.*

DOROTHY, DOROTHEA, DORA, THEODORA, FEODORE. Theos, the Greek for placer or arranger, combined with doron, the Greek for a gift, gives us Theodorus, Theodore, Tudor (Welsh), Theodora, and—reversed—Dorothea, and Dorotheus.

These names must not be confounded with those derived from the Gothic word Theod, such as Theodoric, Theodosia, Derrick, and Dirk. The English derivatives of Theodora or Dorothea are: Theodosia, Dorothy, Dorinda, Dora, Doralicia, Dolly, Doll, and Dodo. It has been suggested that Doll came originally from the old Norse döll, a woman, or from the Anglo-Saxon *dolh*, a wound. In Brittany the name is written Doll, Dolle, and De Doll most likely after the town of Dol in that country, or after Dole in Franche Comté; but, be this as it may, our modern Dolls and Dollys are representatives of Dorotheas and Dorothys.

DOROTHY

There was a period when Dorothy and Dorothea ceased to be popular names in this country; but in olden times, as now, it was one of the most popular of all girls' names in England, and in such common use, indeed, that Dolly became the name of the most beloved of all children's toys, which were originally called "puppets", not "dolls".

There is no cause to wonder at the frequency of the name: it is natural that parents should look upon their children as "divine gifts", as "God-given", and, in their gratitude and love, to so name them; but it is a little curious that in England at any rate the incorrect and reversed form of the name should have become so much the more popular. There have certainly been two Saints Dorotheus, but it is Theodore that our boys are called, whilst Theodoras are rare, and Dorotheas are very frequently met with. In Germany and France, too, the name has been reversed, so that Dorotheas and Dorlisas in Germany, Dorothées, Dorettes and Doralises in France, are constantly found, whilst Ireland still clings to Dorinda.

According to Miss Yonge, Wales, Greece and Venice are the only places where the name is really hereditary. The Ancient Britons were probably acquainted with the name under its still common Welsh form *Tewdwr*.

The beauty of the legend attaching to St. Dorothy has doubtless added much to the popularity of the name and to its wide diffusion. She is reported to have been a native of Cæsarea in Cappadocia, and noted there for her piety and holiness. Her parents had both suffered martyrdom under the Diocletian persecution.

Fabritius caused Dorothy to be most cruelly tortured, because she declined to marry, and would not worship idols. "Christ", she said, "is my only spouse, and death is my desire". Two women who had abjured the Christian religion were appointed to take charge of her, and to turn her from Christianity, but her ardour in the cause of Christianity was so strong, and her skill in argument so great that instead of their converting her to idolatry she re-converted them to the Christian Faith. Fabritius then caused her to be placed on the rack, but thereupon she rejoiced that she should "soon be with the Angels in heaven"; and, as Fabritius watched her being tortured, he was "amazed at the heavenly look" she wore. She was condemned to death and beheaded and afterwards converted one Theophilus to Christianity by sending him fruits and flowers by angelic hands direct from Paradise in testimony of the bliss she was there enjoying.

A second Saint Dorothy is said to have existed, a noble Alexandrian lady; but her story is so similar to that of Saint Catherine of Alexandria, and the periods at which they lived so nearly coincide, that by many authorities they are supposed to have been one and the same person.

Of the two Saints Theodora, one was a martyr, the other a Greek Empress. The latter by her patience and gentleness, reformed the cruel nature of her husband, Theophilus. Upon his death she became regent during the minority of her son Michael III., and for twelve years governed the Empire with great glory. Her son and his uncle Bardas then banished her, and she retired to a monastery, where she died in the year 867. In the Greek Calendar she ranks as a Saint.

Another Empress of the name of Theodora was the wife of Justinian the Great. She was not, however, a woman of good reputation, though her influence over her husband was unbounded. Justinian himself was of obscure birth, but until his marriage was distinguished for his devotional austerity. Theodora became Empress in the year 527, and died in 547 or 548.

Among other Dorothys and Dorotheas worthy to be mentioned here, the Lady Dorothea Sidney, eldest daughter of the Earl of Leicester, must find a place. To her it was that Waller dedicated the bettei part of his poetry during his long and unsuccessful suit, and amongst others she inspired his graceful song.

Go, lovely rose!
Tell her that wastes her time and me
That now she knows,
When I resemble her to thee,
How sweet and fair she seems to be.

Tell her, that's young,
And shuns to have her graces spied,
That, hadst thou sprung
In deserts, where no men abide,
Thou must have uncommended died.

Small is the worth
Of beauty from the light retired;
Bid her come forth,
Suffer herself to be desired,
And not blush so to be admired.

> Then die! that she
> The common fate of all things rare
> May read in thee,
> How small a part of time they share
> That are so wondrous sweet and fair!

Then Dorothy Osborne, as the writer of some of the most charming seventeenth century letters in the English language, deserves to be remembered too. After a long and singularly trying courtship of seven years, during which time, she was by the ravages of smallpox changed from a very handsome woman into a plain one, she became the wife of Sir William Temple.

The Queen of King George I. was named Sophia Dorothea, and the Queen of George II. was Wilhelmina Caroline Dorothea, and of other modern women of the name Felicia Dorothea Hemans, to whom a national memorial is just being erected at Liverpool, and Dorothy Wordsworth, sister of the poet, should be noted.

Except the mimic babies that inhabit our nurseries, and one town—Dorothea, in Sweden—the name does not seem to have been bestowed on any outside object unless we count the "Dorothea"—a ship which was sent under command of Captain Buchan, with the "Trent" under Franklin, in 1818, on an expedition to the Arctic regions, but in literature it occurs frequently.

Massinger founded his play *The Virgin Martyr* on the legend of Saint Dorothy, making Dorothea the heroine, and from the lips of her servant Angelo, on whom she had taken pity, as a beggar-boy, we may gather some idea as to what Massinger pictured Saint Dorothy to have been.

I could weary stars,
And force the wakeful moon to lose her eyes,
By my late watching, but to wait on you.
When at your prayers you kneel before the altar
Methinks I'm singing with some quire in heaven,
So blest I hold me in your company.

Besides this, we have in Drama, Dol Common in *The Alchemist* by Ben Jonson; Dolly Trull in *The Beggar's Opera* by Gay; Doll Tearsheat in *Henry IV*. by Shakespeare; Dorinda in *The Beaux' Stratagem* by Farquhar; Doris in *The Confederacy* by Vanbrugh; Dorothea in *Monsieur Thomas* by Beaumont and Fletcher; Dorine in *Le Tartuffe* by Molière; Dorothea in *Hermann und Dorothea* by Goethe; Dorothea [" The peerless Queen of Scots " who escapes from her faithless husband, in man's attire. War was declared on account of her disappearance, and she therefore gave herself up to ensure peace for her country.] in *James the Fourth* by Robert Greene; Dorothy (Mrs. Hardcastle) in *She Stoops to Conquer* by Goldsmith; *Théodora* by V. Sardou. In Poetry: Verses to Sacharissa (Lady Dorothea Sidney) by Edmund Waller; *Dora* by Lord Tennyson; Dorinda in verses by the Earl of Dorset; Doris in verses by Congreve; Theodora in *Orlando Furioso* by Ariosto; *Dora* —— by Wordsworth; and Herrick's lines *To Mistress Dorothy Parsons*

If thou do ask me, dear, wherefore
I do write of thee no more,
I must answer, sweet, thy part
Less is here than in my heart.

In Fiction: Doralicia in *Arbasto* by Robert Greene; Dolly Varden in *Barnaby Rudge*, Dora in *David Copperfield*, and Dot in *The Cricket on the Hearth* by Dickens; Dolly Winthrop in *Silas Marner*, and Dorothea Brooke in *Middlemarch* by "George Eliot"; Dorothy in *The Fair Maid of Perth*, and Dorothy in *The Fortunes of Nigel* by Sir Walter Scott; Dorothea of Andalusia in *Don Quixote* by Cervantes; *Dodo* by E. F. Benson; and *Dorotea*, a dramatic prose romance (1632), by Lope de Vega: the most beloved by him of all his works.

> Margaret's beauteous—Grecian arts
> Ne'er drew form completer,
> Yet why, in my heart of hearts,
> Hold I Dora's sweeter?
>
> Dora's eyes of heavenly blue,
> Pass all painting's reach,
> Ring-dove's notes are discord to
> The music of her speech.
>
> Artists! Margaret's smile receive,
> And on canvas show it;
> But for perfect worship leave
> Dora to her poet.
>
> *Margaret and Dora* (Thos. Campbell.)

Feodore, or, as it should be spelt, Phaedora, is really nothing more than the Russian form of Theodora, the *th* being in that language changed into *ph*. It is occasionally given under the impression that it is a distinct name.

DRUSILLA. Drusus was a Latin cognomen. According to Roman belief, it was introduced by one of the Livian *gens*, who adopted the name of a Gallic chieftain whom he had slain, and who was called Drausus. Others, including Miss Yonge, believe the name to be of Keltic origin, and to be derived from the word *drud*, signifying strong. The meaning generally attributed to the name is *dew-watered*; but, if the last derivation be correct, it should be *strong*.

Drusilla is the feminine diminutive of Drusus, and even at the present day is sometimes met with in England, yet not very often, since Drusilla of *Acts*, xxiv. 24, though reputed one of the loveliest women of the age, was not admirable in more essential ways. She was first the wife of Azizus, King of Emesa, in Syria, and afterwards of Felix, Governor of Judea.

DULCIBELLA, Ducia, Dulce, Dulcie, Dulcena, Douce, and later Dowsabel, are all forms of the same name, which was at one time very popular in England, and is even now occasionally met with.

Originally a Spanish name, it is derived from *dulcis*, meaning *sweet*; and was the name chosen by Cervantes for Don Quixote's lady-love, whom Sancho Panza thus describes: "Her flowing hair is of gold, her forehead the Elysian fields, her eyebrows two celestial arches, her eyes a pair of glorious suns, her cheeks two beds of roses, her lips two coral portals that guard her teeth of oriental pearl, her neck is alabaster, her hands are polished ivory, and her bosom whiter than the new-fallen snow".

> Ask you for whom my tears do flow so?
> 'Tis for Dulcinea del Toboso.
>
> *Don Quixote*, I. iii. 2.

DULCIBELLA

Douce, the Proud, is one of the characters in Ben Jonson's *Sad Shepherd*, and Dowsabell appears in Michael Drayton's *Nymphidia*:

> Farre in the countrey of Arden,
> There won'd a Knight, hight Cassemen,
> As bolde as Isenbras:
> Fell was he, and eger bent,
> In battell, and in tournament,
> As was the good Sir Topas.
>
> He had, as antique stories tell,
> A daughter cleaped Dowsabel;
> A mayden fayre and free;
> And for she was her father's heire,
> Full well she was y-cond the leyre
> Of mickle curtesie.

The following lines are attributed to Sir W. Raleigh:

> As at noone Dulcina rested
> In her sweete and shady bower;
> Came a shepherd, and requested
> In her lapp to sleepe an hour.
> But from her looke
> A wounde he tooke
> So deepe, that for a further boone
> The nymph he prayes.
> Whereto shee sayes,
> Forgoe me now, come to me soone.
>
> But in vayne shee did conjure him
> To depart her presence soe;
> Having a thousand tongues to allure him,
> And but one to bid him goe:
> Where lipps invite,
> And eyes delight,
> And cheeks as fresh as rose in June,
> Persuade delay;
> What boots, she say,
> Forgoe me now, come to me soone?

EDITH, Ada, Ida. Of the Teutonic or Anglo-Saxon names which have come down to us, none are more beloved in modern England than Edith, Ada, or Ida, with the diminutive Edie. Ada and Ida are contractions of Edith, and all mean rich-gift, blessing, or happiness. Ida is sometimes given from a mistaken notion that it is derived from Mount Ida in Phrygia, and Ada is often supposed to be the same as the Hebrew name Adah, which signifies ornament.

In Germany, where Ida first occurred, the name is now extremely popular, and with us it is growing more and more in favour.

As the name of Tennyson's *Princess*, it has especial claims to our affection.

> Liker to the inhabitant
> Of some clear planet close upon the Sun,
> Than our man's earth ; such eyes were in her head,
> And to much grace and power, breathing down
> From over her arch'd brows, with every turn
> Lived thro' her to the tips of her long hands,
> And to her feet.

Ead, signifying happiness or riches, is a very common commencement to Anglo-Saxon names. Eadwig = rich war, Eadwine or Edwin = happy or rich friend, Eadgar or Edgar = happy spear, Eadmunds or Edmund or Edmond = happy protection, and, most popular of all, Eadward or Edward = happy guardian, are only a very few of the names which occur with this prefix in the ancient chronicles of England.

Among women's names we find Eadgyth, Eddeva, Edeva, Eddid, Edgytha, Eaditha and Edith, Ada and Ida. Edgith was the daughter of King Ethelred II., and wife of Edric, ancestress of the great Earl Godwine.

Of the feminine forms, Edith, Ada, and Ida are the only ones which have retained their popularity through the long centuries which have intervened between the days of the Norman Conquest and the present, but they are as popular now as ever: they mean "blessed (or perfect) happiness".

In spite of the popularity of Edith, however, it is in both history and literature remarkable for its absence, an absence all the more noticeable from its having been borne by two women distinguished for their piety and beauty. Perhaps the misfortunes which seemed to dog their steps made the superstitious Kings of the Middle Ages avoid their name for their daughters.

The first Eaditha we really seem to know is the Queen of the last but one of our Saxon Kings, and through him it is connected with our national Valhalla, Westminster Abbey:

"The Kingliest abbey in all Christian lands,
The lordliest, loftiest minster ever built
To Holy Peter in our English isle"!

Around King Eadward the Confessor's name a kind of halo seems to hover, for in him England welcomed back her line of native Kings. His gentleness and piety, the womanly type of his beauty, with his slender body, delicate complexion, golden hair, blue eyes and small, fragile hands proclaimed him at once a man unfit to govern in those rude days; and he had moreover passed his youth in exile at the Norman Court, but he was of English birth, the descendant of English Kings, and his people therefore welcomed him and loved him.

An old contemporary Chronicle relates how the timid, nerveless Eadward, terrified at the thought of the difficulties which he would, as King of England, be called upon to face, besought Earl Godwine to aid him in the abdication of his uneasy throne and in his return to Normandy, whereupon the stout earl answered, "You are the son of Ethelred, grandson of Edgar. Reign; it is your duty; better to live in glory than die in exile. You are of mature years, and, having known sorrow and need, can better feel for your people. Rely on me, and there will be none of the difficulties you dread; whom I favour, England favours".

Earl Godwine, faithful to his promise of support, bore the burden of government on his own broad, capable shoulders, and gave Eadward his own fair daughter Eaditha to wife.

But, though Godwine aggrandized his house by making his daughter a Queen, he did not make her happy, for, although Eaditha was beautiful in both mind and person, in the eyes of all who knew her, Eadward never loved her, and six years after her marriage—a marriage in name alone—he put her from him and seized all her property. The following year, however, he restored her to honour, and at the consecration of his great Abbey in 1065 Queen Eaditha represented the King, who was too ill to be present in person.

The old chronicles tell of Eaditha's beauty,

and of her intellectual mind. The eldest of all Earl Godwine's many children, she alone shared with her gifted brother Harold the distinction of a genuine love of letters, and was very learned for the time in which she lived, finding, in theological studies more especially, some solace for the lonely, loveless life to which she was condemned by Eadward. Harold's noble nature found its natural sphere in a life of action, whilst his sister's had to be circumscribed and was that of a recluse.

Monk Ingulph tells how, as a schoolboy at Westminster, he used now and again to meet Queen Eaditha on his way home from school, and to be questioned by her in logic and grammar, and how if he answered well he was rewarded with silver pieces and a feast in the royal larder. History does not support this pretty story, but it points to the kind of reputation enjoyed by the gentle Queen, much given to active kindness, whilst her husband was a kind of Shadow-King in every relation of life.

Closely connected with Queen Eaditha is another Eadith, more unhappy still, the daughter of a Saxon Earl called Ethelwolf and the beloved of Harold. She was betrothed to him, and according to some chroniclers secretly married to him, though never during his short reign recognised as Queen, for, for state purposes, he afterwards married Aldwyth. She is mentioned as "Edeva the Fair" in the Domesday Roll, and stated to be the "god-daughter of the Lady of England".

Her piteous story is told by Lord Lytton in

his historical novel *Harold, the last of the Saxon Kings*, and Lord Tennyson gives us a slight outline of her meek and gentle character in his drama *Harold*. That Harold loved her there is no doubt, but owing to their cousinship King Eadward opposed their union on the grounds of its illegality. Whether there ever was a secret marriage between them, we shall probably never know with any certainty. In both novel and drama Edith seeks on the field of Senlac for the body of her beloved, on the night following the battle of Hastings, and, having found it, dies. It is recorded that Harold's mother, Githa, offered William of Normandy the "weight in gold" of her noble son's corpse, but with a taunt the offer was refused; and, giving orders that Harold should be buried on the beach, the Conqueror said, "Let him guard the coasts which he madly occupied".

An Irish St. Edana or Edaena is the titular Saint of New Tuamia, and a famous holy well much resorted to by the sick, bears her name.

Edna, a name made popular by being borne by the gifted authoress of "Donovan", is probably a contraction of Edana.

One of our pagan King Penda's four holy daughters was St. Idaberga or Edberga. As a nun she dwelt at Dormundescaster, and her remains are now supposed to lie at Peterborough.

Mrs. Hemans wrote a pretty little poem entitled *Edith*, founded on an incident related in an American work called *Sketches in Connecticut*. It is the story of a fair young English girl who leaves a home of luxury and ease to share the life of one she loves in the wilds of America. Her husband is wounded in battle, and at nightfall she goes out to seek him on the battle field,

. . . . . . the love
Which fill'd her soul was strong to cast out fear:
And by its might upborne all else above,
She shrank not—mark'd not that the dead were near.
Of him alone she thought, whose languid head
Faintly upon her wedded bosom fell;
Memory of aught but him on earth was fled,
While heavily she felt his life-blood well
Fast o'er her garments forth, and vainly bound
With her torn robe and hair the streaming wound—
. . . . To her eye,
The eye that faded look'd through gathering haze,
Whence love, o'ermastering mortal agony,
Lifted a long, deep, melancholy gaze,
When voice was not; that fond, sad meaning pass'd—
She knew the fulness of her woe at last!
One shriek the forests heard—and mute she lay
And cold . . . .
. . She woke from that long dreamless trance,
The widow'd Edith: fearfully her glance
Fell, as in doubt, on faces dark and strange,
And dusky forms. A sudden sense of change
Flashed o'er her spirit, even ere memory swept
The side of anguish back with thoughts that slept;
. . . .

Where was she? Midst the people of the wild,
By the red hunter's fire: an aged chief,
Whose home look'd sad—for therein play'd no child—
Had borne her, in the stillness of her grief,
To that lone cabin of the woods; and there,
Won by a form so desolately fair,
Or touch'd with thoughts from some past sorrow sprung,
O'er her low couch an Indian matron hung;

Edith's gratitude for their kindness, and patient

resignation, win the hearts of the aged couple, until "they again seem'd parents".

And gentle cares
Th' adopted Edith meekly gave for theirs
Who loved her thus. Her spirit dwelt the while
With the departed, and her patient smile
Spoke of farewells to earth.

She gradually converts her protectors to Christianity, then dies.

. . by slow degrees
Light follow'd on as when a summer breeze
Parts the deep masses of the forest shade,
And lets the sunbeam through. Her voice was
Even such a breeze; and she, a lowly guide,
By faith and sorrow raised and purified,
So to the Cross her Indian fosterers led,
Until their prayers were one. . . .
Now might she pass in hope—her work was done:
And she was passing from the woods away—
The broken flower of England might not stay
Amidst those alien shades.

"My father"!—to the grey-haired chief she spoke—
"Know'st thou that I depart"? "I know, I know",
He answer'd mournfully, "that thou must go
To thy beloved, my daughter"!

Sir Walter Scott, in three of his novels, introduces the name of Edith. Edith, the "maid of Lora" in *The Lord of the Isles*, whose marriage was interrupted by an unseemly quarrel between her brother and Robert Bruce, and The Lady Edith, mother of Athelstane, in *Ivanhoe*; also The Lady Edith Plantagenet called "The Fair Maid of Anjou", who marries David, Earl of Huntingdon, in *The Talisman*. Once at least Scott uses the diminutive Edie for one of his characters, viz. Edie Ochiltree in *The Antiquary*.

EDITH

Queen Edith occurs in *Hereward the Wake*, Charles Kingsley's famous historical novel, and another Edith in fiction is Edith, Mr. Dombey's second wife, in *Dombey and Son* by Charles Dickens. Edith is also one of the characters in the play of *The Bloody Brother*, by Beaumont and Fletcher. Ida is one of the female characters in Lord Byron's drama *Werner*, and his only child was named Ada, the following lines being addressed to her.

Is thy face like thy mother's, my fair child?
Ada! sole daughter of my house and heart?
When last I saw thy young blue eyes they smiled,
And then we parted,—not as now we part,
But with a hope.

Childe Harold (LORD BYRON.)

Lord Byron in an unpublished letter, dated November 6th, 1816, says, "By the way, Ada's name (which I found in our pedigree under King John's reign), is the same with that of the sister of Charlemagne, as I redde, the other day, in a book treating of the Rhine".

Poor Pinky petals, crushed and torn!
  Did heartless Mayfair use you,
Then cast you forth to lie forlorn,
  For chariot-weels to bruise you?

I saw you last in Edith's hair,
  Rose, you would scarce discover
That I she passed upon the stair
  Was Edith's favoured lover.

A month—"a little month"—ago
  O theme for mortal writer!—
'Twixt you and me, my Rose, you know,
  She might have been politer;

But let that pass. She gave you then—
  Behind the oleander—
To one, perhaps, of all the men—
  Who best could understand her—

Cyril, that, duly flattered, took,
  As only Cyril's able,
With just the same Arcadian look
  He used, last night, for Mabel.

. . . .

Roman de la Rose (AUSTIN DOBSON.)

EFFIE: see EUPHEMIA.

EILEEN: see ELEANORE, ELLEN, ELAINE, HELEN, etc.

ELIZABETH, ELIZA, LIZZIE, ISABEL, BETTY, ELSPETH. The name Elizabeth can boast more forms, changes, and abbreviations than any other woman's name.

Like Mary, and so many of our most popular "Christian" names, Elizabeth is of Hebrew origin.

Aaron's wife was called Elisheba, which means "God hath sworn", or "oath of God", in memory of the covenant made with Abraham. Some now interpret the name as signifying "one who worships God", or "God is her oath". Elisheba developed into the Greek Elisabet, whence the Latin Elisabeth. The Russian form of the name is Lescinska; the most common French form Isabelle, or Isabeau, with its diminutives Lisette, Gisella, Babette, Babichon, Babet, Babel.

In England it has given us Eliza, Elsie, Bess, Bessie, Betsy, Betty, Lizzie, Isabel, Bella, Bell, Ibbott, Tibbie, Libby, Elspeth and Sib. Germany has kept the original Elizabeth very generally, with its Lieschen and Lisette, Elise, Lise, Elsabet, Elsabe, Bettine, Betta and Ilse as pet-names.

The popularity of the name probably originated in its having been borne by the mother of John the Baptist, but its fame has been worthily carried on by more than one of her successors.

The first of these to win renown was Elisavetta, the Muscovite Princess, whose name has been handed down to posterity by her royal lover, Harold Hardràda of Norway, who wrote a series of songs in her honour; and the Scandinavian inheritors of her name—the Elsebins, Lisbets, Helsas, and Bettys, are innumerable. The Slavonic nations have, however, loved the name the best, and have passed it down to modern times through Germany and Holland.

The popularity of Saint Elizabeth of Hungary has preserved the original form of the name in Germany, for the good mothers of Germany have loved to think that their little girls might perhaps, in receiving her name, receive with it some of the pure and gentle piety of the woman who daily fed the poor in her palace, relieved distress wherever she heard of it, built hospitals, and with her own hands dressed the wounds of the suffering. Saint Elizabeth died at the age of 24 after having herself known hunger and cold, and what it was to wander through the streets with her little children by her side. Daughter of the King of Hungary, she was wedded to Ludwig, Landgrave of Thuringia, and on his death was driven from his palace, the Wartburg at Eisenach, afterwards so famous as

Martin Luther's place of retreat from persecution. Many miracles are told of her, but the prettiest is, perhaps, that describing how, as she set out one day down the steep path leading from the "Wartburg" to the town, bearing meat and bread in her mantle, to give to the poor, she met her husband returning from the chase. Astonished to see his wife so laden, he drew her mantle aside to see what it was she was carrying so carefully. He was amazed to find nothing but the most beautiful red and white roses he had ever seen, though it was in the winter season. At the same moment he saw above her head a luminous image of a crucifix. He bade her pass on, but took one of the roses which he kept all his life. Once she gave her ducal mantle to a poor man, and an angel restored it to her. She lived from 1207 to 1231.

Another Saint Elizabeth, born in 1271, and niece of Elizabeth of Hungary, was a daughter of Pedro III., King of Aragon, and by her marriage with King Denis, became Queen of Portugal. As a tiny child she was noted for her piety, and, as she grew up, for her works of charity, her seven fastings and her forgiving spirit and sweetness of disposition, by her virtues at last winning her husband from his evil ways and dissipated life. She died at the age of 65.

Yet a third saint of the name was St. Elizabeth of Sconauge who died in 1165 at the age of 36. She was much favoured by heavenly visions.

Elizabeth of Hainault on her marriage to Philippe Auguste of France, consented to her name being converted from Elizabeth into Isabella: this is the first instance on record of this change, which has since taken place on nearly every occasion when our princesses bearing the name of Elizabeth have gone over to France. In fact, Isabelle has become the more popular name in that country, and there is one French Saint known under this form of the name. Saint Isabel the Virgin was a daughter of Louis VIII. of France and sister to St. Louis. Born in 1225, she lost her father when she was little more than an infant. Early remarkable for the piety of her nature, and for her skill in the Latin tongue, she, from the age of 13, spent her life in almost constant prayer, study and good works. In opposition to the wishes of her brother St. Louis, and of the pope, she stedfastly declined to marry, saying, she "would rather be the last amongst the virgins consecrated to God, than an Empress and the first woman in the world". She founded a nunnery at Longchamps, four miles from Paris, which she named "Of the Humility of our Lady", humility having been, she said, the most marked trait in the Virgin Mary's character. After some years of suffering Saint Isabel died on February 22, 1270, and was in 1316 beatified by Pope Leo X.

The French princess, Isabella of Angoulême, brought the name over to England, upon her marriage to King John, and her daughter carred it, in the form of Isabella, to Germany, when she was married to Frederick II.

Isabel or Ysabel are now the most popular

forms of the name in Spain and Portugal, the piety and goodness of Isabella of Aragon being doubtless partly responsible for this.

We have had Queen Isabelles here, besides Isabelle of Angoulême, but in spite of this England has on the whole remained faithful to Elizabeth, with all its contractions. The ugly abbreviation of Eliza was introduced by the Elizabethan poets in their laudations of "Good Queen Bess"; but "Bess" is of far older date, and Elisabeth Woodville, Queen of Edward IV., the "White Rose of York", was, in her time, called "Queen Bess".

In Scotland things French have always had an attraction, and there accordingly Isabel is the popular form of the name, and the favourite contraction—Tibbie; they also have Isbel.

A few words are derived from the name, though nothing like as many as from "Mary".

There is, of course, the adjective "Elizabethan" applied to the most flourishing period of English history and especially literature. Then there is a Spanish gold coin called Isabellino (equivalent to 100 reals), and the colour known as Isabelle or Isabel, a brownish-yellow colour, with a shade of red in it, named after Isabelle of Austria (1566-1633) who, at the siege of Ostend, swore she would not change her linen until the siege had been successful. As the siege lasted something like three years the devoted Princess's linen became somewhat discoloured, and hence the "Couleur Isabelle". Some discourteous historians assert that the name of the shade was suggested by the young lady's complexion!

Many places bear the name, as for instance, to mention a few: in Africa, Port Elizabeth, Elizabeth Point, Elizabeth Bay; in America, Elizabeth town, Elizabeth City, Cape Elizabeth; in Russia, Elisabetpol, Elizatbetgrad; in Austria and Hungary, Elisabeth Salzbad, Elisabethstadt.

Amongst the more noted bearers of the name may be mentioned, in addition to those named above:

Elizabeth, Queen of England: 1533-1603.
Elizabeth of York, Queen of Henry VII.
Elizabeth Stuart, daughter of James I. of England, and Queen of Bohemia.
Elizabeth Petrovna, Empress of Russia: 1709-1761.
Mme. Elizabeth, of France, wife of Louis XVI.: Guillotined.
Elizabeth Claypole, Cromwell's favourite daughter.
Elizabeth Fry, (the female Howard): Prison Reformer.
The Lady Elizabeth Fitzgerald, the heroine of the Earl of Surrey's Love Sonnets, under the name of Geraldine.
Lady Elizabeth Hastings, whom "to love", according to Sterne, was "a liberal education".
Elizabeth Barrett Browning, the poetess, and
Elizabeth Inchbald, the dramatist.
Elizabeth Montague, authoress, and founder of the "Blue-Stocking Club", lived in Portman Square, and thus gave her name to

two places in that neighbourhood, Montague Street and Montague Square.

As heroines of poems and novels Elizabeths, Isabellas, &c., are innumerable; of these some of the best known are the *Verses to Isabel, Countess of Lauderdale*, by Drummond of Hawthornden; Elissa (Dido), Queen of Carthage, in Virgil's *Æneid*; *Bessie Bell and Mary Gray* (a ballad); *Lady Elspat* (a ballad); Elsie, the heroine of *The Golden Legend*, by Longfellow; Elspie, the heroine of *Bothie of Tober-na-Vuolich*, by Clough; *Lizie Lindsay* (a ballad); *The most Pleasant song of Lady Bessie* (a ballad, 1484); *Song of the most pleasant Lady Bessy* [Elizabeth of York] (a ballad); Elizabeth, the heroine of *The Saint's Tragedy*, by Charles Kingsley; *Elizabetha Triumphans* (Queen Elizabeth), by James Aske (1588); *Letters to Eliza*, by Sterne; *Eliza: or an elegy upon the unripe decease of Sir Anthony Irby*, by Wm. Browne; *Isabel*, by Lord Tennyson; *Isabella, or the Pot of Basil*, by Keats; *Iseult of Brittany* (Last Tournament), by Tennyson; *Tristram and Iseult*, by Matthew Arnold; Elise in *L'Avare*, by Molière; Elisabeth in *The High Tide on the Coast of Lincolnshire*, 1571, by Jean Ingelow; *Betsy and I are Out* in *Farm Ballads*, by Wm. Carleton. In Drama: Lady Betty Modish in *The Careless Husband*, by Colley Cibber; Isabella in *Measure for Measure*, by Shakespeare; *The Lady Isabella's Tragedy*; Isabel, or Sib, in *The Tragedy of Edward II.*, by Marlowe; Eliza in *The Plain Dealer*, by Wycherly; Isabella in

The Mistake, by Congreve; *Isabella, or The Fatal Marriage*, by Thos. Southern (1694); and Isabel in *The Revenge*, by Young. In FICTION: Elspeth in *The Antiquary*, Elspeth in *The Monastery*, and Elspeth in *Guy Mannering*, all by Sir Walter Scott; Betsy Prig, the friend of the immortal Mrs. Gamp, in *Martin Chuzzlewit*, by Dickens; *Elsie Venner*, by Oliver W Holmes; and *Thoughtless Miss Betsy*, by Eliza Haywood.

ELLA, ELLE, AELLA, is a contraction of the Saxon word *aelf* = elf, and is an ancient name, now only given to girls; but it was originally used as a man's name. Its probable meaning is "friend of elves".

ELSIE, ELSPETH: see Elizabeth.

EMILY, EMELINE, AMELIA, EMMA, etc. The true origin of this name seems to be a moot point amongst those who have studied the question. Some derive it from a Greek word meaning "flattering" or "witty", whilst others carry it back to the Teutonic *Amal* = work: the second theory is probably the correct one. Miss Yonge in her *Christian Names* suggests that the *Aemilii* of Rome and the *Amaler* of the Goths have a common ancestor in the Teutonic *amal*, meaning work; the same writer points out that *maal* or or *âmal* means "works" in Hebrew also, and *aml* is Old-Norse for "work".

Thus, from this remote Teutonic forefather *amal*, through the Greeks and Romans, have descended our household names of Emily, Emilie, Emmeline, Emeline, Emilia, Amelia, Millie,—and for boys Emmery and Amery.

Emma, though often classed with these, is probably an entirely different name. It is so often thought to be the same name as Emily that it is treated of here, but it is most likely derived from the Icelandic *Emm*, and means a "nurse": *Amme* is the current word for nurse in Germany now.

The English masculine forms are not very common now, though the present writer knows a peasant family in Sussex where the boys are still named Emmery; and in France Emile is exceedingly common.

Emily is the Latin, Amelia the Teutonic, form of the name, and all three names, Amelia, Emily and Emma have been popular amongst the Royal families of Europe, though simple Emma is now often considered too plain for the daughters of the highly-placed. Several minor Saints have borne the name, and Amerigo Vespucci is the great representative of its Spanish masculine form, which through him came to be the name of the vast continent of the Western Hemisphere.

St. Emiliana (A.D. 1246) is one of those Saints to whom Christ is said to have appeared in the image of a child. We are told that as Emiliana was lying in bed ill, she saw a child of about four years of age playing in her room. Emiliana thought it was an angel, and asked if it had nothing better to do than to play, whereupon the child answered by another question: "What would you have me to do instead"? "I should like you to speak to me of God", said the Saint, but the child replied: "In speaking of God, one can only speak in praise, and it is not well to praise one's self", and, so saying, vanished. Of this same Saint it is told that on one occasion she prayed that God would transfer to her the illness of a sick boy whom she had visited, so that the child might be healed, and that her prayer was granted.

St. Emiliana was always careful not to utter a single unnecessary word, and kept absolute silence during the forty days of Lent, and during three days in every week throughout the year.

Emily Becchieri (1238-1314) was another to whom visions were granted, Christ informing her in person that His greatest agony had been the three hours during which He hung on the Cross, and He promised Emily that He would grant the three theological virtues to all those who, at the third hour of the evening, repeated three *Paters* and three *Avés*, in memory of His Crucifixion. On another occasion, whilst Emily was meditating on the Crown of Thorns, she prayed that she might be made to feel in her own person the anguish which Christ had suffered, whereupon Christ answered her by the mouth of her crucifix, saying that He would grant her wish; and forthwith Emily suffered such excruciating pain that for three days she had to keep her bed, and at the end of that time was restored to health only by some mysterious draught administered to her by Mary Magdalen and St. Catherine.

In England the name of Emma was known in very early days, "The Lady of England" at the close of the tenth and beginning of the eleventh century being an Emma. The daughter of Richard Duke of Normandy, she became the Queen of Ethelred the Unready in 1002. In 1013 she was sent with her two sons to Normandy for safety, and upon the death of Ethelred married Canute soon after his accession to the English throne. Harold I. banished her, but she returned to England when her son Edward the Confessor succeeded to the crown. He, however, deprived his mother of her property in 1043, and nine years later she died at Winchester, where she was buried. She is sometimes known by the name of Aelfgiva.

Later, we have Emma Plantagenet, who married King David of Wales, whom Southey celebrates in his *Madoc*.

In Germany there have been many notable women of the name, including Amalie of Mansfield (1493), Amalie of Wurtemburg (1550), and Amalie of Saxe-Weimar, Goethe's friend. The last named was born in Italy in 1739, and died of a broken heart in 1807, for she never recovered from the anguish she suffered at Germany's humiliation at the hands of Napoleon Buonaparte at the battle of Jena in 1806. A Guelph by descent, she, at the age of seventeen, married the Duke of Saxe-Weimar, and at the age of nineteen was left a widow. During her son's minority she held the reins of government, and her little Court at Weimar was, during her reign, the centre of German literary activity. Goethe settled in the town, and amongst those who were to be met in the Duchess' circle were Wieland, Herder, Musæus, and Schiller.

EMILY

In England, from the days of Chaucer downwards, Emilys, Amelias, and Emmas have been sung of by the poets, and in later days written of by novelists; whilst in modern life, Emily Brontë, Emily Faithfull, Amelia B. Edwards, one of our leading Egyptologists as well as a novelist, Emma Marshall, and Emma Albani, are worthy representatives of the name.

Thus passeth yere by yere, and day by day,
Till it fell ones in a morwe of May
That Emilie, that fayrer was to sene
Than is the lilie upon his stalke grene,
And fresher than the May with floures newe
(For with the rose colour strof hire hewe;
I n'ot which was finer of hem two),
Er it was day, as she was wont to do,
She was arisen, and all redy dight.
For May wol have no slogardie a-night.
The seson priketh every gentil herte,
And maketh him out of his slepe to sterte,
And sayth, arise, and do thin observance.
  This maketh Emelie han remembrance
To don honour to May, and for to rise.
Yclothed was she freshe for to devise.
Hire yelwe here was broided in a tresse,
Behind hire back, a yede long I gesse.
And in the gardin at the sonne uprist
She walketh up and doun wher as hire list.
She gathereth floures, partie white and red,
To make a sotel [subtle] gerlond for hire hed,
And as an angel hevenlich she song.

The Knightes Tale (GEOFFREY CHAUCER.)

In literature the first character that occurs to us is *Amelia*, the heroine of Henry Fielding's novel of that name; to the heroine of this famous book S. T. Coleridge wrote his sonnet:

Virtues and woes alike too great for man
In the soft tale oft claims the useless sigh;
For vain the attempt to realize the plan,
On Folly's wings must Imitation fly.
With other aim has Fielding here display'd
Each social duty and each social care;
With just yet vivid colouring portray'd
What every wife should be, what many are.
And sure the Parent of a race so sweet
With double pleasure on the page shall dwell,
Each scene with sympathizing breast shall meet,
While Reason still with smiles delights to tell
Maternal hope, that her loved progeny
In all but sorrows shall Amelias be!

Then there is Amelia in Thomson's *Seasons*, who, struck by lightning, dies in her lover's arms; Amelia in Schiller's tragedy of *Die Räuber*, to whom Thomas Campbell refers, in his *Pleasures of Hope*, when he says:

Or they will learn how generous worth sublimes
The robber Moor, and pleads for all his crimes;
How poor Amelia kissed with many a tear
His hand, blood-stained, but ever, ever dear.

It is to an Emelia that Shelley addressed the following lines:

Madonna, wherefore hast thou sent to me
Sweet basil and mignonette?
Embleming love and health, which never yet
In the same wreath might be.
Alas, and they are wet!
Is it with thy kisses or thy tears?
For never rain or dew
Such fragrance drew
From plant or flower—the very doubt endears
My sadness ever new
The sighs I breathe, the tears I shed for thee.

To Emelia Viviáni (P. B. Shelley.)

EMILY

Æmilia, in Spenser's *Faëry Queene*, Emilie or Emelye in *The Knight's Tale* in *The Canterbury Tales*, by Geoffrey Chaucer; Emilia, the wife of Iago in *Othello*, by Shakespeare; Emilia in *The Winter's Tale*, by the same; Emilia in *The Adventures of Peregrine Pickle*, by Tobias Smollett; Emily in *The Deuce is in him*, by George Colman, Sen.; *Emma*, by Jane Austen; Emma in *Madoc*, by Robert Southey; Emma in Matthew Prior's version of *The Nut Browne Maid*; Little Emily in *David Copperfield*, by Charles Dickens; and Emily in *The White Doe of Rylstone*, by William Wordsworth.

From fair to fairer; day by day
A more divine and loftier way!
Even such this blessed Pilgrim trod,
By sorrow lifted towards her God;
Uplifted to the purest sky
Of undisturbed mortality.
Her own thoughts loved she; and could bend
A dear look to her lowly Friend;
There stopped; her thirst was satisfied
With what this innocent spring supplied:
Her sanction inwardly she bore,
And stood apart from human cares:
But to the world returned no more,
Although with no unwilling mind
Help did she give at need, and joined
The Wharfdale peasants in their prayers.
At length, thus faintly, faintly tied
To earth, she was set free, and died.
Thy soul, exalted Emily,
Maid of the blasted family,
Rose to the God from whom it came!
—In Rylstone church her mortal frame
Was buried by her Mother's side.

Then we have Lord Byron's *Emma*:

Since now the hour is come at last,
  When you must quit your anxious lover;
Since now our dream of bliss is passed,
  One pang, my girl, and all is over.

Alas! that pang will be severe,
  Which bids us part to meet no more,
Which tears me far from one so dear,
  Departing for a distant shore.

Well! we have pass'd some happy hours,
  And joy will mingle with our tears;
When thinking on these ancient towers,
  The shelter of our infant years;
. . . .

These times are past—our joys are gone,
  You leave me, leave this happy vale;
These scenes I must retrace alone:
  Without thee what will they avail?

Who can conceive, who has not proved,
  The anguish of a last embrace?
When, torn from all you fondly loved,
  You bid a long adieu to peace.

and lastly, Emmeline in the sweet old ballad of *The Child of Elle*:

The Child of Elle to his garden wente,
  And stood at his garden pale,
Whan, lo! he beheld fair Emmeline's page
  Come trippinge downe the dale.
. . . . .

Nowe Christe thee save, thou little foot-page,
  Nowe Christ thee save and see!
Oh telle me how does thy ladye gaye,
  And what may thy tydinges bee?

My ladye shee is all woe-begone,
  And the teares they falle from her eyne;
And aye she laments the deadlye feude
  Betweene her house and thine.

. . . . . .

For, ah ! her gentle heart is broke,
  And in grave soone must shee bee,
Sith her father hath chose her a new love,
  And forbidde her to think of thee.

. . . . . .

Nowe hye thee backe, thou little foot-page,
  And let thy fair ladye know
This night will I bee at her bowre-windowe,
  Betide me weale or woe.

. . . . . .

Awake, awake, my ladye deare,
  Come, mount this faire palfraye:
This ladder of ropes will lette thee downe,
  Ile carry thee hence awaye.

. . . . . .

Faire Emmeline scant had ridden a mile,
  A mile forth of the towne,
When she was aware of her father's men
  Come galloping over the downe;

. . . . . .

Faire Emmeline sighed, faire Emmeline wept,
  And did all tremblinge stand:
At lengthe she sprang upon her knee,
  And held his lifted hand.

"Pardon, my lord and father deare,
  This faire yong knyght and mee:
Trust me, but for the carlish knyght,
  I never had fled from thee.

"Oft have you called your Emmeline
  Your darling and your joye;
O let not then your harsh resolves
  Your Emmeline destroye".

The baron he stroakt his dark-brown cheeke,
  And turned his head asyde
To whipe awaye the starting teare,
  He proudly strave to hyde.

. . .

"Here, take her, Child of Elle", he sayd,
And gave her lillye white hand;
"Here take my deare and only child,
And with her half my land.
"Thy father once mine honour wrongde
In dayes of youthful pride;
Do thou the injurye repayre
In fondnesse for thy bride".

ENID = spotless purity, was, as a name, first borne by one of the heroines of King Arthur's court. Enid was the personification of all that is noble and true in womanhood, and conspicuous also for her resplendent beauty and noble bearing. The bard of the Middle Ages could pay no higher compliment to his Mistress than to call her a "second Enid".

And there was no maiden more esteemed than she in the Island of Britain.

The Mabinogion.

The old Arthurian romances exist in several forms.

The version best known to English readers is that known as *The Mabinogion*, a series of Welsh Tales, chiefly relating to Arthur and his Round Table.

About 700 pages of the *Mabinogion* in manuscript are still preserved in the library of Jesus College, Oxford, and are known as *The Red Book of Hergest* from the place in which the MS. was discovered. This manuscript dates from the fourteenth century and contains Welsh versions of three French Arthurian romances, two British tales ascribed to the same age, a history of Taliesin not older than the thirteenth Century, and a few other tales.

ENID

According to Professor Morley, the title *Mabinogion* is the plural of the Welsh word *Mabinogi*, which means amusements or instruction for the young, from *Mab* = child, or *Maban* = a young child. Copies of the *Mabinogion* have been published, both in the original Cymric and in an English translation, by Lady Charlotte Guest.

In this old Arthurian Romance moves Enid, the daughter of Yniol, and wife of Geraint—the beloved and admired of all—whose beauty of character so far outshone even her beauty of person, that jealousy itself was fain to hide its head in her presence.

The old story tells us how Arthur desired to revive the custom of hunting the White Stag, but that his nephew Gawain steps in to crave that the victor in the chase may be permitted indeed to present the head of the stag to his Lady Love, but to dissuade the king from "adhering to the ancient custom of permitting the fortunate victor the privilege of claiming a salute from the fairest Lady of the Court" fearing that "this might lead to dissensions".

Arthur does not, however, like to break his promise and the chase takes place.

Geraint kills the stag, and Enid is judged by the Queen to be the "fairest Lady of the Court".

"Then spake Gwenhwyvar, 'Rightly did I judge', said she, 'concerning the head of the stag, that it should not be given to any until Geraint's return; and behold here is a fit occasion for bestowing it. Let it be given to

Enid the daughter of Ynywl, the most illustrious maiden. And I do not believe that any will begrudge it her, for between her and every one here there exists nothing but love and friendship'".

Tennyson founded his great cycle of poems *The Idylls of the King* on these old romances, though he did not in all cases closely adhere to the Welsh versions.

The tale of Geraint and Enid allegorizes the fatal contagion of distrust and jealousy, which, having its root in the infidelity of Guinevere and Launcelot, spread downwards through King Arthur's Court with fatal destructiveness, at last undermining all the noble projects of the King.

Geraint, "when a rumour rose about the Queen", was alarmed

> "lest his gentle wife,
> Thro' that great tenderness for Guinevere,
> Had suffer'd, or should suffer, any taint
> In nature"

for Geraint loved Enid "as he loved the light of Heaven". He therefore removed Enid from Arthur's Court and the presence of the Queen, and took her to his own country, Devon, on the plea that it needed his care,

> "Where, thinking, that if ever yet was wife
> True to her lord, mine shall be so to me,
> He compass'd her with sweet observances
> And worship, never leaving her, and grew
> Forgetful of his promise to the King,
> Forgetful of the falcon and the hunt,
> Forgetful of the tilt and tournament,
> Forgetful of his glory and his name,
> Forgetful of his princedom and its cares".

Geraint was in short "molten down in mere uxoriousness", and Enid, troubled by her husband's loss of manhood, found his forgetfulness "hateful to her", but through bashfulness did not like to speak.

"I hate that he should linger here;
I cannot love my lord and not his name.
Far liefer had I gird his harness on him,
And ride with him to battle and stand by,
And watch his mightful hand striking great blows
At caitiffs and at wrongers of the world.
. . . .
O me, I fear that I am no true wife".

Geraint in his sleep overhears and misinterprets these last words, and at once jumping to the conclusion that she has indeed become corrupted by the companionship of Guinevere, submits her to all manner of shame and suffering to put her constancy to the proof.

Enid passes through the ordeal as only an Enid could have passed, and a perfect trust in his gentle wife and contrition at his own base thought of her, spring up in Geraint's breast.

"Enid, I have used you worse than that dead man;
Done you more wrong: we both have undergone
That trouble which has left me thrice your own:
Henceforward I will rather die than doubt.
. . . .
You thought me sleeping, but I heard you say,
I heard you say, that you were no true wife:
I swear I will not ask your meaning in it:
I do believe yourself against yourself,
And will henceforward rather die than doubt".

And Enid could not say one tender word,
She felt so blunt and stupid at the heart:

. . . .

And never yet, since high in Paradise
O'er the four rivers the first roses blew,
Came purer pleasure unto mortal kind
Than lived thro' her, who in that perilous hour
Put hand to hand beneath her husband's heart,
And felt him hers again: she did not weep,
But o'er her meek eyes came a happy mist
Like that which kept the heart of Eden green
Before the useful trouble of the rain.

. . . .

They pass'd to their own land
And there he kept the justice of the King
So vigorously yet mildly, that all hearts
Applauded, and the spiteful whisper died:

. . . .

They call'd him the great Prince and man of men,
But Enid, whom her ladies loved to call
Enid the Fair, a grateful people named
Enid the Good.

ERNESTINE is the natural feminine of the name Ernst or (English) Ernest. The name is a Teutonic one, and is probably in the majority of cases given under the impression that it means *earnest* or *serious*; but Mr. H. A. Long, among others, does not hesitate to derive it from *Arn = eagle*.

Arnust was the old German name, which seems in its journey to Italy to have got changed into Ernesto, of which name there are examples as early as the eighth century in that country.

In Germany the name soon began to appear in its altered form, in the persons of sundry dukes and Margraves, and, thus introduced, steadily gained ground, until now, when it is one of the most popular of all German names and is becoming almost as common in England, though here we have not taken kindly to the feminine—Ernestine—which may, however, occasionally be recognised under its diminutive Tine.

In the twelfth century the Minnesinger Heinrich von Veldig sang of the adventures of *Duke Ernst*, the son-in-law of the Emperor Konrad II., who went on a pilgrimage to the Holy Land to expiate the crime of murdering his feudal lord.

ESMERALDA means an emerald. This is a "jewel" name. The emerald is supposed to have the peculiar power of rendering blind any serpent or snake so ill-advised as to fix its gaze upon it.

> Blinded like serpents when they gaze
> Upon the emerald's virgin blaze.
>
> *Lalla Rookh* (MOORE.)

Towards mankind, however, the emerald exercised a totally opposite power, and, according to popular belief, strengthened the eyes of those who looked into its green depths, so that the ancients never wearied of fixing their eyes upon the emeralds in their rings, if they were so fortunate as to possess any.

Yet another virtue did this precious jewel call its own—that of testing true and faithful love:

> It is a gem which hath the power to show
> If plighted lovers keep their troth or no.
> If faithful, it is like the leaves in Spring;
> If faithless, like those leaves when withering.
>
> (MRS. MACLEAN.)

Esmeralda is the name of the beautiful gipsy girl in *Notre Dame de Paris*, by Victor Hugo.

ESTHER, Hester, Stella, Estelle. This name came originally from the Assyrian word Sitarch = star. The Assyrian name was adopted by the Persians, and was given by King Ahasuerus to his Jewish captive Hadassah, in the Hebrew form of Esther, when he, in anger with his Queen Vashti, raised the Hebrew maiden to the throne.

And he brought up Hadassah, that is, Esther, his uncle's daughter: for she had neither father nor mother, and the maiden was fair and beautiful.—*Esther* ii. 7.

There are many forms of the name, which seems to have a dual parentage in the Assyrian Sitarch and the Persian Astarte, whence Asteria, Hester, Esther, Eoster, Estelle, Stella, is an easy descent: they all signify "star", and are allied to *aestus* = tide, or rising waters; and from that come our words estuary and East (place of the rising sun). Eoster gives Easter, the time at which special honours were paid to Astarte, and which afterwards became devoted to one of the great Christian festivals that happened to fall at that season of the year: thus, as has so often been the case, the heathen festival became gradually merged in the Christian, just as the remains of Druidical rites survive in our Yule log and misletoe at Christmas.

Our English diminutives of Esther are Etty, and Ettie, and of Hester, Hetty and Harty.

It was Racine who first made the name popular on the Continent, by his play of *Esther*; but in England, ever since the days of the Puritans, the people have loved to give their children "Bible names", and Esther early became a favourite.

Both the women beloved by Dean Swift bore this name: Esther Johnson, whom he always addressed as Stella, and Esther Vanhomrigh, whom he called Vanessa.

Often Swift wrote to Esther Johnson, to whom he was secretly married in 1706, in verse, and in 1718, on her birthday addressed the following lines to her:—

Stella this day is thirty-four
(We shan't dispute a year or more)
However, Stella, be not troubled,
Although thy size and years are doubled
Since first I saw thee at sixteen,
The brightest virgin on the green.
So little is thy form declined;
Made up so largely in thy mind.
Oh, would it please the gods to split
Thy beauty, size, and years, and wit,
No age could furnish out a pair
Of nymphs so graceful, wise, and fair:
With half the lustre of your eyes,
With half your wit, your years and size.
And then, before it grew too late,
How should I beg of gentle fate,
(That either nymph might lack her swain),
To split my worship too in twain.

Stella was the name by which Sir Philip Sydney addressed the Lady Penelope Devereux, of whom he was deeply enamoured, and to whom he refers in Astrophel and Stella:

Stella! whose voice, when it singeth,
Angels to acquaintance bringeth;
Stella, in whose body is
Writ each character of bliss;
Whose face all, all beauty passeth,
Save thy mind, which that surpasseth.

ESTHER

Charles Lamb wrote a poem to Hester Savory, "a young Quaker you may have heard me speak of as being in love with for some years, while I lived at Pentonville, though I had never spoken to her in my life".

When maidens such as Hester die,
Their place ye may not well supply,
Though ye among a thousand try,
  With vain endeavour.

A month or more she hath been dead,
Yet cannot I by force be led
To think upon the wormy bed
  And her together.

A springy motion in her gait,
A rising step, did indicate
Of pride and joy no common rate,
  That flushed her spirit.

Her parents held the Quaker rule,
Which doth the human feeling cool;
But she was trained in Nature's school;
  Nature had blest her.

A waking eye, a prying mind,
A heart that stirs, is hard to find,
A hawk's keen sight ye cannot bind,
  Ye could not Hester.

My sprightly neighbour! gone before
To that unknown and silent shore,
Shall we not meet, as heretofore,
  Some summer morning?

When from thy cheerful eyes a ray
Hath struck a bliss upon the day,
A bliss that would not go away,
  A sweet forewarning.

Other instances of the name in literature are Estella in *Great Expectations*, by Charles Dickens; Esther Hawdon in *Bleak House*, by Charles Dickens; Esther Lyon, who marries *Felix Holt*, by "George Eliot"; Esther, the housekeeper to Muhldenau in *The Maid of Marienderp*, by Sheridan Knowles; and the touching figure of Hetty Sorrel in *Adam Bede*, by "George Eliot".

Stella and Flavia, ev'ry hour,
  Unnumbered hearts surprise;
In Stella's soul lies all her power,
  And Flavia's, in her eyes.

More boundless Flavia's conquests are,
  And Stella's more confined.
All can discern a face that's fair;
  But few, a lovely mind.

Stella, like Britain's monarch, reigns
  O'er cultivated lands:
Like Eastern tyrants, Flavia deigns
  To rule o'er barren sands.

Then boast, fair Flavia! boast your face!
  Your beauty's only store.
Your charms will ev'ry day decrease!
  Each day gives Stella more!

(Mary Barber.)

ETHEL, Alice, Adelaide, Adeline, Audry, Awdry.

Our Anglo-Saxon ancestors held women in honour, believing them to be inspired, and this belief is often shown in the names they bestowed upon them.

Perhaps there is no name more popular at the present day than Ethel, a name which has descended to us from Anglo-Saxon times, though then it did not stand alone but always had some second meaning attached to it, thus Ethelburga Ethel = noble Burga = protectress.

It may surprise many who now hear the name of Ethel to learn that it is really the same as two other names, which though they seem to be falling a little into disuse now, were more popular than Ethel some twenty or thirty years since, *i.e.* Adelaide and Alice with all their many variants. Alice, indeed, is the true modern English form of the name, Ethel, the Anglo-Saxon.

Before the Norman Conquest it was a royal name in England, and the Aetheling was generally used as the title of the heir to the crown, just as our modern heirs apparent are entitled Prince of Wales.

Ethel, Adel, or Edel signifies noble. Our Aethelric or Alaric, meaning noble king, has in Germany been contracted into Ulrich, just as our Ethelbert has been contracted into Albert by the Germans. Here, however, we have only to deal with the feminine forms of the name, and they alone supply us with quite a formidable list. The usual modern English name is simply Ethel, as before stated; some of the older combinations are Edeline, Ethelswytha, meaning *most noble*, Ethelinda = *noble maiden*, Ethelwyne = *noble and beloved*, Ethelfleda or Ethelfledh = *noble increase*, Ethelburga (a very favourite name amongst Anglo-Saxon ladies) = *protectress*, Ethelgiva = *noble gift* or *royal bounty*, Ethelgifa = *noble helpgiver*, Etheldred, Etheldreda, or Aethelthryth = *noble threatener* or *counsellor*. This last name also takes the form of Audry. At the fair named after Saint Aetheldreda or Saint Audry, cheap finery used to be sold to the country lads and lasses, and hence has come the word *tawdry*. The German name Edel or Adelhilda = *noble heroine* became Adelheid, and Adelheid became Adelaide, meaning noble maiden, shining dew, and hence we have Adelgonde = *noble warrioress*, Aldegonde = *noble lady*, Adelina, Adeline, Adele, Adela, Adeliza, Adeliz, Alix, Alisa, Alicia, Alice, Elsa and Else, all signifying *noble maiden*. Some interpret Adelinde and Adeline as *noble-serpent*.

At least three English Saints have borne this noble old Anglo-Saxon name, and of these the most noted is Saint Etheldreda or Ediltrudis, more generally known as Saint Audry. She lived in the middle of the seventh century and was the third daughter of Annas, king of the East Anglians, and of his wife Saint Hereswyda. Three of her sisters were also Saints—namely, Saint Sexburga, Saint Ethelburga and Saint Withburga. Etheldreda was born at Ermynge in Suffolk, and became the wife of Prince Tonbercht, one of the Girvij, who inhabited Rutland, Northampton, Huntingdon and part of Lincolnshire. Tonbercht died after three years, leaving the Isle of Ely to his widow, as her dowry, and thither Etheldreda retired, living for five years a life of solitude, poverty, and humility, striving to overcome the sins of the flesh by fasting and prayer, and praising God. All her efforts to conceal herself from the eyes of the world were, however, fruitless,—the brightness of her virtues pierced the veil of her seclusion, and her holy way of life attracted the attention of Egfrid the King of Northumberland, who became an ardent suitor for her hand. She at length consented to wed him, but only on condition that she should live with him as his sister, not his wife, and for twelve years these two reigned in Northumberland together. At the end of that time her desire to withdraw from the world became so strong that Etheldreda took the veil and retired to the monastery of Coldingham. In 672 she returned to Ely and there founded a double monastery, herself governing that allotted to women. She ate only once a day, wore only woollen clothes, and always rose at midnight. She died after great sufferings in 679.

Saint Edelburga or Ethelburga, an elder sister of Saint Etheldreda, never married, but early crossed over to France and entered the nunnery of Farmoutier, in the forest of Brie, of which she ultimately became the Abbess. She was accompanied to France by her niece (the daughter of Saint Sexburga and Earçonbercht, King of Kent) Earcongata, who also became a Saint.

The third and last English Saint of the name is Etheldritha or Alfrida, daughter of Offa, King of Mercia. She was so desirous of devoting herself to a life of prayer that she declined to marry Ethelbert, King of the East-Angles.

She bade farewell to the allurements of Court life and withdrew into a small cell near Croyland in Lincolnshire where she dwelt for forty years. She died about 834.

Just about one hundred years after the death of Etheldritha in 931, was born one Adelheid, who at the age of sixteen married Lothaire, King of Italy; three years later Lothaire was poisoned, and his widow invited King Otto I. of Germany into Italy, to fight against her enemy Duke Berengarius or Berenger who had seized the crown.

Adelheid was taken prisoner by Berengarius, but escaped, and again inviting Otto over, finally married him in 951-2. In 973 Otto died and Adelheid was appointed Regent during the minority of her grandson, Otto III. Adelheid was canonized and is known as Saint Adelheid or Adelaide. Nearly two hundred years after the death of Etheldritha the name again appears among the Saints under the form of Alice or Adelaide. Saint Alice or Saint Adelaide, as she is variously called, was, like her predecessors, of noble birth, and daughter of Megendose, Count of Guelders. Her father had founded two nunneries, and of both of these in succession Saint Alice became the governor; the first was at Bellich or Velich on the Rhine, and here she instituted a nunnery of the order of Saint Bennet which afterwards was converted into a Church of Canonesses; the second was that of our Lady at Cologne, and of this Saint Alice died Abbess in 1015. Ethelfleda, the "Lady of the Mercians", has not been canonized as a Saint, but she too did work in the world worth recording. She assisted her brother Edward the Elder against his enemy Ethelwald 901-5, rebuilt the city of Chester in

907, built forts at Tamworth and Stafford, 913, defeated the Welsh at Brecknock in 916, took possession of Leicester in 918, and caused York to surrender to her in that same year. On June 22nd, 922, she died, a very notable, active woman surely, and worthy to be classed amongst the noble ladies of England.

All these were women whose lives were governed by a stern and noble sense of duty which did not belie their names, but there have been heroines of the name of a later date who claim our admiration too. Of these was noble Lady Alicia Lisle, one of Judge Jeffrey's victims. A daughter of Sir White Beconsaw, she married Viscount Lisle, one of Charles I.'s judges. Upon the accession of Charles II. Lisle together with other republicans fled to Switzerland, and was there assassinated by royalists just as he was entering a church at Lausanne. After the Monmouth insurrection Lady Alicia Lisle was brought before Judge Jeffreys at Winchester on the charge of having sheltered fugitives from the battle of Sedgemoor. She was over seventy years of age, too deaf to hear the evidence, and no help of counsel was allowed her. She pleaded in vain, that the man she had sheltered, one Hickes, a nonconformist minister, had not been proved to have borne arms, nor if he had, had she known of his treason. She was known to be loyal, but with Jeffreys that mattered little, and he condemned the grand old woman to be burnt alive that same day. A respite of some days was however obtained, and this was used to petition the king

James II. to allow her to be beheaded instead of burnt; this petition was granted, and Alicia Lisle died at Winchester on September 2nd, 1685.

Coming down to quite modern, and less stirring, times we must remember "Good Queen Adelaide" who also had her cross to bear. As Duchess of Clarence she had led a retired life at Bushby Park, but on the death of George IV., she was suddenly called upon to preside over the English court. It was many years since there had been a queen consort there, the licence of George IV.'s court had been notorious, and Queen Adelaide had a painful, and invidious task to perform when she determined to raise the moral tone of her surroundings. She achieved the task she had set herself with gentleness and tact, and when she died in 1849 she had won the respect and love of all by her goodness and benevolence.

The second name of the Empress Frederick of Germany is Adelaide, and the most beloved of all of our Queen's daughters was the Princess Alice, who married Prince Louis, afterwards Grand Duke of Hesse-Darmstadt. The name of the popular Duchess of Teck was Mary Adelaide.

In Germany the noble Adelheids and Adelaides have been countless.

In less exalted spheres of life we might record Adelina Patti, the brilliant songstress, and Adelaide Anne Proctor, the poetess, and Alice Carey, American novelist, also Adelaide Kemble, novelist, who became Mrs. Sartoris.

In literature the name does not occur so often as might have been anticipated, but appended are some instances: In DRAMA: Alice, sister of Valentine, in *Monsieur Thomas*, by Beaumont and Fletcher; Alicia in *Jane Shore*, by Nicholas Rowe; Adelaide in *The Count of Narbonne*, by Robert Jephson; Alicia in *Arden of Feversham*, by Lillo; Audry in *As You Like it*, by Shakespeare. In POETRY: *Adeline*, "mystery of mysteries, faintly smiling Adeline", by Lord Tennyson; Alice in *Queen of the May*, and Alice in *The Miller's Daughter*, also by Tennyson; Alice Brand in *The Lady of the Lake*, by Sir Walter Scott; Adeline Amundeville in *Don Juan*, by Lord Byron; *Alice du Clos* (a ballad), by Coleridge; and *Alice Fell* (a ballad), by Wordsworth. In FICTION: Alice in *Peveril of the Peak*, the Lady Alice in *The Monastery*, Old Alice Grace in *The Bride of Lammermoor*, the Lady Alicia in *Ivanhoe*, all by Sir Walter Scott; Alice in *Ernest Maltravers*, by Lord Lytton; Ethel Newcome in *The Newcomes*, by Thackeray; *Ethel Churchill*, by Letitia E. Landon; *Alice's Adventures in Wonderland* and *Alice Through the Looking Glass*, by "Lewis Carroll"; *Alice Lorraine*, by R. D. Blackmore; and *Ethelinda*, by W. C. Smith.

One of the oldest London churches is dedicated to St. Ethelburga, and is situated in Bishopsgate Street, City. The City of Adelaide in South Australia, Adelaide Island, and The Adelaide Tavern, Haverstock Hill, are all named after Queen Adelaide, consort of William IV.

EUNICE comes from the Greek 'Εὐνίκη, which means "good, or happy, victory", and may be taken symbolically to mean "one who wins by virtue". It was the name of one of the Nereids, those sea-nymphs, who generally had their altars on the sea-coast, where offerings of milk, oil, and honey, and sometimes even goat's flesh, were made to them. Their duties consisted chiefly in attending on the more powerful deities of the sea, and they were absolutely at the service of Neptune. They had the power of making the waters either rough or calm, and as they were very fond of raising storms, were prayed to by all sailors before starting on a voyage, that they might vouchsafe them a safe return.

The Nereids were represented as young and beautiful maidens, sitting on dolphins, and holding either tridents or garlands of flowers in their hands.

From the Greeks the name Eunice was passed down to the Hebrews, and it occurs in the *New Testament* as that of the mother of Timothy. Paul, in his *Epistle to Timothy*, writes of the "unfeigned faith that is in thee; which dwelt in . . . thy mother Eunice".

It is one of those names which the Bible-loving English have adopted, but which never seems to be met with on the Continent, though so musical in sound; nor does it occur in literature.

EUPHEMIA, Euphame, and their contractions, Effie, Eppie, and Phemie, mean "pleasant spoken". The first recorded Euphemia was the virgin-martyr who suffered under Diocletian, and who by her constancy won the admiration of the whole Christian world. Scotland especially was captivated by her character, and made her name her own. To this day Euphemia is met with in Scotland in all ranks of life, and her literature gives many examples of this fact.

The auldest o' five, whan a lassie o' ten,
She had baith the hoose an' the bairnies to fen';
The mither had gane whan she was but a bairn,
Sae Effie had mony sad lessons to learn.

At hame, had ye seen her amang the young chips,
The sweet law o' kindness was aye on her lips;
She kamed oot their hair, wash'd their wee hackit feet,
Wi' sae tentie a haun that a bairn wadna greet.

She was to her faither the licht o' his een,
He said she wad be what her mither had been—
A fair an' sweet sample o' true womanhood,
Sae carefu' an' clever, sae bonnie an' guid.

From *Effie—A Ballad* (JANET HAMILTON.)

The best known example is perhaps Effie Deans in *The Heart of Midlothian*, by Sir Walter Scott. As an English example we have Eppie in *Silas Marner*, by "George Eliot".

An' O! my Eppie,
My jewel, my Eppie!
Wha wadna be happy
Wi' Eppie Adair?

By love, and by beauty,
By law, and by duty,
I swear to be true to
My Eppie Adair!

EVA

An' O! my Eppie,
My jewel, my Eppie!
Wha wadna be happy
    Wi' Eppie Adair?

A' pleasure exile me,
Dishonour defile me,
If e'er I beguile thee,
    My Eppie Adair!

(ROBERT BURNS.)

EVA, EVELEEN, EVELYN, ZOE, etc. There can be no question as to the origin of the name Eve. It is Hebrew, and comes from the word *chavah*, or *chavva* = life, for the first Eve was to be "the mother of all living". The Arabic word denoting the same idea is *howwa*, the Alexandrian Jews rendering it in their translation *Zoe* = life, though they afterwards called it simply *Eva*. It seems natural to suppose that hence came Evelina, Eveline, and Eveleen, but Miss Yonge, who has made a careful study of the question, seems inclined to think that the popularity of these names in Ireland and Scotland is to be attributed to their being the true descendants, not of Eve, but of the Keltic names Aoiffe and Aoibhiun. Though at first sight a rather forced and unnatural conclusion, having regard to the authority it merits consideration; it seems difficult, however, in this case to account for the extreme frequency of Evalines and Evalinas amongst the old Norman nobility, who, one would suppose, would scarcely turn to the Kelts and Gaels, whom they despised as races, for their daughters' names. That Keltic and Gaelic names are occasionally met with amongst them is true, perhaps due to some pre-historic intercourse between their countries; but in the case in point it seems more natural to suppose that they took the name from Eve.

Under her forming hands a creature grew,
Man-like, but different sex, so lovely fair
That what seemed fair in all the world seemed now
Mean, or in her summed up, in her contained
And in her looks, which from that time infused
Sweetness into my heart unfelt before,
And into all things from her air inspired
The spirit of love and amorous delight.
. . . .
Grace was in all her steps, heaven in her eye,
In every gesture dignity and love.

Paradise Lost, Bk. viii. (JOHN MILTON.)

In Germany there is a popular superstition that to give a child the name of Eve secures to it long life, and hence its frequency in that country.

As regards Ireland and Scotland themselves Aoiffa = pleasant, seems certainly to have often been the equivalent of Eva. Aoiffa being of even greater antiquity in the Emerald Isle than Eva, and that occurs extremely early; whilst in Scotland, whither, according to our authority, it had travelled with other Gaelic names, Eva has been for centuries very common and is found in some of the oldest and noblest genealogies.

Eve and Eva have always had their representatives in England since remote antiquity, but they have never been common with us; and Evelina was made fashionable only through the popularity of Miss Burney's (Mme. D'Arblay's) novel *Evelina; or a Young Lady's Entrance into the World* (1778). This book created quite a sensation, was praised by Burke, Reynolds, Mr. Thrale and other people of literary note, and pronounced by the great Dr. Johnson himself to contain "passages worthy of the pen of Richardson": what wonder then that the heroine's name became fashionable?

Just now it is Eveline or Evelyn that is fashionable, but, spelt with a "y", the name has a different history, and comes from Avellana = a hazel. It is rightfully a masculine name, the true feminine form being spelt Eveline. On this point all authorities are agreed.

The names Eva and Evaline occur in the genealogies of the Diarmids, the Campbells, the Earls of Lennox, the Plantagenets, and the Stuarts, the best known of these being Eva or Aoiffe (for in her case both names appear) the daughter of Dermot MacMurrogh, the deposed King of Leinster.

When Dermot came to England to obtain aid in his distressful circumstances, Richard de Clare, Earl of Pembroke, better known as Strongbow, undertook to effect his restoration upon condition that Dermot should give him his daughter Eva in marriage and nominate him his successor to the Leinster throne. In about 1150 accordingly and in defiance of the express commands of Henry II., Strongbow embarked for Waterford, which he straightway besieged and took, and then, hastily celebrating his nuptials with Eva, marched on to Dublin, which he also conquered. On Dermot's death Strongbow was proclaimed King of Leinster, and became reconciled to

Henry II. on making certain concessions and acknowledging his suzerainty. He and Eva left one child, Isabella, who carried their vast estates and her father's title to William Marshall, Regent of England, to whom she gave her hand in 1189.

With regard to Evelyn, which has in recent years been adopted as a girl's name, the most noted bearer is John Evelyn the diarist, and author of a book, important in its day (1664), on forestry, entitled *Sylva: or a discourse of Forest Trees, and the propagation of Timber in His Majesty's Dominions*, besides other technical and miscellaneous works.

TO EVA.

O Fair and stately maid, whose eyes
   Were kindled in the upper skies
   At the same torch that lighted mine;
For so I must interpret still
Thy sweet dominion o'er my will,
   A sympathy divine.

Ah! let me blameless gaze upon
Features that seem at heart my own;
   Nor fear those watchful sentinels,
Who charm the more their glance forbids,
Chaste-glowing, underneath their lids,
   With fire that draws while it repels.

RALPH WALDO EMERSON.

In literature the name does not occur with great frequency, but there are other examples besides Milton's Eve in *Paradise Lost*, and Emerson's lines quoted above, as for instance Eva, daughter of Torquil of the Oak in *The*

Fair Maid of Perth by Sir Walter Scott; Evaline in *The Betrothed*, originally published as one of the *Tales of the Crusaders*, also by Sir Walter Scott; Eva in *Uncle Tom's Cabin* by Harriet Beecher Stowe; Eva in *The Little People of the Snow* by William Cullen Bryant.

Eva was the name
Of this young maiden, now twelve summers old
. . . .
One little maiden, in that cottage-home,
Dwelt with her parents, light of heart and limb,
Bright, restless, thoughtless, flitting here and there,
Like sunshine on the uneasy ocean-waves.

John Greenleaf Whittier, too, has some lines to *Eva* beginning

Dry the tears for holy Eva,
With the blessed angels leave her;
Of the form so soft and fair
Give to earth the tender care;

whilst of the name of Evelyn we have examples in Alfred Evelyn, in *Money* by Lord Lytton; Sir George Evelyn, in *Wives as they Were, and Maids as they Are* by Mrs. Inchbald; and finally *Evelyn Hope* by Robert Browning.

Beautiful Evelyn Hope is dead!
Sit and watch by her side an hour.
That is her book-shelf, this is her bed;
She plucked that piece of geranium flower,
Beginning to die too, in the glass;
Little has yet been changed, I think:
The shutters are shut, no light may pass
Save two long rays thro' the hinge's chink.

EVA

Sixteen years old when she died!
  Perhaps she had scarcely heard my name;
It was not her time to love: beside,
  Her life had many a hope and aim,
Duties enough and little cares,
  And now was quiet, now astir,
Till God's hand beckoned unawares,—
  And the sweet white brow is all of her.

Is it too late then, Evelyn Hope?
  What, your soul was pure and true,
The good stars met in your horoscope,
  Made you of spirit, fire and dew—
And, just because I was thrice as old
  And our paths in the world diverged so wide,
Each was nought to each, must I be told?
  We were fellow mortals, nought beside?

No, indeed! for God above
  Is great to grant, as mighty to make,
And creates the love to reward the love:
  I claim you still for my own love's sake!
Delayed it may be for more lives yet,
  Through worlds I shall traverse, not a few:
Much is to learn, much to forget
  Ere the time be come for taking you.

But the time will come,—at last it will,
  When, Evelyn Hope, what meant (I shall say)
In the lower earth, in the years long still,
  That body and soul so pure and gay?
Why your hair was amber, I shall divine,
  And your mouth of your own geranium's red—
And what you would do with me, in fine,
  In the new life come in the old one's stead.

. . . .

I loved you, Evelyn, all the while!
  My heart seemed full as it could hold!
There was place and to spare for the frank young smile,
  And the red young mouth, and the hair's young gold.

So, hush,—I will give you this leaf to keep:
  See, I shut it inside the sweet cold hand!
There, that is our secret: go to sleep!
  You will wake, and remember, and understand.

EVANGELINE and EVANGELISTA are derived from Evangelist = preacher, or bringer of good tidings. The name Evangelista exists in Italy, and Evangeline in America, the latter having been first introduced by Longfellow as the name of the heroine of his famous poem in hexameters:

Benedict Bellefontaine, the wealthiest farmer of Grand-Pré,
Dwelt on his goodly acres; and with him directing his household,
Gentle Evangeline lived, his child, and the pride of the village. . . .
Fair was she to behold, that maiden of seventeen summers.
Black were her eyes as the berry that grows on the thorn by the wayside,
Black, yet how softly they gleamed beneath the brown shade of her tresses!
Sweet was her breath as the breath of kine that feed in the meadows.
When in the harvest heat she bore to the reapers at noontide
Flagons of home-brewed ale, ah! fair in sooth was the maiden.

FAITH, HOPE, CHARITY. "Faith, Hope, and Charity, but the greatest of these is Charity". Faith, Hope, and Charity were the names of the three daughters of St. Sophia, who had thus called them out of reverence for those virtues. They lived during the reign of Adrian, and all three laid down their lives for the truth.

Spenser in *The Faëry Queene* translates these names into Fidelia, Speranza, and Charissa:—

> . . . three daughters well upbrought
> In goodly themes, and godly exercise:
> The eldest two, most sober, chast, and wise,
> Fidelia and Speranza, virgins were;
> Though spous'd yet wanting wedlock's solemnize;
> But faire Charissa to a lovely fere
> Was lincked, and by him had many pledges dere.

The Puritans loved all these names, which to their piously austere minds appeared eminently edifying. Bunyan, in whom Puritan aspirations had their fullest articulate embodiment, personified all these virtues, and placed Charity in the "Palace Beautiful".

Charity is sometimes contracted into Chatty, and Cherry: in the latter form it occurs in Farquhar's *Beaux's Stratagem.* To this class must be added the name Truth, and the pretty Cornish name Loveday.

Another of the "abstract-virtue names" is Patience, from the Latin *patientia* = endurance or submission. There once was a Saint of the name St. Patience of Lyons, and we all know Patience in *The Pilgrim's Progress.*

FELICITY and Felicia are two English feminine names based on the Latin *felix*, meaning *happy.* The personification of this idea was Felicitas = *happiness,* who amongst the early Romans was worshipped as a goddess.

Two Saints of this name suffered martyrdom, one in the second century, the other very early in the third.

Except in view of what their martyrdom may

have won for them in a happier world than this, their name cannot be said to have been of good omen, for the first was doomed to see her seven sons all tortured, then flung over a rock, and afterwards beheaded, whilst she was herself cast into boiling oil. Whilst watching her children's death, it is said she exhorted them to be "faithful in Christ's love, and to fight courageously for their souls".

The second Felicitas suffered at Carthage with St. Perpetua, during the reign of the Emperor Severus, and was exposed to wild beasts in the amphitheatre there.

Felicitas in Italy, and Félicités in France have always abounded, being called after these two martyrs; but in England the name has never gained any real foot-hold, though now and then we come across a Felicia, as in the case of Felicia Dorothea Hemans, the poetess, and in recent years the name Felicity is occasionally given.

In the old romance of *Sir Guy of Warwick*, Sir Guy's wife is called Felice, but here the name is really Phillis.

FINELLA. Finn, signifying "white", is a favourite prefix to Irish names, as witness the many Irish Saints whose names have begun thus, such as St. Fintan, Abbot of Cluainednach; St. Finian, surnamed Lobhar; St. Finbar, Bishop of Cork; St. Finan, of Keann-Ethich; and St. Finghin, the Patron Saint of Ulster. Amongst Irish women's names, we have Fionn-ghuala, or Finnuala, which has become contracted into Finella, or Fenella, and means "white, or fair-shoulders", a name still in use; Finvola and Finola used to be common too, but are now falling out of use; whilst a host of other names with this prefix are now almost forgotten.

Scott, in *Peveril of the Peak*, gave the name Fenella to the little deaf-and-dumb dwarf, attached to the Countess of Derby's household, in the Isle of Man.

FLORENCE, Flora. The Latin word *flos* (genitive *floris*) means a flower. From this root sprang the name of Flora, the Latin goddess of the spring and of flowers, who was of Sabine origin, her worship having been introduced into Rome by Titus Tatius, a Sabine King. Flora was also the goddess of youth and of youthful pleasures. Numa is credited with having appointed her a special priest, Flamen Floralis, and a temple was erected to her in 238 B.C. In accordance with the decrees of the Sibylline books a theatrical festival was also instituted in her honour, and for this festival men decked themselves and their animals in flowers, roses being especially selected, and women, setting aside their more sombre garments, also appeared on this occasion in gay attire.

It is to be feared that at this festival the merriment was boisterous enough to over-step the bounds of modesty, consisting as it did of five days of games and coarse farces, the sixth being devoted to the hunting of goats, hares and other animals, in the circus. Porridge, peas and lentils were supplied to the multitude by way of refreshments.

The masculine forms of this name are Florus,

Florentius, and Florence; the feminine Flora, Florence = flourishing, Florentia, Flo, Florentina, Flossie, Florrie, Florinda, and in poetry Florimel. Florence was a common male name amongst Anglo-Norman nobles in mediæval days, and is very occasionally met with even now. The mediæval men who bore the name were probably named after St. Florentius, but the modern Florences, both men and women, are often, like Percy Bysshe Shelley's son for instance, simply so named because they chanced to be born in the beautiful Italian city of that name.

The name of the American State, Florida, arose in a different way. The Spaniards call Easter-Day *Fascua Florida*, because of the custom of scattering flowers upon the church floors upon that festival, and Ponce de Leon, who discovered Florida, first landed there on Palm Sunday 1513.

There was a St. Florentia who suffered martyrdom, like so many other early Christians, during the Diocletian persecution in Gaul; and also a St. Flora (A.D. 1309-47), who was subject to ecstacies or trances which were of quite unusual duration. On one occasion it is reported of her "that her soul remained out of her body for twenty-two days", during which period she was favoured by many visions; of the same Saint it is related that, being greatly harassed by visits from the devil, and her fidelity having been sufficiently tested, the Lord sent an angel to her with the gift of a two-edged sword. This was so sharp that, not only could it cut joint and marrow asunder, but could also part soul and spirit. Armed with this deadly weapon, the young maiden felt secure for the future against any further attacks from the Evil One. A Gaul, St. Florentinus, who was sent to preach the Gospel in Poitou, was one of the numerous Saints who achieved the feat of hanging a pair of gloves on a sunbeam; whilst St. Florus was of the number of those who brought forth a fountain of water in an arid land.

We need not, however, go back to heathen days, nor yet to remote Church history, in search of a noble prototype for those who bear the name of Florence—for has there not been a Florence Nightingale, one of the noblest in the band of heroic women?

Born at Florence in 1820, she was the daughter of a Derbyshire gentleman, and received a liberal education, being proficient in both classical and modern languages. She early took an interest in the welfare of the suffering poor, and went to London for the express purpose of acquiring an efficient knowledge of nursing in both hospitals and reformatories, afterwards going to the Continent to complete her studies, and entering as a voluntary nurse in the Society of Protestant Sisters of Mercy at Kaiserswerth on the Rhine. There she remained for six months, and then, on her return to England, interested herself in the organisation of the Governesses' Home in Harley Street, London.

Whilst still engaged on this work, she was called upon by the English War Office to see if she could suggest anything for the amelioration of the terrible sufferings of the wounded in the Crimea, the horrors of which were driving the English public frantic. Miss Nightingale at once volunteered to go out to the East with a staff of nurses under her direction, to do what might be done; and accordingly in October 1854 she sailed with ninety-two nurses, many of whom were the daughters of noblemen, for Scutari, whither the wounded were transported from the scenes of battle.

Three weeks after the arrival of these devoted women, they had as many as three thousand wounded under their care. In spite of almost insurmountable difficulties, Miss Nightingale's hospital was a model of order and good management, and all the hospitals on the Bosphorus were ultimately placed under her control. Her own health was, however, permanently undermined by an attack of hospital fever, and in 1856 she returned to England.

The public, in their gratitude to her, subscribed £50,000, which was devoted at her request to the foundation of the Nightingale Training Institute for nurses. Her own health has never recovered sufficiently to enable her to take any active part in public work again; but she has always been ready with advice and sympathy, and has published several books upon the subject so near her heart.

Flora Macdonald, too, was possessed of qualities which all must respect, admire, and wish themselves to share. After the defeat of the Young Pretender, Prince Charles Edward, at Culloden in 1746, she risked her own life that she might save his; and, dressing him as a woman, and pretending that he was her serving-maid, conveyed him safely to the Isle of Skye, whence, after many hardships and perils, he at last succeeded in making good his escape to France. Flora Macdonald, who was afterwards imprisoned for a short time in the Tower of London, did not die until 1790. The following lines were written, of course, with reference to this incident in her life:—

He is gone, she has done it bravely,
  She has saved him from his foes;
How great the risk she took has been
  Well the brave maiden knows.
He is gone—the curl is in her hand,
  'Twas all he had to give,
When he is passed from earthly life,
  That bright brown curl will live.
Eyes yet unborn will weep o'er it,
  When they hear his sad, sad story;
That story of a wasted life,
  Long grief, and bright short glory.
. . . .
But Flora stands and dreams her dream
  Of mountains hid in cloud,
Of open boats, and beating rain,
  Of wretched hut and cave,
Of perils they have bravely faced
  By moor, and strath, and wave;
But at last Flora wakes again,
  What has the old dame said,
"Flora, we must keep those sheets,
  The sheets upon his bed".
"Yes, we will keep them", Flora spoke,
  "And when at last I die,
In mine they shall hap me for the grave".
  The tear stood in her eye.

The Prince (T. Robertson.)

FLORENCE

Ye shepherds, tell me, have you seen
My Flora pass this way?
In shape and feature beauty's Queen,
In pastoral array;
Shepherds, tell me, have you seen
My Flora pass this way?
A wreath around her head she wore—
Carnation, lily, rose,
And in her hand a crook she bore,
And sweets her breath compose.
The beauteous wreath that decks her head,
Forms her description true.
Hands lily-white,
Lips crimson red,
And cheeks of rosy hue.

Old Glee.

The above is a well-known old glee, and in poetry the name of Flora also occurs in several of William Shenstone's poems, and in a short poem of Drummond of Hawthornden, who has also two epigrams on Flore, and Lord Byron has lines *To Florence.* There is a Flora in Mrs. Centlivre's play, *The Wonder*; a Fiorinda in *The Duke of Florence*, by Massinger; a Floria in Ford's *Fancies Chaste and Noble*; a Flora in J. P. Kemble's *The Farm House*; a Donna Floranthe in *Octavian*, by Geo. Colman; Florimel the Fair in Spenser's *Faëry Queene*; Florinda in Robert Southey's *Roderick*; Florise in *The Talisman*, by Sir Walter Scott; Flordelice and Flordespina in Ariosto's *Orlando Furioso*; and, familiar to us all, Florence Dombey in Charles Dickens' story of *Dombey and Son*, and Flora MacIvor in Sir Walter Scott's *Waverley*. A Miss Flo' is the heroine in *Going to Propose*, by C. C. R.[hys]

in his *Up for the Season*; and there is an old ballad called *Flora's Farewell.*

In midst of silent night,
When men, birds, beasts do rest,
With love and fear possest,
To heaven and Flore I count my heavy plight.
Again, with roseate wings
When morn peeps forth, and Philomela sings,
Then void of all relief,
Do I renew my grief:
Day follows night, night day, whilst still I prove
That Heaven is deaf, Flore careless of my love.

A Lover's Plaint (Drummond of Hawthornden.)

FRANCES, Fanny, etc. The suggestion has been made that France, known to the ancients as Gallalia, or Gallia, and finally Gaul, became in later times Franconia, because the Cherusci—new settlers in the country—carried a kind of javelin called a *franca*; but it is much more probable that the name really comes from the High-German Frang – free lord, a title which these gentlemen arrogated to themselves after their successful expedition into Gaul from Franconia, in Germany, where they had previously dwelt. Hence the name Francis = free man, Frances = free woman.

Gradually, as the new nation grew in importance, and at last became for a long period the leading nation in modern Europe, the names of François and Françoise multiplied amongst men and women. In Germany it became Franz and Franziske, in England Francis and Frances, though the alteration of the "i" in the last syllable to an "e", to indicate the feminine name, is a comparatively modern innovation. The at one time fashionable Fanny dates back, according to Miss Yonge, only to the days of Good Queen Anne, though, like Frank, it is now often given to children as an independent name, and is of frequent occurrence in both France and Germany, where it seems to be now preferred to their native contractions of Fanchon, Fanchette, Franze and Sprinzchen. The name became very fashionable in England after the "Field of the Cloth of Gold", when our Merry Monarch met the Merry Monarch of France, after which burst of national enthusiasm and display, English men and women began calling their children—boys and girls indiscriminately—Francis, in compliment to the French King. The name used occasionally to be spelt Frauncis. There had, however, been instances of the name occurring in England before 1520, for England had been faithful to the Papal See until then, and the list of Saints Francis and Saints Frances is a long one.

Amongst so many it is difficult to make a selection, but Saint Francis of Assisi, as the earliest, may not be omitted. He was born in Assisi in Umbria in 1182 of a respectable trading family, his father and mother both most worthy people being so occupied with their business as to somewhat neglect the education of their little son. In the way of business, however, his parents had much intercourse with France, and therefore had their boy, as a matter of policy, taught French. In this language he became so proficient that he was called Francis instead of by his baptismal name of John, and by the name of Francis he has ever since been known.

Though much given to pleasure in his youth, one characteristic always marked the future Saint, and that was his undeviating charity to the poor and suffering. When quite young he made a vow never to refuse to the poor anything for which they should ask "for the love of God", and to this vow he remained faithful until the day of his death. During a war between Perugia and his native city, Saint Francis was taken prisoner, a misfortune which he bore with great patience during the year which his confinement lasted. Shortly afterwards he was called upon to bear another trial in the shape of a severe illness. Upon his recovery from this, St. Francis had a dream, in which he saw a magnificent palace filled with rich arms all marked with a cross, and in his dream he heard someone say that these arms all belonged to him and his soldiers, if they would "take up the Cross and fight courageously under its banner". St. Francis, feeling himself inspired, pondered in his mind how he should do this thing. One day, when out riding, he met a leper, whose sores were so loathsome that St. Francis recoiled from the sight, but struggling with himself he overcame his revulsion and ministered to the sufferer's needs; and after this frequently visited hospitals and waited on the poor and sick, at times even giving them the very clothes from his own back. Whilst thus dividing his time between helping those in trouble and attending to his father's business, he went one day to pray at the old, tumble-down church of St. Damian, without the walls of Assisi: whilst praying, he seemed to hear a voice saying "Francis, go and repair my house, which thou seest falling"; whereupon St. Francis rose, and went home, and took from his father's warehouse a horse-load of cloth, and sold it and the horse, and took the proceeds to the priest of St. Damian's; but the priest declined the money so obtained, and his father, enraged at what his son had done, beat him, put fetters on his feet, and locked him in his room. Ultimately Francis renounced his paternal inheritance, dedicating himself to a life of poverty, charity, and labour, working in person at the rebuilding of the Church of St. Damian, and afterwards at that of Portiuncula. In 1209, St. Francis founded his Order of Franciscan Friars, whose members dedicated themselves to lives of poverty, prayer and good works. He composed a rule for his Order consisting of the Gospel counsels of perfection, to which he added a few rules for the ordering of their lives, and exhorted his brethren to manual labour and to take nothing in payment therefor beyond things necessary to life.

If any part of his rough garment seemed to him too soft, he sewed its seams with packing-thread, and either slept on the ground, with a block of wood for a pillow, or in a sitting posture. Unless ill, he ate no cooked food, strewed ashes and water on his bread, and drank nothing but water. He spoke of his body as "brother Ass", because it was destined to carry burdens, to be beaten, and to be coarsely and meagrely fed; and, if he saw an idle man, he addressed him as "brother Fly", because doing no good himself he yet spoilt the good that others did. His favourite saying was "what every one is in the eyes of God, that he is, and no more".

In his humility, he, to the end of his days, declined to be ordained priest, but remained a deacon. He travelled to Spain, Syria, and Egypt, preaching penance to all the world, and in Spain alone founded several convents—indeed in less than three years from the time of its foundation his Order possessed sixty monasteries, exclusive of the Convent of St. Clair, which was for women. St. Francis died with the words of the 41st Psalm on his lips, at the age of 45, and was canonized two years later.

Not a Saint, but mentioned in this place because a contemporary of Saint Francis, was Francesca da Rimini, an Italian lady of noble birth, the daughter of Guido de Polenta, Lord of Rimini, and wife of Giovanni Malatesta. She fell in love with her husband's brother Paolo, and, with him, died by her husband's hand about 1288. Her tragic history is told by Dante in his *Inferno*; Silvio Pellico wrote a tragedy based upon it, and Leigh Hunt wrote a poem on it.

Returning to the Saints, we shall find that next in chronological order stands a woman—the foundress of the Collatines, and known as Saint Frances, the Widow. Born at Rome in

1384, of an illustrious family, she early gave signs of exceptional piety, had an aversion to childish amusements, and at the age of 11 evinced a desire to enter a convent. In obedience to her parents she, however, set aside this wish, and married a young Roman nobleman of the name of Laurence Ponzani, and for forty years these two lived together in mutual love and respect. Saint Frances used to say that "a married woman must, when called upon, quit her devotion to God at the altar, to find him in her household affairs". She imposed many and heavy mortifications upon her own body, amongst other things making mouldy bread her staple diet; but was kind and indulgent to her household, and treated her servants with great tenderness. Her dress was of coarse serge, beneath which was a hair shirt and a horse-hair girdle. Her example and influence made many Roman ladies forsake their lives of luxury and idleness for one of good works, and her whole endeavour was to train her own children well. With her husband's sanction, she in 1425, founded a monastery for nuns, called Oblates, and gave them the rule of St. Benedict, and, owing to the large number who sought admission, enlarged the building in 1433. The Oblates make no solemn vows, but only promise obedience to the Mother-President, and are permitted to retain property, and, with leave, to go about. Their Abbey in Rome is filled with ladies of the first rank. After her husband's death St. Frances herself entered the monastery, but was seized with sickness and died at the age of 56 when on a visit to her son John Baptist, who was ill. Immediately after her death, she was canonized by Pope Paul V.

In 1416, about mid-way between Naples and Reggio, in Calabria, was born of poor but devout parents, a little boy called after St. Francis of Assisi. At the early age of thirteen, he was placed by his father in the Convent of Franciscan Friars at St. Mark's. At the age of fifteen this boy retired to a cave on the sea-coast, sleeping on the bare rock, and eating nothing but the herbs he found in the neighbourhood. Before he was twenty years of age two friends joined him, and some neighbours built them three small cells and a chapel, and thus was founded the Order of St. Francis of Paula. By the time seventeen years had passed these three cells and the tiny chapel had developed into a large monastery and a church. The Order of St. Francis of Paula was remarkable for its poverty, austerity and holy zeal, but especially for its humility, which its founder regarded as the groundwork of all Christian virtues. The Order steadily grew in importance, until it owned many monasteries, and many miracles are attributed to St. Francis, his fame as a healer of the sick being so great that when Louis XI. of France was seized with apoplexy, he, greatly dreading death, sent an urgent message to the Saint, saying that if he would visit him and restore him to health, he would ever after serve him and his Order; but the Saint declined to "work a miracle which was asked for low and merely human motives". Louis then begged the intercession of Pope Sixtus IV., and upon his command St. Francis travelled to Plessis-les-Tours, where the French King then was. Louis received him with great joy, only to be told that "the lives of kings have their limits just as those of their meanest subjects"; and to be exhorted to prepare himself for death. The king died in the Saint's arms, perfectly resigned. St. Francis passed the remainder of his life in France, and died at Plessis-les-Tours in 1508, at the age of ninety-one.

St. Francis Xavier, known as the Apostle to the Indies, was a native of Navarre, and born in 1506. At the age of eighteen he went to Paris to study philosophy and logic, becoming a teacher in those subjects at the Beauvais College at the age of twenty. St. Ignatius now obtained a great influence over the hitherto somewhat worldly young man, and thenceforth his main endeavour was to curb and humble his own proud spirit by fasting and other austerities.

In 1538 we find him at Rome consulting over the foundation of the Order of the Jesuits, and in 1540 he was sent on a mission to the East Indies to convert the heathen. He performed the journey on foot as far as Lisbon, and waiting there for eight months set sail from that port, and on May 6, 1542, reached Goa after a voyage of thirteen months, in which he had to endure many hardships. For over eleven years St. Francis Xavier laboured successfully in the midst of a population of depraved

Portuguese and natives, whose chief characteristics were revenge, ambition, avarice and debauchery, during that time visiting Ceylon, the Pearl Coast, Travancore, Macassar, the Moluccas, Cochin, and Japan. He was arranging an expedition into China when he was seized with his last illness. He died on the 2nd December 1552. St. Francis de Sales was the founder of the Order of the Visitation, an Order which spread rapidly throughout Europe. This Saint is credited with having converted 72,000 Calvinists to the Church of Rome, and became at last Bishop of Geneva. Amongst other works, he wrote a book named *Introduction to a Devout Life*, originally in the form of letters to a lady; it has exercised a wide influence. St. Francis de Sales died at Avignon in 1622.

In his great work one of his chief fellow-workers had been the lady now known as St. Jane Frances de Chantal, who received the name of Frances upon her confirmation. It is recorded that upon her death St. Vincent de Paul saw her soul ascend to heaven as a ball of fire.

Yet two more Saints of this name are St. John Francis Regis, and St. Francis Borgia; but space is lacking for any detailed account of them.

Two French Kings of the name, and two Austrian Emperors, bear witness to the popularity of the name on the Continent amongst the highest in the land. In England it was in considerable vogue during the time of the Tudors, and was borne amongst many others by Frances Brandon, Duchess of Suffolk, the daughter of Mary Tudor, and the mother of unhappy Lady Jane Grey; by our great seaman, Sir Francis Drake; by Elizabeth's faithful councillor, Sir Francis Walsingham; and by the philosopher, Sir Francis Bacon. The celebrated beauty, Lady Fanny Shirley, upon whom Pope has some verses, introduced that form of the name to the world of fashion in the time of Queen Anne, whilst the names of Frances Burney (Mme. D'Arblay), Frances Sheridan, Frances Kemble, Frances Trollope, Catharine Frances Gore, and Frances Power Cobbe uphold it in the world of letters. As a surname, too, it is not unknown—witness Piero della Francesca, di San Sepolcro, the Italian painter; Philip Francis the poet; and his son Sir Philip Francis, the political writer. Everybody who knows anything about our poet Keats will also know the name of Fanny Brawne.

" To see those eyes I prize above my own
Dart favour on another—
Or those sweet lips (yielding immortal nectar)
Be gently pressed by any but myself,
Think, think, Francesca, what a cursed thing
It were beyond expression "!

(Quoted by KEATS in his first letter to Fanny Brawne.)

Little Miss Fanny,
So cubic and canny,
With blue eyes and blue shoes—
The Queen of the Blues!
As darling a girl as there is in the world—
If she'll laugh, skip, and jump,
And not be *Miss Glump!*

(S. T. COLERIDGE.)

The French coin "franc" is called after the country, the Tuscan coin "Francescone" (=4/6) after Francesco, Duke of Tuscany, and the French pastry puff with apricot or peach jam, known as Fanchonnette, has handed down the name of some obscure Francoise, or Fanchonnette, to posterity.

The Franciscan Friars were of course called after their founder, St. Francis of Assisi, but the Franciscan Sisters are known as "Clares", "Poor Clares", Minoresses, and Urbanites.

In Poetry we find Francesca da Rimini in *Il Inferno*, by Dante; *Francesca da Rimini*, by J. H. Leigh Hunt; Francesca in *The Siege of Corinth*, by Lord Byron; *Paolo to Francesca*, by J. Russell Lowell; *To Frances Shirley*, by Alexander Pope; *To my Daughter* (Fanny), by Thomas Hood; *To Fanny Alexander*, by James Russell Lowell. In Drama: *Francesca da Rimini*, by Silvio Pellico; Frances in *The New Inn*, by Ben Jonson; Frances Fitzdottrell in the same author's play, *The Devil is an Ass*; Franceschina in *The Dutch Courtesan*, by John Marston; Frances in *The Beggar's Bush*, by Beaumont and Fletcher; Francelia in *Brennoralt*, by Sir John Suckling. In Fiction: *Frances*, by Mortimer Collins.

> The Colonel has married Miss Fanny,
> And quitted the turf and high play;
> They're gone down to live with his granny,
> In a sober and rational way.
> Folks in town were all perfectly scared
> When they heard of this excellent plan,
> For nobody there was prepared
> To think him a sensible man.

For Fanny two years he'd been sighing,
 And Fanny continued stone-cold ;
Till he made her believe he was dying,
 And Fan thought herself growing old.
So one very fine night, at a *fête*,
 When the moon shone as bright as it can,
She found herself left *tête-à-tête*
 With this elegant sensible man.

There are minutes which lovers can borrow
 From Time, ev'ry one worth an age ;
Equivalents each to the sorrow
 They sweetly combine to assuage.
'Twas so on this heart-stirring eve ;
 He explained ev'ry hope, wish, and plan ;
She sighed, and began to believe
 The Colonel a sensible man.

He talked about roses and bowers,
 Till he dimmed her bright eye with a tear ;
For though "Love cannot live upon flowers",
 Miss Fan had four thousand a year ;
'Twas useless, she felt, to deny,
 So she used her bouquet for a fan ;
And averting her head, with a sigh,
 Gave her heart to the sensible man.

(THEODORE HOOK.)

FREDERICA, the feminine form of Frederick, though not what is usually called a "pretty" name, is historically one of the most interesting that we have. In its present form it means *peaceful ruler*, not, as is so often assumed, *rich in peace*. It has had a chequered history in its long descent from the Sanskrit *pri* = love, Zend *frî*, and Greek *φίλος* = loving ; *freon* or *frigon* means to be free and to love ; the Norse word is *fri*, the Gothic *frige*, the High-German *frei*, the Low-German *freoh*.[1]

[1] Miss Yonge, *Christian Names*.

From this root comes not only the Modern-German word *frei* = free, but also *Frau* = woman, and *Freude* = joy.

The direct ancestors of our Fredericks and Fredericas are Freyer, the son of Niörder, one of the Wanes, a race of gods worshipped by the earlier inhabitants of Germany and Scandinavia, and his sister Freya, or, as she is variously called, Frea, Frey, Frealaf, Frigg and Frigga, the Queen of Heaven, who was elevated to the position of Odin's wife, and who bore him seven sons, who were the founders of the Anglo-Saxon Kingdom. Amongst the Germans she was worshipped as Mother Earth, and she had for her attendants Fulla, or Plenty, by some believed to be her sister, such a favourite was she; Gna her messenger, who, riding on her steed Hoof-flinger, with trappings all of gold, bore her mandates to the uttermost parts of the earth, and Hlyn the protectress of those who worshipped Freya and owned her power.

Freya's palace was known as Fensaler, or Hall of the Sea, and by the dwellers on the coast Freya was looked upon as the ruler of the sea and protectress of ships. To Fensaler, where a soft twilight always reigned, Freya would bring all sorrowing husbands and wives whom an early death had parted, and there they were reunited for ever. This shows that even in those far-away days the belief in a life after death existed. Freya used to sit in her beautiful palace every night, spinning the finest of silken threads, which she would afterwards give to the best wives and mothers in token of her love;

and every starlight night those on earth might watch her at her loving, self-imposed task, for was not what we call Orion's Belt the spinning-wheel of the Queen of Heaven?

Some of the stories told of Freya do not quite redound to her credit, as, for instance, when she secretly caused part of Odin's golden statue to be destroyed, that the gold might furnish her with a splendid necklace. We must hope that this was done during what was only a passing fit of inordinate feminine vanity!

To her worshippers, in spite of these little weaknesses, Freya appeared in the light of a mighty goddess, who as the wife of Odin or Wodan sat high enthroned by his side, above the worlds, ruling heaven and earth, and deciding on the fate of nations, hovering over battlefields, and meting out victory or defeat as seemed to her just and right. Freya divided the fallen warriors with her husband, and led those who fell to her share to her beautiful palace, where she gave them refreshing draughts of mead.

The Scandinavian legends relating to Freya are modifications of these, varying in some details, but in all alike she is the goddess of beauty, love, and plenty — the great Earth Mother, wearing the shining necklace Brisingamen, and the bright flowers of spring, and when moved to tears, weeping tears "golden as the blaze of the new spring sun", and hence Freya's tears—golden tears—have grown to be proverbial.

It is uncertain whether Friday is named after Freya or after Frey: in all probability it is Fraya (*dies Veneris*).

Some students of Norse Mythology hold that Frigg and Freya are quite distinct conceptions: Frigg is a *mother's* love, they say, whilst Freya is the love of a *youth* or *maiden.*

Turning from these heroines of the shadowy past to the comparatively historical days of Saxon England, we shall find amongst the Saxon Saints a Frithswith (strong in peace), who, the daughter of a nobleman of that part of the country, dwelt in a lonely cell at Thornbury, and afterwards became the patroness of a priory at Oxford, which stood upon the site now occupied by Christ Church. She is often called Frideswide, and it is to her that Chaucer refers in *The Milleres Tale.*

> The carpenter to blissen him began,
> And said: Now helpe us Seinte Frideswide.
> A man wote litel what shal him betide.

Though the name Frederic occurs in Domesday Book, it did not gain much hold upon the people until the Middle Ages, when its popularity amongst the ruling classes of Germany became very great, and amongst the Hohenzollerns especially, was the commonest name of all.

It is a moot point whether the name Frieda, or Frida, should be spelt with or without the "e", the balance of opinion rather leaning towards the omission of the second vowel. It is a favourite name in Germany, and means "peace" or "peaceable".

Notable Fredericks are almost countless, but the Fredericas are rare, though one thinks at once of the Swedish novelist, Frederica Bremer, and Gœthe's first love was Friederike Brion.

GABRIELLE and GABRIELA are the feminines of Gabriel, which is variously given as meaning *God is my strength*, *God is my excellency*, and *hero of God*.

As a woman's name this is far more popular in France than in England, possibly because of La belle Gabrielle, the beautiful daughter of Antoine d'Estrées, with whom Henry IV. of France fell so violently in love.

With us it has been conferred on children, chiefly in rural districts, by those who have been captivated by the character of him whom Milton calls "chief of the angelic guards". The angel Gabriel is also called "the Messenger of the Messiah", because of his being chosen to execute the Messiah's orders upon earth.

In *The Golden Legend* Longfellow makes Gabriel "the angel of the moon" and the bearer to man of "the gift of hope". In spite of all this, however, although boys are often called Gabriel, Gibby, or Gab, girls are rarely found amongst us bearing the name of Gabriela or Gabrielle. In Italy the name is more popular, and Ariosto in *Orlando Furioso* calls one of his characters Gabrina, whilst the Portuguese Vasco de Lobeira introduces a Gabrioletta in *Amadis de Gaul.*

GEORGIANA, GEORGINA and GEORGY are feminine forms of George, a Greek name, signifying "earth-worker", husbandman, or cultivator of the soil. "I am the true vine and my Father is the Γεόργιος".

The first George, or Georgos, that we hear of is supposed to have been the Damascene sentinel who aided in St. Paul's escape from prison, and for this he is supposed to have been put to death: nothing is, however, really known about him. Here, in England, we are more concerned with our Patron Saint—the renowned slayer of the dragon—who furnished us with our national battle-cry:

> Our ancient word of courage, fair St. George
> Inspire us with the spleen of fiery dragons.
> *Richard III.*, Act V., Sc. iii. (SHAKESPEARE.)

The dragon must of course be taken as the symbol of sin and unbelief.

St. George ranks as one of the seven great Champions of Christendom, and the special Patron Saint, not only of England, but also of Portugal, Burgundy, Aquitaine, and, together with St. Mark, of Venice.

Gibbon, the historian, makes the error of supposing George of Cappadocia to be one and the same as St. George of Coventry, the English hero. That St. George of Coventry was a veritable person who actually lived, there is little doubt, but mystery, miracles, and legends of all kinds have clustered so thickly round his name that it is now quite impossible to winnow the wheat from the chaff, the truth from fiction.

> A gentle Knight was pricking on the plaine,
> Ycladd in mightie armes and silver shielde,
> Wherin old dints of deepe woundes did remaine,
> The cruell markes of many a bloody fielde;
> Yet armes till that time did he never wield.
> His angry steede did chide his foming bitt,
> As much disdayning to the curbe to yield:
> Full jolly knight he seemed, and faire did sitt,
> As one for knightly giusts and fierce encounters fitt.

And on his brest a bloodie Crosse he bore,
  The deare remembrance of his dying Lord,
  For whose sweete sake that glorious badge he wore,
  And dead, as living, ever him ador'd:
  Upon his shield the like was also scor'd,
  For soveraine hope which in his helpe he had.
  Right faithfull true he was in deede and word;
  But of his cheere did seeme too solemne sad;
Yet nothing did he dread, but ever was ydrad.

Upon a great adventure he was bond,
  That greatest Gloriana to him gave,
  (That greatest Glorious Queene of Faery lond)
  To winne him worshippe, and her grace to have,
  Which of all earthly thinges he most did crave:
  And ever as he rode his hart did earne
  To prove his puissance in battell brave
  Upon his foe, and his new force to learne
Upon his foe, a Dragon horrible and stearne.

The Faëry Queene (SPENSER.)

According to our old English legend, St. George was born at Coventry, the son of Albert, Lord High Stewart of England, and his wife. His mother died at his birth, and he, being handed over to the care of three nurses, was mysteriously spirited away by "the weird lady of the woods", who brought him up carefully, and trained him to deeds of arms.

From the first a great destiny had been predicted for him, and he was born with three marks on his body, *i.e.* a dragon on his breast, a garter round one leg, and a blood-red cross on his right arm. When arrived at man's estate, St. George fought the Saracens; and when in Libya, hearing that there was there a huge dragon, to which a young girl was daily sacrificed as food, he went in search of it, and arrived on the very day on which the King's own daughter, Sabra, was to be handed over to the monster. Sabra was already bound to the stake, and awaiting her cruel end, when her deliverer arrived. Thrusting his lance down the dragon's throat, St. George killed him on the instant. The maiden whom he had thus rescued afterwards became his wife, and he brought her over to England, where they dwelt in St. George's native town of Coventry.

It is said that the ghost of St. George came to the aid of the Christian army before Antioch, and that the success of the siege was due to him. He also appeared before Richard I., Cœur de Lion, and assured him of victory, and hence his battle-cry of "St. George for Merrie England!".

Two ballads printed among the *Percy Reliques* record our national hero's birth and deeds. Both are far too long to give in full here, but we may quote a few of the verses.

The Birth of St. George.

Listen, lords, in bower and hall,
  I sing the wonderous birth
Of brave St. George, whose valorous arm
  Rid monsters from the earth:

Distressed ladies to relieve
  He travell'd many a day;
In honour of the Christian faith,
  Which shall endure for aye.

His wife, having forbodings of evil, Lord Albert goes forth to consult the "weird sisters"; and on his return finds that his wife is dead, and that he has a little son:

He beat his breast, he tore his hair;
And shedding many a tear,
At length he askt to see his son;
That son that cost so dear.

New sorrowe seiz'd the damsells all;
At length they faultering say:
"Alas! my lord, how shall we tell?
Thy son is stoln away.

"Fair as the sweetest flower of spring,
Such was his infant mien;
And on his little body stampt
Three wonderous marks were seen:

"A blood-red cross was on his arm;
A dragon on his breast:
A little garter all of gold
Was round his leg exprest.

. . . . .

"But lo! all in the dead of night,
We heard a fearful sound:
Loud thunder clapt; the castle shook;
And lightning flasht around.

"Dead with affright at first we lay;
But rousing up anon,
We ran to see our little lord:
Our little lord was gone"!

. . . . .

There the weird lady of the woods
Had borne him far away,
And train'd him up in feates of armes,
And every martial play".

GEORGIANA

St. George and the Dragon.

Of Hector's deeds did Homer sing,
  And of the sack of stately Troy;
What griefs fair Helena did bring,
  Which was Sir Paris' only joy:
And by my pen I will recite
St. George's deeds, an English knight.

. . . .

Now, as the story plain doth tell,
  Within that countrye there did rest
A dreadful dragon fierce and fell,
  Whereby they were full sore opprest;
Who by his poisonous breath each day,
Did many of the city slay.

. . . .

No means there were, as they could hear,
  For to appease the dragon's rage,
But to present some virgin clear,
  Whose blood his fury might asswage;
Each day he would a maiden eat,
For to allay his hunger great.

. . . .

The king and queen and all their train
  With weeping eyes went then their way,
And let their daughter there remain,
  To be the hungry dragon's prey:
But as she did there weeping lye,
Behold St. George came riding by.

. . . .

St. George then looking round about,
  The fiery dragon soon espy'd,
And like a knight of courage stout,
  Against him did most fiercely ride;
And with such blows he did him greet,
He fell beneath his horse's feet.

For with his launce that was so strong,
  As he came gaping in his face,
In at his mouth he thrust along;
  For he could pierce no other place:
And thus within the lady's view
This mighty dragon straight he slew.

A figure of St. George on horseback is worn by the Knights of the Garter.

George of Cappadocia flourished at a much earlier period than the English champion, and could hardly rank as a Saint, if all we are told about him by St. George of Nazianzen be true. The son of a fuller, George of Cappadocia was himself what we should now call an army contractor apparently, and performed his duties so badly that it was with difficulty that he escaped being torn to pieces by the soldiers.

He fled to Alexandria and there joined the Christian Church, and ultimately became an Arian Bishop; once more incurring the hatred of the populace, he had for the second time to flee for his life; but was captured, paraded through the streets on a camel's back, and finally torn to pieces and burnt.

There are isolated instances of the name of George in England, from the time of Harold downwards; but it really did not gain any true vogue here until the advent of the House of Hanover, since which time it has been one of our most common names.

As a woman's name, it is quite modern, and has never been very popular, though Lord Lytton chose it as the name of his heroine in *Money;* and the name George was chosen as the pseudonym of two of the greatest women writers that have ever lived, *i.e.* "George Sand" and "George Eliot". Of recent examples of the name may be mentioned Mrs. Georgina M. Craik and Lady Georgiana Fullerton.

GERTRUDE, GERALDINE. The histories of these two names reach back into the old Valkyr days, and, like Hilda, have to do with strife and battle. A Gêrdrûd, or Geirthrud, appears in the Nibelungen Cycle, and, though Geraldine cannot in its present form lay claim to such antiquity or to unbroken descent, it may at least claim to be related in the first degree of cousinship through Gerald and Gerhold. Gertrude means "spear-maiden"; Geraldine means "firm-spear". The family of "spear" names, as we may call them, is fairly extensive, including as it does Geraud, Gerard, Garreth, Jarrett, Jareth, Gerhard, Gerald, Giraud, Jerold, Jerome, and others; but the feminine forms are scarcer far, being comprised of Gertrude, with its diminutives of Gerty and Gatty, Gerlinda, and Geraldine in England; Gerhardine, Gerts, Gertruda, Gertrudes, Gerty, Giralda, and Trudchen, with some others, are familiar in different parts of the Continent, but not here.

Many who have called their girls Gertrude have imagined the name to mean "a maiden trusted and true", but this is an error.

From Gar = a spear, we have War, which is precisely the same word as the French guerre. Gher, or gier, in Valkyr days meant "spear", and trude or thrüdr (also a Valkyr name) means "maiden" and not "truth".

Ghere was the name in the *Nibelungen Lied* of the messenger sent to invite Siegfried and Chriemhild to Wurms.

Geraldine—in German Gerhardine—is much more modern in its present form than Gertrude, and, according to Miss Yonge, was first introduced by Henry Howard, Earl of Surrey, when he selected the Lady Elizabeth Fitzgerald as the object of his poetical addresses, under the name of the "Fair Geraldine"; this lady's Anglo-Saxon name-ancestor was probably a Gerhold = firm-spear.

Gerlinda, or Girlint, the mother of Harmuth, King of Norway, appears as the evil genius of the story in an old Anglo-Saxon poem dating back to the thirteenth century.

The generic name "Germans" probably means "spear-men", for though they called themselves "Deutschen" ("Teutons" with the initial letter flattened into "D"), signifying "multitude", we know that the Romans called them "Germani" at least two hundred years before the Christian era. A tablet dated 222 B.C. was discovered in A.D. 1547, recording the victories of Marcellus over Veridomar "dux Gallorum et Germanorum" (General of the Gauls and Germans).

In the realm of Church history and legendary lore we find four St. Gertrudes, each of whom did much towards popularizing their name.

The first of these was the daughter of Pepin of Landen, and a younger sister of St. Beggha.

Born in A.D. 626, she was brought up in her father's palace, but early evincing a preference for a single life was not pressed to marry. By her mother Itta's desire a nunnery was built for St. Gertrude at Nivelle in Brabant, and she became its abbess at the early age of twenty, performing the onerous duties of the office with "prudence, zeal, and virtue". She courted poverty in her own person, but enriched the poor, and by much prayer and meditation "obtained wonderful lights from heaven". At the age of thirty she resigned her office in favour of a niece, and during the three years of life which remained to her spent her days in preparing for her death. More than one miracle is ascribed to her during her life, and ten years after her death her spirit is said to have "appeared visibly" in the College of Nivelle, for the purpose of extinguishing a fire, which would otherwise have destroyed the entire building.

Gertruydenberg, a town in the Netherlands, is named after her, her father Pepin having made her a gift of it in 647. It has suffered many vicissitudes since during times of war.

Perhaps the most popular of all the Saint Gertrudes was born at Eisleben (Luther's birthplace) in Upper Saxony: she at the early age of five years was dedicated to a religious life and placed in the Benedictine Nunnery of Rodalsdorf, where twenty-five years later she officiated as Abbess. It is said that she was subject to ecstacies and visions, and spent much time in watching, fasting and all forms of self-denial, being remarkable for her profound humility and her devotion to the service of others. She published a much esteemed devotional book called *Divine Insinuations, or Communication and Sentiments of Love*, and was a good Latin scholar. After faithfully fulfilling the duties of abbess for forty years, Saint Gertrude died in 1292. Her memory is still held dear in the land of her birth.

Saint Gertrude of Ostend was of lowly parentage, and was at one time betrothed to a young man who jilted her for the sake of another woman with a larger dowry. She was famed for her ecstacies, in which she would sometimes remain wrapped for weeks, for having had the stigmata or five wounds, and for having worked many miracles. She died in 1358.

Finally there was Saint Gertrude of Vaux-en-Dieulet, she who on arriving in the valley of Argonne, on the borders of the Vaux, could find no water anywhere. Thereupon Saint Gertrude touched the earth with a stick and a fountain of clear water bubbled up, which has continued to flow until this day, and is known as the "Fountain of Saint Gertrude", lying somewhere to the west of Dieulet.

There are a few striking examples of both names in literature. Besides the old Anglo-Saxon poem mentioned above, there is Gertrude, Hamlet's mother, the guilty Queen of Denmark; the Fair Geraldine of Surrey's verses, who was the daughter of Gerald Fitzgerald, ninth earl of Kildare, and wife of the Earl of Lincoln. Sir Walter Scott refers to this poet and his mistress in *The Lay of the Last Minstrel*:

"That favoured strain was Surrey's raptured line:
That fair and lovely form, the Lady Geraldine".

Then there is Gertrude in *Eastward Ho*, a drama by John Marston; Lady Geraldine, an orphan, and ward of her uncle Count de Valmont, in *The Foundling of the Forest*, by W. Dimond, and Thomas Campbell's poem on the destruction of the village of Wyoming in Pennsylvania in 1778, called *Gertrude of Wyoming*.

From Tuscan came my lady's worthy race;
Fair Florence was sometime their ancient seat;
The Western isle whose pleasant shore doth face
Wild Camber's cliffs, did give her lively heat:
Fostered she was with milk of Irish breast;
Her sire, an earl, her dame of princes' blood;
From tender years, in Britain doth she rest
With King's child, where she tasteth costly food.
Hudson did first present her to my eyen:
Bright is her hue, and Geraldine she hight:
Hampton me taught to wish her first for mine;
And Windsor, alas! doth chase me from her sight.
Her beauty of kind, her virtue from above—
Happy is he that can obtain her love!
(Henry Howard, Earl of Surrey.)

O Susquehana's side, fair Wyoming!

. . . . . .

Sweet land! may I thy lost delights recall,
And paint thy Gertrude in her bower of yore
Whose beauty was the love of Pennsylvania's shore!

. . . . . .

Young, innocent, on whose sweet forehead mild
The parted ringlet shone in simplest guise,
An inmate in the home of Albert smiled,
Or blest his noon-day walk—she was his only child.
Gertrude of Wyoming (Thos. Campbell.)

GERTRUDE

Gertrude of Wyoming is the daughter of the patriarch of the village, Albert. An Indian brings a boy of nine years, named Henry Waldegrave, to the patriarch, to be cared for, at the wish of the boy's dying mother. Waldegrave remains at Wyoming for three years, but is then claimed by relatives in England, and sent to them. When he attains manhood, he returns, and marries Gertrude; but three months afterwards Gertrude and her father are both killed during an attack made upon the settlement by the British and Indian forces. Waldegrave thereupon joins George Washington's army, and fights for American independence. In a play by Thomas Heywood called *The English Traveller* the heroine's name is Geraldine.

Further there is *Lady Geraldine's Courtship*, by Elizabeth Barrett Browning, the poem which is said to have led to the authoress' friendship and subsequent marriage with Robert Browning.

There's a lady, an earl's daughter,—she is proud and she is noble,
And she treads the crimson carpet and she breathes the perfumed air,
And a Kingly blood sends glances up, her princely eye to trouble,
And the shadow of a monarch's crown is softened in her hair.

. . . .

There are none of England's daughters who can show a prouder presence;
Upon princely suitors praying, she has looked in her disdain,
She was sprung of English nobles, I was born of English peasants;
What was I should love her, save for competence to pain?

I was only a poor poet, made for singing at her casement,
As the finches or the thrushes, while she thought of other things.
Oh, she walked so high above me, she appeared to my abasement,
In her lovely silken murmur, like an angel clad in wings!

. . . . . .

She has voters in the commons, she has lovers in the palace,
And of all the fair court-ladies, few have jewels half as fine;
Oft the prince has named her beauty twixt the red wine and the chalice;
Oh, and what was *I* to love her? my beloved, my Geraldine!

Yet I could not choose but love her:

Lady Geraldine invites him down to her country seat in Sussex, and he goes.

With a bunch of dewy maple, which her right hand held above her,
And which trembled a green shadow in betwixt her and the skies,
As she turned her face in going, thus she drew me on to love her,
And to worship the divineness of the smile hid in her eyes.

For her eyes alone smile constantly; her lips have serious sweetness,
And her front is calm, the dimple rarely ripples on the cheek;
But her deep blue eyes smile constantly, as if they in discreetness
Kept the secret of a happy dream she did not care to speak.

. . . . . .

'Tis a picture for remembrance. And thus morning after morning,
Did I follow as she drew me by the spirit to her feet.

. . . . . .

In her utmost lightness there is truth—and often she speaks lightly,
Has a grace in being gay, which even mournful souls approve,
For the root of some grave earnest thought is understruck so rightly
As to justify the foliage and the waving flowers above.

Bertram, the poet, accidentally overhears an Earl press his suit on Lady Geraldine.

What he said again, I know not: it is likely that his trouble
Worked his pride up to the surface, for she answered in slow scorn,
" And your lordship judges rightly. Whom I marry, shall be noble,
Ay, and wealthy. I shall never blush to think how he was born".

There I maddened! her words stung me.

The poet losing all self-control goes in to her presence, and raving at her worldliness cries—

" What right have you, madam, gazing in your palace mirror daily,
Getting so by heart your beauty which all others must adore,
While you draw the golden ringlets down your fingers, to vow gaily,
You will wed no man that's only good to God, and nothing more?

Why, what right have you, made fair by that same God, the sweetest woman
Of all women he has fashioned, with your lovely spirit face

Which would seem too near to vanish if its smile
  were not so human,
And your voice of holy sweetness, turning common
  words to grace?

What right *can* you have, God's other works to
  scorn,

. . . . . .

But at last there came a pause. I stood all vibrating
  with thunder
Which my soul had used. The silence drew her face
  up like a call.
Could you guess what word she uttered? She looked
  up, as if in wonder,
With tears beaded on her lashes, and said—"Bertram"! it was all.

Bertram faints, and returns to consciousness to find he has been carried to his room. Whilst meditating a speedy leave-taking, he seems to see her vision in his room, and addresses it; it is the Lady Geraldine who asks—

Dost thou, Bertram, truly love me? Is no woman
  far above me
Found more worthy of thy poet-heart than such a
  one as *I?*

. . . . . .

Bertram, if I say I love thee, . . . "'tis the vision
  only speaks".

Softened, quickened to adore her, on his knee he fell
  before her,
And she whispered low in triumph, "It shall be as I
  have sworn.
Very rich he is in virtues, very noble—noble certes;
And I shall not blush in knowing that men call him
  lowly born".

(E. B. Browning.)

The devotion of Gertrude Von der Wart to her husband, who was accused, perhaps falsely, of having taken part in the murder of the Emperor Albert, and who was bound alive on the wheel, has been the subject of two poems; she attended him during the whole time of his torture, and described his terrible sufferings in a letter to a friend, which was published afterwards at Haarlem. Mrs. Hemans has written a poem of seven verses on it, of which we give the two last.

She wiped the death-damps from his brow
  With her pale hands and soft,
Whose touch upon the lute-chords low
  Had still'd his heart so oft.
She spread her mantle o'er his breast,
  She bathed his lips with dew,
And on his cheeks such kisses press'd
  As hope and joy ne'er knew.

Oh! lovely are ye, Love and Faith,
  Enduring to the last!
She had her meed—one smile in death—
  And his worn spirit pass'd!
While even as o'er a Martyr's grave,
  She knelt on that sad spot,
And, weeping, bless'd the God who gave
  Strength to forsake it not.

GILLIAN: see JULIA.

GITHA, GYTHA: see AGATHA.

GLADYS, CLAUDIA. This name, in its Latin form, is Claudia, in French Claudine, in English (Cornish) Gladuse, and Welsh Gladys, and means "lame". With this somewhat depressing signification it is curious that the name of Gladys has of late years become so popular in this country, unless people have been misled by a mistaken interpretation which is sometimes given, to the effect that the name signifies "brilliant" or "splendid". In Scotland the masculine form got altered into Glaud, and still is in use; this came back to England again as Claud, and probably at no time in their history have Claud and Gladys been so popular as now.

Its original introduction into Britain was probably due to the Emperor, who, born at Lyons in 9 B.C., bore the high-sounding name of Tiberius Drusus Nero Germanicus Claudius, and who, on the murder of his nephew Caligula, was, at the age of fifty suddenly raised from the position of a mere officer in the army to that of Emperor of the Romans.

Ninety-seven years after the second invasion of Britain by Julius Cæsar and two years after his own accession to the Roman throne Claudius determined to invade this island, coming over in person. The invasion was vigorously resisted by the Britons, but Hampshire and Dorset were, after a desperate struggle, conquered, and leaving the completion of the task of conquest to his generals, Claudius hastened back to Rome to celebrate his triumph, to add Britannicus to his title, and to declare Britain a Roman province. The Roman generals Plautius and Ostorius were for a long time successfully resisted by the British Prince Caractacus, but Ostorius at last defeated the British at Caer-Caradoc, in Shropshire, and Caractacus, with his father Bran, all his brothers, his wife and his daughter were sent in chains to Rome. When Claudius saw them there, he was so touched by their noble and independent bearing that he set the prisoners free, probably retaining Bran as a hostage. This was in A.D. 51.

They became Christians, and if we may believe tradition one of Caractacus's daughters, after baptism received the name of Claudia, in token of gratitude to the Emperor for his generous treatment of the captives. This Claudia it is who is mentioned in St. Paul's Epistle to Timothy. Claudia never returned to Britain; she married one Pudens, who is also named by St. Paul, and she and her husband received St. Peter into their house and were baptised either by St. Peter or St. Paul. They became the parents of four children, all of whom were canonised, *i.e.*, Novatus, Timotheus, Praxodes and Prudentiana.

Claudia died, after a long life, at her husband's villa of Sabinum in Umbria early in the second century, and was by her sons buried at Rome by the side of Pudens. She is alluded to by Martial in his epigrams. The Emperor after whom she was called, died by poison administered by his niece Agrippina, who had become his fourth wife. His conquests in Britain were in the course of years lost, but his name has remained down to the present day.

Another Saint of the name was St. Claudia of Ancyra, one of the seven virgins who suffered martyrdom by drowning, during the height of the Christian persecutions (c. 303). The Rev. G. E. Mason has dramatised the life of this St. Claudia, and recently published his drama under the title of *Claudia (The Christian Martyr)*: A tragedy in four acts. After her death one who loved her thus speaks of her:

Cold is that generous heart that glowed abroad
In merciful and most compassionate love
To the slaves, the poor, the sad. They worshipped thee.
Oh! I have marked them, how they thronged thy doors,
Kissing thy sandal, clinging unrebuked
To the hand that fed them; thy grave eyes the while
Wide-wondering with pity, and thy face
Magnificent with tears. When thy retinue
Bore thy patrician litter through the street,
I have heard them cry "'Tis she, our lady comes;
Heaven bless our patroness". The Esquiline,
Thronged with a squalid crowd, the dregs of Rome,
Turned fondly after thee, as Autumn flowers
Turn lingering looks upon the passing sun.
Oh! thou wert ever pitiful to all.

Long before the Saint Claudius, of whom we have been speaking, there was another woman of the name, one Claudia Quinta, who, though no Christian Saint, was in her time and by her people, looked upon with veneration. She lived 206 B.C., and was probably the sister of Appius Claudius Pulcher. When the ship which was conveying the image of Cybele from Pessinus to Rome stuck fast in a shallow at the mouth of the Tiber, and the soothsayers announced that only a chaste woman could move it, she cleared herself from accusations that had been levied against her by stepping forward from the midst of the matrons who were with Scipio to receive the image, and towed the vessel to Rome.

A third Christian Saint of the name was Claudia, the sister of Sulpicius Severus, who lived about 420 A.D. Both were disciples of St. Martin, and two or three letters are still extant which passed between the brother and sister on questions of faith and love and duty; nor in the list of those who have made the name popular must we omit Saint Claude, Archbishop of Besançon. He was born at Salins about the year 603; he was held in great veneration by the clergy of Besançon, and upon the death of Archbishop Gervaise, was elected as his successor. Afraid of the responsibilities attaching to the office, Claude fled, but was discovered in his place of hiding and compelled to accept the onerous position, acquitting himself therein with great zeal for seven years. The opportunity for retirement then presenting itself, he resigned his See and withdrew to the monastery of St. Oyend, or Ouyan, on Mount Jura, and there assumed, in 690, the monastic habit, being soon afterwards appointed Abbot. Spending the remainder of his life in silent prayer, in reading, fasting, and mortification, he died about 696.

One of the sects of the Donatists call themselves Claudianists.

Other noteworthy bearers of the name have been Claudius II., surnamed Gothicus on account of his brilliant victories over the Goths; Claudius Claudianus, a Latin poet, supposed to have been a native of Alexandria; three Roman Consuls named respectively Curtius Quintus Claudius, 271; Pulcher P. Claudius, 249; and Crassus Appius Claudius, 394. Claude

Gelée, generally known as Claude Lorraine, the great French landscape painter; Jean Claude, a great French Protestant Divine; Matthias Claudius, the German poet and friend of Klopstock, and author of the famous song *Rheinweinlied*, to whom Longfellow alludes in his *Drinking Song*.

> " Claudius, though he sang of flagons,
> And huge tankards filled with Rhenish,
> From the fiery blood of dragons
> Never would his own replenish ".

Also Claudine, Queen of Francis I., and daughter of Louis XII., and in contemporary times, Mme. Claude Vignon, an artist, journalist, and song writer, but best known as a sculptor, many of whose works occupy prominent positions in the streets and public galleries of Paris.

Claudia and Gladys, Claudio and Claud, all have their representatives in literature, though Gladys, being for England so modern, has no classic to support it.

An old ballad, called *Amintas and Claudia*, the first verse of which runs:

> Calm was the evening and clear was the sky
> when the new budding flowers do spring,
> When all alone went Amintas and I,
> to hear the sweet nightingales sing;
> I sate and he laid him down by me,
> and scarcely his breath he could draw,
> But when with a fear
> He began to draw near,
> He was dasht with a ha, ha, ha, ha, ha, ha,
> ha, ha, ha, ha, ha, ha, ha.

Claudia Rufina and the Death of Ahab, by

M. E. R., and Claude, the hero of *Amours de Voyage*, by A. H. Clough, represent poetry; whilst in drama we have *The Statelie Tragedie of Claudius Tiberius Nero, Rome's Greatest Tyrant, truly represented out of the purest records of those times*—1607; Claudio in *Measure for Measure*, Claudio in *Much Ado About Nothing*, and Claudius in *Hamlet*, all by Shakespeare; Claudine in *The Deaf and Dumb*, by Thomas Holcroft; Claudius in *Virginius*, by J. Sheridan Knowles; and Claude Melnotte in *The Lady of Lyons*, by Lord Lytton. In FICTION: *Gladys of Harlech*, by Anne Beale; *Gladys the Reaper*, by the author of *Simplicity and Fascination*; *Gladys Fane*, by T. Wemyss Reid; *Gladys's Vow*, by Mrs. Reaney; *Gladys Anstruther*, by Louise Thomson; *Claude and Claudia*, by Mrs. H. Martin; *Gladys*, by Edith M. Dauglish; *Gladys Woodley*, by "Eglantine"; and *Claudia: a Tale*, by A L[ady] O[f] E[ngland].

GRACE. This name is not connected with the Latin word *gracilis*, signifying slight, slender, slim, meagre, or lean, which came originally from the Greek *grao* = to consume. It is not even distantly allied to it.

The Latin word *grates* is the real origin of our English name, and this means thanks, thanksgiving (especially to the gods). The noun *gratia* = favour, esteem, love, or friendship, and the adverb *gratiis*, the old form of *gratis*, formed from it, and meaning "without reward" (whence our common expression "to do a thing gratis" or gratuitously), has the same origin, namely, the primitive root GRA-. Thus is it that the

Greek "Charites" are known as the Graces. They were the goddesses of grace and of everything that lends beauty to nature or to human life, and according to Hesiod were the daughters of Zeus.

Their names are Euphrosyne = joy, Thalia = bloom, and Aglaia = brilliance; of these Aglaia is the youngest. The inspiration of these Graces was considered essential to all the arts, and to their appreciation; and the Graces therefore dwelt with the Muses on Mount Olympia.

Sometimes they were called the daughters of the Sun, because of their bright and happy natures. They were worshipped at Orchomenus in Boeotia, together with Aphrodite and Dionysus, where their shrine was of great antiquity, and where their oldest images were said to have fallen direct from heaven. Here the feasts of the Charitesia were held.

At Sparta and at Athens only two Graces, or Charites, were worshipped, namely, at Sparta Cleta = Sound, and Phaenna = Light; at Athens Auxo = Increase, and Hegemone = Queen. It was on these goddesses that the youth of Athens swore faith to their country, on receiving their spear and shield. The Graces are generally represented as beautiful maidens, linked hand in hand.

Thus it is a spiritual rather than a physical quality which should be implied by this name —in fact the present meaning of our word "gracious" more nearly conveys the idea than what is now commonly understood by "grace".

The name became common in England in

Puritan days, and was meant by our grave and reverend old forefathers to imply thanks or gratitude, just in the same sense as the "grace" which, in English households, is spoken before the family joins in a meal. The Puritan fathers thought, with Charles Lamb, that there were other things to be grateful for besides food, and tried to show it in their daughters' names.

Charles Lamb, in his *Essays of Elia*, writes, "I own I am disposed to say grace upon twenty other occasions in the course of the day besides my dinner. I want a form for setting out upon a pleasant walk, for a moonlight ramble, for a friendly meeting, or a solved problem. Why have we none for books—those spiritual repasts—a grace before Milton, a grace before Shakespeare, a devotional exercise proper to be said before reading the 'Fairy Queen'"?

Grace, and Gracie, are especially popular in Ireland, owing in the first place to its supposed relationship to their name Grainé = love. To this confusion, no doubt, Grace O'Malley, the Irish pirate Queen, owed her name. Grace O'Malley, the famous Queen of Connaught, better known as Granuaile, has her memory preserved to this day by a custom which has been scrupulously observed for upwards of three centuries. When Grace was returning to Connaught from a mission to England, she wished to visit the Lord Howth of the day. On calling at Howth Castle, she was informed that the family were at dinner. Enraged at not being invited to join them, she stole the heir, a child whom she found playing on the strand, and took him with her to Connaught. The door of Howth Castle has ever since been kept open at dinner time, and its present occupant, Lord Ashbourne, observes the custom.

The Spanish form of this name, Engracia, obtained some degree of popularity in that country through its having been that of a young girl who was tortured to death at Saragossa in in 304; and one of her name-descendants, Grace of Valentia, must have also commanded some respect, for she attained to such an ethereal condition of body that each year she lived all through the forty days of Lent on nothing but the Eucharistic bread, and on other occasions too abstained from all but this "angel's food". She was a member of the Order of Saint Francis of Paula, and it is asserted that for seven years previous to her joining this community, and during the whole of the twenty-four years during which she belonged to it, nothing liquid ever passed her lips, not even water. This dry diet seems to have agreed with her constitution, however, for born in 1494, she did not die until 1606, so that she lived to the unusual age of 112 years!

The real glory of the name of Grace is, however, that true heroine in humble life, Grace Darling, the daughter of the Lighthouse-keeper on the Longstone Rock, one of the Farne Islands lying off the wild Northumberland coast.

Grace, one of a large family, was born at Bamborough in or about 1816, and lived with her parents in the lighthouse. On the night of September the fourth, 1838, a fearful storm had raged, and when in the early morning of the fifth, Grace looked out to sea, she saw in the distance a wreck, and could dimly distinguish some living forms still clinging to it.

She pointed them out to her father, but he declared rescue to be impossible: she urged him, however, to make the attempt with her, and at last, inspired by her enthusiasm, he consented.

Her father followed her into the boat as it tossed on the still raging sea; and, after a fearful struggle against the elements, these two, a middle-aged man and a girl of two and twenty, succeeded in reaching the wreck and in saving the lives of the nine men still clinging to all that remained of the steamboat *Forfarshire*.

Grace Darling "awoke to find herself famous", and her praises were sung throughout the length and breadth of the land. A subscription, too, was raised for her benefit; but her fame and her comparative riches, did not spoil Grace Darling, who was too noble to be influenced by anything so passing as public enthusiasm. She went on living her own quiet life in the lighthouse just as before, until four short years afterwards she was carried off by consumption, dying on October the fourth, 1842.

She was buried in Bamborough Churchyard, where a monument stands to her memory.

Her father, William Darling, lived until 1865.

A Maiden gentle, yet, at duty's call,
Firm and unflinching, as the Lighthouse reared
On the Island-rock, her lonely dwelling place;
Or like the invincible Rock itself that braves,
Age after age, the hostile elements,
As when it guarded holy Cuthbert's cell.

GRACE

All night the storm had raged, nor ceased, nor paused,
When, as the day broke, the Maid, through misty air,
Espies far off a Wreck, amid the surf,
Beating on one of those disastrous isles—
Half of a Vessel, half—no more; the rest
Had vanished, swallowed up with all that there
Had for the common safety striven in vain,
Or thither thronged for refuge. With quick glance,
Daughter and Sire through optic-glass discern,
Clinging about the remnant of this Ship,
Creatures: how precious in the Maiden's sight!
For whom, belike, the old Man grieves still more
Than for their fellow-sufferers engulfed
Where every parting agony is hushed,
And hope and fear mix not in further strife.
"But courage, Father! let us out to sea—
A few may yet be saved". The Daughter's words,
Her earnest tone, and look beaming with faith,
Dispel the Father's doubts: nor do they lack
The noble-minded Mother's helping hand
To launch the boat; and with her blessing cheered,
And inwardly sustained by silent prayer,
Together they put forth, Father and child!

. . . . .

True to the mark,
They stem the current of that perilous gorge,
Their arms still strengthening with the strengthening heart,
Though danger, as the Wreck is neared, becomes
More imminent. Not unseen do they approach;
And rapture, with varieties of fear
Incessantly conflicting, thrills the frames
Of those who, in that dauntless energy,
Foretaste deliverance; but the least perturbed
Can scarcely trust his eyes, when he perceives
That of the pair—tossed on the waves to bring
Hope to the hopeless, to the dying, life—
One is a Woman, a poor earthly sister,
Or, be the Visitant other than she seems,
A guardian Spirit sent from pitying Heaven,
In woman's shape.

. . . . .
Shout, ye Waves,
Send forth a song of triumph. Waves and Winds,
Exult in this deliverance wrought through faith
In Him whose Providence your rage hath served!
Ye screaming Sea-mews, in the concert join!
And would that some Immortal Voice—a Voice
Fitly attuned to all that gratitude
Breathes out from floor to couch, through pallid lips
Of the survivors—to the clouds might bear—
Blended with praise of that parental love,
Beneath whose watchful eye the Maiden grew
Pious and pure, modest and yet so brave,
Though young so wise, though meek so resolute—
Might carry to the clouds and to the stars,
Yea, to celestial Choirs, *Grace Darling's* name!
(William Wordsworth.)

Lady Grace, the sister of Lady Townly, in *The Provoked Husband*, by Vanbrugh and Cibber; Grace-be-here Humgudgeon (a man), in *Woodstock*, by Sir Walter Scott; Graciosa, a lovely princess in an old fairy tale—the object of the ill-will of a step-mother, and the beloved of a fairy prince named Percinet; Gratiano, the brother of Brabantio in *Othello*, by William Shakespeare, and Gratiano, the friend of Antonio and Bassanio, in *The Merchant of Venice*, also by Shakespeare; and Grace O'Malley, in *The Dark Lady of Doona*, by W. H. Maxwell, are some of the very few instances of this name met with in general literature.

To the Handsome Mistress Grace Potter.

As is your name, so is your comely face
Touch'd everywhere with such diffused grace,
As that in all that admirable round
There is not one least solecism found;

> And as that part, so every portion else
> Keeps line for line with beauty's parallels.
> (ROBERT HERRICK.)

GRISELDIS is a Teutonic name derived from *gries* = a stone, and *hilda* = battle-maid. It occurs also in the following forms: Griselidis, Griselda, Grizzell, Grizzie, Girzie, or Gritty.

This was at one time one of the commonest of Scottish names, and will be found in most of the popular Scottish writers of the early nineteenth century, as for example Susan Ferrier and John Galt.

The heroine of the old French fable of the twelfth or thirteenth century was proverbial for her patience. Her humility, which, according to our modern notions, transcended the desirable, captivated the somewhat overbearing gentlemen of past ages, and "patient" Grizzell's story was taken up by Boccaccio and Petrarch, and through them passed on to Chaucer, who handed her name down to succeeding generations as a model for all wives:

> Pearless! the paragon of womankind!

> Upon Grisilde, this poure creature,
> Ful often sithe this markis sette his eye,
> As he on hunting rode paraventure:
> And whan it fell that he might hire espie,
> He not with wanton loking of folie
> His eyen cast on hire, but in sad wise
> Upon hire chere he wold him oft avise
> *The Clerkes Tale* (CHAUCER.)

GUIDA, GUIETTE. Guy is a name derived from the Keltic Gwion, one of the knights of

Arthur's court. Its meaning is doubtful, but according to Miss Yonge, one of our best authorities, it signifies "sense".

For long the name was thought to come from the French *guidon*, and to mean "standard-bearer", but this theory has long been rejected.

The English feminine, rarely met with, is Guida, the French Guiette.

GWENDOLEN, WINIFRED.

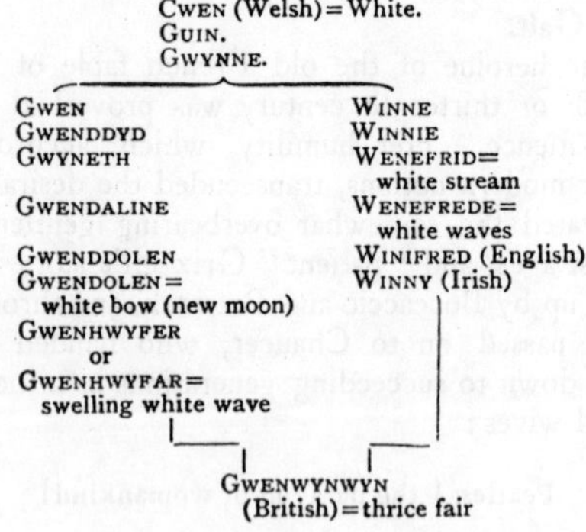

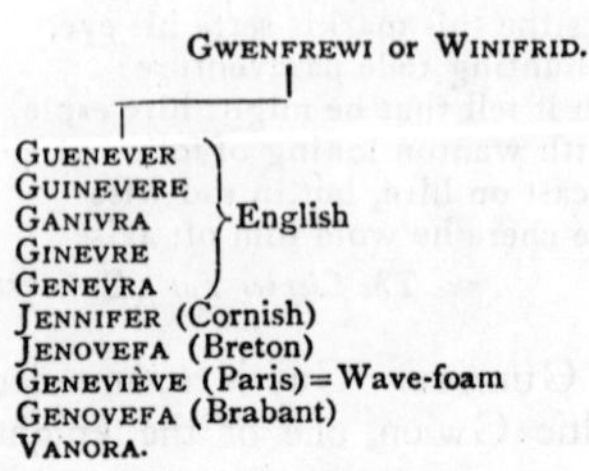

Teutonic and unconnected with any of the above are

WINFRED = friend of peace.
WINFRITH = " " " (Anglo-Saxon)

Gwen also means "woman".

The above somewhat elaborate table has no pretentions to being scientific, and is only given in order to show as clearly as possible to the passing reader the common origin and meaning of the two names of Gwendolen and Winifred, which are daily growing in popularity with the English people. It should be borne in mind that in Welsh in composition *gwen* becomes *wen*, as for example Cain Gwen becomes Cainwen, the feminine of Cain. The name Gwendolen is of great antiquity and occurs several times in the Keltic Arthurian Cycle which is still extant in various forms and fragments, but most perfectly in the Welsh *Mabinogion*, the Scottish *Brut*, and the Breton *Barzaz-Breiz*.

According to Welsh legend, King Arthur married three times, all his three Queens bearing the name of Gwenhwyvar (Guinevere). This would, however, be such an unlikely coincidence, that we may be permitted to in dulge our sentimental feelings about King Arthur, and still believe that in all his life he loved but one who, though frail, was surpassingly beautiful, and in whom he believed until almost the end of his life.

Yet think not that I come to urge thy crimes,
I did not come to curse thee, Guinevere,
I, whose vast pity almost makes me die
To see thee, laying there thy golden head,
My pride in happier summers, at my feet.

. . . .

And all is past, the sin is sinn'd, and I
Lo! I forgive thee, as Eternal God
Forgives: do thou for thine own soul the rest.
But how to take last leave of all I loved?
O golden hair, with which I use to play
Not knowing! O imperial-moulded form,
And beauty such as never woman wore,
Until it came a kingdom's curse with thee.

. . . .

My love thro' flesh hath wrought into my life
So far, that my doom is, I love thee still.
Let no man dream but that I love thee still.
Perchance and so thou purify thy soul,
And so thou lean on our fair Father Christ,
Hereafter in that world where all are pure
We two may meet before high God, and thou
Wilt spring to me, and claim me thine, and know
I am thy husband—not a smaller soul,
Not Lancelot, nor another. Leave me that,
I charge thee, my last hope.

. . . .

And while she grovell'd at his feet,
She felt the king's breath wander o'er her neck,
And in the darkness o'er her fallen head,
Perceived the waving of his hands that blest.

Guinevere (*Idylls of the King*, Tennyson.)

In Guinevere's repentance and flight to Ambresbury Tennyson has closely followed the details given in the old story.

According to the *Brut* and Geoffrey of Monmouth the first Gwendolen that we know of was the daughter of Corineus, Duke of Cornwall, and the wife of "Locryn the son of the Trojan Brutus and Sovereign of these realms". Locryn "fell in love with Astrild, the King of Germany's beautiful daughter; as soon as he beheld the damsel, he determined to wed her, but unfortunately he had before become betrothed to Gwendolen, the daughter of Corineus, Duke of Cornwall". This Corineus had the reputation of being fierce and revengeful, and was unlikely to overlook any insult offered to his house, "so Locryn deemed it expedient to marry Gwendolen". He had, however, "a secret habitation contrived", wherein he concealed Astrild until, Corineus dying, Locryn "dismissed Gwendolen and elevated Astrild to the rank of Queen". But Gwendolen was not the sort of woman to submit tamely to such an indignity, so she forthwith brought "her father's Cornish vassals to her aid", and led them "against her faithless husband" who was slain. Robert of Gloucester says she was a "sturne wommon", a true saying, if indeed she did as is related of her, and caused her rival Astrild, with her daughter Averne, to be drowned in the Severn. In no accounts of her does this lady appear in a very gracious aspect.

Turning from legend and romance to legend and church history for an early instance of one of the names under discussion, we find St. Gwenfrewi, or St. Winifrid, who is said to have been the daughter of a Welsh noble, named Thevith, who was second to none in North Wales save the King. She was niece, too, to St. Beuno, and, her parents rejoicing greatly when the Saint settled in their neighbourhood, handed their daughter Winifrid over to her Uncle to be educated. The little girl used to sit at her Uncle's feet as he preached to the people, eagerly drinking in all the wisdom which fell from the Saint's lips. Winifrid early took the veil, and entered a nunnery built expressly for her by her father in the neighbourhood of what is still known as Holy-Well. After a time Winifrid was appointed Abbess of the Monastery of Gutherin in Denbighshire, and whilst she was there Caradoc, or Cradoc, a prince of that country, fell violently in love with her; she steadily declining to wed him, the prince became so enraged that he rushed after her, and, as she fled from him towards a church which St. Beuno had built for her at Holy-Well, cut off her head. According to Robert of Shrewsbury, Caradoc was instantaneously swallowed up by the earth, and where Winifrid's head fell there sprang up a well (famed ever since for its healing properties) "with pebble stones and large parts of the rock at the bottom, stained with red streaks"; and he adds how the martyr was raised to life again by St. Beuno, and how she ever after bore the mark of a red circle round her neck.

St. Geneviève, the gentle and the brave, Patron-Saint of Paris, was a native of Nanterre and born in 422. At the early age of seven years she attracted the attention of St. Germanus, who, to her parents, foretold her future sanctity; and at the age of fifteen she took the veil. Upon the death of her parents she left Nanterre, and went to reside with her grandmother in Paris, making occasional journeys thence to the provincial towns for purposes of charity and religion, ofttimes working miracles. At one period of her life she suffered greatly from the scoffing of unbelievers and the charge of being a visionary, and was on one occasion only saved from drowning by the intervention of St. Germanus. At the time of the Frankish invasion of Gaul, when Chilperic besieged Paris, the citizens were threatened with famine. Thereupon St. Geneviève went at the head of a company to procure provisions, and returned with several boat-loads of food from Arcis-sur-Aube and Troyes: later on she interceded successfully with the conqueror for the lives of many of his prisoners, and when Chilperic's son Clovis became King and embraced the Christian faith, Clovis also "granted liberty to several captives at her request" as his admiration for her was great. St. Geneviève is credited with the first designs for the magnificent church begun by Clovis, completed by St. Clotilde, and dedicated to SS. Peter and Paul, but now known by her own name. St. Geneviève died the same year as King Clovis, at the age of eighty-nine, and was buried near him in the church towards the building of which they had both done so much.

Passing from legendary lore to pure literature, we have the fragment of a poem entitled *Ginevra*, written by Shelley and founded on an old Florentine tale, wherein the bride, forcibly wedded to one whom she does not love, dies on her bridal day; whilst two of the very few sonnets from Lord Byron's pen are *To Genevra*, and represent that form of the name in English literature; one runs:

Thy cheek is pale with thought, but not from woe,
  And yet so lovely, that if Mirth could flush
  Its rose of whiteness with the brightest blush,
My heart would wish away that ruder glow:

And dazzle not thy deep-blue eyes—but, oh!
  While gazing on them sterner eyes will gush,
  And into mine my mother's weakness rush,
Soft as the last drops round heaven's airy bow.
For, through thy long dark lashes low depending,
  The soul of melancholy Gentleness
Gleams like a seraph from the sky descending,
  Above all pain, yet pitying all distress;
At once such majesty with sweetness blending,
  I worship more, but cannot love thee less;

whilst the other commences

  Thine eyes' blue tenderness, thy long fair hair,

Every one knows Gwendolen Harleth, the chief woman's figure in "George Eliot's" novel *Daniel Deronda*, whilst the shorter name of Gwen has been made familiar to many through the works of the first of living Welsh bards, Lewis Morris. First, we have *Gwen ; a Drama in Monologue*, in six acts:

I see a lithe girl-figure, tall,
With grave blue eyes and hair of gold,

and after marriage:

. . . but Gwen my wife
Is dearer even than Gwen the maid.
We walk by hidden deeps of life,
And no man maketh us afraid;

Secondly, *The Curse of Pantannas*, a weird story in which another Gwen figures as the heroine; and thirdly, *The Foster Brother*, which opens with the lines

Of all the noble damsels, in all our Brittany,
Gwennola was the sweetest far, a maiden fair to see.

Scarce eighteen summers shed their gold upon her
shapely head,
Yet all who loved the fair girl were numbered with
the dead—

. . . .

For three long years she watched in vain, hoping
each day would send
The only heart which beat to hers, her lover and her
friend.

"Go, get you gone and tend the kine", the cruel
step-dame said;
"Leave brooding over long-past years; go, earn
your daily bread".

One dark winter morning a noble knight rides up and says that in three weeks' time he will come and claim her for his bride:

All breathless ran she homeward, when, lo, a wondrous thing!
For on her slender finger blazed her foster brother's
ring.

But though the maiden waits, the knight does not return, and her step-mother drives her to church to wed "Giles the neat-herd"

Not a dry eye was around her, save step-dame stern
alone,
Who looked on with an evil smile, as from a heart of
stone.

The marriage-feast being over,

The ring from off her hand she flung, the wreath
from off her head,
And with wild eyes that spoke despair, and locks
that streamed behind,
Into the darkling night she fled, as swiftly as the
wind.

Her foster-brother of course appears on a white charger, and carries her off

And lo, within a land they were, a land of mirth and pleasure
Where youths and maidens hand in haud, danced to a joyous measure;
. . . .

But when the next sun on the earth, broke from the gathered gloom,
From the white church, the young maids bore the virgin to her tomb.

Other examples in literature are: Guenevra in Scott's *Talisman*; Gineura, the bride of Ariodantes in *Orlando Furioso* by Ariosto; and Ginevra, a young Italian bride, in *Italy* by Samuel Rogers, who, playing hide-and-seek, hid herself in a trunk, and, the lid falling down and being held fast by a spring lock, died. Her skeleton was discovered many years afterwards.

Coleridge twice writes of Genevieve, once in his poem *Love*, and again in his sonnet *Genevieve*

Maid of my Love, sweet Genevieve!
In Beauty's light you glide along:
Your eye is like the star of eve,
And sweet your voice as seraph's song.

Winifred does not often occur in literature, but in John Crowne's drama of *The Country Wit* there is a Winnifride or Wynnifride Rash (spelt both ways in the play!). John G. Cooper wrote a poem entitled *Winifreda*, and finally among *The Percy Reliques* there is the beautiful old ballad of *Winefreda*.

Away; let naught to love displeasing,
 My Winifreda, move your care;
Let naught delay the heavenly blessing,
 Nor squeamish pride, nor gloomy fear.

What tho' no grants of royal donors
 With pompous titles grace our blood;
We'll shine in more substantial honors,
 And to be noble we'll be good.

. . . .

Through youth and age in love excelling,
 We'll hand in hand together tread;
Sweet-smiling peace shall crown our dwelling,
 And babes, sweet-smiling babes, our bed.

How should I love the pretty creatures,
 While round my knees they fondly clung;
To see them look their mother's features,
 To hear them lisp their mother's tongue.

And when with envy time transported,
 Shall think to rob us of our joys,
You'll in your girls again be courted,
 And I'll go a-wooing in my boys.

Vanora is a Keltic name still in use in Wales, and closely allied to Gwenever and Guennola: it means "white wave".

HARRIET, HENRIETTA, HETTY, DETTA. Heimdal or Riger, the third sword-god of the old Teutonic mythology, who always appears with his sword girded to his side, was the mysterious watchman who was stationed at the rainbow — the bridge of Bifröst to protect Asgard, and who in wisdom resembled the Wanes, that race of gods before whom the yet earlier inhabitants of Germany had bowed down.

Heimdal dwelt on a heavenly hill near the

bridge, and when not actively engaged in his occupation of guarding the brave, sat and sipped sweet mead the livelong day. He could hear the faintest sounds, and his piercing sight could penetrate rocks and forest: without any effort he could perceive all that was passing around him within a distance of a hundred leagues, either by day or by night.

Heimdal blessed the human race, and kept the distinctions between the different classes clearly defined. He was the son of nine mothers, the wave-maidens.

His alternative name of Riger shews his connection with the Scandinavian Eoric or Eric, and the German Erich, Erk, Hern, or Chern, —the Sword-God. In the *Edda* he is called the Sword-Ase.

Living in Himinbiörg (Heaven-hall), he protected the brave, and though he took many journeys he always returned to Himinbiörg, mounted on his horse Gulltop, and riding down the Iring's road, now called by men the Milky Way.

Heimdal was, in short, the old Teutonic Peter, who kept watch at the door of their Valhalla or Heaven.

His name comes from *Heim* = home, and *dallr* = powerful, so that the complete name may be taken to mean home-ruler, or lord-of-home. Whilst the Greeks adored the Muses and the Graces, in fact, all that was beautiful, the old Teutonic race gave its homage only to the brave and strong: its chief characteristics were love of war, love of freedom, and love of home, and these distinctive marks are clearly brought out in their names.

Germany is the only country, not excluding even Scandinavia and England, in which names occur with the prefix of *heim* or *home*.

The precise date or period when Heimerich or Heinrich, the original forms of our names Henry and Harry, first took shape as a personal name is forgotten in the mists of the past, but Heinrich der Vogler (876) (Henry the Fowler), the husband of Matilda the Good, covered the name with glory; of such noble descent to begin with, and so adorned, what wonder that it speedily spread through the length and breadth of the land?

Indeed the name hardly needed the added glory of saintship to urge its claims to popular favour amongst the nations of Western Europe. Yet even this was granted it, for Henry the Fowler's son, Henry Duke of Bavaria, had also a son called Henry, who has since been canonized as a saint.

Born in 972, the child was early placed under the care of St. Wolfgang, Bishop of Ratisbon, and from his earliest years gave promise of great intellectual strength and piety. Henry succeeded his father as Duke of Bavaria in 1002, and was chosen Emperor upon the death of his cousin Otho III. In the following year he was crowned King of Germany, and soon after his accession to the throne resigned his Duchy in favour of his brother-in-law Henry surnamed senior.

St. Henry did much towards fixing the canons of the church, and by his courage, prudence, and clemency was instrumental in quelling rebellion and enforcing justice.

In 1014 he went to Rome, where ten years after his election he was formally crowned Emperor by Pope Benedict VIII., amidst great pomp and rejoicing.

Henry restored the sees of Hildesheim, Magdeburg, Strasburg and others, and endowed many churches and monasteries: he warred continually against paganism and barbarity, and made Poland, Bohemia, and Moravia tributaries of the Empire.

Henry died after a reign of twenty-two years, in 1024, and was canonized in 1152.

St. Henry of Treviso was a very different man. Of humble parentage, his father's poverty deprived him of the means of education, and he began life as a day-labourer. All his time that was not employed in an actual struggle for existence, he spent in acts of devotion, and leading a life of great privation he gave all he could to those poorer even than himself. In Italy he is known as St. Rigo, the Italian diminutive of Arrigo or Henry.

The English feminine forms of this name, Henrietta, Harriet, Harriot, Harty, Hatty, Hetty, Etta, and Detta, did not become common until the sixteenth century, when the Queen of Charles I., Henrietta Maria, daughter of Henry IV. of France, made it fashionable. She was a beautiful and high-spirited woman, and though her levity and attachment to the Romish Church made her very unpopular in England with a certain party, the royalists were her warm adherents and her English namesakes were innumerable. Even one of Oliver Cromwell's daughters was named after the Queen; but that was before Englishmen had realized the coming troubles of the reign of Charles I.

Her daughter Henrietta Maria of England, as she is called, added to the charm of beauty that of great sweetness of character. She married Philip Duke of Orleans, but the marriage was not a happy one. She was induced to take an active part in the intrigues between the French and English courts during her brother Charles II.'s reign.

She died at the early age of twenty-six, probably from the effects of poison.

Harry is the true native English form of the name Henry, and it is therefore not surprising that Harriet has always been more popular in England than Henrietta. The names Harry and Harriet are confined to English-speaking peoples.

Many English surnames are derived from Heimdal or Heimerich, as, for instance, Herrick, Herries, Hamly, Hamlyn, Hamo, Harris and Hall.

Harriet Martineau and Harriet Beecher Stowe may be mentioned as having brought new honour to the name they bore.

In Tobias Smollett's play, *The Reprisal*, there is a Harriot, and in George Crabbe's poem, *Squire Thomas*, a Harriot is the heroine.

Harriot was in truth
A tall fair beauty in the bloom of youth;
And from the pleasure and surprise, a grace
Adorn'd the blooming damsel's form and face;

"How fair, how gentle", said the Squire, "how meek,
And yet how sprightly, when disposed to speak!
Nature has bless'd her form, and Heaven her mind,
But in her favours fortune is unkind;
Poor is the maid—nay, poor she cannot prove
Who is enrich'd with beauty, worth, and love".

There is Henriette in *Les Femmes Savantes*, by Molière; Henrietta Maria in *Peveril of the Peak*, by Sir Walter Scott; and Sir Charles Hanbury Williams has written *An Ode to Miss Harriet Hanbury, six years old.*

Why should I thus employ my time
  To paint those cheeks of rosy hue?
Why should I search my brains for rhyme
  To sing those eyes of glossy blue?

The power as yet is all in vain,
  Thy numerous charms and various graces:
They only serve to banish pain,
  And light up joy on parents' faces.

But soon those eyes their strength shall feel,
  Those charms their powerful sway shall find;
Youth shall in crowds before you kneel,
  And own your empire o'er mankind.

The following lines were addressed by the poet Shelley to his first wife:

Beneath whose looks did my reviving soul
Riper in truth and virtuous daring grow?
Whose eyes have I gazed fondly on
And loved mankind the more?

Harriet! on thine: thou wert my purer mind;
Thou wert the inspiration of my song;
Thine are these early wilding flowers,
Though garlanded by me.

To Harriet (SHELLEY.)

HELEN, Ellen, Eleanore, Leonora, Eileen. Helen, daughter of Zeus and Leda and wife of Menelaos, kind of Sparta, of whom Homer wrote "she moves a goddess, and she looks a queen", and who by eloping with the Trojan prince, Paris, her husband's guest, brought about the siege of Troy—a siege which lasted ten years, before the town was burned to the ground—has been from time immemorial accepted as the type of perfect female beauty, of a beauty so glorious and so rare as to make not one man only but many men lay down their lives for it.

"The Helen of one's Troy" has become a saying to signify anything for which one would live or die, and thus, in spite of her frailty and the misery that she brought on others, Helen of Troy has had countless namesakes throughout the civilized world.

The name springs from the Greek root *ele.* Seleucus whence Selene (the moon) and Helios (the sun), both mean the shiner or giver of light. In England, Ireland and Scotland, the name under one or another of its numerous forms has been popular for centuries. Helena, Helen, Elaine, Eleanore, Eleanor, Ellen, Elinor, Lena, Nelly, Nellie, Nell, Lenora, Leonora, Annora or Anora, are only some of the English versions of the name; whilst in Ireland they have the pretty form of Eileen and Aileen; in Scotland the most popular is Ellen. The Spaniard has remained faithful to Helena, the French have Heléna and Hélène, the Germans Helene, and the Italians Elena, Eleonora and Leonora.

HELEN

As the ages have rolled on, and woman, who at one time was denied even the personal possession of a soul, has come to be admitted more and more to an equal place in society with man, mere personal beauty has ceased to be regarded as the only essential attraction for a woman to possess, and therefore the probability is that few of the modern bearers of her name are or would wish to be really called after Helen of Troy, and they will like to feel that other Helens have lived, not indeed devoid of personal graces, but in whom these have been quite secondary qualities.

Our thoughts turn at once to Helena, Saint and Empress.

English people have long loved to think that they might claim St. Helena as their countrywomân, and, though some French historians have tried to upset this theory and to establish their claim that Helena was a native of Bithynia, our old chroniclers, such as William of Malmesbury and Henry of Huntingdon, and old historians of repute like Leland, uniformly maintain that she was born at Colchester, and was the daughter of king Coilus or Coël, who first built walls round the city of Colchester, and whose jovial memory is kept alive in all our nurseries under the name of "Old King Cole". According to some, York was the place of her birth. It is only fair to add that not a few indirect evidences exist as to her British birth, though modern historians are inclined to the Bithynian theory. We know positively that she became the wife of the Emperor Constantius

Chlorus, when he was only a private officer in the Roman army quartered in Britain, though he was afterwards created co-Emperor with Maximian Herculens, ruling over that division of the Empire which included Gaul and Britain. Helena became the mother of Constantine the Great, who is believed to have been born in Britain, and whose education she herself superintended. On his elevation to the throne, Constantius was forced to divorce Helena and to marry Theodora, the daughter-in-law of Maximian, but when Constantius succeeded his father, he conferred on his mother the title of Augusta, and caused her to be proclaimed Empress throughout his armies, and ordered that medals should be struck in her honour. He always treated her with the greatest respect and deference.

Constantius was early converted to the Christian Faith, but his mother did not follow in his footsteps until some time later. Her conversion, when it did occur, was so entire that she at once embraced all the tenets and all the observances of the Christian Church, and especially those of public worship and almsgiving: forgetting her high estate she laboured amongst the poor and lowly, and was "the common mother of the indigent and distressed". She built a convent at Jerusalem for maidens, built and endowed many churches; and in 326, though then already ninety years of age, went to Palestine and personally superintended the building of a magnificent church on Mount Calvary. She is credited with the discovery of the Cross on which our Saviour was crucified, and according to St. Ambrose, when she discovered it "she adored not the wood, but the king, Him who hung on the wood". She sent a part of the cross to her son Constantine, then at the city he had founded—Constantinople,—and of the nails, she put one in a bridle, a second in a diadem, which she also gave to the Emperor, and a third she threw into the Adriatic during a storm. "Though Empress of the world and mistress of the Empire, she looked upon herself as a servant of the hand-maids of Christ". St. Helena died in the presence of her son and her grand-children on 18th August 326, or 328, at Rome, and was buried with great pomp. In 1672 the urn containing her remains was discovered near the road to Palestrina, about three miles from Rome. Her ashes are now preserved in a rich porphyry shrine under the high altar of the church of Ara Coeli.

In the Middle Ages Eleanor was the favourite form of the name and closely connected with the royal houses of France and England. Eleanor of Provence, the Queen of Henry III., did not, alas! bring much credit to her name; but her daughter-in-law "Good Queen Eleanor" was a worthy namesake of St. Helena. The daughter of Ferdinand III. of Castile, known as St. Ferdinand, and sister to Alfonso X. surnamed the Wise, she was, at the age of ten, betrothed to Edward I., then Prince of Wales. In 1269, she accompanied Edward to the Holy Land, and there saved her husband's life, it is said, by sucking poison from a wound inflicted by a poisoned Saracen dagger. Throughout her long and happy married life her influence on her noble husband was always exercised for good, and when she died at Grantham in 1290 at the age of forty-six, Edward, broken-hearted, had her body brought all the way to Westminster Abbey, and erected memorial crosses at all the places where the melancholy procession rested on the road to London. "I loved her tenderly in her lifetime and I do not cease to love her now she is dead", he wrote to her friend, the Abbot of Cluny. A monument to her memory still stands in Westminster Abbey.

At least one more, an Eleanor, there is whose name will go down to all time, and that is Leonora d'Este, the sister of the Duke of Ferrera, Alfonso II., with whom Torquato Tasso fell hopelessly in love. She either never knew of his love or scorned it; but she never married anyone else; the poet had that consolation at least, and in the episode of Sophronia and Olindo in *Jerusalem Delivered*, he told the story of his ill-fated passion.

Sweden boasts a St. Helene whose relics are preserved in Zealand, near Copenhagen.

One of our Queen's daughters, H.R.H. the Princess Christian, bears the name of Helena, and two of our greatest modern actresses are Lady Theodore Martin, née Helen Faucit, and Ellen Terry. We all know of Nell Gwynne.

Objects bearing the name are few. Of these the most obvious are Helen's Fire, or Feu d'Hélène, electric lights which sometimes play about the masts of ships, and which if seen singly are supposed to presage bad weather, and if two or more are seen at a time are supposed to indicate that the worst of the storm is over; and some towns, of which the first is Helenopolis, which was named after St. Helena by her son Constantine, she having a particular regard for that city on account of its connection with St. Lucian. There are several places in England and Scotland of the name, as for example Great St. Helen's in the City of London; St. Helens, Lancaster; St. Helens, Isle of Wight; and Helensburgh on the Clyde. In America the name is most popular, there being no fewer than fifteen places bearing the names of either Helene or Helen, besides several Ellens, and there is the Island of St. Helena where Napoleon the Great was kept in captivity.

In literature almost every form of the name occurs, and of some literary characters we subjoin a list. In DRAMA: The Spirit of Helen of Troy, in *Doctor Faustus*, by Marlowe; Helena in *A Midsummer Night's Dream*, Helena, the heroine in *All's Well that ends Well*, and Elinor in *King John*, all by Shakespeare; Leonora, the usurping queen, in *The Spanish Fryar*, by Dryden; Leonora in *The Mistake* by Congreve; Leonora in *The Revenge* by Young; Leonora in *The Padlock*, by Isaac Bickerstaff; Leonora in *Two Strings to Your Bow*, by Jephson; Nell in *The Devil to Pay*, by C. Coffey; Helen in *The Hunchback*, by Sheridan Knowles; Helen Mowbray in *Woman's Wit*, by Sheridan Knowles; Lady Helen in

The Iron Chest, by George Colman; and Elena in *Van Artevelde* Book II., by Sir Henry Taylor. In OPERA: Leonora in *Il Trovatore*, by Verdi; Leonora de Guzman in *La Favorita*, by Donizetti; Leonora in *Fidelio*, by Beethoven. In POETRY: *Elene or the finding of the Vercelli Book*, attributed to Cynewulf; Elaine, the lily maid of Astolat, in *Idylls of the King*, and *Eleanore* by Tennyson; Lenore in *The Raven*, by Poe; *Helen of Kirconnell* (a ballad); *Ellen Irwin* (a poem founded on Helen of Kirconnell), by Wordsworth; Ellen in *The Excursion*, by Wordsworth; *Ellen Burd* called *Childe Waters* in *The Percy Reliques; Lenore* in a German ballad by Burger; *William and Helen* imitated from Burger's *Lenore*, by Sir W. Scott; Helen of Corinth in *Arcadia*, by Sir P. Sidney; and Dame Helinore in the *Faëry Queene*, by Edmund Spenser. In ROMANCE: Elein and Elain, sister of King Arthur and mother of Mordred, in *History of Prince Arthur*, by Sir Thomas Malory. In FICTION: *Helen*, a novel by Maria Edgworth; Helen Hesketh in *Reginald Dalton*, by J. G. Lockhart; *Helenore or The Fortunate Shepherd*, by Alexander Ross; Little Nell in *The Old Curiosity Shop*, by Dickens; Nelly in *Guy Mannering*, by Sir Walter Scott; Leonora in *Joseph Andrews*, by Fielding; Helen Pendennis in *Pendennis*, by Thackeray; and Helen Burns in *Jane Eyre*, by Charlotte Brontë.

HELOÏSE: see LOIS.

HENRIETTA: see HARRIET.

HEPHZIBAH. This name, with its beautiful meaning "My delight is in her", has fallen out of favour in the British Isles, where in Puritan days the wife of Hezekiah had many namesakes.

> Thou shalt be called Hephzibah, and thy land Beulah: for the Lord delighteth in thee, and thy land shall be married . . . as the bridegroom rejoiceth over the bride, so shall thy God rejoice over thee.—*Isaiah* lxii. 4.

In America it is still often given, and Nathaniel Hawthorne selected it as the name of one of his most pathetic characters—Hephzibah Pyncheon, in *The House of Seven Gables*.

HERMIONE and HERMIA, meaning "maiden of high degree", are Greek names, supposed to be derived from ἕρα (*era*) = the earth. Many Greek names for men begin with *her*. The name is not, as is so often assumed, the same as Erminia or Hermine, which are of Latin origin.

Two Hermiones are the heroines of Greek legends: the one was said to be a daughter of Mars and Venus, and the wife of Cadmus, the founder of Thebes. Juno was the only one amongst the gods and goddesses who absented herself from her nuptials, and as bridal gifts Hermione received a rich veil and a magnificent necklace, which had been made for her by Vulcan. She and her husband were both transformed into serpents, and placed in the Elysian fields.

The second Hermione was the only child of Menelaus and Helen. She married Neoptolemus, the son of Achilles, immediately on her father's return from Troy, in obedience to his wish. According to a later legend she had previously been promised in marriage to her cousin Orestes, who claimed her from Neoptolemus, who declined to resign her. Orestes, accordingly, slew Neoptolemus with his own hand at Delphi, and carried off Hermione to his own home.

HERMIONE.

If it be as they said, she was not fair,
Beauty's not beautiful to me,
But sceptred genius, age inorbed,
Culminating in her sphere.
This Hermione absorbed
The lustre of the land and ocean,
Hills and islands, cloud and tree,
In her form and motion.

I ask no bawble miniature,
Nor ringlets dead,
Shorn from her comely head,
Now that morning not disdains
Mountains and the misty plains
Her colossal portraiture;
They her heralds be,
Steeped in her quality,
And singers of her fame
Who is their Muse and dame.

. . . .

Once I dwelt apart,
Now I live with all;
As shepherd's lamp on far hillside
Seems, by the traveller espied,
A door into the mountain heart,
So didst thou quarry and unlock
Highways for me through the rock.

. . . .

(R. W. EMERSON.)

Shakespeare chose the name of Hermione for

one of the most beautiful of all his characters, the injured Queen in *The Winter's Tale.*

> Chide me, dear stone, that I may say indeed
> Thou art Hermione ; or rather, thou art she
> In thy not chiding, for she was as tender
> As infancy and grace.

The other form of the name—Hermia—is that given by the same poet to one of his heroines, a Greek maiden, in *A Midsummer Night's Dream.*

Hermioniae was the name of a city near the Riphaean Mountains.

> 'Tis cruel to prolong a pain !
> And to defer a bliss,
> Believe me, gentle Hermione !
> No less inhuman is.
>
> (SIR CHARLES SEDLEY.)

HESTER : see ESTHER.

HILDA, MATILDA, MAUDE, CLOTHILDA. Hilda is one of the very oldest of Teutonic names and has come down to us from the Valkyrs.

It is derived from Hildr, the war-goddess of the north, and signifies "battle-maid". After a long hiatus, it has again become a very popular name in England, there being just now a tendency to revive old names, from a growing feeling for and interest in the poetry of the past, and a sense too of the need for a change, a need for something distinctive.

The name of Hilda used not generally to stand alone, but had either some prefix or addition, and throughout the Teutonic nations

Hilda is still a frequent termination to a woman's name, and as often a prefix to a man's, though as a prefix it is by no means confined to masculine names. It is noteworthy that the three most common terminations to old Teutonic feminine names all denote attributes or proofs of courage — Hilda = battle, Gunda = brave, -trud = fortitude—a token that the women of those days were worthy helpmeets to one of the bravest races of men that have dwelt on the earth: they were women who did not even shun the horrors of war, but were ready when occasion served, to wield the sword side by side with their husbands and brothers.

Hildiridur = battle - hastener (Valkyrie); Hildelildis = battle-spirit (Anglo - Norman); Hildegunnr, Hildegunda, or Hildegonda = battle-maid-of-war, or female-warrior; Hildegarde = lady protectress, or, according to another authority, a woman guarded by the Asir Goddess Hilda, Ollegaard being the Danish form; Hildewig, Hildegar, Hildebjorg, the Scandinavian; and Hiltibraht and Hillibrand the Low German forms of the name. Hildemar means glory of Hilda, as Hercules means glory of Hera. Bathilda means commanding battle-maid; Berghild, protecting battle-maid.

Hilduara, a Spanish form of the name, means "battle-prudence", and the second and most common Spanish form is Hildefuns, meaning "battle - vehemence", or wealth of warlike attributes. This name, introduced into the country by the Visigoths, became gradually altered into Ildefonso and Illefonso, and thence into Alfonso and Alonzo, the most popular of all names with the reigning houses of Castile and Aragon. The present King of Spain is Alfonso XII.

Alphonse is now a very popular name in France, where its feminine counterpart is Alphonsine. The English never took much to this form of the name, and Alphonsos and Alonzos have always been rare amongst us.

Hildegonda became Aldegonda in the Netherlands. Philippe Marnix, who defended Antwerp against the great Duke of Parma, was Baron de St. Aldegonde.

The prefix of the letter "C" before Hilda at one time denoted royal rank: thus Brunehilda = lady of rank; Brunechilda = royal lady; Hildebert = illustrious lord; Childebert = illustrious prince. Hiltrude is made up of two old Valkyr names, Hildur = battle, and Thrudr = truth.

A few years back one of the commonest English girl's names was Mathilda, or Matilda = maid of Hilda, or might of Hilda, some deriving the first syllable from the German word *Magd* (maid), others from the German word *Macht* (might). The present generation has, however, preferred the prettier form of Maude, or Maud. Matty, Tilly, Tilda, and Mall, have all been common in England, but the last four names are now rare except amongst cottagers. The French and German have for the most part remained constant to Mathilde, though the former have Mahaud which is a parallel to our Maud. The Italians, like the

English, have dropped the "h", and spell the name Matilda.

A pretty Frankish form of the name is Clothilda or Clothilde, common in France, though unusual in England.

Swanhilda has become almost extinct.

Several things have combined to make the name popular from the earliest days in Germany: to begin with Hildebrand = *battle-sword* was the name of one of the heroes in the great *Nibelungenlied*, part of whose story is also told in the *Hildebrandslied*, and quite enough alone to make the name eagerly adopted by the knighthood of the entire Teutonic race on the Continent of Europe; then, secondly, it was the name of the popular Pope who is now generally known as Gregory VII., but who was first known as the monk Hildebrand of Cluny.

It was of him that Longfellow wrote when he said:

> We need another Hildebrand to shake and purify us. (*The Golden Legend.*)

Saint Hildegard, or Hildegarda, the beloved Abbess of Rupertsberg, near Bingen on the Rhine, and foundress of the Convent at that place, so popularized the name that in Germany at the present day it is still of frequent occurrence. Saint Hildegard, who lived about 1090-1180, was beautiful and virtuous, but so delicate in health that "her whole life was the image of a blessed death". In her capacity of Abbess, she was a great disciplinarian, but so tender-hearted and sympathetic withal that she understood and entered into the inmost thoughts of each member of the community over which she presided. She was favoured with many visions, knew Latin accurately by inspiration (never having learnt it), and was a great theologian. She is taken as the type of the absence of self-consciousness.

A second Saint Hildegard much venerated at Kempten and St. Gall, was one of the five wives of Charlemagne, and the mother of his sons Charles, Pepin, and Louis, the third being the only one to survive his father. It is said, that she was accused of infidelity by a servant named Taland, and was therefore divorced by Charlemagne, whereupon she retired to Rome, and there led a life of great piety, devoting herself to tending the sick. Whilst so engaged she met Taland, wandering about, blind, and restored him to sight, and he, overcome by gratitude and stricken by remorse, confessed his crime and led her back to Charlemagne.

Nearly two hundred years before Saint Hildegard of Rupertsberg, another form of the name had been popularized amongst the Germans by their good Queen Saint Maud, or Saint Mathilda. She lived from about 900-968, and was the daughter of Theodoric, a Saxon nobleman. Maud was brought up in the Monastery of Erfurt, by her grandmother Maud, and in 913 was married to Henry, surnamed the Fowler, who in 916 succeeded to his father's title of Duke of Saxony, and in 919 was elected King of Germany. Henry the Fowler was a pious and merciful King and greatly beloved by his people, and was aided in all his good works by his noble wife. Queen Maud comforted the sick and afflicted, taught the ignorant and succoured the poor, setting prisoners free and pointing them the way to heaven. After twenty-three years of a happy married life Henry died (936). Two of the three sons of this noble pair, disputed for the crown, which was elective, and the elder—Otho—obtained it, the Queen having favoured her younger son Henry. For this she afterwards suffered severely. The brothers combined (under the pretext that their mother gave too much in charity) to strip their mother of all her possessions, though they eventually repented of their injustice, and made restitution. Maud founded many churches and five monasteries, one of these, at Polden, in Brunswick, being of such extent that it held 3000 monks. The second in importance was the monastery of Quedlinburg, in Saxony. Here Maud buried her beloved husband, and here, after the completion of the building, she spent most of her own time in prayer, penance, and good works.

Her third son was Saint Brune, Archbishop of Cologne. She died on March 14th, 968, and was canonized.

In France the name spread under the form of Clothildis, Clotildis, or Clothilde, through the influence of Saint Clotildis, the daughter of Chilperic, the murdered brother of Gondebald, King of Burgundy. Gondebald, with the object of usurping their dominions put all his brothers, their wives, and their children to death, sparing however, in the general family massacre the two infant daughters of his brother Chilperic. One of these became a nun, but the other, Clotildis, was brought up at her uncle's court. By some means not recorded, she became a Christian. Clotildis is reported to have been beautiful, modest, meek, witty, and pious, and to have been sought by crowds of suitors. She was, however, bestowed by her uncle upon Clovis I., surnamed the Great, who had asked her hand in marriage and who granted to her the free and secure exercise of her religion. Clovis and his bride were married at Soissons in 493, and the Queen made herself an oratory in the palace there, wherein she spent much of her time. She, however, neglectd none of her worldly duties;—she watched over her household, was charitable to the poor, and devoted to her husband, endeavouring to soften and sweeten his fierce and warlike temper. Finally she succeeded in converting Clovis from heathenism to Christianity in 496. It was under his good Queen's influence that Clovis built the Church of SS. Peter and Paul, now known as St. Geneviève at Paris, and sent his royal diadem to Pope Hormisdas as a token that he dedicated his kingdom to God. Clovis the Great died in 511, Clotildis surviving him many years and suffering great tribulation by reason of dissensions between her sons. She spent the last years of her life at Tours, in praying, fasting, penance, and almsgiving. When on her death-bed, she exhorted her sons, Childebert, King of Paris, and Clotaire, King of Soissons, to honour God, protect the poor and to be as fathers to their people. Clotildis died on 3rd June, 545, and was buried by the side of her husband in their church of St. Geneviève, Paris.

Saint Hiltrude of Liessies should be named, and also Saint Hildeletha, the Abbess of Barking. This Saint early consecrated herself to religion and entered a monastery in France, there being at that time none in England. When Saint Erkonwald founded the monastery of Chertsey for himself, he founded a convent at Barking for his sister Saint Ethelburga, and, sending to France for Saint Hildeletha, committed his sister to her care. Saint Ethelburga, who died before her instructress, preceded her as Abbess of Barking.

The last Saint in this long list to be recorded here, shall be one who seems to belong peculiarly to England: Saint Hilda, Abbess of the beautiful monastery founded by King Oswy in 657 at Whitby in Yorkshire. The ruins of the building may still be seen standing on the top of the cliff at whose feet the waves of the North Sea break.

Saint Hilda, who was born in the West Riding of Yorkshire in 614, was descended from the royal line of Northumbria. Dedicating her life to the service of God, she in 649 became Abbess of Hartlepool, but in 658 removed to Whitby. King Oswy had endowed the Abbey there, but to St. Hilda belongs the chief credit of its foundation and she became its first Abbess. To her care King Oswy committed his beautiful daughter Edelfled, whom, in gratitude to Heaven for his great victory over Penda, the pagan King of

Mercia, in 655, he had dedicated to the service of God. Many learned men and women were educated at Whitby Abbey, and the reputation of its Abbess for piety and holiness of life was great.

The story goes that in Saint Hilda's time the Abbey and its neighbourhood were over-run by serpents, and that through the prayers of the holy Abbess (as the monks asserted), these serpents were miraculously deprived of their heads, and turned into stones, to the no small amazement of the onlookers. These stones may still be seen by thousands as you walk at the foot of the Whitby cliffs, both in the cliffs and beneath your feet, and in the gullies round about—each serpent being enclosed in a sort of stone matrix. Modern naturalists call them ammonites. Sir Walter Scott refers to the miracle in *Marmion :*

> They told, how in their convent-cell
> A Saxon princess once did dwell,
> The lovely Edelfled ;
> And how, of thousand snakes, each one
> Was changed into a coil of stone,
> When holy Hilda pray'd ;
> Themselves, within their holy bound,
> Their stony folds had often found,
> They told, how sea-fowl's pinions fail,
> As over Whitby's towers they sail,
> And, sinking down, with flutterings faint,
> They do their homage to the saint.

Saint Hilda died on November 17th, 680.

The greatest name connected with the Abbey, however, hardly owed its greatness to the education there received, for, of lowly birth, and employed in some menial office about the Abbey, its owner was illiterate even for those days. In spite of this—the name of Caedmon, our first great English poet, will ever be associated with the Yorkshire Monastery.

In 867 the monastery was destroyed during an inroad of the Danes, and most of its inmates lost their lives, but Titus, the then abbot made good his escape to Glastonbury, bearing with him the relics of Saint Hilda. The Abbey was refounded as a priory by William de Percy in the time of William the Conqueror, and dedicated to St. Peter and St. Hilda, and during the reign of Henry I., was again advanced to the dignity of an Abbey. Leland in his *Collectanea* says that in the painted windows of the Abbey it was shown, that before the advent of William I., the bordering Scots were cannibals, and were for that savage practice punished by William. The building was of extreme magnificence, and measured 220 feet long and about 56 wide. Much of the ruin fell in 1830, yet enough even now remains to indicate its early grandeur.

Turning from the Saints to general history, we find that at one time Matilda was a pre-eminently royal name. William the Conqueror's consort was Queen Matilda, daughter of Baldwin IV., Count of Flanders, and of Adela, a French princess. She was crowned Queen of England in 1068. Of her eleven children one became Robert, Duke of Normandy, and two became Kings of England, viz., William Rufus and Henry Beauclerc. To Queen Matilda's industry we owe, it is believed, the celebrated Bayeux Tapestry, which represents the leading events in the history of the conquest of England by the Normans, and history also credits her with having exercised great influence over her crafty husband.

Henry I., son of the above, also married a Matilda, generally known as Good Queen Maud, who was a daughter of King Malcolm III. of Scotland.

These two in their turn had a daughter, also called Matilda, or Maud, who when still a child was wedded to the Emperor Henry V. of Germany. On the Emperor Henry's death, Matilda married Geoffrey Plantagenet, Earl of Anjou, and was by her father, Henry I. of England, nominated as his successor to the English crown. Her cousin, Stephen of Blois, however, during Matilda's absence from England usurped the title, and though she strenuously opposed him, the conflict between the cousins resulted finally in a victory for Stephen, though it was Matilda's son who succeeded Stephen on the English throne as Henry II., surnamed Plantagenet.

Stephen was himself married to a Matilda—Matilda of Boulogne, the daughter of Count Eustace of Boulogne and Mary of Scotland, the daughter of St. Margaret, and niece of Edgar Atheling. Stephen's Queen was therefore of royal English descent, and on her father's side own niece to Godfrey de Bouillon and Baldwin—both Kings of Jerusalem. She founded St. Katharine's Hospital in memory of her two eldest children, who died in infancy, and in conjunction with her husband founded the Abbey of Faversham in Kent, where, in 1151, she was interred.

Henry II.'s eldest daughter was again a Matilda, and was married to Henry the Lion, Duke of Saxony.

Another Matilda was the "Great Countess" of Tuscany, who succeeded her father, Boniface II., in that dukedom. She became the wife of Godfrey the Hunchback, Duke of Lorraine, and was noted for her staunch adherence to the Papacy, giving an asylum to Pope Gregory VII. (Hildebrand) during his disputes with her cousin, the German Emperor, Henry IV. In 1101 she led her army in person against Ferrara, and in 1114 herself conducted the siege of Mantua, until overtaken by illness. She died in 1115.

Another princess of the name was Maud of Hainault, who, if she did nothing else worthy of note, at least, in a comparatively short life, contrived to have almost as many husbands as our "bluebeard" Henry VIII. had wives! She first married Guy II., Duke of Athens, then Louis of Burgundy, then (secretly) Hugh de la Palisse, and, lastly, John of Gravina. She died at Naples, in prison, in 1324, at the age of thirty-one.

The name was revived in England by our present Queen — Her Majesty Victoria — who called her second daughter by the name of Alice Maud, and it has been continued by His Royal Highness the Prince of Wales in the person of his third daughter, the Princess Maud of Wales, now Princess Charles of Denmark.

But O I loved you, Hilda, and will love you evermore;
I cannot choose but love you, be the anguish what it will,
For the very pain of loving is all other joys before:
Though you broke my heart in pieces, every bit would love you still.

Though you broke my heart in pieces, I would love you more than all
Who might seek to bind it up again; for love alone can bind
What only love can break; and all the fragments broken small
Would but glass as many Hildas in the mirror of my mind.

Hilda amongst the Broken Gods (WALTER C. SMITH.)

In literature the name does not, under any form, appear very frequently, but there is in POETRY: Hildebrand in *The Nibelungen-Lied*; *Hiltibrant and Hadubrant* (an old romance); *Matilda . . .* by Michael Drayton; Maudlin in *The Sad Shepherd*, by Ben Jonson; *Maud*, "faultily faultless, icily regular, splendidly null", by Lord Tennyson; *Hilda Among the Broken Gods*, by Walter C. Smith; Hilda in *Marmion*, by Sir Walter Scott; and *Maud Muller*, by J. G. Whittier. In DRAMA: Maude in *The Passe-Tyme of Pleasure* (1515), by Stephen Hawes; Mathilde, sister of Gessler, in *Guglielmo Tell* (Opera), by Rossini. In FICTION: Mathilde, heroine of a tale, by Sophie Ristaud; Matilda in *Rokeby*, by Sir Walter Scott; Hilda the vala in *Harold*, by Lord Lytton; Tilly Slowboy in *The Cricket on the Hearth*, by Charles Dickens; Miss Matty in *Cranford*, by Mrs. Gaskell;

and finally Hilda in *The Marble Faun* (*Transformation*), by Nathaniel Hawthorne.

Hildersheim, Hanover, means of course Hilda's home, and is renowned for its examples of mediæval and German Renaissance architecture; and there is a town named Hildburghausen, in the Duchy of Saxe-Meiningen. A tower is still shewn in Rome as "Hilda's Tower", with the Virgin's image, before which Hilda is fabled to have kept a perpetual light burning, and where the doves came to be fed.

HONOR: see Nora(h).

HOPE: see Faith, etc.

HORATIA. One of the most ancient of the Roman *gens* was the Horatian: some derive the name from *hora*, "an hour", others from *oro*, "I pray", probably neither of these interpretations is correct. Horatius was the name of the hero who

> Kept the bridge
> In the brave days of old,

and Horatio and Horace have always been rather popular names in England, whilst Horace is used in France, Orazio in Italy, and Goratij in Russia.

England seems to be almost unique in her use of the feminine Horatia.

HORTENSE is derived from the Latin *hortus* = "a garden". This name has enjoyed some popularity in France by being that of the daughter of the Empress Josephine by her first marriage with the Viscount Beauharnais, who suffered death by the guillotine. Hortense became the unhappy wife of Louis Buonaparte, then King of Holland, and the mother of the future Emperor of the French, Louis Napoleon. In Italy the name occurs as Ortensia, but it is rarely met with in this country, and then as Hortensia.

Vanbrugh has a character named Hortensia in his play *Æsop*, and Dickens introduces the name as that of the French lady's-maid in his novel *Bleak House*.

IDA: see Edith.

IMOGEN is presumably an old English name, but the only authority who attempts to give it a meaning is Mr. H. A. Long and he believes it to signify "last born".

> I'll disrobe me
> Of these Italian weeds and suit myself
> As does a Briton peasant: so I'll fight
> Against the past I come with; so I'll die
> For thee, O Imogen, even for whom my life
> Is every breath a death; and thus, unknown,
> Pitied nor hated, to the face of peril
> Myself I'll dedicate.
>
> *Cymbeline* (SHAKESPEARE.)

Shakespeare's beautiful creation is the only instance we have of this name occurring in English literature, but there are a few cases of Imogine, and Imagina seems to be not unknown in Germany.

The lady Imogine is the heroine in C. R. Maturin's tragedy of *Bertram*; and Imogine is the heroine of M. G. Lewis's ballad *Alonzo the Brave and the fair Imogine*.

A warrior so bold, and a virgin so bright,
  Conversed as they sat on the green;
They gazed on each other with tender delight:
Alonzo the brave was the name of the knight—
  The maiden's, the Fair Imogine.

"And, oh!" said the youth, "since to-morrow I go
  To fight in a far-distant land,
Your tears for my absence soon ceasing to flow,
Some other will court you, and you will bestow
  On a wealthier suitor your hand"!

. . . .

"If e'er I, by lust or by wealth led aside,
  Forget my Alonzo the Brave,
God grant that, to punish my falsehood and pride,
Your ghost at the marriage may sit by my side,
May tax me with perjury, claim me as bride,
  And bear me away to the grave"!

. . . .

But scarce had a twelvemonth elapsed, when, behold!
A baron, all covered with jewels and gold,
  Arrived at Fair Imogine's door.

. . . .

  And carried her home as his spouse.

. . . .

Then first with amazement Fair Imogine found
  A stranger was placed by her side:
His air was terrific, he uttered no sound—
He spake not, he moved not, he looked not around—
  But earnestly gazed on the bride.

. . . .

The lady is silent; the stranger complies—
  His visor he slowly unclosed;
O God! what a sight met Fair Imogine's eyes!
What words can express her dismay and surprise
  When a skeleton's head was exposed!

Alonzo the Brave and the Fair Imogine (LEWIS.)

INEZ: see AGNES.

IRENE. This pretty name signifying messenger of peace, comes from the Greek

Eirene, of which Irene is the Latin form: Eirene was one of the Horae and the Greek goddess of peace. She was worshipped as the goddess of wealth, and she is accordingly represented in art with Plutus in her arms: her other attributes are the cornucopia, an olive branch, the staff of Hermes, and ears of corn in her hair and hand. Irene's symbolic flower is the Iris = rainbow or uniter, the messenger of peace, the link between the earth and sky.

In mythology she is said to be the daughter of Thaumas = wonder and admiration, and Electra = brightness, and is represented as a Virgin-goddess, swift as the breeze and with wings of gold, the messenger of the gods and especially of Zeus and Hera, bearing their commands from the uttermost ends of the earth even as far as the river Styx, and down into the depths of the ocean wave.

Upon the advent of Christianity Irene was adopted as a Christian name, on account of its appropriate meaning, and it has always been especially popular amongst the Greeks, and wherever the Greek section of the Christian church prevails—notably in Russia where it becomes Eereena.

Many of the Greek empresses bore the name, and in some cases where it was not their baptismal name, they not being always Greeks by birth, it was assumed by them on the occasion of their marriage, when, in conformity with the custom of the Greek Church, they changed their names. This custom still obtains, the Emperors of Russia, for instance, still claiming this act of grace on the part of their brides, upon their becoming Empresses of Russia.

In illustration of this we will instance the case of Pyrisca, the daughter of Ladislas, King of Hungary, who, upon her marriage with the Emperor John Commenus, became the Empress Irene. Their son, Alexius Commenus, also had an Irene for his Empress.

A second Empress who changed her original name for that of Irene, upon ascending the Greek throne, was Violante, the daughter of William V., Marquis of Montferrat, surnamed the Great, and of Isabella of Cornwall. She became the Empress of Andronicus Palaeologus.

Amongst noted Irenes must be named the beautiful Greek Princess, the daughter of Maurice, Emperor of Greece.

She married Khosru Purviz, a Prince of Persia, whilst he was a fugitive in Constantinople, his father Hormuz, King of Persia, having been dethroned. Khorsu embraced the Christian faith and married one of the most lovely women in Europe, whose name moreover proved prophetic, for after Khosru's marriage his country was restored to peace, and he was called upon to ascend the throne of his forefathers. Queen Irene so charmed the people in the land of her adoption, by her grace, beauty, and virtues, that to this day she and her husband are celebrated in Eastern Song in *The Loves of Khosru and Shireen*. Shireen signifies sweet, and was the name into which the Persians transformed Irene. One other Irene we will name, celebrated for her beauty too, but alas! still more for her crimes.

An Athenian by birth, she married, in 769, the Emperor Leo IV., and upon his death, her son Constantine V. being then only nine years old, assumed the reins of government herself. To make her position more secure, she arrested her four brothers-in-law, caused one to be blinded, and the tongues of the three others to be cut out, and then sent them to Athens and caused them to be strangled. She displayed great capacity for governing, however.

When her son Constantine V. had arrived at manhood and expressed a wish to assume the government, this monster in woman's shape caused him also to be deprived of sight.

She endeavoured to win the people by lavish expenditure and display, and great liberality to the poor, but to no purpose, for in 802 a conspiracy was formed against her, and she was deposed, and exiled to the Isle of Lesbos, where she died in the following year. Irene was the first woman to occupy the throne of the Cæsars.

She caused the convocation of the seventh General Council at Nice in 787, by the decrees of which the worship of Images was restored.

There have been two men who have borne the name of Irenaeus, who must be mentioned here, both prominent members of the early Christian Church, and one Irene, a saint who suffered martyrdom at Thessalonica in 303, and another, a widow who cared for Saint Sebastian after his first martyrdom.

IRENE

St. Irenaeus, Bishop of Lyons, ranks as one of the Fathers of the Church. Born about 120 A.D. at the beginning of the Emperor Adrian's reign, he was a Grecian by birth, and of Christian parentage.

He was placed under the care of the great St. Polycarp, Bishop of Smyrna, for his education, and St. Polycarp at once recognised his genius.

Irenaeus made a close study of pagan mythologies that he might be the better able to refute the prevailing heresies which were a confused medley of heathenism and Christianity, and earned for himself the reputation of being "the most diligent searcher of all doctrines", and "the light of the western Gauls".

St. Polycarp sent Irenaeus into Gaul, and at Lyons, where the zeal of the Christians had stirred up the animosity of the heathen to such a degree that persecution and bloodshed were the result, Irenaeus gave signal proof of his zeal, though for part of the time he was absent at Rome.

Whilst Irenaeus was in Rome the Bishop of Lyons died, and Irenaeus was elected his successor.

By the eloquence of his preaching he soon converted nearly the whole of that part of Gaul to the Christian faith, and then, more peaceful times succeeding, devoted himself to the propagation of the Gospel by the writing of books, notably five against heretics, which earned him a high reputation for piety and learning. He also wrote a treatise concerning the unity of God and many other works. He raised his voice, too, in favour of toleration, deprecating the excommunication of Asiatics.

St. Irenaeus died at Lyons together with many other Christians during the fifth persecution of the Church set on foot by the Emperor Severus, in about A.D. 202. He is supposed to have been beheaded.

The second S. Irenaeus, who lived just about a century later, was Bishop of Sirmium (now called Sirmish) in Hungary. During the Diocletian persecutions he was taken before the Governor of Pannonia, one Probus, who accosted him thus: "The divine laws oblige all men to sacrifice to the gods", whereupon Irenaeus boldly answered, "But the law of my God commands me rather to suffer all torments than to sacrifice to the gods". The Proconsul commanded him to be put on the rack, and whilst he was tortured he said to him, "What do you say now, Irenaeus? Will you sacrifice?"

Irenaeus answered, "I sacrifice to my God by confessing His holy name, and so have I always sacrificed to Him". Irenaeus had been married before he entered the priesthood, and, whilst he was being subjected to torture, he was attended by his wife and children who besought him for their sakes to save his life by offering up sacrifices, but he would not, nor would he yield to the earnest entreaties of Probus himself: "Throw not yourself away", he urged, "if you will not sacrifice I cannot avoid condemning you".

It was ordered that his head should be struck off, and his body be cast into the river. He died in A.D. 304. In the Greek Empire a certain officer bore the title of Irenarch, nearly corresponding to our Chief Justice of the Peace.

> Angry if Irene be
> But a minute's life with me:
> Such a fire I espie
> Walking in and out her eye,
> As at once I freeze and fry.
>
> (ROBERT HERRICK.)

In literature Irene does not occur very frequently, but Spenser alludes to Iris in his *Faëry Queene*, Bk. V., c. 3, thus:

> As when the daughter of Thaumantes faire
> Hath in a watry cloud displayed wide
> Her goodly bow, which paints the liquid ayre.
> That all men wonder at her colours pride;
> All suddenly, ere one can looke aside,
> The glorious picture vanisheth away,
> He any token doth thereof abide:
> So did this Ladies goodly forme decay,
> And into nothing goe, ere one could it bewray;

and the same author has written a dialogue between Eudoxus and Irenaeus, *Concerning a View of the State of Ireland*, which is of value as giving a picture of the manners and circumstances of that country in the Elizabethan age.

An Irene occurs in J. Brown's play *Barbarossa*; in Sir Walter Scott's *Count Robert of Paris*; and in a poem by E. A. Poe, where he thus describes her:

All beauty sleeps: and lo! where lies
With casement open to the skies,
Irene with her destinies!
Thus hums the moon within her ear,
"O lady sweet! how camest thou here?
Strange are thine eyelids; strange thy dress!
And strange thy glorious length of tress!
Sure thou art come o'er far off seas,
A wonder to our desert trees"!

There is Irenus in *The Purple Island*, by Phineas Fletcher; and Dr. Johnson wrote a tragedy which he called *Irene*: he took years to write it, and it was put on the stage by David Garrick, but was a failure and only ran for nine nights. Finally J. R. Lowell has a poem entitled *Irené*.

IRMENTRUDE. Irmintrudis was the name of the sister of Charles the Great. She married Isembert, Count of Altdorf, and became the mother of Guelf, the founder of both the Italian and the German branches of that famous family. The younger branch established itself in Germany, and became Dukes of Brunswick. Hence Irmentrudis or Irmentrude was the direct ancestress of our Queen Victoria. Irmentrude died in 820.

The name is supposed to come from *eormen* meaning "great", or "noble", and *trudr* meaning "a maid".

ISABELLA: see ELIZABETH.

JACOBINA, JAMESINA, JACQUELINE, with their variants Jacuita, Jacquetta, Jaquenetta, and Jaculin, are all feminine forms of Jacob or James, a name which signifies "the supplanter", and which was chosen by Rebekah for her second son, because she had a presentiment that he would supplant his elder brother.

If the namesakes of Jacob may be numbered by the thousand, the number of those called after the Great Apostle James, the son of Zebedee, is even larger; and it has followed as a matter of course that some feminine forms have been evolved.

In France the pretty name of Jacqueline is still greatly beloved; but in England and Ireland none of the women's names have taken strong hold, though in Scotland Jamesina and Jacobina are often found.

Jacuita occurs in a play by Vanbrugh called *The False Friend*; Jacquenetta is the name of a country-girl in Shakespeare's *Love's Labour's Lost*; Jaculin, of a character in *The Beggar's Bush* by Fletcher; and Miss Sara Tytler has a novel entitled *Citoyenne Jacqueline*.

> Oh! she was good as she was fair.
> None—none on earth above her!
> As pure in thought as angels are,
> To know her was to love her.
> When little, and her eyes, her voice,
> Her every gesture said "rejoice",
> Her coming was a gladness;
> And, as she grew, her modest grace,
> Her downcast look 'twas heaven to trace,
> When, shading with her hand her face,
> She half inclined to sadness.
> Her voice, whate'er she said, enchanted;
> Like music to the heart it went.
> And her dark eyes—how eloquent!
> Ask what they would, 'twas granted.
>
> *Jacqueline* (S. Rogers.)

JANE, Janet, Joan, Jean, Jessie, etc.

Jessie is so generally accepted now as a separate name, that one pauses before stating it to be identical with Johanna, Joan, Jane, Jean or Janet. Such is, however, the case; and these names must therefore be treated together.

Johanna, Jane, or Jessie, then, are derived from the same root as Hannah or Anne, namely the Hebrew word *Chaanach*, signifying "favour", "mercy", "grace", which, combined with the contraction of Jehovah, *Iah* or *Jah*, give Johanna = grace of the Lord.

Johanna is, of course, the feminine of Johannes, of which John is our English contraction. When we recollect, therefore, those who have borne this name — St. John the Baptist, St. John the Evangelist, with a whole host of martyrs following in their steps, and Joanna the wife of Herod's steward who "ministered to Christ", and who was one of those permitted to behold the two angels at the Saviour's tomb (Luke viii. 23; xxiv. 10), we could not have marvelled had the name rapidly become one of the most popular in the Christian world.

This, however, was not the case with us, perhaps owing to its somewhat unmusical sound, which may have stood in its way until the religious fervour of the Middle Ages, which sacrificed all else to religious associations, came to the rescue. Since those days no name has been in more universal use in these islands, unless it be Mary.

As John, Jack, or Jock were our contractions of Johannes, so Joan, Jane and Jean became our contractions of Johanna; and of these, in England, Joan was for a long period the most usual, until, adopted at last too universally by the very poor, it was in Tudor days discarded in favour of Jane by the nobility. Jane is now in its turn giving way to the far prettier forms of Jean, Janet, and Jessie amongst those who still cling to old associations, yet hesitate before giving their child a name which they cannot feel is pretty.

In Germany Johanna with its diminutive Hanne is still the only form of the name, and very common, the Germans apparently caring more for association than for musical sound.

Perhaps the prettiest of all the developments of the name is the Spanish Juanita.

Joan was for long a royal name in England, many of the daughters of our Kings having borne it. The first of these princesses was a daughter of Henry II., and another, Joan Makepeace, the daughter of Edward II., whilst Edward the Black Prince married Joan, "the Fair Maid of Kent".

The name cannot, however, lay claim to the added charm that most of its bearers have been fortunate in their lives—on the contrary, if it can be shown that the meaning attaching to it = Grace of God has been a talisman to its owners, then it must be in a purely spiritual, not worldly, sense—at least as regards those recorded in history.

Amongst so many, it is difficult to make a selection; but the striking figure of Joan of Arc, the Maid of Orleans, stands out in such bold relief that her claims to notice seem paramount. One of the most extraordinary characters in the whole history of the world, she is an example of what may be accomplished by an enthusiastic belief in a divine mission.

Of obscure parentage, herself a servant at a village inn, she was enabled to save her country from being trodden under-foot by the English. Placing herself at the head of the French soldiers, dispirited as they were by a long series of defeats, she led them on to victory, doubtless aided by the general belief amongst both friends and foes that she was inspired from above. To the everlasting disgrace of the English, they burnt this brave woman as a sorceress on May 30th, 1431.

Though she attained her goal only at the cost of her own life, yet who shall venture to say it was not by the "Grace of God"?

The great German poet Friedrich Schiller has based one of his dramas, *Die Jungfrau von Orleans*, on her life.

But who alone
And unapproach'd, beside the altar-stone,
With the white banner forth like sunshine streaming,
And the gold helm through clouds of fragrance gleaming,
Silent and radiant stood? The helm was raised,
And the fair face reveal'd, that upward gazed,
Intensely worshipping—a still, clear face,
Youthful but brightly solemn! Woman's cheek
And brow were there, in deep devotion meek,
Yet glorified, with inspiration's trace
On its pure paleness; while, enthroned above,
The pictured Virgin, with her smile of love,
Seem'd bending o'er her votaress. That slight form!
Was that the leader through the battle-storm?

Had the soft light in that adoring eye
Guided the warrior where the swords flashed high?
'Twas so ; even so ! and thou, the shepherd's child,
Joanne, the lowly dreamer of the wild !
Never before, and never since that hour,
Hath woman, mantled with victorious power,
Stood forth as *thou* beside the shrine didst stand,
Holy amidst the knighthood of the land,
And, beautiful with joy and with renown,
Lift thy white banner o'er the olden crown,
Ransom'd for France by thee!

A sermon is now annually preached in France towards the beatification of the Maid of Orleans, who will eventually perhaps prove Shakespeare's prophecy true, that she will displace St. Denis as the Patron Saint of that country :

No longer on St. Denis will we cry,
But Joan la Pucelle shall be France's Saint.

Another Jane whom we must not ignore is Jane Seymour, Henry the Eighth's third wife ; fortunate in this that, though she died young, she died a natural death—neither beheaded nor divorced. Jane Seymour, as the mother of the only son of Henry VIII., was indirectly connected with the fate of that other Jane, the nine days' Queen. Edward VI., for some reason overlooking the claims of both his sisters to the English throne, appointed as his successor the Lady Jane Grey, a great-granddaughter of Henry VII. and his own cousin. She, urged thereto by her nearest relatives, accepted the crown, only to lose it again at once, by laying down her life on the block, a victim to the ambition and folly of others.

Three Queens of the name of Jeanne, or

Jane reigned in Navarre, the last of them being Jeanne d'Albret, the mother of Henry IV. of France. She it was who, dying suddenly on the eve of St. Bartholomew, was said to have been done to death by her bitter enemy Katherine de Medici, through the medium of a pair of poisoned gloves. It is only fair to state, however, that, though rumour supported this charge, history offers no trustworthy evidence of its truth. All that we positively know is that Queen Jeanne d'Albret died with suspicious suddenness at a comparatively early age. The incident is alluded to by Christopher Marlowe in his drama, *The Massacre at Paris*.

True to the sorrowful fate which seemed to hang round royal Joans, Joanna, the wife of Henry IV. of England, too, had more than the usual mead of sorrow allotted to humanity. First married to John de Montfort, Duke of Brittany, a man many years her senior, by whom she had nine children, she, upon de Montfort's death, married King Henry IV. of England, having become acquainted with him during her first husband's lifetime.

Left a widow a second time, she was at first honourably treated by Henry V., and even allowed a share in the government; but the English victory at Agincourt brought her much personal sorrow, for her son-in-law, the Duke of Alençon, was slain, as well as her brother Charles of Navarre, and her son Arthur taken prisoner. She was permitted one interview with her son—but one only; and all her efforts to obtain his release were fruitless. In 1418 she herself was suddenly arrested on a charge of witchcraft, and, though the charge was evidently a mere pretext for depriving her of her liberty, she was not released until 1422, being kept a close prisoner in Pevensey Castle. Upon her death, however, she was interred in Canterbury Cathedral by the side of her husband, Henry IV.

Yet one more Joanna we will name—one around whose name a strange atmosphere of fable has gathered, so that it is difficult to disentangle truth from fiction. This Joanna, who is said to have been of English birth, but of whose origin we really know nothing, is reported to have clothed herself in man's attire and to have, in the company of a Fulda Monk, lead a life of desperate adventure, finally ascending the Chair of St. Peter at Rome as Pope John VIII. She died suddenly during a religious procession in which she was taking part. She lived in the middle of the ninth century.

Jane Austen, Jane Porter, Jenny Lind, Janet Hamilton, Jean Middlemass, Jean Ingelow, Jessie Fothergill, have all, in more recent days and more humble walks of life, done their part in maintaining the reputation of their name, whilst in works of literature the number of Janes, Jessies, Jeans, and Joans is almost overwhelming.

> To equal young Jessie seek Scotland all over;
> To equal young Jessie you seek it in vain;
> Grace, beauty, and elegance fetter her lover,
> And maidenly modesty fixes the chain.
>
> (Robert Burns.)

In Drama we have: *Jeanne d'Arc* by Soumet; *Die Jungfrau von Orleans* by Schiller; Jeanne of Alsace, in *The Courier of Lyons* by Edward Stirling; Jenny Diver, in *The Beggar's Opera* by John Gay; Joanna, in *The Deserted Daughter*, afterwards called *The Steward*, by Thomas Holcroft; *Jane Shore* by Nicholas Rowe; and Jessica, in *The Merchant of Venice* by William Shakespeare. In Fiction: Jeanie Deans, and Jennie, the housekeeper, both in *The Heart of Midlothian*; Janet in *The Fortunes of Nigel*; Janet of Tomahourich in *The Two Drovers*; Princess Joan in *Quentin Durward*, all by Sir Walter Scott; Jane, the heroine in *Harry Lorrequer* by Charles Lever; *Jane Eyre* by Charlotte Brontë; and *Janet's Repentance*, one of the *Scenes from Clerical Life* by "George Eliot". In Poetry: the old nursery rhyme of *Cock Robin and Jenny Wren*; Janet, in *Tamlane*, an old ballad; Jessy, in William Shenstone's *Elegies*; *Jane Shore*, a ballad quoted by Pepys, and included in *The Percy Reliques*; *Jenny Kissed me when we met*, a lyric by Leigh Hunt; *Joan of Arc, or The Vision of the Maid of Orleans* by Robert Southey; *Jessie and Colin, a Tale in verse* by George Crabbe; several short poems to Jessy Lewars by Robert Burns, and one or two to *Jean* by the same author, amongst them the exquisite little song of *I Love my Jean*, which runs:

Of a' the airts the wind can blaw,
I dearly like the west,
For there the bonnie lassie lives,
The lassie I lo'e best;

There wild woods grow, and rivers row,
And monnie a hill between;
By day and night my fancy's flight
Is ever wi' my Jean.

I see her in the dewy flowers,
I see her sweet and fair;
I hear her in the tunefu' birds,
I hear her charm the air:
There's not a bonnie flower that springs
By fountain, shaw, or green;
There's not a bonnie bird that sings,
But minds me o' my Jean.

Then we have a poem by D. G. Rossetti called *Jenny*; Jane in Jack's song in *Sunrise* by William Black; Lady Jenny in Matthew Prior's *The Female Phaeton*; *Jenny, I'm not jesting* by A. P. Graves; *To Jane*, by Tom Hood; *Jenny's Bawbee*, and the well-known *Jenny dang the Weaver*, by Sir Alexander Boswell, and Motherwell's beautiful lyric *Jeanie Morrison*:

I've wandered east, I've wandered west,
Through many a weary way;
But never, never can forget
The love of life's young day!
The fire that's blawn on Beltane e'en,
May weel be black gin Yule;
But blacker fa' awaits the heart
Where first fond love grows cool.

O dear, dear Jeanie Morrison,
The thoughts o' bygane years
Still fling their shadows owre my path,
And blind my een wi' tears!
They blind my een wi' saut, saut tears,
And sair and sick I pine,
As memory idly summons up
The blithe blinks o' langsyne . . .

Oh, mind ye, love, how aft we left
The deavin' dinsom toun,
To wander by the green burn-side,
And hear its water croon?
The simmer leaves hung o'er our heads,
The flowers burst round our feet,
And in the gloaming o' the wood
The throssil whistled sweet.

I've wandered east, I've wandered west,
I've borne a weary lot;
But in my wanderings, far or near,
Ye never were forgot.
The fount that first burst frae this hear
Still travels on its way;
And channels deeper as it rins,
The love o' life's young day.

O dear, dear Jeanie Morrison,
Since we were sindered young,
I've never seen your face, nor heard
The music o' your tongue;
But I could hug all wretchedness,
And happy could I dee,
Did I but ken your heart still dreamed
O' bygane days and me!

JEMIMA (or JEMIMAH), Keziah, and Kerenhappuch, were the names of Job's three daughters. Jemima in Hebrew means "handsome as the day"; in Arabic "a dove", and this last translation is the more popular: Keziah means "cassia", and Kerenhappuch signifies "horn of stibium" (a cosmetic used by eastern ladies for the beautifying of their eye-lashes) and figuratively "beautiful-eyed". All three names are rapidly falling into disuse now, though formerly in vogue amongst the Puritans.

He (Job) had also seven sons and three daughters. And he called the name of the first Jemimah; and the name of the second, Keziah ; and the name of the third, Kerenhappuch. And in all the land were no women found so fair as the daughters of Job.—*Job* xlii. 14 and 15.

Jemima occurs as a character in *My Aunt Margaret's Mirror*, by Sir Walter Scott.

JENNIFER: see GWENDOLEN.

JOYCE, JOCELYN, etc. Jocunda, Jocosa, whence Joyce, are from the Latin *jocus*, which means "sport" or "gladness", and is the same word as our *joy* and the French *joie*. The Welsh form is Jodoca, and is still occasionally met with in Wales, though Jocunda and Jocosa are obsolete with us. Joyce still holds its own, however, and is a favourite name in some families.

Joscelyn, Josselyn, or Joceline is often mistakenly classed with Joyce; but it really comes from the Latin *jus* = right, law, and is the same as Justa, Justina, Justinianus, Justinus, and Justia.

Unlike Joyce, which, in spite of its beauty, seems, like a violet, to have always kept modestly in the shade, Joscelyn can boast some illustrious progenitors, and of these may be mentioned the virgin martyr Justa and St. Justina, who lived in the reign of Claudius II. of Rome, and who shared the martyrdom of St. Cyprian. With him she was first torn from head to foot with hooks, and then cast into a cauldron filled with boiling pitch and oil. It is averred that neither Saint felt any pain, and that both escaped uninjured from the fearful ordeal, though only to be beheaded afterwards. St. Justina's emblem is the unicorn, for it is said that a unicorn will suffer none but a spotless maiden to control him.

Two Emperors of the East bore the name Justinianus, and there was a Latin historian called Justinus ; but it is St. Justin Martyn's name that will first occur to most of us. Carefully trained in the schools of Greek philosophy, he at the age of thirty became a convert to Christianity. When a persecution of the Christians was commenced under Antoninus Pius, St. Justin pleaded their cause with the Emperor, and later on published *A Dialogue with Trypho the Jew*, with the object of proving the Messiahship of Jesus. Not long afterwards Justin was scourged and beheaded.

Justin is a name still beloved in the Emerald Isle, and amongst modern writers the name of the author of *The History of Our Own Times* will at once occur to all—Mr Justin McCarthy.

Both Joyce and Joceline exist as surnames, but are not common: Jeremiah Joyce [1764-1816] was the author of some *Letters on Natural Philosophy* and some *Scientific Dialogues*, and a Jocelin of Brakelonde [1173-1202] wrote a *Chronicle of the Monastery of St. Edmund*.

In literature there is a play entitled *Jocasta*, adapted from the *Phœnissæ* of Euripides, by George Gascoigne, Francis Kinwelmersh, and Christopher Yelverton, which is remarkable for having been the second drama written in blank verse in the English language ; Joyce is a minor character in Ben Jonson's drama, *A Tale of a Tub* ; and there is a Sir Josceline, an English knight in the army of Richard I., in *The Talisman*, by Sir Walter Scott.

JOSEPHINE and JOSEPHA are the English

feminine forms of Joseph, which is a Hebrew name meaning "increase": if we include the Spanish, Italian, German, Russian, and French forms, with all their derivatives and diminutives, they will be found to be almost countless; and England stands almost alone in not numbering Josephine, in some form or other, among her commonest names. Joseph, as a boy's name, is, of course, very common.

The reason of this popularity is not far to seek, for Joseph, Rachel's first-born, is, by his early misfortunes, endeared to our children even before they leave their nurseries, and his later triumphs over seemingly insuperable difficulties, and his final attainment of an almost princely rank in the land of the Pharoahs, all combine to make him one of the most fascinating characters in the Old Testament.

Then again, in England a sort of personal interest attaches to St. Joseph of Arimathea, for is he not said to have visited Glastonbury in person, and to have died and been buried there, and to have taken thither from the Holy Land a mystic vessel containing some of the blood that trickled from our Saviour's wounds at the time of His crucifixion? The legend says that he also had with him some of the wine left over from the Last Supper. This mystic vessel plays an important part in the Arthurian legends, where it is often alluded to as the Holy Grail, or San Graal, in Malory's *Morte d'Arthur*, and in Tennyson's *Idylls of the King*; Drayton, too, refers to it in his *Polyolbion*. The Glastonbury Thorn, which is said to blossom every year on

Christmas Day, is alleged to have sprung from St. Joseph's staff, which he had stuck into the ground.

O three times famous isle, where is that place that might
Be with thyself compar'd for glory and delight,
Whilst Glastenbury stood? exalted to that pride,
Whose Monastery seem'd all other to deride?

. . . . .

To whom didst thou commit that monument to keep,
That suff'reth with the dead their memory to sleep?
When not great *Arthur's* Tomb, nor holy *Joseph's* Grave,
From sacrilege had power their sacred bones to save;

. . . . .

For rev'rence to that seat which hath ascribed been,
Trees yet in winter bloom, and bear their summer's green.

Polyolbion, III. 203-314 *passim* (DRAYTON).

Then again, St. Joseph of Nazareth was Mary's husband, and St. Joseph Barsabas, St. Joseph of Leonissa, and St. Joseph of Cupertino were all men after whom the devout would name their children, hoping thereby to call down blessings upon them.

In England, since the days of the Puritans, when almost all children were given names chosen from the Bible, Joseph has been one of the most popular; but, except in Ireland, where Fifine is often met with, the feminine forms of Josephine and Josepha have never been common here, though everywhere on the Continent they abound.

One of the first amongst Royalties was Maria Josepha, the daughter of Maria Theresa; but the one best known of all was the unhappy Empress of Napoleon Buonaparte. A native of Martinique, she was taken to France by her father when still quite a girl, and at the age of sixteen married the Viscomte de Beauharnais, and became the mother of two children —Eugène and Hortense. In 1779 she returned to Martinique to attend on her mother, who was ill; but three years later, on the revolt of the Colony, was obliged to go back to Paris, where she experienced all the horrors of the Revolution. In 1794 her husband was beheaded, and she was herself condemned to die; but was rescued from prison by Tallien, upon the fall of Robespierre, and she shortly afterwards met Napoleon, then a General, at Barras' house, and in 1796 married him.

The friend of many emigrants, several kindly and generous acts are recorded of her, and she did her best to encourage the arts and industries; but, after Napoleon's elevation to the throne, he was advised to obtain a divorce on account of her having no children. Josephine had been crowned Empress at Paris and Queen of Italy at Milan; but when she learnt what the wishes of the nation were, she declined to let her own feelings stand in the way of the public good, and herself suggested that Napoleon should marry the Archduchess Maria Louisa. Instead of leaving France, as would have seemed natural under the circumstances, Josephine retired to her beautiful estate of Malmaison, with the title of Empress-Queen-Dowager, and there she lived until her death in 1814. Her daughter Hortense became

Queen of Holland, and was the mother of Napoleon III.

In literature Josephine hardly ever occurs, but in Lord Byron's play of *Werner* the hero's wife is called Josephine. Another noted literary example is Robert Browning's *Fifine at the Fair*, and the American poet, J. W. Watson, has a poem to

MY DARLING JOSEPHINE.

The stars are countless in the skies,
The earth a flood of light;
The cream-white moon in beauty flies
Along the path of night;
I sit alone, but not alone:
A spirit all unseen
Has to my welcome bosom flown—
My darling Josephine.

JUDITH, JUDY, is either the feminine of Judah, meaning "the praise of the Lord", or only "a Jewess".

This name became popular through the story of the lovely Jewess of Bethulia, who assassinated Holofernes, Nebuchadnezzar's general, in order to save her native town.

Though a Hebrew name, it very early found its way to Europe, and occurs in English history before the reign of King Alfred the Great. Judith, the daughter of Charles the Bald, when about twelve or thirteen years of age, was given in marriage to Aethelwulf, King of Kent and Wessex; and upon his death she became the wife of Aethelbald, King of Wessex. For her third husband she married Baldwin I., Count of Flanders. Thereupon the name became a hereditary one in that house, and was re-introduced into this country by the marriage of Tostig, the third son of the great Earl Godwine and brother of King Harold II., for he married Judith, the sister of Count Baldwin V. of Flanders.

A few years later and we meet the name again; for Waltheof II., Earl of Bernicia, upon his submission to William the Conqueror, was rewarded with the hand of the Conqueror's niece Judith, a daughter of the Count Aûmale: this lady certainly lent more terror than lustre to the name!

From those remote days down to the present the name has held its own amongst us, and steadily reappears in every generation, amongst Christians as often as amongst those of the Jewish faith, and in Ireland it has always been exceptionally popular. One of Shakespeare's daughters bore the name. There exists a fragment of an old English religious poem, entitled *The Story of Judith*, and Isaac Bickerstaff's oratorio *Judith* is founded on the Apocryphal Book.

Sir Walter Scott introduces a Judith into *The Fortunes of Nigel.* The diminutives are Jugge and Judy.

JULIA, Juliana, is one of those names so often met with among the Latins, which have had their origin in some personal peculiarity. It means soft-haired or downy-cheeked, from *iulus*, derived from the Greek *ioulos*, signifying the downy or soft hair of early youth. The name is said to have been assumed by Ascanius of

Troy when he, while yet in early manhood, came off the victor in a combat.

Some derive the name *Iulus* from Ilium, the citadel of Troy, and quote in support of their theory the line *Julius a magno demisum nomen Julo* [Julius, a name descended from the great Julius], Julius or Ascanius having been the son of Aeneas and Lavinia.

Certain it is, that the Julian gens was older than Rome itself, and one of its members bore the cognomen of Julus, namely, Aeneas' son.

The family was not originally a Roman one, and it did not migrate to Rome until the time of Tullus Hostilius, the third and somewhat mythical King of Rome, the successor of Numa, and, though the Julian family was a noble one, it was undistinguished until it burst into glory in Caius Julius Caesar.

After the time of Julius Caesar every family that had a representative who ascended the Imperial throne was supposed to be adopted into the Julian gens or clan, and thenceforward Julius, Julian, and Julia became common names whereever the wide-embracing arms of the Roman Empire reached.

England at once had her full quota of Julius's, and in Wales, especially in the form of Jolo, it lingered long. In England it never became obsolete, and during the eighteenth century, when nothing was thought beautiful that was not classical, it enjoyed a vigorous revival in both its masculine and its feminine forms: with our seventeenth and eighteenth century poets Julia was quite exceptionally popular. The true English form of the masculine name is Julian, of the feminine Julia, Juliet (Julietta), Juliana, Gillian, and Gill.

Julius Cæsar had a daughter Julia, and so had Augustus—she who married Vipsanius Agrippa, and the emperor Septimus Severus married a Julia, and we might go on enumerating the Imperial Julias of Rome almost *ad infinitum*, but the name has also been ennobled by many women of a later age.

There was a Saint Juliana of Nicomedea, who suffered martyrdom under Galerius, and she has had many namesakes, more especially in the Low Countries and in Normandy.

St. Juliana's troubles first began through her having rejected the addresses of a young nobleman named Evilatius. He in revenge denounced her as a Christian to the prefect, whereupon she was subjected to the most excruciating tortures. But whilst at the height of her sufferings, she only repeated the words, "As is thy day, so shall thy strength be"; and, when sorely tempted by the devil, she heard a voice from heaven exhorting her thus "Juliana, be of good courage; for I am with you, and will never leave you, nor forsake you"; and as these words were spoken she not only felt comforted in spirit, but her wounds began to heal.

When, therefore, she next appeared before the prefect, he was amazed to see her in excellent health, and looking more beautiful than ever.

Her tormentors then caused her to be cast into a furnace, but the fire at once went out and thereupon the people shouted "There is no God like Juliana's God", and more than five hundred people were on that day converted to the Christian Faith.

The following lines were written to commemorate her triumph over her sufferings, by Brantius, who wrote a life of her in verse:

The boiling cauldron but new strength supplies;
Hung by her hair she laughs; fused lead defies;
War with the devil wages day and night,
Nor ceases till she joins the Saints in light.

In the time of Diocletian another Saint appears. This is Saint Julitta. She was a Cæsarean woman possessed of great wealth. A leading man in Cæsarea seized a great part of her property, and, upon her endeavouring to obtain legal redress for the outrage, he denounced her as a Christian.

The Judge at once ordered her to sacrifice to the idols, but Julitta stoutly declined, declaring she "would rather have her body cut in pieces than offend the God that made her".

The Judge, exasperated at her undaunted bearing, at once handed over her estates to the man who had unlawfully seized them, and condemned Julitta to be burnt.

Upon hearing her doom, "a most heavenly joy flushed her countenance"; and, when all had been made ready, Julitta laid herself cheerfully upon the funeral pile and there expired, stifled, it was supposed, by the smoke, for the flames did not appear to touch her body.

Her body was lifted up entire, and afterwards buried in the principal church of Cæsarea.

Saint Basil assures us that "the earth which received the body of this blessed woman sends forth a spring of most pleasant water, whereas all the neighbouring waters are brackish and salt. This water preserves health and relieves the sick".

In A.D. 439 a noble maiden of Carthage, called Julia, was taken captive by Genseric, and sold as a slave to one Eusebius, a pagan merchant of Syria.

Though compelled by her situation to perform many menial offices, she was faithful in the discharge of her duties; and, as she resisted all her master's entreaties to renounce her faith, he, out of the regard he bore her, allowed her the free exercise of her religion.

Eusebius had occasion, however, to make a voyage into Gaul, and saw fit to take Julia with him.

Having reached Capo-Corso in Corsica, he cast anchor and went on shore to take part in some pagan festival then in course of celebration.

Julia remained at a distance from the scene, openly protesting against the superstitious ceremonies.

Felix, the Governor of the island, observing her, asked Eusebius who the woman was who dared to insult their gods, and, upon being told that she was a Christian, Felix offered Eusebius four of his best female slaves in exchange for her.

Eusebius declined the offer, saying that all Felix possessed would not equal Julia in value, so faithful and true was she.

Felix, however, whilst Eusebius was sleeping,

took upon himself to force Julia to sacrifice to his gods, and offered her her liberty if she would comply with his wishes.

Julia answered that in being "free to serve Christ she had all the liberty she required". Felix, thwarted in his purpose, caused her hair to be torn from her head, ordered that she should be struck in the face, and finally had her hanged on a cross.

In Italy, during the Renaissance period, Julia was a common name, and some of its bearers achieved renown, as, for instance, Julia or Giulia Gonzaga, the patroness of art, and Julia Farnese, the beloved of Roderigo Borgia, afterwards Pope Alexander VI.; whilst in France the Christian name of the celebrated and beautiful Mme. Recamier (1777-1849) was Julie. It was in her rooms that much of the coming Revolution was planned.

Mme. Recamier was, however, distinguished from most of her contemporaries by the purity of her motives and her absolutely unsullied personal reputation: the breath of scandal never touched her name, and neither the favour of Napoleon nor the admiration of Prince August of Prussia had any attraction for her.

Her *salon* was, like that of Mme. de Staël, frequented by all the leading characters of the day; but she exercised her power over men by calling out their talents and rousing to action all that was noblest in them. Goethe said of her that "so much disinterestedness, modesty, and renown have never been seen united in one person before".

When, after the restoration of the Bourbons, M. Recamier became poor, and he and his wife had to adopt a different style of living, her hold on the true affections of her contemporaries was so genuine that her reverse of fortune had no other effect than to draw after her, into her humble abode, those who had frequented her brilliant *salon.* Throughout her life Mme. Recamier had shewn a generous sympathy with the oppressed, and had never failed to plead their cause.

In England we can boast of Dame Juliana Berners, the Prioress of Sopewell Nunnery, near St. Albans. She lived in the second half of the fifteenth century, and published *The Bokys of Hawking and Hunting, and also of Cootarmuris at St. Albans* (1486), but only part of the book is ascribed to her own pen.

In the English literary world of to-day Juliana Horatia Ewing, and in America Julia Howe are worthy representatives of the name.

No real person has, however, conduced more to the popularity of a name than has Shakespeare's Juliet. Of her, Mrs. Jameson wrote "All Shakespeare's women, being essentially women, either love, or have loved, or are capable of loving; but Juliet is love itself"—and Hazlitt affirms that "Juliet's character is one of perfect truth and sweetness".

O! she doth teach the torches to burn bright;
It seems she hangs upon the cheek of night
Like a rich jewel in an Ethiop's ear:
Beauty too rich for use, for earth too dear!
So shows a showy dove trooping with crows,
As yonder lady o'er her fellows shows.

What wonder then, that she has had namesakes galore?

Long, long before Juliet, or even her creator Shakespeare, was dreamt of, Cynewulf wrote a poem, which may be found in *The Exeter Book* called *The Legend of St. Juliana.* Other examples of its use are:

Julia in *The Two Gentlemen of Verona*, by Shakespeare; Julia in *The Rivals*, by Sheridan; Julia in *The Hunchback*, by Sheridan Knowles; Donna Julia in *Don Juan*, by Lord Byron; Juliana in *The Double Marriage*, by John Fletcher; Juliet in *Measure for Measure*, by Shakespeare; Juletta, *The Pilgrim*, by Beaumont and Fletcher; Gillian in *The Chances*, by the same; Gillian in *The Betrothed*, by Sir W. Scott; Juliana in *The Honeymoon*, by J. Tobin; Julie in *Mons. de Pourceaugnac*, by Molière; Julie in *La Nouvelle Héloïse*, by Rousseau; Julie de Montemar in *Richelieu*, by Lord Lytton; Juliet in *The Sea Voyage*, by Beaumont and Fletcher; Juliana in *Charles the Eighth of France*, by John Crowne; Juliana in *Sir Clyomon and Sir Clamydes*, by George Peel; Julia in *Theodric*, by Thomas Campbell; *Vandracour and Julia*, by Wordsworth; *Julia*, a short poem by Coleridge; innumerable lyrics and sonnets, by Robert Herrick; Juliet in *The Demon of the Pit*, by Frederick Langbridge, and *Julia de Roubigne*, by Henry Mackenzie. All these bear testimony to the popularity of the name, especially amongst dramatists and poets.

Julia I bring
To thee this ring
Made for thy finger fit;
To show by this
That our love is
(Or should be) like to it

Close though it be
The joint is free;
So, when love's yoke is on,
It must not gall
Or fret at all
With hard oppression.

But it must play
Still either way
And be, too, such a yoke
As not too wide
To overslide,
Or be so straight to choke.

So we who bear
This beam must rear
Ourselves to such a height
As that the stay
Of either may
Create the burden light.

And as this round
Is nowhere found
To flaw, or else to sever;
So let our love
As endless prove
And pure as gold for ever.

(Robert Herrick.)

KATHERINE, Catherine, Kathleen, Kitty, etc. Katherine, like Margaret, is a "jewel-name", it is derived from the Greek *Katharos* (Crystal), and signifies spotless purity. This is, however, only one of the four attributes associated with the name, for beauty, grace and intellectual devotion are also now supposed to cluster round it.

The English, Scottish and Irish forms of the name are Katharine, Katherine, Katharina, Catherine, Catherina, Kate, Kitty, Katie, Katty, Kathleen, Katren and Rina. Various German derivatives from Katharina are Käte, Käthe, Kathi, Kathei, Katrein, Katinka and Katterle, and in France we find Cathérine, Catant, Trinette, whilst graceful Catalina rules in Spain, and the Danes favour Karina. In Italy Caterina stands alone, and the Russians have Ekaterina and Katinka.

As the cause of the popularity of the name cannot be sought in the Bible, we must conclude that it is in this case due to its own intrinsic merits—its beauty of sound and beauty of meaning, enhanced in the Middle Ages by sincere admiration and wonder for the virtues of St. Catharine of Alexandria to whose marvellous history our remote forefathers gave implicit credit.

The true story of St. Catharine of Alexandria is lost in the mists of the ages: that which has come down to us is a strange jumble of romance, allegory and superstition—with perhaps some slight sub-stratum of truth. Even so early as in the 15th century, when the popular capacity for swallowing marvels was still unbounded, doubts had been advanced as to the authenticity of the legend, and at any rate some German and French prelates doubted enough to suppress some of the festivals held in honour of the Saint. She still retains her place, however, in the English Calendar, and churches are still dedicated to her. She is supposed to have lived somewhere about 300 A.D., but her name and fame did not travel to Europe until the 11th century, when the Crusaders brought tidings of her from the East, and even in the East nothing had been heard of her until the 8th century.

Her story, as it has come down to us, is, that she was of noble birth, and that, at one of the Emperor Maxentius's sacrificial festivals, she set herself in opposition to the heathen religious rites there performed, declaring them to be ridiculous, and loudly proclaiming her belief in the Christian religion. Maxentius, who was in love with her, and whose proffers of love Catharine had declined to entertain, stung by the rejection of his suit and furious at her derision of his religious rites, caused her to be stripped, scourged and fastened to wheels studded all over with nails, with which she was to be torn in pieces. At the last moment, however, the wheels collapsed, miraculously broken, and Catherine, escaping, fled to the mountains of Arabia. There she was overtaken by soldiers, who tortured and finally slew her. According to the legend, Angels bore her body through the air to Mount Sinai, and there buried it, in answer to her prayer that her body might be neither seen nor touched by men after her death. There still stands a monastery at the foot of Mount Sinai, dedicated to her and erected over her shrine.

Her offences were enhanced in the eyes of her enemies by the fact that, besides being one of the most beautiful she was also one of the most learned maidens of her time, and succeeded in converting to the Christian Faith not alone the Emperor's wife Faustina and two hundred soldiers of the Imperial bodyguard, but also the fifty heathen philosophers especially commissioned by the Emperor to refute her doctrines. It was in deference to her learning and powers of persuasion that she was chosen as the patron saint of the Faculty of Philosophy at the University of Paris.

Saint Catharine of Alexandria's chief successor is Saint Catharine of Sienna.

This saint was born in 1347, and was the daughter of James Benincasa, a dyer of Sienna. Her intellectual gifts added to her personal beauty won for her the name of Euphrosyna. When still a child, she adopted a solitary life, withdrawing to a distance from the town. At the age of twelve her parents were desirous she should marry, but she had already secretly resolved on a single life, and her devotion and humble spirit were such that she saw only blessings in the hardships and humiliations imposed upon her by her parents, who, in the hope of bending her will to their purpose, insisted on her performing many menial offices. Overcome by her patience and piety, they were at last prevailed upon to sanction her entrance into the Order of St. Dominic when in her eighteenth year. She still, however, lived at home and devoted her life to the poor. The fame of her piety gradually spread, until she was sent on one mission after another on behalf of her Order, or the Church, until at last Pope Gregory XI., from his banishment at Avignon, appealed to her to aid in quelling the disturbances at Florence caused by the factions between the Guelphs and the Gibellines. Armed with the Papal authority, she travelled through Italy, reducing rebellious cities to obedience to the Holy See; and finally going to Avignon, she induced the Pope to quit that place and to return to Rome, she herself returning to Sienna and quietly resuming her retired way of life, converting sinners and reconciling enemies. In 1378 she was again called upon to intervene in questions of State, but, worn out with anxieties, fastings and many sufferings, she died in 1380 at the age of thirty-three. She was canonised in 1461. The French proverb

"Coiffer Ste. Cathérine" (to become an old maid) may be traced to St. Catharine of Sienna.

We know yet three other saints of the name: St. Catharine of Ricci, St. Catharine of Genoa and St. Catharine of Bologna. The first of these, at the age of thirteen, entered the Third Order of St. Dominic. She was especially attracted to the Passion of Christ, in which she was permitted to participate, and during twelve years passed every Friday in ecstacy. She is said to have known of the arrival of a soul in Purgatory and the time of its release. She died in 1589.

St. Catharine of Genoa, having been refused admission into a convent at the age of thirteen, owing to her youth, was forced into an unhappy marriage with a dissolute nobleman. The beauty of her life, and her devotion to the sick and suffering so influenced her husband that he was converted to a better life. After great suffering, borne with much fortitude, this holy woman died in 1510.

The third is Catharine of Bologna (1413-1463), the authoress of "Revelationes Catharinae Bononiensi factae".

Leaving the world of Saints, we find many women of mark who have borne the name in less difficult walks of life, and some have suffered martyrdom without wearing the martyr's crown.

Catherine of France, Queen of Henry V. of England, who was the mother of the ill-fated Henry VI., and through her second marriage with Owen Tudor, the grandmother of Henry VII., may perhaps have led a fairly happy life.

But what of the dismal trio of Catherines committed to the tender mercies of Henry VIII.? Katharine of Aragon was divorced, Catharine Howard beheaded, whilst Catharine Parr escaped committal to the Tower on a charge of heresy only through the exercise of singular tact and good sense.

Catharine of Braganza, daughter of John IV. of Portugal, became the neglected Queen of Charles II. of England. She maintained her own reputation unstained in the midst of a dissolute Court, and afterwards, as Regent of Portugal, acquitted herself well.

In France the beautiful and accomplished Queen of Henry II., Catherine di Medici, did her best to make her name the watchword for cruelty and deceit. The mother of three kings, she brought them up of set purpose in such a manner as to make them mind-less and will-less, that she might still rule.

Through her persecution of the Huguenots and her connection with the Massacre of St. Bartholomew she earned the odium of all succeeding generations.

In Russia, too, Catherines have left their mark. Catherine I., Empress of Russia, was of low birth. After having been in domestic service, she attracted the notice of Peter the Great. He married her, and upon his death she was proclaimed his successor. Her reign was short, however, for she gave way to habits of intemperance, and died at the age of thirty-eight.

Catherine II., Empress of Russia, was of noble German parentage, and became the wife of Peter III. Both she and her husband were of dissolute habits, and she, hearing that Peter III. contemplated divorcing and imprisoning her, had him seized and imprisoned, and finally connived at his death. A month afterwards she was solemnly crowned "Empress of all the Russias", and, whatever her failings as a woman were, she ruled wisely and did her utmost to civilize her people.

Other Catherines there have been who stood near to thrones, but who did not wear a crown, such, for instance, as Lady Catherine Grey, sister of Queen Jane, and Jane's sister-in-law, Lady Catherine Dudley, sister of Lord Guildford Dudley. Then there was "the Pale Rose of England", Lady Catherine Gordon, daughter of the Earl of Huntley, who, through the instrumentality of James IV. of Scotland, was married to Perkin Warbeck, the Pretender.

Lastly we will name Catherine de Bora, who became the wife of Martin Luther, the Reformer, and Katharine Gladstone, the devoted wife and companion of our great English statesman.

In France the name is sometimes given to men.

Namesakes of "Catherine" are few, but we may mention the Order of Knights of St. Catherine, instituted in Palestine in 1063; the Order of Catherine, founded by Peter the Great of Russia in 1714 for women, in honour of his Empress and enjoining on all its members a life as pure as the name implies.

Catherine Wheels, a kind of firework well-known to boys, are named after the instruments of the martydom of St. Catharine of Alexandria. "Catherine-wheel windows" is another name for the "rose-windows", with radiating divisions, in ecclesiastical architecture. The tavern sign "The Cat and Wheel" is a corrhption of "Saint Catherine's Wheel".

St. Catherine's Flower is the Nigella or Love-in-a-Mist, sometimes called Devil-in-a-Bush, probably because of the resemblance of the flower to the shape of a wheel,—and St. Catherine's Pear, which ripens some time about St. Catherine's Day (November 25) is another instance of the use of the name in the vegetable world. At one time a kind of crinoline was called a "Catherine-Wheel farthingale".

Places of the name are numerous all over the world, *e.g.*, Saint Catherine's Hill and Point (England), Loch Katrine, Santa Caterina (Switzerland, Sicily, Italy), Santa Catharina and Santa Catharina Islands (S. America), Catharine Bay (New Ireland), Saint Catherine Island and Sound (United States), Saint Catharines (Canada), Catherine Hill Bay (New South Wales), Catherine Peak (Jamaica), Cape Saint Catherine (N. W. Africa), Katerina (Maçedonia) and so on.

> In every mood she's to be wooed,
> Gay, tender, wise, or witty,
> But don't—this counsel I'd intrude—,
> Try sentiment with Kitty.
>
> *Up for the Season* (C. C. Rhys.)

Subjoined is a short list of poems, dramas, and works of fiction in which people bearing the name of Katharine figure. In Poetry: *Life of*

St. Katharine by John Capgrave (1393-1464); *Mrs. Katharine's Lantern* by W. M. Thackeray; *Kittie's Confession* by Sir David Lindsay; *Praise of the Fair Brydges* (Lady Catherine Chandos) by George Gascoigne; *Katherine Janfaries*, the ballad on which Sir Walter Scott's *Young Lochinvar* is founded; *Kate Kearney* (one of the twelve most pathetic Irish melodies) by Lady Morgan; *Kathleen Mavoureen*, a very popular Irish ballad; Katenka, a Georgian, in *Don Juan* by Lord Byron; *Kathleen* by J. G. Whittier. In DRAMA: *Katharine* was the subject of a mystery play (acted at Dunstable before 1119); Katharine of France in *King Henry V.*, Katharina in *Taming of the Shrew*, Katharine in *Love's Labour's Lost*, all by William Shakespeare; Kitty, daughter of Sir David Dunder, in *Ways and Means* by George Colman; Kitty Pry in *The Lying Valet* by David Garrick; Kitty Willis in *The Belle's Stratagem* by Mrs. Cowley; Catherine, the Queen Mother, in *The Massacre of Paris* by Christopher Marlowe; and Katharine in *The Jew of Malta* by Christopher Marlowe. In FICTION: Kitty, servant of Peregrine Lovel, in *High Life Below Stairs* (1759) by Rev. James Townley; *Katharine Ashton* by Mrs. Sewell; *Catherine: A Story* by Thackeray; Corinthian Kate in *Life in London* by Pierce Egan; *Kitty* by M. Betham-Edwards; *Katherine's Trial* by Holme Lee; and Katie Glover the *Fair Maid of Perth* by Sir Walter Scott.

LAURA. There is some doubt as to the true origin of the name of Laura, but the generally accepted theory is that it is the feminine form of

Laurence, and that it means a bay or laurel tree. According to Miss Yonge, in her exhaustive researches regarding the origin of this name, which was at one time very fashionable in England, and which has enjoyed great popularity amongst poets, we ought to go much further back than we usually do for its first beginnings—even as far back as remote Roman mythology, when the Romans adopted the Etruscan idea of guardian spirits around their hearths, and with it the word *lars* signifying *lord* or *master*. The images of these *lares*, covered with dog-skins, were set beside the Roman hearths, and beside them again figures of dogs were placed.

A special feast was held each year (December 22nd) in honour of these *lares*, which was closely followed by another to Lara, Larunda, or Laurentia, to whom dogs were sacrificed. Later on, Laurentia was supposed to be the wife of Faustulus, a shepherd, who brought up Romulus and Remus. The Greeks converted Laurentia into a nymph, who talked so incessantly that, in punishment, her tongue was cut out, and she was by Mercury conducted down to the nether regions.

The Greek counterpart of this nymph was called Daphne, of whom it is affirmed that, upon being pursued by Apollo, she entreated the assistance of the gods in her escape from Apollo's importunities, and was by them transformed into a laurel bush.

The laurel was considered by the Romans to be a protection against lightning, just as the white vine, when planted against a house, was supposed to have the power of shielding it against a thunder-storm; palm-branches, when laid upon coals, were also credited with this power. Tiberius, who stood in terror of lightning, was, we are told, in the habit of crouching under his bed during a heavy storm, and of sheltering his head under branches of laurel, in the belief that that would save his life, and he also nearly always wore a sprig of laurel, hoping it might act as a talisman against this, to him, most dreaded danger.

The laurel was noted in more ways than this, however. In heraldry, for example, it was used to form the triumphal crown for the warrior who had gained a victory, and had brought his army home in triumph, whilst it is even now almost universally regarded as the symbol of fame and glory; again, in funeral processions it used to be used as the emblem of immortality.

To poets, the laurel wreath has been accorded from time immemorial, and we, in England, actually have the title and office of *Poet Laureate*, supposed to be held by the greatest poet of the day. The great Italian poet, Petrarch, loved to imagine some connection between the poet's laurel wreath and his Laura; and was never tired of playing upon this idea, even though some of his critics fancy that Laura was a fictitious name—an imaginary person set up by him as a convenient "peg whereon to hang a tale". Petrarch's Laura is, however, commonly supposed to have been the wife of Hugues de Sade of Avignon, who died of the plague in 1348. Byron alludes to her in *Childe Harold*.

Our academic term Bachelor (of Arts) is by many supposed to be derived from *Baccalaureat*, or Bay-laureate.

Our modern Lauras are assuredly not called after either the Roman or the Greek nymph, but have received their name in the trust that they may become the guardian spirits of their homes, the true descendants of the Etruscan *lares*. It is possible, too, that the laurel being an evergreen, some may attach the figurative meaning of perpetual youth to the name.

Saints of the Christian Church have added to the renown of the name, for, though there have been no canonized Lauras, there have been three or four St. Laurences, one of whom became Archbishop of Dublin in the twelfth century, and who is doubtless the ancestor of the numerous Irish Laurences. This St. Laurence was of true Irish birth, and was the son of Prince Maurice O'Tool, who, when the child was only ten years old, was handed over as a hostage to Dermod Mac Murchad, King of Leinster. Two years later he was given into the care of the Bishop of Glenduloch, and upon the Bishop's death was chosen as his successor, as Abbot of the Monastery of St. Coemgen, and in 1162 was appointed Archbishop of Dublin. Several times he acted as mediator between the Irish and King Henry II. of England. He died when on a visit to Normandy.

The other Saints have been a St. Laurence, who suffered martyrdom in A.D. 258, and St. Laurence Justinian, the first Patriarch of Venice, who died in 1455.

LAURA

Laura was at one time a fashionable name with us, and, though not nearly so popular now as it was a generation or two ago, it still has many admirers.

LAURA SLEEPING.

Winds, whisper gently while she sleeps,
  And fan her with your cooling wings,
Whilst she her drops of beauty weeps,
  From pure, and yet-unrivall'd springs.

Glide over beauty's field, her face,
  To kiss her lips and cheek be bold,
But with a calm and stealing pace,
  Neither too rude, nor yet too cold.

(CHARLES COTTON.)

In literature Laura has representatives from the days of Elizabeth down to the present. There is a Laura in *Gondibert*, by William Davenant; Laurana, the "King's daughter of Thessaly", in *The History of Parismus*, by E. Foord; and William Drummond of Hawthornden, Charles Cotton, William Shenstone, Lord Byron (in *Beppo*), W. Mackworth Praed, all have added their tributes to the beauty of the name. Laura Bell is the heroine of Thackeray's *Pendennis*.

Little Laurette was sitting beside
  Her dressing-room fire, in a dream, alone;
A mignonne mixture of love and pride
  She seemed, as she loosed her zone.

She combed her tresses of wondrous hair,
  Her small white feet to the fire peeped out,
Strangely fluttered her bosom fair,
  And her lips had a wilful pout.

Whoever had seen that little Laurette,
  Looking so innocent, tender, and sweet,
Would have long'd to have made her his own, own pet,
  To lie at her fair young feet.

Is it fear that dwells in those weird blue eyes?
  For it is not love, and it is not sorrow.
Ah! little Laurette, from your dream arise,
  You must be married to-morrow.

Married to one who loves you well,
  Whose wealth to your life will a glory be.
Yet I guess you are thinking—who can tell?—
  Of Frank, who is over the sea.

Pooh, pooh! her heart? Why, she hasn't a heart;
  She waltzed that night with Sir Evelyn Vere:
Into the greenhouse they strolled apart—
  He's got twenty thousand a year.

The news will go out by the *Overland Mail*:
  In a month or two poor Frank will hear
That London has nothing to do but hail
  The beauty of Lady Vere.

From *Little Laurette* (MORTIMER COLLINS.)

LAVINIA simply means "a woman of Latium". In Virgil's *Æneid* she appears as the daughter of Latinus and the betrothed of Turnus, King of the Rutuli; when Æneas landed in Italy, Lavinia's father promised her in marriage to him. The rivalry thus created between Turnus and Æneas resulted in a war, which was settled by single combat; and in this Æneas came off victor. He wedded Lavinia, and afterwards founded the town of Lavinium in her honour.

The lovely young Lavinia once had friends;
And fortune smil'd, deceitful, on her birth.

Her form was fresher than the morning rose,
When the dew wets its leaves; unstain'd and pure,
As is the lily, or the mountain snow.
. . . A native grace
Sat fair-proportion'd on her polish'd limbs,
Veil'd in a simple robe, their best attire,
Beyond the pomp of dress; for loveliness
Needs not the foreign aid of ornament,
But is when unadorn'd adorn'd the most.
Thoughtless of beauty, she was beauty's self,
Recluse amid the close-embow'ring woods.

Autumn (THOMSON.)

In Shakespeare's play, *Titus Andronicus*, Lavinia is the name of the daughter whom Titus feels called upon to slay; and in Rowe's play, *The Fair Penitent*, the sister of Lord Altamont and wife of Horatio, is called Lavinia. Mackenzie used the name as the title of a pastoral. At one time it enjoyed a considerable share of popularity, though it is falling into disuse now.

LEAH, meaning "wearied", was the name of Laban's elder and less favoured daughter, whom he passed off on to Jacob after his first seven years of service.

The name of the elder was Leah.

It has a pathetic interest, for not only was Leah the less loved daughter, but she was also the less loved wife, though more blessed with children.

In English literature it occurs in a most touching little passage, where Shakespeare, with one touch of his magic pen, gives us a glimpse of the capacity for tenderness in Shylock's heart. It is after Jessica's flight:

Tubal. One of them showed me a ring that he had of your daughter for a monkey.

Shylock. Out upon her! Thou torturest me, Tubal; it was my turquoise; I had it of Leah when I was a bachelor: I would not have given it for a wilderness of monkeys.

LEILA, LELA, is probably of Arabic origin, and amongst the Arabs and Moors it is a great favourite. In Mohammedan romance, too, it stands for the type of Oriental beauty. In Beckford's *Vathek* these words occur: "When he sang the loves of Megnôun and Leilah . . . tears insensibly overflowed the cheeks of his auditors".

It is beloved amongst all Eastern poets, and probably signifies "darkness", or "night", a not unfitting symbol for the dark-eyed beauties of the East.

In *Don Quixote* Lela Marien stands for the Virgin Mary.

Lord Byron celebrates the name in *Don Juan*, where it is the name of the little girl rescued by Don Juan at the siege of Ismail.

. . . but at his side
Sat little Leila, who survived the parries
He made 'gainst Cossacque sabres, in the wide
Slaughter of Ismael. Though my wild Muse varies
Her note, she don't forget the infant girl
Whom he preserved, a pure and living pearl.

The same poet also selects Leila as his heroine's name in *The Giaour*.

Oh! who young Leila's glance could read
And keep that portion of his creed,
Which saith that woman is but dust,
A soulless toy for tyrants' lust?

On her might Mufts gaze, and own
That through her eye the Immortal shone;
On her fair cheek's unfading hue
The young pomegranate's blossoms strew
Their bloom in blushes ever new;
Her hair in hyacinthine flow,
When left to roll its folds below,
As midst her handmaids in the hall
She stood superior to them all,
Hath swept the marble where her feet
Gleam'd whiter than the mountain sleet
Ere from the cloud that gave it birth
It fell, and caught one stain of earth.
The Cygnet nobly walks the water;
So moved on earth Circassia's daughter.
The Giaour (LORD BYRON.)

Leila or The Siege of Granada is the title of a work by Lord Lytton.

LEONORA (LENA): see HELEN(A).

LETITIA, LAETITIA, or LETTICE, is a name of Latin origin, and belongs to a rather large class which denotes "joy" or "gladness". Letitia means "gaiety", "gladness", and is now more common in Ireland than in England, though the pretty old English form of Lettice was at one time a favourite here, and at the present time signs are not wanting of its return to favour. Letty, in both England and Ireland, is the common diminutive of both Letitia and Lettice.

Lettice sometimes occurs as a surname, as in the instance of John Lettice, the author of a poem published in 1764 on the Conversion of St. Paul.

Welcome! but yet no entrance, till we bless
First you, then you, and both for white success.
Profane no porch, young man and maid, for fear
Ye wrong the threshold-god that keeps peace here:

Please him, and then all good-luck will betide
You, the brisk bridegroom, you, the dainty bride.
Do all things sweetly, and in comely wise;
Put on your garlands first, then sacrifice:

From *The Entertainment*; *or porch-verse, at the marriage of Mr. Henry Northly and the most witty Mrs. Lettice Yard.*

(Robert Herrick.)

In William Wycherley's drama *The Plain Dealer* there is a Lettice, and in George Congreve's *The Old Bachelor* there is a Laetitia.

LILIAN, Celia, Rosalie. The Lily, in Christian Art, is an emblem of chastity, innocence and purity—a vase of lilies being frequently placed, in pictures, by the side of the Virgin; and St. Joseph is also represented holding a lily-branch in his hand to show that his wife Mary was the personification of purity.

The name of Lilian or Lily, as now used, signifies purity, but in its original form of Cœlius it meant "heaven".

Miss Yonge shows how Cœlius got changed into Celio and Celia, which in the Venetian tongue became Zilia and Ziliola, in the Neapolitan, Liliola. Celia, the descendant of Cœlius, and Lilian, the descendant of the Neapolitan Liliola, are amongst the most musical and graceful of all English women's names, and deservedly beloved. In Scotland Lilias is a very popular name. In France Céline and Célie are very commonly met with.

I saw fair Celia walk alone;
When feathered rain came softly down,
As Jove descending from his tower
To court her in a silver shower:

The wanton snow flew to her breast,
Like pretty birds into their nest,
But overcome with whiteness there,
For grief it thaw'd into a tear:
  Thence falling on her garment's hem,
  To deck her, froze into a gem.

(THOMAS CAREW.)

Rosalie might be called a "portmanteau name" for it is a combination of Rose and Lily.

In regard to the Lily being the Virgin's flower, it is interesting to know that in Buckinghamshire the White Lily (Lilium Candidum) is dedicated to her under the name of Lady-Lily, and the Order of the Lily of Navarre has also reference to the Virgin. This order was instituted by Prince Garcia VI. in 1048, in the City of Nagera, "where the image of the Virgin Mary issuing out of a Lily was discovered in the time of the King's sickness, who thereupon suddenly recovered his health; and in token of gratitude instituted the Order of Knights of St. Mary of the Lily, consisting of eight-and-thirty knights whereof he was chief. Each of these weareth a Lily on his breast, made of silver, and a double chain of gold enterlaced with the Gothish letter M, which stands for Mary. At the end of the chain hangeth a Flower-de-luce, carrying the same letter crowned".

A pretty old custom that used to obtain in this country, of decorating the Lady Chapels with Lilies of the Valley, during the time of their blossoming, has died out:

The lily, of all children of the spring
The palest—fairest too, where fair ones are;

and as an architectural ornament the Lily is constantly used in these Chapels.

Rightly or wrongly, the Common White Lily is supposed to be a native of the Holy Land, and to represent the return of happiness, and unconscious sweetness. So-called Lily-Work ornamentation adorned the top of the pillars of Solomon's temple, and the ancient Jews believed that witchcraft and enchantments could be counteracted by the use of the Lily; and Christ Himself referred to them.

> Consider the lilies how they grow, they toil not, neither do they spin, and yet I say unto you that even Solomon in all his glory was not arrayed like one of these. *Matthew*, Chap. VI., v. 28, 29.

The Lily and the Rose have for ages been emblematical of the relation of mother and son, and it was in connection with this that the Lily was adopted into the shield of Normandy, and the Rose into that of England, in the days of the Norman invasion. Later the Lily became the royal emblem of France, and the Rose the emblem of England, the parallel being carried even further, for the Dauphin was often styled "The Lily of France" and the Prince of Wales "The Rose of Expectancy of this fair State".

Leaving the flower-world and returning to the human bearers of the name, we find that there has been one Saint who bore it: St. Coelina, a Virgin of Meaux, who was converted to a holy life by St. Geneviève.

As a surname, too, it has its representatives of

note. John Lilly or Lyly, the dramatist, who lived 1553-1601, and wrote the celebrated *Euphues or Anatomy of Wit*, and some exquisite little lyrics, such as

By the moon we sport and play;
With the night begins our day:
As we dance the dew doth fall;
Trip it, little urchins all.
Lightly as the little bee,
Two by two, and three by three,
And about go we, and about go we.
Song of the Fairies.

Other instances are:

William Lilly, the seventeenth-century astrologer and magician, Sir Peter Lilly or Lely, the great Court-painter of the Restoration, to whom Lovelace addressed a poem, and William Lilly, the first Head-Master of St. Paul's school.

Celia was once the poetical name for any lady-love, as for instance, "Would you know my Celia's charms"?

Five hours, and who could do it less in,
By haughty Caelia spent in dressing.
(Swift.)

In literature Celia and Lilian, under their various forms, occur not infrequently, exclusive of Celia, as the generic name for lady-loves. The most generally-known instances are in Poetry: *Coelia in Love*, anonymous; Dame Celia, the mother of Faith, Hope, and Charity, in *The Faëry Queene*, by Spenser; *Roswal and Lillian*; *Celia Singing*, by Thomas Carew; Celia, in *Ungrateful Beauty Threatened*, by the same; *The*

Lily in a Crystal, by Herrick; *To Celia*, by Waller; *Lilli* [= Anna Elizabeth Schonemann], by Goethe; Celia in *The Distracted Lover*, by Henry Carey; *Lilian*, by Lord Tennyson; *Celia*, by Thomas Hood; Laura Lily in *The Belle of the Ball-Room*, by W. Mackworth Praed; and *Celia: a Song*, by Sir Charles Sedley. In DRAMA: Celia in *As You Like It*, by Shakespeare; Celia in *The School for Lovers*, by Whitehead; Lilly in *The Elder Brother*, and Lillia in *The Wild-Goose Chase*, both by Beaumont and Fletcher; and Coelia in *Croesus*, by William Alexander. In FICTION: Celia Brooke in *Middlemarch*, by "George Eliot"; Sheila Mackenzie in *A Princess of Thule* carried on in *The Marriage of Moira Fergus*, by William Black.

The following poem gives Celia fair warning that it were wiser not to give herself too many airs or she may repent.

> Know, Celia, (since thou art so proud)
> 'Twas I that gave thee thy renown;
> Thou hadst, in the forgotten crowd
> Of common beauties, liv'd unknown,
> Had not my verse exhal'd thy name,
> And with it impt the wings of fame.
>
> *Ungrateful Beauty Threatened* (CAREW.)

"Rare" Ben Jonson's beautiful lines to Celia are known to all:

> Drink to me only with thine eyes,
> And I will pledge with mine;
> Or leave a kiss but in the Cup,
> And I'll not look for wine.

LILIAN

The thirst that from the soul doth rise,
Doth ask a drink divine;
But might I of Jove's nectar sup,
I would not change for thine.

I sent thee late a rosy wreath,
Not so much honouring thee,
As giving it a hope that there
It could not withered be.
But thou thereon didst only breath,
And send'st it back to me;
Since when it grows, and smells, I swear,
Not of itself, but thee.

Not less well-known are Lord Tennyson's lines :—

Airy, fairy Lilian,
Flitting, fairy Lilian,
When I ask her if she love me,
Claps her tiny hands above me,
Laughing all she can;
She'll not tell me if she love me,
Cruel little Lilian.

When my passion seeks
Pleasance in love-sighs,
She, looking thro' and thro' me
Thoroughly to undo me,
Smiling, never speaks:
So innocent-arch so cunning-simple,
From beneath her gather'd wimple,
Glancing with black-beaded eyes,
Till the lightning laughters dimple
The baby-roses in her cheeks;
Then away she flies.

. . . . .

Praying all I can,
If prayers will not hush thee,
Airy Lilian,
Like a rose-leaf I will crush thee,
Fairy Lilian.

LILITH stands for Lind-ith, and means "a serpent". Burton in his *Anatomy of Melancholy* mentions an old Talmudical legend, to the effect that a snake was transformed into a woman, and became Adam's first wife, and was named Lilith; but, because her offspring all turned out to be snakes too, Lilith was deposed and Eve put in her place, and Lilith in revenge became a serpent again, and tempted Eve to her destruction. Dante Gabriel Rossetti has a well-known poem entitled *Lilith.*

LIZZIE: see ELIZABETH.

LOÏS or ALOISIA comes from Heloïse, the feminine form of the provençal name of Aloys, from Louis, the contraction of Lludevicus, and means "famous war". The man's name Loiz is the Breton form of Louis. Heloïse gained considerable vogue in France owing to the very wide favour that was accorded to Rousseau's romance, *La Nouvelle Heloïse.*

LOIS (without the diæresis) is a Hebrew woman's name meaning "better". It occurs in the New Testament (2 *Timothy* i. 5) as the name of Timothy's grandmother, in whom dwelt "unfeigned faith".

LOTTIE: see CHARLOTTE.

LOUISA, LOUISE, ALISON. The Salic prefix *hlod*, Greek κλύω (*kluo*), Latin *cluo*, Anglo-Saxon *hlowan*, may possibly have originated in the noise of the cow, which we in English try to render by the verb *to low*. All these words represent noise, even figuratively in the case of *hlod* or *hlud*, for they are Old-German for renown.

The first Christian King in France, Clovis, was known amongst his Franks as Hluodowig = "famous-war", just as his wife, that good Queen Clotilda, was known by the name of Hluodhild. Not until after his conversion to Christianity did Hluodowig go by the name of Clovis, when the Pope who baptized him thus rendered his name into French. By the Germans Hluodowig got changed into Hlodwig and Hlodwig into Ludwig, the form the name still bears in their country—but the French changed Hlodwig into Lluduicus, and then Louis, whilst the soft-tongued Provençals of the South converted the name into Aloys. Aloys has passed back again into Austria as Alois.

Louis has been the pre-eminently royal name of France, no less than nineteen Louis having sat on her throne, exclusive of those of the line of Buonaparte.

The saintly reputation of the son of "good Queen Blanche", Louis IX., did much to popularise the name, and his descendants have carried it on.

Louis IX. had made a vow in 1244, when suffering from a dangerous illness, that, in the event of his recovery, he would march against the infidels in the Holy Land: accordingly in 1248 he embarked with an army of 50,000 men, accompanied by his Queen and almost all the chivalry of France, leaving his mother to act as Regent in his absence.

After winning some victories over the Saracens he was himself taken prisoner by them in 1250. A heavy ransom having been paid for the royal prisoner, he was allowed to leave with all that remained of his once noble army—about 6000 men. He went to Acre, and spent four more years in Palestine, but never beheld Jerusalem.

In 1270 Louis undertook a fresh crusade, but, together with one of his sons and many of his soldiers, fell a victim, during the siege of Tunis, to a pestilence then raging in the army.

Louis IX. in character displayed a most unusual combination of punctilious honour, fortitude, humanity and personal courage, and when in France governed his kingdom with great good-sense, impartiality and justice.

The Welsh and the Irish are both fond of the name of Lewis which is a form of the name that has been also widely adopted amongst the English Jewish community, and Lodowick is common in Scotland.

The feminine forms of the name in use in these islands are Louisa, Louise, Louie and Alison.

Alison, very common in Scotland, has no doubt descended direct from the French Aloys and Heloïse.

Alison or Alisoun was however brought over from Scotland to England in very early days. It is the name of one of Chaucer's heroines—the carpenter's wife in *The Milleres Tale*, one of the *Canterbury Tales*.

That the royal Saint, Louis IX. of France, was chiefly instrumental in popularising this name, is no doubt true, but there have been others who have done their part towards ennobling it.

Among these must be numbered Saint Louis Bertrand. He was born at Valencia, in Spain, and was the eldest of nine children.

From early childhood he showed a retiring disposition, was inclined to shun all frivolous amusements, and, when still a mere lad, assumed the habit of the Order of Saint Dominic.

He was an eloquent preacher, but chiefly distinguished himself by his noble self-devotion during a pestilence which raged in Valencia in the year 1557.

In 1562 St. Louis obtained permission from his superiors to visit South America, and for seven years he laboured assiduously among the natives there. Returning to his own country in 1569, he was appointed Prior to two Dominican Convents in succession, and in 1581 died at the age of fifty-five.

Of Louisas, too, there have been several who deserve notice. The first of these is Louisa of Lorraine, the Queen of Henry the third of France.

Louisa of Savoy, Duchess of Angoulême, and the mother of Francis I. of France, must also be mentioned. This Louisa was unhappily more remarkable for her bad than for her good qualities. Her ambition, avarice, and revengeful spirit were notorious, and they caused many evils to France.

Amongst other indefensible acts of which she is accused, is that of her having seized upon money intended for the payment of the army, and devoted it to her own private uses, and then allowing the Superintendent of Finance to be condemned and hung for peculation.

Again, she offered her hand in marriage to the Constable de Bourbon, and upon his declinal of her offer, she in revenge instituted a lawsuit against him, which not only impoverished him for life, but also obliged him to quit France.

During her son's absence on a military expedition she acted as Regent, and Francis I. always loved and believed in his mother, and sincerely mourned her loss when she died, but by the country at large Queen Louise was hated.

Another Queen of the name was Louisa Ulrica of Sweden, and lastly we name Louisa of Mecklenburg Strelitz, who, born in 1776, married the Crown Prince, Frederick William of Prussia, in 1793, and in 1797 was crowned Queen.

Louisa was a model wife, mother, and Queen. Her noble bearing whilst Prussia lay under a cloud, and the fortitude with which she bore the insults offered her by Napoleon Bonaparte, when he was at the height of his power and Prussia lay prostrate at his feet, won for her an intense affection, almost amounting to adoration, amongst her husband's people. Her son, the late Emperor William, always held her memory in the greatest veneration. She died in 1810.

Mrs. Hemans wrote some lines to her memory.

Amongst our contemporaries mention should be made of Louise Jopling, one of our leading lady artists; Louisa May Alcott, the popular

American authoress, who was born in 1833 in Germantown, Pennsylvania, and whose best books are *Little Women*; *Good Wives*, and *Little Men*; and Mary Louisa Molesworth, our most popular writer of children's stories. She was born abroad but is really of pure Scottish descent, and spent much of her childhood in Scotland. She commenced to write for magazines at the early age of sixteen, Mr. Gaskell, husband of the novelist, taking great pains in helping her to achieve a good literary style.

As a child she had suffered much from excessively Calvinistic surroundings, and determined that no child with whom she was brought in contact should, if she could prevent it, be taught the religion of fear. Hence, her one leading motive in her children's stories has been to make Sundays pleasant for the little people for whom she chiefly writes. Some of her best known stories are *Carrots*, *Just a Little Boy*; *The Cuckoo Clock*; *The Adventures of Herr Baby*; and *Grandmother Dear*.

We must also name Louisa de la Ramé, better known as "Ouida". This pseudonym originated in a baby mispronunciation of Louisa. This lady is a native of Bury St. Edmunds, and, carefully trained by her father, she began to write at a very early age.

Strathmore; *Under Two Flags*; *Two Little Wooden Shoes*; *Moths*; and many other well-known works bear testimony to her power and industry.

Louisa, Marchioness of Waterford is another, who, by her talents, virtues and public spirit, has made her name beloved and respected wherever known.

Finally, there was born in 1850, in Hainault, Louise Lateau, who afterwards became one of the mysteries of the nineteenth century.

Her father was a working man, and she herself a sempstress. When she was sixteen years of age, cholera broke out in the village of Bois d'Haine, and Louise distinguished herself by the devotion with which she nursed those attacked by the disease.

Two years later she suffered from great pain in the localities of Christ's five wounds, and blood flowed from hands, feet, and side, and a "crown of thorns" made its appearance on her head.

For ten years this occurred on every Friday regularly, and though a committee of well-known Church dignitaries was appointed to examine the marks, and above a hundred medical men of recognised position and of all nationalities visited Louise, and thoroughly examined her during those ten years, no fraud of any kind could be detected, and neither did Louise Lateau appear to be suffering from any kind of illness. *The Lancet* of April 22, 1871; *The British Medical Journal*, 1871 and October 1875; and *The Times*, August 29, 1878; besides many other papers of undoubted respectability, referred to her case.

As literary examples of the name we may mention *La Nouvelle Héloïse*, by Jean Jacques Rousseau; Alison in *The Miller's Tale*, by Geoffrey Chaucer; Louisa in *The Duenna*, by Richard Brinsley Sheridan; Louisa in *The*

Deserter, by Thomas Dibdin; Louise, the glee-maiden, in *The Fair Maid of Perth*, by Sir Walter Scott; Louise de Lascours in *The Orphan of the Frozen Sea*, by Edward Stirling; and *Alison Gross*, a ballad, printed by Robert Jamieson "from the recitation of Mrs. Brown"; some lines to *Louise*, by William Wordsworth; and some lines to *Louise Schepler*, by Mrs. Hemans.

Louise Schepler was the faithful servant and friend of pastor Oberlin. The last letter ever addressed by him to his children alludes in touching terms to her devotion and untiring zeal in teaching the children of the mountain hamlets, through all seasons, and undaunted by any dangers.

A fearless journeyer o'er the mountain snow
Wert thou, Louise! The sun's decaying light
Oft, with its latest, melancholy glow,
Redden'd thy steep, wild way: the starry night
Oft met thee, crossing some lone eagle's height,
Piercing some dark ravine: and many a dell
Knew, through its ancient rock-recesses well,
Thy gentle presence, which hath made them bright
Oft in mid-storms, oh! not with beauty's eye,
Nor the proud glance of genius keenly burning;
No! pilgrim of unwearying charity!
Thy spell was *love*—the mountain-deserts turning
To blessed realms, where stream and rock rejoice
When the glad human soul lifts a thanksgiving voice!

LUCY, Lucinda, Lucretia, etc. The name of Lucy is derived from the Latin word *lux* [genitive *lucis*] = light—the masculine form of Lucius, meaning "one born at day-light". According to Cicero, Lucina is identical with luna = the moon, both being derived from luceo = I shine, and the name has synonyms in all languages. There are many masculine forms of the name besides Lucius, including Lucinus, Lucien, Lucan, Luke, Lucretius, and Lycidas.

It was for long a most popular name with the Romans, until abandoned by them on account of the crimes committed by two bearers of the name, one a thief, the other a murderer.

After the advent of Christianity, however, it again came into fashion, owing chiefly to the popularity of a virgin martyr of the name, the patron Saint of the Italian fishermen, who called their daughters after her. To Saint Lucy, too, those afflicted with blindness appealed for aid, owing to some confusion in their minds between the meaning of her name, her supposed power to confer benefits, and their own misfortunes.

Hence gradually arose the legend that Saint Lucy was deprived of her eyes, but of this no mention whatever is made in the histories of the early Christian Church. In old paintings she may be identified by the representation of an eye, or a lamp, attention being thus drawn by the artist to the meaning of her name.

The name of Lucy has been popular in England from before the days of the Norman Conquest, the fancy form of Lucille never having been very common, and Lucinda and Lucasta being chiefly affected by eighteenth-century poets in their amorous poems. Lucretia, though never popular, perhaps because of the notoriety of Lucrezia Borgia, the daughter of Pope Alexander IV., has always had a few representatives in this country. Donizetti founded his opera *Lucrezia di Borgia* on this lady's history.

Saint Lucy, as she is called in England, Santa Lucia as she should really be called, because a Sicilian by birth, was born of wealthy parents in the city of Syracuse late in the second century, and was from the first brought up as Christian. Her father died during her infancy, and her upbringing therefore devolved entirely upon her mother, who spared no pains to instil into her mind all virtuous thoughts.

When still quite young, Lucia secretly dedicated herself to a religious life. Her mother, not knowing this, arranged a marriage for her; but Lucia did all she could to prevent the ceremony taking place. Upon her mother being seized with a severe illness, Lucia joined her prayers with those of the sufferer for her restoration to health, whereupon she was healed. Lucia then confided her vows of virginity to her mother, and she, in gratitude for her own restoration, consented to leave her daughter free to choose her own path in life.

The young nobleman to whom her mother had sought to wed Lucia, furious with disappointment, denounced her as a Christian to the authorities, who forthwith subjected her to many tortures and persecutions. Lucia firmly declined to renounce her faith, however, and she died in prison of the wounds her tormentors had inflicted, about 304. She was buried at Syracuse, but her body was afterwards removed to Metz by order of the Emperor Otto I.

Amongst the tortures to which this Saint was subjected was, it is said, that of being plunged into a cauldron full of boiling pitch and molten lead. She is said to have remained therein for many hours without taking any harm, and it is also recorded that she stood uninjured, tied to a stake around which burnt a fire built up of faggots steeped in resin, pitch and oil. After this her tormentors grew desperate and thrust a sword down her throat, which proved fatal. One saying credited to this Saint is that "Everyone who leads a chaste and holy life is a temple of the Holy Ghost".

Lucifer means light-bringer. Dante describes Lucifer in his *Inferno* as a huge giant with three faces; one red, denoting anger; one yellow, denoting envy; one black, denoting melancholy: from between his shoulders sprang two enormous bat-like wings, quite featherless, which when "he flapped i' the air, Cocytus to its depths was frozen", but before his fall Lucifer had excelled all other angels in brightness, and hence his name.

Lucifer is also the name of the morning-star. Venus when she *follows* the sun in the evening is called the evening-star, or Hesperus; when she *precedes* the sun and appears before sunrise, she is called Lucifer or the morning-star, the light-bringer.

The Earl of Mercia, in Edward the Confessor's time, had a daughter Lucy, and King Stephen had a sister Lucie, who was drowned.

Under one form or another this name occurs with great frequency in literature. There is a

Lucinda, and also a Lucy in Spenser's *Faëry Queene*:

" Then did my younger brother, Amidas,
Love that same Damzell, Lucy bright,
To whom but little dowre allotted was:
Her vertue was the dowre that did delight.
What better dowre can to a dame be hight?"

Then did Sir Terramont unto them shew
His Lucida, that was full faire and sheene.

Lucasta, really Lucy Sacheverell, celebrated by Richard Lovelace in his poems, of which we here quote one:

To Lucasta, on going to the Wars.

Tell me not, sweet, I am unkinde
That from the nunnerie
Of thy chaste breast and quiet minde,
To warre and armes I flie.

True, a new mistresse now I chase,
The first foe in the field;
And with a stronger faith imbrace,
A sword, a horse, a shield.

Yet this inconstancy is such,
As you too shall adore;
I could not love thee, deare, so much,
Lov'd I not honour more.

Other examples are: Lucetta in *The Two Gentlemen of Verona*, Luciana and Luce in *Comedy of Errors*, by Shakespeare; and *The Rape of Lucrece*, by the same author; *The Rape of Lucrece*, by Thomas Heywood, and a French drama by A. Vincent Arnault, called *Lucrèce*: these three last are all founded on the story of Lucretia, the daughter of Spurius Lucretius, prefect of Rome, and the wife of Tarquinius

Collatinus. Nathaniel Lee's *Lucius Junius Brutus*, and John Payne's *Brutus, or the Fall of Tarquin*, deal with the same subject.

Then we have Lucia in Addison's *Cato*; Lucia in *The Cheats of Scapin*, by Thomas Otway; Lucinda in *Don Quixote*, by Cervantes; Lucinda in *Love in a Village*, by Isaac Bickerstaff; Lucinda in *Love and a Bottle*, by Farquhar; Lucinda in Thomson's *Spring*, who was in reality Lucy Fortescue, and who became the wife of Lord George Lyttelton:

O Lyttelton. . . .
Courting the muse, thro' Hagley Park thou strayst. . . .
Perhaps thy loved Lucinda shares thy walk,
With soul to thine attuned.

The Seasons: Spring.

Lucinde in *L'Amour Médecin*, by Molière, and Lucinde in *Le Médecin malgré Lui*, by the same author; Lucippe in *The Mad Lover*, by Beaumont and Fletcher; Lucy in *The Recruiting Officer*, by Farquhar; Lucy in *Love in a Wood*, by Wycherley; Lucy in *The Old Bachelor*, by Congreve; Lucy Wealthy in *The Minor*, by S. Foote; Lucy Goodwill in *The Virgin Unmasked*, by Henry Fielding; Lucy Lockit in *The Beggar's Opera*, by John Gay, the original of this character being Lucy Fenton, Duchess of Bolton.

Herrick's lines to a child begin:

At stool-ball, Lucia, let us play
For sugar-cakes and wine:
Or for a tansy let us pay,
The loss, or thine, or mine.

Wordsworth has a touching little lyric on

Lucy Gray; D. G. Rossetti a sonnet *Concerning Lucy*; Lucy Ashton the ill-fated *Bride of Lammermoor*, whose tragic history, in the hands of Sir Walter Scott, has thrilled the hearts of thousands, and was used by Donizetti as the basis of his opera *Lucia di Lammermoor.* The real name of this character was not Lucy Ashton, but Janet Dalrymple, the daughter of the first Lord Stair. *Lucile* is the name of a poem by Robert Lord Lytton.

Other examples are Lucilia in *Lucretius*, by Lord Tennyson; *Lucretia or The Children of the Night*, by Lord Lytton; Lucretia in *Coningsby* by Lord Beaconsfield; Lucy in *The Man of the World*, by Henry Mackenzie; Lucy in *The Parish Register*, by George Crabbe; Lucy Deane in *The Mill on the Floss*, by "George Eliot"; *Lucy's Flittin*, a song by William Laidlaw.

Ah, weel may young Jamie gang dowie and cheerless!
  And weel may he greet on the bank o' the burn!
For bonny sweet Lucy, sae gentle and peerless,
  Lies cauld in her grave, and will never return.

J. G. Whittier's beautiful lines to the memory of Lucy Hooper begin:

They tell me, Lucy, thou art dead,—
. . . .

That true and loving heart,—that gift
  Of a mind, earnest, clear, profound,
Bestowing, with a glad unthrift,
  Its sunny light on all around,
Affinities which only could
Cleave to the pure, the true, and good;
  And sympathies which found no rest,
Save with the loveliest and best.

and Thomas Tickell has a famous ballad called

LUCY

LUCY AND COLIN.

Of Leinster, fam'd for maidens fair,
  Bright Lucy was the grace;
Nor e'er did Liffy's limpid stream
  Reflect so fair a face.

Till luckless love, and pining care
  Impair'd her rosy hue,
Her coral lip, and damask cheek,
  And eyes of glossy blue.

. . . . .

Three times, all in the dead of night,
  A bell was heard to ring;
And at her window, shrieking thrice,
  The raven flapp'd his wing.

Too well the love-lorn maiden knew
  That solemn boding sound;
And thus, in dying words, bespoke
  The virgins weeping round.

"I hear a voice you cannot hear,
  Which says I must not stay:
I see a hand you cannot see,
  Which beckons me away.

"By a false heart, and broken vows,
  In early youth I die.
Am I to blame, because his bride
  Is thrice as rich as I?

. . . . .

"To-morrow in the church to wed,
  Impatient, both prepare;
But know, fond maid, and know, false man,
  That Lucy will be there.

"Then bear my corpse; ye comrades, bear,
  The bridegroom blithe to meet
He in his wedding-trim so gay,
  I in my winding-sheet".

Then what were perjur'd Colin's thoughts?
  How were those nuptials kept?
The bride-men flock'd round Lucy dead,
  And all the village wept.

Confusion, shame, remorse, despair
  At once his bosom swell:
The damps of death bedew'd his brow,
  He shook, he groan'd, he fell.

After this tragedy we may close with Tom Hood's more cheerful lines:

Young Love likes to knock at a pretty girl's door:
So he call'd upon Lucy—'twas just ten o'clock—
Like a spruce single man, with a smart double knock.

Now a handmaid, whatever her fingers be at,
Will run like a puss when she hears a rat-tat:
So Lucy ran up—and in two seconds more
Had question'd the stranger and answer'd the door.

The meeting was bliss; but the parting was woe;
For the moment will come when such comers must go.
So she kiss'd him, and whisper'd — poor innocent thing—
"The next time you come, love, pray come with a ring".

LYDIA simply means a woman of Lydia, after the cities of that name, there being two, one in Asia, the other in Africa.

English women have been called Lydia after the woman who sold purple dye or silks in Philippi: she became a convert to Christianity, and St. Paul, upon her begging him to do so, dwelt in her house.

At the end of the last and beginning of the present century the name was a great favourite in England; now it has fallen out of fashion.

Massinger in *The Duke of Florence*; Wycherley in *Love in a Wood*; and Sheridan Knowles in *The Love Chase*, all introduce a Lydia, whilst Brinsley Sheridan's Lydia Languish in *The Rivals* is a household name.

In Ariosto's *Orlando Furioso* it was Lydia whom Alcestes sought in marriage.

Lydia Maria Child, an American authoress and ardent anti-slavery writer, is the lady to whom J. G. Whittier addressed the following lines:

> O, woman greatly loved! I join thee
> In tender memories of our friend;
> With thee across the awful spaces
> The greeting of a soul I send!

MABEL, MABLE, etc. Most people when they give their little children this pretty name, probably think that it is a French one, and that, for the meaning to be discovered, it need only be literally translated: that it means "my beautiful", "my fair one"; but this is a mistake, and the name is not in use in France. Its real origin is Irish, and its meaning "merry". Meadhbh, Meave or Mab are the original forms of the name, and are of great antiquity, being derived from either meadhail = joy, or mear = merry—it is uncertain which.

Meadhbh was a heroine of Irish romance, who gradually developed into the Queen of the Fairies in popular lore, under the name of Mab, and it was in that character that she was transplanted from Irish on to English soil, by the Elizabethan poets.

MABEL

Romeo: I dreamt a dream to-night . . .
Mercutio: O! then, I see, Queen Mab hath been with you.

she comes
In shape no bigger than an agate-stone
On the forefinger of an alderman,
Drawn with a team of little atomies
Over men's noses as they lie asleep;
Her waggon-spokes made of long spinners' legs;
The cover, of the wings of grasshoppers;
The traces, of the smallest spider's web;
The collars, of the moonshine's watery beams;
Her whip, of cricket's bone; the lash, of film;
Her waggoner, a small grey-coated gnat,
Not half so big as a round little worm
Prick'd from the lazy finger of a maid.
Her chariot is an empty hazel-nut,
Made by the joiner squirrel, or old grub,
Time out of mind the fairies' coachmakers—
And in this state she gallops night by night
Through lovers' brains, and then they dream of love:
O'er courtiers' knees, that dream on court'sies straight.
O'er lawyers' fingers, who straight dream on fees:
O'er ladies' lips, who straight on kisses dream;
Which oft the angry Mab with blisters plagues,
Because their breaths with sweetmeats tainted are.
Sometimes she gallops o'er a courtier's nose,
And then dreams he of smelling out a suit:
And sometimes comes she with a tithe-pig's tail,
Tickling a parson's nose as 'a lies asleep,
Then dreams he of another benefice.
Sometimes she driveth o'er a soldier's neck,
And then dreams he of cutting foreign throats,
Of breaches, ambuscadoes, Spanish blades,
Of healths five fathom deep; and then anon
Drums in his ear, at which he starts and wakes;
And, being thus frighted, swears a prayer or two,
And sleeps again. This is that very Mab,
That plats the manes of horses in the night;
And bakes the elf-locks in foul sluttish hairs,
Which, once untangled, much misfortune bodes.

Romeo and Juliet (SHAKESPEARE.)

From the scene given above from *Romeo and Juliet* the reader will see that Mab was, in the popular fancy, employed to inspire men's brains with dreams, and Sir Walter Scott in *The Antiquary* assumes the same thing:

"I have a friend who is peculiarly favoured with visits from Queen Mab", he says, meaning that his friend was a great dreamer.

Titania, as we all know, was really the Queen of the Fairies, and the word "Queen", when used in connection with Mab, is not really queen at all, but *quén* or *cwén*, a saxon word for *woman* or *nurse*, and the Danish word *ellequinde* means female elf, not queen of elves. "Mab" in Welsh means baby. According to Prof. Morley, Mabinogion is the plural of the Welsh word Mabinogi, which means entertainment or instruction for the young, the word being derived from Mab, a Child, or Maban, a young child. *The Mabinogion*, the celebrated collection of Welsh romances, now preserved at Jesus College, Oxford, contains versions of three French Arthurian romances, two British tales, a history of Taliesin, and other matter.

Some people have erroneously supposed that Mabel and Amabel were one and the same name; but there is no true connection between them, Amabel being derived from Aimable, an old French name.

The name was not in use in England till after the time of Elizabeth, though very popular in Ireland. The roll-call of celebrated Mabels or Mabs is, as far as England is concerned, non-existent; but the name has become so popular with us during the last ten or fifteen years, that erelong there will doubtless be many celebrated "Mabels" to chronicle.

At present, even in literature, though "Mab" has been written of by Shakespeare, Ben Jonson, Drayton, Herrick, and Shelley, the "Mabels" are restricted to some unimportant novels and children's stories, with the exceptions perhaps of *Mabel Stanhope* by Kathleen O'Meara; *Mabel Vaughan* by Maria S. Cummins; and in poetry, Mabel in *Sam Green's Love*, by Frederick Langbridge; Mab in *L'Allegro*, by Milton, and certainly J. G. Whittier's graceful poem called *Mabel Martin: a Harvest Idyll*, which first appeared under the name of *The Witch's Daughter*. Of this we give a few short extracts below:

For Mabel Martin sat apart,
  And let the hay-mow's shadow fall
  Upon the loveliest face of all.

The school-boys jeered her as they passed,
  And when she sought the house of prayer,
  Her mother's curse pursued her there.

. . . . . .

That mother, poor and sick and lame,
  Who daily by the old armchair,
  Folded her withered hands in prayer:—

Who turned, in Salem's dreary jail,
  Her worn old Bible o'er and o'er
  When her dim eyes could see no more!

. . . . . .

And *she* was with us, living o'er again
  Her life in ours, despite of years and pain—
  The autumn brightness after latter rain.

Beautiful in her holy peace as one
  Who stands, at evening, when the work is done,
  Glorified in the setting sun!

Her memory makes our common landscape seem
  Fairer than any of which painters dream;
  Lights the brown hills and sings in every stream;

For she whose speech was always truth's pure gold
  Heard, not unpleased, its simple legends told,
  And loved with us the beautiful and old.

MADELINE, Magdalen. Unlike so many names whose beautiful signification is alone enough to account for their popularity, Magdalen or Madeline, with its contraction Maun, is not from its first meaning particularly attractive, or even appropriate to those dwelling in Europe.

Its true interpretation is "of Magdala", and the second name of the penitent in Holy Scripture was probably only given to distinguish her from the other Marys, with whom she has sometimes been confounded.

Mrs. Jameson, in her *Sacred and Legendary Art*, says that this question as to the identity of the Marys is open to discussion; but "where Origen and Chrysostom have ranged themselves on one side, and St. Clement and St. Gregory on the other, who may affirm anything positively? One can only in this, as in all other cases, speak to the best of one's belief. I fully believe, with the Eastern Church, that Mary of Bethany was a virtuous woman, and a distinct person from Mary Magdalene: or why, in her home of Bethany and in connection with Martha and Lazarus, should Mary never be called Mary Magdalene? We know that out of Mary Magdalene were cast seven devils, but whether she was indeed the woman who was a "sinner", I do not think Scripture has made so plain. But

I would say, as one has said who carefully studied the subject: "The woman who, under the name of Mary Magdalene—whether her name be rightfully or wrongfully bestowed—stands before us sanctified in the imagination and in the faith of the people in her combined character of sinner and saint, is a reality and not a fiction. Even if we would, we cannot do away with the associations inseparably connected with her name and her image".

The name Magdalen comes from the word *migdol*, which signifies "watch-tower", whence the name of the Decapolitan city Magdala, and of the Abyssinian Acropolis; but obviously in Europe it has been given in memory of the touching Bible narrative, or on account of its musical sound.

Its popularity was afterwards increased by the admiration felt in Roman Catholic countries for St. Mary Magdalen of Pazzi, who was born in Florence in 1566 and who was of noble parentage.

Catherine, not Mary, Magdalen had been the name given her at her birth, but she changed it to Mary Magdalen when she took the vows of the Carmelite Order, and entered the monastery of St. Fridian, near Florence, at the age of fifteen.

Her early piety, her humility, devotion, and sufferings, and her unwearied striving after a high ideal, in the face of many temptations, won for her the veneration of those who came in contact with her. At the age of thirty-one she was appointed Sub-Prioress of the House wherein she had passed so many years of her life, as a nun, and when she died of consumption, at the comparatively early age of forty-one, it was to the deep sorrow of those who knew her, whose hearts she had won by her patience under suffering.

The name Magdalen got transformed into Madeline, and the later form is now the more popular of the two in England ; it also contracted into Maudlin—and by this contraction the Oxford College, though always spelt Magdalen, is known.

No Oxford College presents a more dignified front to the world than does Magdalen, with its fine old trees, its deer-park, and above all its magnificent tower rising by the side of the Cherwell and above all surrounding objects.

The proportions of this tower are so perfect that it takes rank as one of the finest in the land.

Magdalen was Cardinal Wolsey's College, and some credit him with having designed the tower, but its architecture points to a somewhat earlier date. True to the original meaning of its name, watch-tower, the choir-boys of Magdalen College watch from the top of the tower for the dawn of each first May morning, and at five o'clock usher in the day with the singing of an anthem. An old custom which has been carried down to modern days.

There is also a Magdalen Hall at Oxford, and a Magdalen College at Cambridge.

In literature Dr. Hake has a poem called *Madeline*, and Keats made a Madeline the heroine in his poem *The Eve of St. Agnes*, considered by judges to be one of the finest efforts of his genius.

My Madeline! sweet dreamer! lovely bride!
Say, may I be for aye thy vassal blest?
Thy beauty's shield, heart-shaped and vermeil dyed?
Ah, silver shrine, here will I take my rest
After so many hours of toil and quest,
A famish'd pilgrim,—saved by miracle
Though I have found, I will not rob thy nest
Saving of thy sweet self; if thou think'st well
To trust, fair Madeline, to no rude infidel.

Mrs. Hemans also wrote *Madeline: a Domestic Tale.* Magdalen Murdochson is a character in *The Heart of Midlothian* by Sir Walter Scott; in Molière's drama *Les Précieuses Ridicules* one of the heroines is Madelon; and the heroine of Lord Lytton's novel *Eugene Aram* is a Madeline. In conclusion we quote from Lord Tennyson's beautiful little word-portrait of *Madeline.*

Smiling, frowning, evermore,
Thou art perfect in lovelore.
Revealings deep and clear are thine
Of wealthy smiles: but who may know
Whether smile or frown be fleeter?
Who may know?
Frowns perfect-sweet along the brow
Light-glooming over eyes divine,
Like little clouds sun-fringed, are thine,
Ever varying Madeline.

Thy smile and frown are not aloof
From one another,
Each to each is dearest brother
Hues of the silken sheeny woof
Momently shot into each other.
All the mystery is thine;
Smiling, frowning, evermore,
Thou art perfect in love-lore,
Ever varying Madeline.

MARCELLA, with its prototype Martial and its variants Marcius, Marcellus, Marcus, Mark, Martin, Martyn, Marcia, Marcellina, Marcelline, Marcelia, and Martina. This name is supposed to mean "disciplinarian", and is by some derived from *mas* = male, by others from Mars, Mavors or Mamers, the principal deity of the Latins, and particularly reverenced by them, as they regarded him as the father of Romulus, the founder of Rome.

One of the attributes of Mars being strength, the Romans, by emphasizing this, came to look upon him as the God of War.

In Greece, the Greek form of the name—Markos—has ever since the introduction of Christianity been very popular as the name of the Evangelist, and in the Venetian Republic, where St. Marco is looked upon as the patron Saint, Marco is one of the most common of all names.

In England we have the name Marcus, but our usual form is Mark, with its derivatives Martin and Martyn, and the feminine forms of Martine, Marcelia, Marcelline, Marcellina, and Marcella. In Ireland, Marcella is more frequently met with than in England, and Marceline is frequently found in France.

Marcius and Marcellus were common in ancient Rome as names belonging to a noble gens, whose women were called Marcia.

Not a few, too, of the heroes and heroines of the Early Christian Church bore the name in some one of its forms, as for example St. Marcellina, the eldest sister of St. Ambrose and Satyrus. Her father was a prefect of the

Gauls, but upon his death Marcellina with her mother and brothers removed to Rome, and Marcellina charged herself with the education of her brothers.

She inspired them with an ardent thirst for truth and goodness, and endeavoured constantly to impress upon their minds the futility and hollowness of noble birth when compared with that of noble living. She also would point out to her pupils the Socratic doctrine that "man's best knowledge was to know himself".

In A.D. 352 Marcellina assumed the veil, but, instead of entering a nunnery, she lived in a private house with only one companion. The date of Marcellina's death is not known exactly, but she survived her brother, St. Ambrose, for some time, and he died in 397.

In France the name became popularized through Marcella, a widow who was honoured by the friendship of St. Jerome.

A maiden of noble Roman birth, known as St. Martina, suffered martyrdom for the faith in the Imperial city; a chapel was afterwards consecrated to her memory, and in 1634 a new church was built in her honour by Pope Urban VIII.

Amongst men, too, the name has been nobly borne.

In A.D. 179 a Marcellus suffered martyrdom at Châlons, where a monastery and church were dedicated to him.

In A.D. 298 a second Marcellus laid down his life for his faith: he was a centurion in the legion of Trajan, then quartered in Spain, and declined to take part in sacrifices made to the Roman gods in honour of the Emperor Maximian's birthday. Throwing down his arms and his vine-branch (the sign of his office of Centurion), he declared that he could make no sacrifices, for he was a soldier in the army of Christ. Marcellus was arrested and cast into prison, and afterwards sent before Aurelian Agricolaus, who was then at Tangiers. By him he was sentenced to death, and was beheaded on October 30th, 298.

In the late third and early fourth century there was a Pope Marcellinus, afterwards canonized; and he was succeeded in the Papal Chair by St. Marcellus, who had been a priest under him: Marcellus occupied the Chair of St. Peter only for about a year and a half, being banished by the tyrant Maxentius for his severity in enforcing the canons of penance. In *The Duke of Milan* (by Massinger) the Duke refers to his wife thus:

> The phœnix of perfection ne'er was seen,
> But in my fair Marcelia.

In spite of its never having been a common woman's name in England, there are several instances of its occurrence in Literature. There is a Marcella in the early play of *Gorboduc*, by Thomas Norton and Lord Buckhurst, and it is sometimes even entitled *Marcella* ; a story treating of early Christianity by Mrs. Knevels (F. Eastwood) is called *Marcella* ; Mrs. Humphrey Ward has also written a *Marcella* ;

Marcellin de Peyras comes in *The Gold Mine, or The Miller of Grenoble*, by Stirling; whilst in *Don Quixote* Marcella is the name of a shepherdess; Marcellina appears in Beethoven's Opera *Fidelio*; and Marcello in Meyerbeer's opera *Les Huguenots*. There is a Marcellus in Shakespeare's *Hamlet*; and in Dibdin's "bibliographical romance", called *Bibliomania*, there is a Marcellus who is intended for Edmund Malone, the critic.

Young Chrysostome had virtue, sense,
  Renown, and manly grace
Yet all, alas! were no defence
  Against Marcella's face!
His love, that long had taken root,
  In doubt's cold bed was laid;
Where, she not warming it to shoot,
  The lovely plant decayed.

Had coy Marcella owned a soul
  Half beauteous as her eyes,
Her judgment had her soul controlled;
  And taught her how to prize.
But Providence, that formed the Fair
  In such a charming skin,
Their outside made their only care;
  And never looked within!
The Dirge of Chrysostome (THOMAS D'URFEY.)

MARGARET, MARJORIE, MAGGIE, PEGGY, META, MAY, DAISY, etc. The beautiful name of Margaret is one of the so-called Jewel Names, and is of Persian origin. Murwari means, in the Persian language, "pearl", or "child of light". The picturesque and fanciful Eastern mind conceived the idea that at night oysters rise to the surface of the water from the depths of the sea for the purpose of worshipping the moon, and, opening their shells, receive within them a drop of congealed dew, which is, by the moon's beams, transformed into a pearl, a realistic touch being given to the legend by the peculiar translucent colour of the pearl, so akin to that of the moon's, called by Dante "*la gran Margherita*".

Murwari became changed in Greek into "Margarites", and that in its turn, into Margaret, and, though of Eastern origin, it is in the West that the name has taken deepest root.

Combining, as it does, beauty of meaning with beauty of sound, the name has become popular throughout Europe. The French form of the name is Marguérite, with the abbreviation of Margot and Goton; the Italian forms are Margherita, Malgherita, and Rita, the German Margarethe, with its abbreviations of Gretchen and Grethel made so familiar to us all by Grimm. In the British Isles the forms, abbreviations, and diminutives seem almost endless, and include Margaret, Margaretha, Margery, Marjorie, Madge, Meg, Mysie, Maisie, Daisy, Maidie, Maggie, Peggy, Gritty, Meta, Meeta and May.

In Germany the name has almost become the symbol of a tender, trustful, and childlike nature, rich in womanly gentleness. For this no doubt Goethe's "Gretchen" is in part responsible, but long before Goethe or the creation of his brain was dreamt of, the "Pearl of Bohemia" and other saintly women had done far more than Goethe ever did to ensure its popularity.

Margaret of Bohemia—the Pearl—an ancestress of our own popular Princess of Wales, who lived in the twelfth century, was wedded to Waldemar, King of Denmark, and rapidly won the love and gratitude of the Danes, by her beauty, goodness and saintly life. The day after her marriage she petitioned the king, as a personal favour to herself, for the repeal of the plough-tax, which pressed heavily on the people, and she also begged for the release of all prisoners; to the end of her life she was constantly striving to ease suffering and relieve distress, so that in their grateful devotion the people christened her "Dagmar", "the mother of the Day".

Another Saint of the name was "Mild Margarete that was God's Maid", generally known as "the maid of Antioch", in Pisidia. It is said that Margaret was converted to Christianity by her nurse, that she was persecuted by her father who was an idolator, and that after enduring bravely many tortures she finally fell a victim to the sword. Her name occurs in the ancient Greek Calendars and in the Litany in the old Roman Order. Her name has become the symbol of innocence and faith. In a legend relating to her she is said to have been swallowed alive by a dragon, whose body was rent in twain by the power of her Christian faith, so that she issued thence unhurt. At Westminster, in Henry VII.'s Chapel, an image of St. Margaret may be seen holding a cross in her hand, whilst she stands on the dragon, to illustrate the power of Christianity over evil.

In reference to the first meaning of her name,

this Saint is often represented wearing a string of pearls, and holding daisies in her lap. Vida, one of the tutelar saints of Cremona, in Hungary, a great hymnologist, honoured St. Margaret with two hymns, and by their means her fame spread through the land; moreover two other Saints of the name, besides St. Margaret of Scotland, are associated with Hungary.

Margaret of Scotland was the daughter of the little English prince who had been sent into exile by Cnut, when that monarch seized the English throne. Brought up by the King of Hungary, he married the Queen of Hungary's sister, Agatha, and became the father of Edgar Outre-mer, or Aetheling, of Christina, a nun, and of Margaret. They were invited to return to England by their great-uncle Edward the Confessor, but upon his death and the death and defeat of Harold at Hastings, Edgar, unable to stand up against the tyranny of the Conqueror, fled from the country with his sister Margaret. Their ship was driven by storms on to the Scottish coast, and there the fugitives were kindly welcomed by King Malcolm, who firmly refused to surrender them to William; the rare beauty, prudence and wit of Margaret, together with her pure, unworldly character, won the heart of Malcolm. He married her, and as Queen of Scotland, and mother of three of the best kings Scotland ever had, Margaret's beneficent influence was of long duration. Malcolm himself, first led by his devotion to her, and admiration of her saintly life, became almost as saintly as she. Malcolm died at the siege of

Alnwick Castle and his good queen died four days later, November 16th, 1093. She was canonized in 1251.

Yet two more saints of the name are St. Margaret of Cortona, who after a dissipated youth led a penitential life and died in the odour of sanctity on February 23rd, 1297, and St. Margaret of England, who died in the Cistertian Nunnery of Seauve Benoite in 1193.

For some reason difficult to discover, the name is more common in Scotland, Ireland and the North of England than in the Southern Counties.

Our first English Margaret was a daughter of King Henry III., and since her time the name has occurred frequently amongst English princesses, and the fame of some of them rests on something more tangible than the accident of royal birth.

Margaret of Anjou, Queen of Henry VI., in 1448 founded the Lady Margaret Professorship of Divinity, at Cambridge; the nobles of her Court wore a daisy in her honour.

Margaret Beaufort, the mother of Henry VII., founded St. John's College and Christ's College, Cambridge.

Margaret, Countess of Richmond and mother of Henry VIII., in 1502 founded the Margaret Professorship of Divinity in the University of Oxford. This lady bore three white daisies on a green turf as her badge.

France can boast of Margaret of Valois, Queen of Navarre, authoress of the *Heptameron*, whom Francis I. called "La Maguérite des Marguérites" (The Pearl of Pearls), and of the beautiful and accomplished Margaret of Navarre, who married Henry IV. of France; whilst Norway has her Margaret too, the "Semiramis of the North" (1353-1412), so called because of her heroic qualities; she it was who made the name so popular in Scandinavia, with its abbreviation of Mette, Maret and Metelill.

Margaret Roper, the devoted daughter of Sir Thomas More, also deserves a place here. The present popular Queen of Italy is a Margaret.

Except the Professorships at Oxford and Cambridge, and St. Margaret's College, Glasgow, the name of Margaret has, unlike that of Mary, been bestowed upon few objects, with the notable exception of the Herb Margaret, or Daisy, so named because it generally first blooms somewhere about St. Margaret's Day, February 22nd. Chaucer tells us how Queen Alceste, who sacrificed her own life to save that of her husband, was tranformed into a daisy as a reward for her noble conduct. In France the flower is always called Marguérite, and in Germany Margarether-blume. There is also the plant known as Queen Margaret, or Chinese Star, and an apple known as the Margaret or Magdalen Apple.

In the matter of place-names Margaret has been more popular. There are three Margaret Rivers (W. Australia, S. Australia, Quebec), three Margaret Mountains (W. Australia, S. Australia, New South Wales), and town-names have been given after St. Margaret in all parts of the world. Our own Margate, St. Margaret's

Bay (which has counterparts in Nova Scotia and Newfoundland), and St. Margaret's Hope must not be forgotten.

The name has been occasionally borne by men. In literature the Margarets are countless, though the present writer knows of only one "Pearl", which is in Nathaniel Hawthorne's *Scarlet Letter.* A few are appended. In POETRY and the DRAMA : *The Miseries of Queen Margaret*, by Michael Drayton ; Peggy, in *The Gentle Shepherd*, by Allan Ramsay ; *Posthumous Fragments of Margaret Nicholson*, by Shelley ; *The Affliction of Margaret*, by Wordsworth ; *Meg Merrilies*, by Keats ; *Margaret*, by Tennyson ; Ladye Margaret, "the flower of Teviot", in *Lay of the Last Minstrel*, and *Proud Maisie is in the Wood*, both by Scott ; *Fair Margaret and Sweet William* (a ballad) ; *Fair Margaret's Misfortunes* (a ballad) ; *Margaret's Ghost*, by D. Mallet (1724) ; *Willie and May Margaret* (a ballad) ; *Peg-a-Ramsay*, alluded to in "Twelfth Night" (a ballad) ; *Peg of Limavaddy* (humorous), by Thackeray ; Margaretha, in *No Song no Supper*, by Hoare ; *Marguerite*, by Whittier ; Margaretha or Gretchen, in *Faust*, by Goethe ; Margaret, who declines Lord Lovel and remains faithful to her humble lover Tom Allworth, in *A New Way to Pay Old Debts*, by Massinger ; Marjorie, in *The Shoemaker's Holiday*, by Dekker ; Madge, in *A Tale of a Tub*, by Ben Jonson ; Margaret de Valois, in *The Massacre of Paris*, by Marlowe ; Margaret, wife of Vandunke the Burgomaster of Bruges, in *The Beggar's Bush*, by

Beaumont and Fletcher; Donna Margeritta, in *Rule a Wife and Have a Wife*, by the same; Margaret Simon, in *The Gold Mine or Miller of Grenoble*, by E. Stirling; Meesa, in *The Maid of Mariendorp*, by Sheridan Knowles; and Pegg Thrift, in *The Country Girl*, by Garrick. In FICTION: Meg Dods, in *St. Ronan's Well*, Madge Wildfire, insane daughter of Meg Murdochson, the Gipsy thief, in *The Heart of Midlothian*, Mysie, in *The Bride of Lammermoor*, Dame Margaret, in *The Betrothed*, Meg Merrilies, a mad woman, in *Guy Mannering*, Peggy, laundry-maid in the same, and Peggy, in *Old Mortality*, all by Sir Walter Scott; *The Trials of Margaret Lindsay*, by Prof. Wilson; Marguerite, in *St. Leon*, by William Godwin; Maggie Tulliver, in *The Mill on the Floss*, by "George Eliot"; Margaret Hales, in *North and South*, by Mrs. Gaskell; Maggy, the half-witted girl, in *Little Dorrit*, Meg, in *The Chimes*, both by Dickens.

MARTHA, with its English diminutive PATTY, like Mary, means "bitterness", and is generally assumed to have been originally the same name. In France the name is Marthe or Marthon, in Russia Marfa, in Germany it is the same as in England. Italy has Marta.

Martha has not enjoyed nearly so great a popularity as Mary, which, in some form or other, has graced every throne in Europe, whilst the royal Marthas have been confined to Russia. The name to us is typical of housewifely cares and thoughtfulness, for was not Martha, the elder sister of Mary Magdalen, "careful and troubled about many things", so that she had little time or thought to give to the more sentimental virtues? She seems, however, to have been amongst those who attended Christ during His Passion,and to have stood at the foot of His Cross.

According to the Roman Calendar, Martha went to France after the Crucifixion, introduced Christianity into that country, and died at Tarascon, in Provence; but so many legends have gathered round her name that it is very difficult to separate the wheat from the chaff.

In Christian art St. Martha is represented wearing a bunch of keys at her girdle and holding a jug of water, or a ladle, in her hand, and accompanied by a dragon.

In Ireland, where the name is very popular, it seems to have got confused with Meabhdh, or Meave, the Queen of the Fairies.

In literature Martha is not uncommon, and Sir Walter Scott alone has six examples of it —in *St. Ronan's Well*, *Rob Roy*, *Count Robert of Paris*, *The Fair Maid of Perth*, *Peveril of the Peak*, and Marthon in *Anne of Geierstein*; a Martha appears in Wycherley's play, *Love in a Wood*; in *Faust*, by Goethe, Margaret's friend is called Martha; Martha is one of the characters in *The Orphan of the Frozen Sea*, by Stirling; there is a Martha in Beaumont and Fletcher's play, *The Scornful Lady*; and two Operas have Marthas—Marthe in Guiraud's Opera *Piccolino*, and the Opera *Martha*, by Flotow. Patty Honeywood becomes Mr

Verdant Green's wife in the third part of "Cuthbert Bede's" famous story of undergraduate life at Oxford.

MARY, MIRIAM, MARIA, MARION, MAUREEN, MOLLY, POLLY. Our English name, Mary, which, judging by its frequency, is the most popular of all our girls' names, is of Hebrew origin, and is derived from Miriam.

The meaning is generally supposed to be "bitterness", from the Hebrew word *Mar*, or *Marah* (?), probably in allusion to the bondage of Israel when the first bearer of the name was born. Gesenius, however, traces the name back to *merî* = "stubbornness", whilst others have connected it with the titles "Myrrh of the Sea", "Lady of the Sea", "Star of the Sea". These explanations were all popular in the Middle Ages, and "Star of the Sea" is still the meaning most popularly attributed to it by Roman Catholics. It has also been suggested that the name is derived from that of the Nereid *Mara* [Odyssey xi. 326], whose name may express the phosphoric flashing of the surface of the sea, just as the same name *Maira* expresses the sparklings of the dog-star Sirius [Iliad xviii. 48].

Whatever the origin, the primary cause of its popularity undoubtedly is, that it was the name of the Virgin, and since it is to the place she holds in the Christian Church that women owe that improved position in the Christian world, which is one of the most distinguishing marks between the ancient and the modern worlds, for this, if for no other reason, those women who bear it, have good cause to rejoice in their name.

It grew to be a common name amongst Jewish women after the Captivity, and, under Greek influence, assumed the forms of Mariam and Mariamne.

The first bearer of the name mentioned in history, is Miriam, the Prophetess, the sister of Moses; then we have Mariamne, the wife of Herod; and, in the New Testament, besides Mary, the mother of Jesus, there is Mary, the wife of Cleophas, the mother of James, Jude, Joses and Simeon—supposed to be the sister of the Virgin; Mary Magdalene, or Mary of Magdala, and Mary of Bethany, etc.

In about the 4th Century A.D., St. Mary of Egypt is supposed to have lived—she who after many years of dissipation is said to have been suddenly brought to a sense of her sins and to have wandered in the desert in humiliation and repentance for forty-seven years. She is said to have died in 421.

Another saint of the name is St. Mary of Oignies, a native of Nivelle, in Brabant—she and her equally pious husband devoted their lives to tending the lepers in a part of their native town known as Villembroke. They were scoffed at and reviled, but nothing could turn them from their pious resolve. She died at the age of thirty-three in 1213.

In 1565 was born Mary of the Incarnation, who after the death of her husband Pierre Acarie, entered the order of the Discalced Carmelites. She died at Pontoise in 1618; and finally there is St. Mary Magdalen of Pazzi, born in 1566 of a noble Florentine family. She made a vow never to marry, when she was twelve years old, and at eighteen entered the Carmelite Monastery of Santa Maria degli Angeli, changing her name from Catherine to Mary Magdalen, and taking as her motto "To suffer or die". She died, after a life of devotion to duty, in 1607.

In A.D. 851 a girl called Maria (the Spanish form of the name) suffered martyrdom at the hands of the Moors, at Cordova, but until the time of the Crusades there are comparatively few examples of the name in the western world. After the Crusades, however, the name rapidly grew in popularity, and the roll-call of celebrated Marys, Marias, or Maries, has increased steadily in every Christian country, year after year, until now, when it is probably far longer than that of any other woman's name.

The increased respect in which the Virgin Mary has been held during the last three hundred years, in Roman Catholic countries, has led to such an increase in the use of the name, that its frequency has become proverbial: "Cercar [to seek] Maria in Ravenna" corresponds to our "to search for a needle in a bottle of hay" (Miss Yonge, *Christian Names*, p. 30), and the name is borne by men almost as frequently as by women. On the Continent some attribute ascribed to the Virgin is frequently attached to the name, so that we constantly come across Maria Assunta, Maria Annunciata, Maria de Dolores, Santamaria, and Maria Immacolato, but as far as I have been able to ascertain, this custom does not prevail in England.

In England the name was spelt after the French fashion—Marie—until the translation of the Bible into English introduced the form of Mary. Mary II. was the first Queen to adopt this mode of spelling, and our Latin form of Maria was introduced during the last century when all things classical appealed to the fashionable taste.

The names derived from Mary are numerous, and include the Spanish Mariana, the French Marionette, Marion, Marriette, Marat, and in English, Marian, Moll, Molly, Polly, Malkin, Mariott, Maryatt, Maro, the month from whom the Maronites (the remains of the Canaanites) take their name. In Scotland we have McMarry, McMurroch, McMurchie, Murchison, Murtoch, Maris, Marr, and from Mary-worship have also come the names of Ladyman and Toplady.

Maureen is another form — the Irish — of Mary.

The hour we parted,
When broken-hearted
You clung around me,
Maureen, aroo,
I swore I'd treasure,
Thro' pain and pleasure,
Thro' health and sickness,
My love for you.

. . .

The night is falling
And you are calling
The cattle homeward
With coaxing tone;

MARY

> In God's own keeping,
> Awake or sleeping,
> 'Tis now I leave you,
> Maureen, Mavrone!
>
> From *The Hour we Parted* (A. P. Graves.)

I have left the most usual abbreviation, *i.e.* May, to the last. Most of the Mays we know (and we all of us know some), really bear the name of Mary, and the month of May is often called "Mary's month", but the true origin of the name of the month is Maia, the Mother of Mercury, to whom, amongst the ancients, sacrifices used to be offered on the first day of this month—and like our Mistletoe at Christmas, which dates back to old Druidical times, our first of May celebrations, May Queens, and Jacks in the Green, now fast dying out, probably had their origin in festivals older than those of the Christian Church. As a surname, according to Mr Lower, the name of May is the old Scottish *maich*, Anglo-Saxon *moeg*, old English *mei*, meaning son-in-law, son, or some other relative. An island and a rivulet in Scotland, and a rivulet in Wales, bear the name, and there is a village of the name "Le May", in the Department of the Maine at Loire, France.

There is also the Anglo-Saxon word *moede*, moedewe, which we now call meadow.

The things and customs named after Mary are many, as for example Mariolatry, a term denoting the worship of the Virgin by Roman Catholics—from this in its turn is derived Marionettes—or puppets, small images of the Virgin being called in French Mariettes; Marotte is the name of the doll carried by court fools in the olden times. Mr. Charnock says that some derive the name of Marionettes from an Italian of the name of Marion, who introduced these puppets into France during the reign of Charles IX.; but the Italian's own name would have come from Marie in the first place too.

Marigold = Mary's gold, flower of the Virgin; Mariola, a shrine, or image of the Virgin; Mariengroschen, an old silver coin with an image of the Virgin on it, which first appeared in Goslar, also Mariengulden = 20 Mark; Marienthaler once existed in some places, and in Hungary, whose patron Saint is the Virgin, we find Marienducaten.

Amongst minerals Germans have Marienglas = Isingglas-stone; and in Zoology the Marienkäfer or Marienwurm = Lady-bird.

For botanical examples we have:

Marien-distel = St. May's Thistle; Marienschuh, lady's slipper (note how often their Marie is rendered in English by lady); Lady's Smock, Lady's Tresses, Our Lady's Hair, Maiden Hair, Lady's Bedstraw, Our Lady's Seal (Black Briony), Lady's Eardrop (Periwinkle).

Marion-fest = Lady day.

The places named after the Virgin are legion, all over the world; but the American Maryland was named by Lord Baltimore after Henrietta Maria, Queen of Charles I.; our 7th Dragoon Guards were nicknamed "the Virgin Mary's Body-guard", after serving under Maria Theresa in Austria. Neither does Mary-le-bone church come from Marie-la-bonne, as many suppose, but from St. Mary-at-the Bourne (Tyburn).

Of course the much beloved exclamation of the Elizabethan dramatists, "Marry", is a corruption of "By St. Mary"; it occurs even earlier, in Chaucer

> Ye? quod the preest, ye, sire, and wol ye so?
> Mary thereof I pray you hertily.

> Send thee my lanthorn, quotha! Marry
> I'll see thee hang'd first.
>
> *Waggoners' dialogue* in *'King Henry V.*
> (SHAKESPEARE.)

Mary Anne is a slang name for the Guillotine, and also the generic name for a secret Republican Society in France.

The Marys whose heads have worn a crown are many, and of these several have been exceptionally famous. In 1370 there was born to King Louis or Ludwig I. of Hungary, a daughter who received the name of Mary. She wedded one Sigesmund of Brandenburg, who in his turn became King, jointly with his wife King Mary, who succeeded to her father's throne. Their rule was marked by its severity. (The Hungarians object to the title *Queen*, so that all women who have ascended their throne have been entitled *King*). King Mary of Hungary ultimately fell into the hands of her rival, the King of Naples, and died in 1395. Another royal Mary was Queen Mary of Hungary, daughter of Philip I. of Castile. She married King Ludwig or Louis II., and after his death in 1526, fled to Vienna; in 1530 she was appointed by her brother the Emperor Charles, Regent of the Netherlands.

Several Queens of the name have sat on the Spanish throne: the best known of these in England is perhaps Maria Christina, who in 1829 became the fourth wife of Ferdinand VII. Through her influence the Pragmatic Sanction (1830) was agreed to, by which females became eligible for the Spanish throne, thus practically disinheriting the King's brother, Don Carlos. After the death of Ferdinand (1833) Maria Christina was appointed Regent during the minority of her daughter Isabella. She died in 1873. The present Queen Regent of Spain is also a Maria, the daughter of the Archduke Karl Ferdinand of Austria.

In Portugal we find Maria II. da Gloria (born 1819), who succeeded to her grandfather's throne, upon the resignation of her father, in 1834.

In France, in pondering over the long line of Marys, our attention is at once arrested by the fierce Marie de Medicis (born 1573) who was crowned Queen just one day before the murder of her husband Henry of Navarre (1610). She became Queen Regent of France during the minority of Louis XIII., afterwards known as the Just.

Maria Theresa, a Spanish princess, became in 1660, the wife of Louis XIV., the Great Dieudonné. She died in 1683.

Who does not know of Marie Antoinette, one of the most tragic characters in all modern history! Her faults may have been great as a Queen: on the wife, mother and woman they brought down most frightful retribution—and we forgive the heartless follies of her youth in admiration of the courage with which she bore her trials, and met her death October 16th, 1793.

The second wife of Napoleon Buonaparte was Marie Thérèse of Savoy, and the Queen of King Louis-Philippe was Maria-Amelia *La Santa.* She died in 1866.

One other Queen there was who by her beauty, follies, and tragic end inevitably challenges comparison with Marie-Antoinette of France. We mean Mary, Queen of Scots.

We here in England have had our Queen Marys too, *e.g.*, Mary VI., daughter of Henry VIII., whose fierce zeal in the Roman Catholic cause, egged on doubtless by the bitter memories of her mother's wrongs at the hands of Protestant King Hal, caused the flame of religious persecution to be relighted throughout the land, and whose name has thus become a byeword for religious intolerance and cruelty; Mary of Modena, the second wife of James II.—and lastly, Good Queen Mary, who ascended the English throne (1689) with her husband William III.

Looking away from thrones, and among the people, Marys may be found gracing every walk of life, but one curious little coincidence is that the three women who have made their mark in female mathematics and philosophy have all borne the name of Mary, *i.e.*, Marie Gaetano Agnesi, a Milanese, born in 1718, Lauria Maria Bassi (1711-1778), who was created Doctor of Philosophy and held a Professor's chair at the University of Bologna, and Mary Somerville (1770-1872).

MARY

The following is a very imperfect list of the poems or books addressed to Marys, or having Marys amongst their characters:

The Ballad of Maid Marian and Robert Hood; *Mary Ambree*, a ballad describing "the valorous acts performed at Gaunt by the brave bonnie lass Mary Ambree, who in revenge of her lover's death (Sir John Major) did play her part most gallantly"; *Arcadia*, written in honour of Mary Sidney, Countess of Pembroke, by her brother Sir Philip Sidney; Mary Ashburton, heroine in *Hyperion* by Longfellow; *Mary, I believe thee true* by Moore; *To Mary in Heaven*, *Highland Mary*, *Mary Morrison*, *Mary Queen of Scot's Lament on the return of Spring*, all by Robert Burns; *Mary's Dream* by John Lowe; Mary Trevellyn, in *Amours de Voyage* by Clough; *To Mary* by Cowper; *Mariana; Mariana in the South* by Tennyson; *Mary the Maid of the Inn* by Southey; May, the girl who married the old Lombard Baron in *The Canterbury Tales* by Chaucer; *Rhyme of the Duchess Mary* by Elizabeth Browning; *May Colvin* (a ballad); *May Collean* (a ballad); *Baby May* by W. C. Bennett; *Molly Mog: or the Fair Maid of the Inn* by John Gay; *Oh Mary Call the Cattle Home* in *The Sands of Dee* by Charles Kingsley; *Mariane* by Whittier; *Willie and May Margaret* (a ballad); and *Marianne's Dream: to Mary Shelley* by Percy B. Shelley. In DRAMA we have: *The Life and Repentance of Marie Magdalene* by Lewis Wager (1567); *Marie Magdalene's Funerale Teares* by Robert Southwell (1594); *Marian the Fair Queen of Jewry* by Lady Elizabeth Carew; *Marie Stuart* by Schiller; *Mary Stuart* by J. Haynes; The "Mermaid" in *A Midsummer Night's Dream* is intended for Mary Queen of Scots; Mary in *Monsier Thomas* by Beaumont and Fletcher; *Mary Tudor* by Victor Hugo; *Queen Mary* by Tennyson; *Queen Mary* by Aubrey de Vere; Marie Beaumarchais in *Clavigo*, and Marie in *Götz von Berlichingen* both by Goethe; Mariana, in *Measure for Measure*, Mariane, in *All's well that ends Well*, and Maria, in *Twelfth Night*, all by Shakespeare; and Maria, in *School for Scandal* by R. B. Sheridan; *Maureen, Maureen* is the title of a lyric by A. P. Graves.

MATILDA, MAUD: see Hilda.

MERCY is one of the English "abstract virtue" names, which were so much in vogue in Puritan times, and, which having become hereditary in many families, is still frequently met with in this country. Its form, as a "pet-name", is Merry.

Whene'er I go, or whatsoe'er befalls
Me in mine age, or foreign funerals,
This blessing I will leave thee, ere I go:
Prosper thy basket and therein thy dough.
Feed on the paste of filberts, or else knead
And bake the flour of amber for thy bread.
Balm may thy trees drop, and thy springs run oil,
And everlasting harvest crown thy soil!
These I but wish for; but thyself shall see
The blessing fall in mellow times on thee.

To my dearest sister, M. Mercy Herrick (HERRICK.)

META: see MARGARET.

MILDRED. This extremely pretty old Anglo-Saxon name had until lately almost fallen into disuse amongst us. The present revival of its popularity is doubtless to be attributed to its musical sound, its supposed meaning and the modern love of reverting to our old Anglo-Saxon names. The meaning generally attributed to it is "one that is gentle of speech", but this is not the true meaning, for though *mild* means mild in Anglo-Saxon and German, *red* is always a masculine termination in Anglo-Saxon names. Furthermore the original name was Mildthryth: now thryth means commanding or threatening, so that the true meaning of the name is "one who is gently or mildly strict".

Merowald, King of Mercia, evidently considered that gentleness should form a large ingredient in a woman's nature, for which we will in no wise quarrel with him, and for which indeed he merits our respect, always supposing that he thought of the strict meaning of the names he bestowed upon his daughters.

He had three daughters and one son, and all the daughters' names began with *mild*, namely, Milburga or Mildburh, Mildgyth or Mildgithe, and Mildred or Mildthryth, whilst he called his son Mervin or Mervyn, signifying "sea-hill" —a Keltic name.

Whether influenced and inspired by their names or not, I cannot say; but all King Merowald's, or Merwald's, daughters became nuns, and two of them were canonised, Milburg and Mildred. They came, indeed, of a family of Saints, and through their mother Eormenburga were the grand-daughters of Queen Emma, several of whose children were canonised—amongst them

St. Ethered, St. Ethelbright and St. Eormenbert. It is with Mildred that we are here concerned, but of her life's history we have only slight outlines and that we may learn what we can of her we must go back a generation, to the days of her great-uncle Egbert, King of the English. Now it is said of this king that he caused his two nephews Ethelred and Ethelbright to be secretly murdered, employing a Count Thunor as his agent in the dastardly act. Count Thunor, after their murder, buried the bodies of the murdered Princes beneath the King's throne in the royal palace of Estria.

Thereafter, the king, whose guilty conscience made him see everything with a distorted vision, was one day terrified by beholding something that was probably no more than an ordinary sunbeam, but which he believed to be a miraculous ray of light that darted direct from heaven on to the grave. "Conscience doth make cowards of us all"—in early Anglo-Saxon days just as now—so, urged to restitution by his guilty terror, Egbert sent for the sister of his victims, his niece Eormenburga, Queen of Mercia, and payed over to her "forty-eight ploughs of land" as *weregild*, which was the fine imposed by the laws of England to be payed by a murderer to the relatives of the murdered. These forty-eight ploughs of land Queen Eormenburga devoted to the founding of a monastery, wherein the repose of the souls of the murdered Princes was to be prayed for. The King himself aided much in the foundation of the monastery, hoping no doubt to thereby further ease his guilty soul. This monastery was called the Menstrey, or Minstre, and was situated in the Isle of Thanet, where the village of Minster near Ramsgate now stands.

Eormenburga sent her daughter Mildred over to France, to the Abbey of Chelles, where she took the veil, and was duly trained in all religious exercises.

Upon Mildred's return to England, she was appointed first Abbess of her mother's newly founded Monastery of Minstre, St. Theodorus, Archbishop of Canterbury, conducting the installation service, and seventy maidens joining the community on the same occasion.

Saint Mildred bore herself with gentleness and humility towards those over whom she had been appointed to rule, and by her own holy life and example pointed them the way to a virtuous life. After a lingering and painful illness, Saint Mildred died at the close of the seventh century.

The monastery over which her gentle spirit had presided was on several occasions plundered by the Danes, and the nuns and clerks murdered; notably in 980 and 1011; after the last date the monastery ceased to be occupied by any but a few secular priests, and in 1033 Saint Mildred's remains were transferred thence to the monastery of St. Austin's at Canterbury, where, according to William of Malmesbury, they were venerated above all other relics, and where, according to the same authority, many miracles were wrought by them.

Two churches in London are dedicated to

Saint Mildred, one in Bread Street (1170), the other in the Poultry (1247).

A daughter of Lord Burleigh was named Mildred, and amongst rising lady artists of the present day Miss Mildred Butler, A.R.W.S., may be mentioned.

The name is variously spelt Mildred, Mildreda and Mildrid.

MILICENT, Melita, Melissa, Melusine. This name has come down to us from the remote past. In the days when the Sagas and Niebelungen stories seemed living realities, this name was already a household word. Mr. Baring-Gould, in his *Curious Myths of the Middle Ages*, tells us that amongst the Carthaginians, Mylitta, the goddess of moisture, was worshipped and regarded as a universal mother and source of life: her servants were called Melitta, Meleto, Milto, and Miletia. In Greece the priestesses of Demeter were called Melissae, and the name was probably a corruption of the names of the servants of Mylitta. He adds that "the name Melissa was probably introduced into Gaul by the Phœcian colony at Massilia, the modern Marseilles, and passed into the popular mythology of the Gallic Kelts as the title of nymphs, till it was finally appropriated by the Melusina of romance".

Melusina changed gradually into Melisenda and Melicerte, and then, in England, into Melisent, Melecent, Milicent, and Millicent. In Spain it is Melisenda.

Some attempts have been made to connect the name with bees and honey (Latin *mel*), but this is probably incorrect; and our Milicents may regard themselves as the true descendants of the lovely Melusina of romance. The original name of Melusine, or Melusina, is still occasionally met with, not only in England, but also in France and Germany.

From Love, from angry Love's inclement reign
  I pass awhile to Friendship's equal skies;
Thou, generous Maid! reliev'st my partial pain,
  And cheer'st the victim of another's eyes.

'Tis thou, Melissa, thou deserv'st my care;
  How can my will and reason disagree?
How can my passion live beneath despair?
  How can my bosom sigh for aught but thee?

Ah! dear Melissa! pleased with thee to rove,
  My soul has yet survived its dreariest time;
Ill can I bear the various clime of Love!
  Love is a pleasing, but a various clime.

To Melissa, his Friend (SHENSTONE.)

The old romance tells us how, one day, Count Emmerick of Poitou hunted boars, accompanied by a large retinue, from which he and one Raymond, a son of Count de la Forêt, got accidentally parted. Suddenly a boar burst out upon them, and Raymond, in endeavouring to strike the brute, struck the Count instead, and slew him. In despair at this evil chance, Raymond wandered through the forest until his steps were suddenly arrested by the sight of three fair young maidens. One of them came up to him, and inquired the cause of his evident distress, and after some hesitation he opened his heart to her. They talked until daybreak, and before they parted had plighted their troth to one another.

One stipulation and only one did the lady make, and that was that her Saturdays should be spent in an absolute seclusion upon which not even her husband was to intrude. With this one condition Raymond readily complied. Many children were born to them, and, though each child suffered from some personal deformity, Melusina and Raymond dwelt together in mutual love.

One Saturday, however, the old Count de la Forêt suddenly asked for his daughter-in-law, and upon Raymond explaining that it was the day on which none might intrude upon her privacy, the old Count hinted at dark stories that were told of her. Raymond, in a fit of unreasoning suspicion and jealousy, rushed to his wife's apartments, and looking through a keyhole beheld his beautiful Melusina in her bath with her lower extremities transformed into the tail of an enormous fish or serpent. In a moment of impatience, Raymond allowed it to transpire that he knew of Melusina's secret, whereupon she uttered a shriek of despair, and, conjuring him to take care of their motherless children, vanished from his sight forever, though for long afterwards she appeared in spirit form at night and hovered round her husband and her children.

Melita was the old name for Malta, and is sometimes given to girls who happen to be born there.

In English literature the name Milicent occurs in *The City Madame* by Massinger, and in *Sir Martin Mar-All*, by Dryden ; and Melissa in the *Ode to Aurora on Melissa's Birthday* by Thomas Blacklock, and in *Secret Love, or the Maiden Queen* by Dryden.

Back started she, and turning round we saw
The Lady Blanche's daughter where she stood,
Melissa with her hand upon the lock,
A rosy blonde, and in a college gown,
That clad her like an April daffodilly
(Her mother's colour) with her lips apart,
And all her thoughts as fair within her eyes,
As bottom agates seen to wave and float
In crystal currents of clear morning seas.

The Princess (TENNYSON.)

MILLIE: see EMILY.

MINNIE is generally used, in England, a a diminutive of Wilhelmina, and in Ireland as a diminutive of Mary; but it has a real and distinct existence and a special meaning of its own, which is "held in memory" or "beloved". The old German singers, called troubadours and trouvères in France, were called "Minnesingers" in that country where the forms Minne and Minna are still common.

Art thou weary, little Minnie?
  Lay thy head upon my knee:
It makes the old man's heart rejoice
  Thy sunny face to see.
Well may the aged falter,
  Who tread life's rugged way,
When even little Minnie
  Grows weary of her play.

. . . . .

Good-night, my little Minnie!
  You're weary now I know:—
Yes, twine your arms around me,
  And kiss me ere you go;

Then hie thee to thy chamber—
Another day is gone;
Good-night, my precious Minnie!
God bless thee, little one!

(ANON.)

MIRANDA is an English name derived from the Latin and meaning "admired", and has been rendered famous by Shakespeare's choice of it for his famous heroine in *The Tempest*:

Admired Miranda!
Indeed the top of admiration! worth
What's dearest to the world! Full many a lady
I have eyed with best regard and many a time
The harmony of their tongues hath into bondage
Brought my too diligent ear: for several virtues
Have I liked several women; never any
With so full soul, but some defect in her
Did quarrel with the noblest grace she owed
And put it to the foil: but you, O you,
So perfect and so peerless, are created
Of every creature's best!

The Tempest (SHAKESPEARE.)

MIRIAM: see MARY.

MONA is the Latinised form of the British word *môn-au*, which means "lonely" or "remote"; and was the name given by the Romans to the Isle of Anglesea, as well as to the Isle of Man.

There once lived a maid in Mona's fair Isle,
Whose sweet face was never lit up by a smile;
She mournfully sighed whilst others were gay,
And seemed to grow sadder as years passed away.

The Fair Maid of Mona's Isle (ROWLANDS.)

Mona is the title of a pleasant Irish novel by Miss Alice Clowes.

MONICA. The origin of this name is doubtful, though it is generally supposed to signify "alone" or "dwelling alone". It has never been common, but has of late gained in popularity, especially amongst members of the High Church party, and Roman Catholics. Some suppose the name to be derived from *Moneo* = I advise or warn. Moncha is the Irish, Monique the French, form of the name.

Such popularity as it enjoys is largely due to its having been the name of the great St. Augustine's mother, who was remarkable for her patience and piety, and to whose influence the conversion of her famous son to Christianity was in great part due. Mrs. Lucy Walford has given the title *The Mischief of Monica* to one of her novels.

MURIEL, Myra, Myrrha. The pretty old English name of Muriel, Meriel, Myra, or Mira, Myrtilla, Myrrha, meaning perfumed, was originally derived from the Greek *muron*, any sweet juice distilling from plants and used for unguents or perfumes, *muron* itself being derived by the ancients from *muro* = to flow or trickle, or, according to Athenæus, from *murra* = the oil of myrrh, though the word is probably of Oriental origin—perhaps connected with the Hebrew *môr*. The word is of not uncommon occurrence in Greek literature, and even enters into a proverbial saying, "*Sweet* oil on lentils", meaning "Pains thrown away".

Met with in old English registers and amongst our old song writers, it had practically sunk into disuse until quite recent years ; but is now surely and deservedly gaining popularity. A fresh impetus was first given to Muriel probably by Miss Dinah Muloch's (Mrs. Craik's) popular book *John Halifax, Gentleman*—where the little blind heroine has the name of Muriel, "Muriel —little unconscious, cooing dove" ! . . . "Yes, those pretty baby eyes were dark—quite dark. There was nothing painful or unnatural in their look, save, perhaps, the blankness of gaze which I have before noticed. . . . She never had seen—never would see—in this world". . . .

"My father sighed, 'Give me thy child for a minute'. . . . God bless this little one ! Ay, and she shall be blessed". . . .

"If I could find a name to describe that child, it would not be the one her happy mother gave her at her birth, but one more sacred, more tender. She was better than Joy—she was embodied Peace.

"Her motions were slow and tranquil—her voice soft—every expression of her little face extraordinarily serene. Whether creeping about the house, with a footfall silent as snow, or sitting among us, either knitting busily at her father's knee, or listening to his talk and the children's play, everywhere and always, Muriel was the same. No one ever saw her angry, restless, or sad. The soft dark calm in which she lived seemed never broken by the troubles of this our troublous world. She was as I have said, from her very babyhood a living peace".

Bright Mira Meyrick, in *Daniel Deronda*,

brought the name of Myra into prominence again.

The first recorded Myrrha was she who in the Greek legend is said to have been enamoured of her own father, Cinyras, King of Cyprus, who, when he became aware of his daughter's feelings, was so enraged, that he attempted to stab her, and she, fleeing into Arabia from her father's wrath, and praying to the gods for protection, was there turned into a myrrh, or myrtle tree. Out of the branches of this tree sprang beautiful Adonis, the beloved of Aphrodite (Venus). Adonis died while yet a youth, wounded by a boar whilst out hunting, and Aphrodite, inconsolable, made anemonies grow out of his blood. Adonis (= lord) was in truth a Syrian god of nature, a symbol of vegetation, which, springing forth each year, after a brief period of activity always dies again.

The myth was celebrated by women in a yearly Feast of Adonis, which, first held in Byblos in Syria, travelled by way of Cyprus to Asia Minor and Greece, thence passed into Egypt, and finally to Rome. When, after the autumn rain, the waters of the river Adonis by Byblos were turned red by the soil washed down from the hills, they were said to be stained by the blood of Adonis slain by the boar, and thereupon the women sallied forth in search of him, and finding some body declared it to be that of the slain Adonis, and performed funeral rites over the corpse. The manner of celebrating the festival varied according to the place where it was held.

Myrtle is the emblem of fertility and purity, and in Germany and one or two other places is regarded as the proper plant for the bridal wreath in spite of its being also associated with sorrow and war, and in mediæval times awarded as a prize to the brave.

The sign of peace who first displays
The olive wreath possesses;
The lover with the myrtle sprays
Adorns his crisped tresses.

says Michael Drayton in his *Muses' Elysium*.

In Somersetshire a flowering myrtle is regarded as the greatest acquisition to a house, and there is a popular saying concerning it, "water it every morning, and be proud of it; for it is the luckiest plant to have in your window. To get the plant to grow (which is often a most difficult matter), you should spread the tail or skirt of your dress when planting the slip, and *look proud*".

Whilst the Romans strewed roses on the graves of those they loved, the Greeks preferred the myrtle, and if none were used it was looked upon as matter for complaint. One of the old Greek writers lamented that the tomb of Agamemnon had never been adorned with the much-prized plant:

With no libations, nor with myrtle-boughs
Were my dear father's manes gratified.

There are two towns of the name of Myra in Asia Minor.

Lord Byron in his drama *Sardanapalus* introduced an Ionian slave-girl, named Myrrha, as the heroine. The character is well sustained —dignified and impassioned, but not overdrawn.

A LOVER'S DAY AND NIGHT.

Bright meteor of day,
For me in Thetis' bowers for ever stay:
Night, to this flowery globe
Ne'er show for me thy star-embroider'd robe;
My night, my day, do not proceed from you,
But hang on Mira's brow;

(WILLIAM DRUMMOND, of Hawthornden.)

I, with whose colours Myra drest her head,
I, that wore posies of her own hand-making,
I, that mine own name in the chimnies read,
By Myra finely wrought ere I was waking,
Must I look on, in hope time coming may
With change bring back my turn again to play?

(LORD BROOKE.)

Robert Herrick has a sonnet to *Myrrha, Hard-Hearted*. The varieties of this name are, Muriel, Mira, Meriel, Myrrha, Myrtah, Myra, Myrrhene, and Myrtle.

Miss Amelie Rives has recently published a novel called *Meriel: a Love Story*; and Dean Stubbs has a poem *Meriel* in his collection entitled *The Conscience and other Poems*. Myrtilla occurs in Cibber's *The Provoked Husband*, and in Massinger's *The Guardian*; Mira in a short poem by Drummond of Hawthornden, called *Eurymedon's Praise of Mira*, and again in his *Lover's Day and Night*.

MYRRHA, MIRA: see MURIEL.

MYSIE: see MARGARET.

NAOMI, one of the most beautiful of all Hebrew women's names, means "my pleasant one". It was the name of the wife of Elimelech, the mother-in-law of Ruth, who, when her husband and two sons were dead, returned to her own country and people, and took Ruth, the daughter-in-law who was "better to her" than "seven sons", with her. When a son was born to Ruth and Boaz, Naomi took the child "and laid it in her bosom, and became nurse to it". Considering its beauty and the pathetic Bible story attaching to it, it is wonderful that the name has not been more popular.

It has never been widely adopted either in everyday life or in literature. Though Mrs. Webb has written a story dealing with Rome and the Fall of Jerusalem, which she has called *Naomi*, and which has enjoyed considerable popularity; and the Rev. S. Baring-Gould has also given *Naomi* as a title to one of his tales.

In Coleridge's tragedy *Remorse* the name occurs; but there it is that of a man.

NELLIE: see HELEN.

NESTA: see AGNES.

NORA(H), HONOR, HONORIA. This name is a Latin one, and comes from *honos* = honour. *Honos* and *Virtus* were the Latin personifications of "honour" and "warlike courage". The great Marcus Marcellus, he who in 212 B.C. conquered Syracuse, added a shrine to Virtus to that already erected to Honos, placing them both in the same building, which he adorned with masterpieces of Greek statuary taken by him from Syracuse. In 101 B.C. Marius built a second temple to Honos and Virtus with the proceeds of the booty taken in the Cimbrian War. Both Honos and Virtus are on coins represented by youthful figures with long hair, Honos with a wreath of bay-leaves and a cornucopia, and Virtus with an elaborately ornamented helmet.

Though Honorius was a Roman name there are not many historical instances of its use. It was certainly one of the names borne by the father of Theodosius the Great, and also conferred upon Theodosius's less worthy son, who succeeded him on the throne, and who was the last of the true Roman Emperors.

The Emperor Honorius did not live up to his name, for, though he was not a vicious man, neither was he a bold one, nor one in any way calculated to win honour or renown. He was of a modest, timid nature, and quite unfit for the high position he was called upon to fill. Any conquests made during his reign were due to the skill of his generals, and, instead of being himself a leader of men, he allowed himself to be ruled by those who took advantage of his indolence.

It was under Honorius and his brother Arcadius that the Roman Empire became divided into two, those who succeeded Honorius and had their seat of government at Rome being called the Emperors of the West, those who succeeded Arcadius and dwelt in Constantinople being called Emperors of the Eastern Roman Empire.

Neither the character of Honorius, nor that of his cousin Justa Grata Honoria, was calculated to render the name they bore very popular, but in spite of them, and for the sake of its own intrinsic merits, it has never under any of its forms quite fallen into disuse, and the pretty Irish form of Nora or Norah has never been more popular than now.

Moreover, there have been some bishops, and at least one female Saint, Saint Honorine, slain during an invasion by the Danes, who have done honour to the name. Honor, Honora, Honoria, Nora and Norah occur oftenest in England, whilst Honorine is popular in France, though the Welsh Ynyr has fallen out of favour in the Principality.

Saint Honoratus, or Saint Honoré, who subsequently became Archbishop of Arles, was a member of a Roman Consular family, and a learned man. He and his brother Venantius, both desired earnestly to join the Christian Church, but their pagan father, who was devotedly attached to them, constantly put obstacles in their way. At last the brothers left their native land, and sailed for Greece, accompanied by a hermit as their director. Venantius, however, died shortly after landing, and Honoratus became so ill that he was forced to return to his own country. There he at first led the life of a hermit amongst the mountains near Frejus, but afterwards settled on the small island of Lerins, now called St. Honoré after him. Here, in about the year 400 he founded a monastery, which afterwards became famous. In it some lived together, whilst others were isolated in separate cells as anchorets.

This Community as a whole is said to have

been conspicuous for its internal harmony, its charity, and its devotion.

In 426 Saint Honoratus was, against his own wish, created Archbishop of Arles, and died three years later from exhaustion caused by overwork and the severity of the austerities he had imposed upon himself.

St. Hilary, his kinsman and successor, tells us that when Saint Honoratus first landed on the island of Lerins, he found a desert, rendered almost uninhabitable by reason of the swarms of serpents with which it was infested; but that, after the Saint had settled there, the serpents soon vanished and the sterile country began to "blossom as the rose". Hence it is that in religious art this Saint is represented as expelling serpents with his pastoral staff.

Saint Honoratus is also said to have repeated the miracle performed by Moses, and to have brought forth water from a rock, when he discovered that Lerins was deficient in that element. The rhyme

Saint Honoré
Dans sa chapelle
Avec sa pelle
Est honoré.

refers to the tradition that, when his old nurse heard that he had been made a bishop, she was so amazed that she exclaimed "I don't believe it, I don't believe it!"; and sticking a piece of peel which she held in her hand, into the ground, added "when that takes root I will believe that my boy is made a bishop", and forthwith from that piece of peel a mulberry tree full of leaves and fruit sprang up.

Worthy Honora, as you have begun
In Virtue's spotless school, so forward run;
Pursue that nobleness and chaste desire
You ever had; burn in that holy fire;
And a white martyr to fair memory
Give up your name, unsoil'd of infamy.
The Loyal Subject (BEAUMONT and FLETCHER.)

In literature the name does not occur often, but there are examples, as for example a play by James Shirley (1594-1666) called *Honoria and Mammon*; Honora, daughter of General Archas and sister to Viola, in *The Loyal Subject* by Beaumont and Fletcher (1618); Mistress Honor, waiting maid to Sophie Western in Henry Fielding's novel *Tom Jones*; Honoria in John Dryden's poem, *Theodore and Honoria*, a fair but haughty dame, the beloved of Theodore of Ravenna. Honoria "hated him" and alas! "the more he loved, the more she disdained", until haunted by a vision (which appeared to her in a dream) of Guido Cavalcanti hunting a girl with mastiffs for despising his love. This poor girl was doomed to suffer this same torture one year for every month that she had resisted Cavalcanti's love, being torn to pieces, disembowelled, and restored to life again every Friday. This vision so appalled Honoria that she resolved to accept the addresses of Theodore. The tale was taken by Dryden from Boccaccio's *Decameron*.

Nora is the name of one of the characters in Mr. A. P. Graves's little poem entitled *Loobeen*, and J. G. Whittier has given the name of Norah in his poem *Kathleen* as that of the person to whom he tells the tale:

> O Norah, lay your basket down,
> And rest your weary hand,
> And come and hear me sing a song
> Of our old Ireland.

In conclusion we append some lines from Mr. Graves's *The Girl with the Cows*. In this poem Nora is the heroine, and an Honor also plays a part.

> O the happiest orphan that ever was seen,
> Was Nora Maguire at the age of eighteen;
> Her father and mother both died at her birth,
> So grief for their sakes didn't trouble her mirth.
> Nora Maguire was the flower of the girls,
> Wid her laughin' blue eyes and and her sunny bright curls,
> Wid her mouth's merry dimple, her head's purty poise,
> And a foot that played puck right and left wid the boys;
> Yes! her looks were a fortun'; yet cur'ous to tell
> Sweet Nora Maguire was an heiress as well,
> For her father had left his dear child at his death,
> Half a hundred of cows at the side of the heath,
> . . . .
> When who should come hurryin' down the boreen
> But Honor O'Connor dressed out like a Queen,
> Wid her hair in one wonderful plait, and upon it—
> Like a bird on its nest—a sweet bit of a bonnet—
> And a green sash that showed her fine figure for'nint,
> And flouncin' behind her, the beautif'lest print,
> Folded into her hand, just enough for a hint
> Of as tidy an ankle as ever set step—

OLGA is a Russian name, which some consider to be the Russian form of the old Teutonic name Aldegonda, meaning "noble war"; whilst others hold that it is derived from the Greek name Helena; and a third school believe it to be a derivative of *oleg*, meaning "holy". It has in recent years taken hold of the English fancy, and often been introduced amongst us.

OLIVE, Olivia. There is a legend that Minerva and Neptune had a dispute. Both deities wished to found a city on the same spot; and, appealing to Jove, the chief of the gods decreed, that whichever would undertake to bestow the most useful gift on the future inhabitants of the contemplated city, should be granted the privilege of founding it. Neptune at once struck the earth with his trident and forth sprang a war-horse: but Minerva produced an Olive-tree, the emblem of peace: Jove awarded Minerva the coveted favour and she became the patron goddess of Athens, and the Olive became the emblem of that city.

> To whom the heavens in thy maturity
> Adjudged an Olive-branch and Laurel crown,
> As likely to be blessed in peace and war.

The *Oliva* or Olive, has for ages been looked upon as the symbol of peace, not only amongst our own people but almost universally.

This general acceptance of it as an emblem of peace is doubtless partly due to the Mosaic record of the return of the dove to the ark, but it will not account entirely for its wide acceptance. The Chinese, the Israelites, and the ancient Greeks and Romans all regarded it as the emblem of peace and joy.

In China the custom exists still, of sending an Olive and a piece of red paper to the aggrieved party in a quarrel; as a sign that peace shall be restored; and in Ancient Greece, branches of Olives were looked upon as tokens of peace and friendship.

In Parkhurst's *Hebrew Lexicon*—antiquated in many respects though it be—many curious facts are recorded, amongst them some having reference to the Olive.

Parkhurst says "The *Olive-tree*, from the effect of its oil in supplying, relaxing, and preventing or mitigating pain, seems to have been from the beginning an emblem of the benignity of the Divine nature; . . . Hence we see a peculiar propriety in the olive-leaf or branch being chosen by Divine Providence as a sign to Noah of the abatement of the deluge; we may also account thus for olive-branches being ordered as one of the materials of the booths at the feast of tabernacles: and whence they became emblems of peace to various and distant nations. So Statius mentions *Supplicis arbor Olivae* = The suppliant Olive-tree. And our late eminent navigators found that green branches carried in the hands, or stuck in the ground, were the emblems of peace universally employed and understood by all the islanders even in the South Seas".

The Greeks held branches of Olive or Laurel in their hands whilst engaged in prayer, and wore crowns of the same plants on their heads.

In the *Song of Roland* the Olive-branch is

spoken of as a sign of peace, and Shakespeare was perfectly cognisant of its symbolic meaning. He mentions the Olive on several occasions and nearly always in reference to its peaceful office.

> Bring me into your city
> And I will use the Olive with my sword,

he says in one place; and in another

> Prove this a prosperous day, the thrice-mocked world
> Shall bear the Olive freely;

and that daintiest of messengers, Viola, in *Twelfth Night* says

> I bring no overture of war, no taxation of homage, I hold the Olive in my hand: my words are as full of peace as of matter.

In Art, St. Agnes is represented with a Palm-branch in her hand, and at her feet a lamb crowned with Olives and holding an Olive-branch in its mouth. The Olive also figures largely on old Greek coins.

Thus Olive is in its significance one of the prettiest of all flower-names, and must not be confounded with Olave, the feminine of the old Teutonic name of Olaf = forefather's relic, which was probably the name of one of Charlemagne's two chief paladins, though it has been transmitted to us as Oliviero or Oliver.

> Froissart, a countryman of ours, records,
> England all Olivers and Rowlands bred
> During the time Edward the Third did reign.
> *Henry VI.* (SHAKESPEARE.)

Oliver was the name of more than one mediaeval hero, and Oliver has always been common in England, the great popular leader, Oliver Cromwell, even to this day having many namesakes.

Olivia was at one time very fashionable, but the prettier anglicised form of Olive has now far more representatives.

Many old customs and superstitions grew around the idea of the Olive, as the emblem of peace and joy. In the Apocryphal Bible we read how, in the general rejoicing at the deliverance wrought by Judith, from Holofernes, and when he had been put to death, "all the women of Israel ran together to see" Judith "and blessed her and made a dance among themselves for her: and she took branches in her hand, and gave also to the women that were with her. And they put a garland of Olive upon her, and her maid that was with her".

This is the only instance related, of the Hebrews placing a crown of Olives on a woman's head.

In some country places women still hang an Olive-branch at the entrance to their homes, as a talisman against witches, and amongst our forefathers the Olive, Yew, or Palm-tree used to be solemnly blessed by the priests, some of their branches reduced to ashes, and then, on the Ash Wednesday of the following year, employed by the priests in their sacred rites, whilst branches were distributed amongst the devout and carried by them in their religious processions.

This custom obtained in this country down

to the time of King Edward VI. It was then discontinued on account of its supposed superstitious tendency.

There being no Olive-trees in England, Box or Yew-trees were substituted for them, and this is by some accounted the cause of old Yew-trees being so frequently found in old country churchyards.

The ancient Greeks had a custom of carrying an olive branch to their neighbours' houses at the New Year, and according to Ovid even ambassadors bore olive branches in their hands in testimony of their peaceful intentions.

In various countries too, the Olive was supposed, together with a few other plants, to possess the power of producing showers; and it was also placed by mourners upon the tombs of those they loved.

> This is a sacrifice, our showre shall crowne
> His sapulcher with Olive, Myrrh, and Bayes,
> The plants of peace, of sorrow, victorie.

Even the study of heraldry leads us back to the Olive, for amongst its mysteries we discover the old custom of sending officers to challenge to battle, or to carry messages between the enemies bearing in their hands staffs of Laurel or of Olive, which were called the *herald's wands* or *sceptres*: Athenian heralds also often employed the *Harvest Wreath* made of an olive or laurel branch, wound round with wool and ornamented with various fruits. This

Harvest Wreath was a symbol or token of peace and plenty.

> The sign of peace who first displays
> The Olive wreath possesses.
> (MICHAEL DRAYTON.)

In literature the name is well represented:

There is Olive Waynflete in *Marquis and Merchant*, by Mortimer Collins, who sings a song beginning:

> Oh, once it was a stately tree
> Whose summit caught the morning star—
> And now it is sole friend to me,
> My sad guitar.

and we all know Shakespeare's Olivia in *Twelfth Night*; then we have Olivia in *The Good-natured Man*, by Goldsmith; Olivia in *The Plain Dealer*, by Wycherly; Olivia in *Evadne* or *The Statue*, by R. L. Shiel (1821); Olivia, the rose of Aragon, in *The Rose of Aragon*, by Sheridan Knowles; and lastly, Olivia Primrose in Goldsmith's *Vicar of Wakefield*, who is described by her father as having "that luxuriancy of beauty with which painters generally draw Hebe; open, sprightly, and commanding", whose beauty "vanquished by a single blow" and who was "often affected from too great a desire to please."

> 'Tis beauty truly blent, whose red and white
> Nature's own sweet and cunning hand laid on . . .
> I see you what you are: you are too proud;
> But, if you were the devil, you are fair . . .
> If I did love you in my master's flame
> In your denial I would find no sense,
> I would not understand it . . .

PATIENCE; PATRICIA

I would
Holla your name to the reverberate hills;
And make the babbling gossip of the air
Cry out, Olivia!

Twelfth Night (SHAKESPEARE.)

PATIENCE: see FAITH, etc.

PATRICIA means "noble", from the Latin *patricius*. The Patricii were the three hundred ruling families of ancient Rome.

It is St. Patrick, the Apostle of Ireland, who has popularised the name in these islands.

Killpatrick or Kirkpatrick on the Clyde in Scotland, Cornwall, and Brittany dispute the honour of being the place of his birth, which probably occurred about the year A.D. 387. Kidnapped in childhood, he was carried as a slave to Ireland, and was there employed in guarding sheep until he was ransomed. Thirty years later he returned as a Christian Bishop to the scenes of his servitude, and there laboured faithfully for some thirty years or more, as a shepherd in another field. St. Patrick's relation to the Irish Church was much the same as that of St. Augustine to the English; and Ireland has rewarded him for his devotion by unswerving and unbounded admiration and love, naming her sons after him, and adopting the diminutive Pat or Paddy as her national *sobriquet*. The feminine form is by no means so common as the masculine, and is indeed more often met with in Scotland than in Ireland.

One of our English princesses, a daughter of the Duke of Connaught, is known as the Princess Patricia.

PAULINA, or PAULINE, is, of course, only the feminine form of Paul, which means "little" or "small", and is a contraction of Pauxillus, in all probability one of the names of the Aemilian gens who happened to be of small stature. The name was not, however, by any means restricted to one gens, but was in very general use amongst the Romans. It is only right to add that some who have studied the question derive the name from the Greek word *παῦλα* meaning "rest".

Paul has gradually got modified and developed into various forms, until now, in England alone, we have such names as Paulet, Pawley, Paley, Palafox, Pollock, Polson, Sampol (a combination of St. Paul), and Paulus; and according to one authority the variations have gone so far afield as to include M'Phail. The Corsicans render the name as Paoli, the Italians give us Paolo, in Spain it appears as Pablo, and in Wales as Peevlin; but, under whatever guise we may meet with it, we may be assured that its popularity from the first has been due to its assumption by Saul of Tarsus, when, after his conversion, he set forth on his journey to Rome. Whether he adopted the name as emphasising some physical peculiarity, or as a sign of humility and the small estimation in which he held himself, is matter for conjecture.

The popularity of the name of Paul is so widespread that under some form or another it is met with throughout the Christian world: its lustre has moreover been added to by the fact that some eleven or twelve other men who have borne the name have been canonised since the days of St. Paul the Apostle.

Of these, the earliest appears to have been St. Paul of Ptolemaïs (A.D. 274). The legend asserts that he, together with his sister Juliana, was, by order of the Emperor Aurelian, subjected to various torments, in the hope that they might turn aside from the Christian faith. The Emperor caused them to be cast into a dungeon "with serpents, adders, vipers, dragons, and other venomous reptiles". In this dungeon they remained for three days and nights, with the creatures crawling around and over them, but making no attempt to do them harm—for after gazing at them fixedly they lay curled up at their feet whilst the brother and sister sang hymns and psalms together. On the third day Aurelian looked through the dungeon window to see how his victims fared, when lo! instead of seeing only two faces there amongst the reptiles, he distinguished three, the third being that of an angel. Aurelian thereupon gave orders that the prisoners should be at once set free; but, when his servants went to obey his mandate and open the dungeon door, the reptiles sprang on them with fury and, killing them, themselves escaped into the desert.

St. Paul the Anchorite (A.D. 330); St. Paul the martyred Bishop of Constantinople (350); St. Paul the Confessor, beheaded July 25, 308; St. Paul of Trois Châteaux; St. Paul the Hermit; St. Paul the Simple; St Paul, Bishop of Leon (492-573); St. Paul de la Croix; St. Paul, Bishop of Verdun (631); and St.

Vincent de Paul (1660) are all names honoured in the Western Church.

Finally there was Santa Paula, a noble Roman woman, who devoted her life to acts of mercy. Her relics are supposed to be in the Metropolitan Church at Sens, where the feast of Santa Paula (27th January) is kept as a holiday.

Two sects have arisen, inspired by one or other of these men: the Paulicians and the Paulianists.

In the more secular walks of life appear such names as Paul Veronese, Peter Paul Rubens, Jean Paul Richter, Paul Delaroche, the mathematician Paul of Middleburg (1445-1534), Paul of Venice, the philosopher (1427), Paul Jones, the Scot who fought against England on the side of America, Paul the murdered Emperor of Russia, besides five Popes of the name, and if not great at least the well-known Paul Kruger!

Some other feminine forms of the name are, in Italy, where it is most common, Paola, Paolina, and Paoletta; in France, Paulette and Pauline; and in Germany, Pauline and Paulinechen. In England as a woman's name it has never been common.

Pauline, the meekly bright! though now no more
  Her clear eye flash'd with youth's all-tameless glee,
Yet something holier than its dayspring wore,
  There in soft rest lay beautiful to see;
A charm with graver, tenderer, sweetness fraught—
The blending of deep love and matron thought.

Through the gay throng she moved, serenely fair,
  And such calm joy as fills a moonlight sky
Sat on her brow beneath its graceful hair,
  As her young daughter in the dance went by,
With the fleet step of one that yet hath known
Smiles and kind voices in this world alone.

The above verses are taken from Mrs. Hemans' poem entitled *Pauline*, which commemorates the self-devotion of the Princess Pauline Schwartzenberg, who, upon the occasion of a fire breaking out in a castle where festivities were in full progress, sacrificed her own life in the endeavour to save that of her daughter. It is a poem of some fifteen stanzas, of which we here give one more:

And bore the ruins no recording trace
  Of all that woman's heart had dared and done?
Yes! there were gems to mark its mortal place,
  That forth from dust and ashes dimly shone!
Those had the mother, on her gentle breast,
Worn round her child's fair image, there at rest.

Of characters in fiction bearing the name, the pathetic little figure of Paul Dombey is perhaps the best known to modern English readers, though Pauline, the beautiful daughter of Mme. Deschappelles, who marries the hero Claude Melnotte, in Bulwer Lytton's play *The Lady of Lyons*, is a household word, too, as is also Paul Pry, the hero of Poole's comedy, whilst St. Pierre's graceful story of *Paul et Virginie* has immortalised the name in French literature. Of this romance Cobb wrote a dramatic version in English. Sir Walter Scott has a Pauline in the *Fortunes of Nigel*, and Shakespeare, in his *Winter's Tale*, gives us Paulina, wife of Antigonus, and true friend to Hermione in her trouble, a "clever, generous, strong-minded, warm-hearted woman" though "heedless and hot-tempered". Paul Flemming in Longfellow's *Hyperion*, *Paul Ferrol* by Mrs. Archer

Clive, and *Paul Clifford* by Lord Lytton, are other instances of the name occurring in literature.

Love me—love me, Pauline, love naught but me,
Leave me not! All these words are wild and weak,
Believe them not, Pauline! I stooped so low
But to behold thee purer by my side,
To show thou art my breath, my life, a last
Resource, an extreme want: . . .
. . . Be still to me
A key to music's mystery when mind fails,
A reason, a solution and a clue!

. . . . . .

And be to all what thou hast been to me!

Pauline (Robert Browning.)

PEGGY: see Margaret.

PENELOPE was the daughter of Icarius, the wife of Odysseus or Ulysses, and the mother of Telemachus. After her marriage, she went with her husband to live in Ithaca, but Ulysses had to leave her soon after the birth of their son, to go to the Trojan war, which lasted ten years. Even after the war was over, Ulysses did not return to her; and Penelope, beset by wooers, who tried to convince her that her husband had been shipwrecked, declared that she would make choice of one of her suitors as soon as a piece of tapestry was finished, upon which she was then engaged. She baffled their importunities by unpicking in the night what she had accomplished in the day: hence the proverb or phrase "Penelope's Web", meaning something which can never be ended.

After twenty years, Ulysses returned to weary,

patient Penelope, who, according to Homer, was a model of female excellence.

Penelope, for her Ulisses sake,
  Deviz'd a Web her wooers to deceave;
In which the worke that she all day did make,
  The same at night she did againe unreave.
Sonnet xxiii. (SPENSER.)

The name comes from $\pi\acute{\eta}\nu\eta$ = thread on the bobbin; $\pi\eta\nu\acute{\iota}\zeta o\mu\alpha\iota$ = to wind thread off.

In both England and Ireland the name has always enjoyed a moderate popularity.

In the old English ballad of *King Cophetua and the Beggar-Maid* the form of Penelophon occurs as the name of the beggar.

"Thou shalt go shift thee cleane.
What is thy name, faire maid?" quoth he.
"Penelophon, O King", quoth she:
With that she made a lowe courtsèy;
  A trim one as I weene.

One of the characters in *St. Ronan's Well*, by Sir W. Scott, is Penelope.

First, for your shape, the curious cannot show
Any one part that's dissonant in you:
And 'gainst your chaste behaviour there's no plea,
Since you are known to be Penelope.
Thus fair and clean you are, although there be
A mighty strife 'twixt form and chastity.
To his kinswoman, Mrs. Penelope Wheeler (HERRICK.)

PHILIPPA, the feminine of Philip, means "love horses" and was at one time a very common name in this country, it having been introduced into England by the popular Philippa of Hainault, Queen of Edward III. Though

Philip still holds its own amongst us, Philippa is rapidly dying out.

PHŒBE, DIANA, CYNTHIA, SELINA, together with SELENE and ARTEMIS, are all names given by the ancients to the Goddess of the Moon, and all, save Diana, which is Latin, are Greek.

Phoebe means "the light of life" or "pure radiance", and Phoebe herself was said to be the daughter of Hyperion and Theia, and sister to Helios and Eos. Twin-sister to Phoebus or Apollo, she rode in a car drawn by horses, mules or cows, the horns of the latter representing the crescent moon; and she is in pictures and statues represented as a huntress, and recognizable by her crescent.

Phoebus and Phoebe had many worshippers in Greece, and gradually grew to be regarded as the deities of the sun and moon, owing probably to the original meaning of their names = to shine, coming from the Greek word φάω (*phao*); and Phoebe is probably of greater antiquity than Artemis.

In France the names of Artémidore and Artémise had their votaries, but England, rejecting them, has clung to the prettier and simpler Phoebe.

Phoebe was in use amongst the Roman women of Greek descent, but the introduction of the name among us was probably due to St. Paul, who commends his "Sister Phoebe" to the Romans. That was quite enough to make the name rank as a "Bible name" amongst our cottagers, who knew nothing of pagan beliefs and "moon-goddesses", nor anything of the beautiful meaning of the word.

First given as a name from the Bible, it was afterwards, through family affection, handed down from one generation to another.

"Sweet Phebe, do not scorn me: do not, Phebe:
Say that you love me not; but say not so
In bitterness. The common executioner,
Whose heart the accustomed sight of death makes
 hard,
Falls not the axe upon the humbled neck
But first begs pardon: will you sterner be
Than he that dies and lives by bloody drops".

As you Like It (SHAKESPEARE.)

The masculine Phoebus has never been used in England, though in the Pyrenees it was, during the Middle Ages, given to some of the Counts of Foix, and Victor Hugo has so named one of his characters (Captain Phoebus) in his celebrated novel *Notre Dame de Paris*. Byron's heroine in his pastoral poem is Phoebe.

In Crabbe's *Parish Register* there is a Phoebe Dawson.

Two summers since, I saw at Lammas fair
The sweetest flower that ever blossomed there,
When Phoebe Dawson gaily cross'd the green,
In haste to see, and happy to be seen:
Her air, her manners, all who saw admired;
Courteous though coy, and gentle though retired;
The joy of youth and health her eyes display'd
And ease of heart her every look convey'd,
A native skill her simple robes express'd,
As with untutor'd elegance she dress'd;
The lads around admired so fair a sight,
And Phoebe felt, and felt she gave delight.

Admirers soon of every age she gain'd
Her beauty won them and her worth retain'd;
Envy itself could no contempt display,
They wish'd her well, whom yet they wish'd away.

Sir Walter Scott, too, has introduced a Phoebe Mayflower into his novel, ***Woodstock***; and J. R. Lowell has a peom on the bird called Phoebe, whose cry resembles that sound.

Thomas Lodge has a quaint little poem about a Phoebe, which is not as well known as it deserves to be, and therefore we will quote it at length.

Phoebe sat,
Sweet she sat,
Sweet sat Phoebe when I saw her;
White her brow,
Coy her eye,
Brow and eye, how much you please me!
Words I spent,
Sighs I sent,
Sighs and words could never draw her.
Oh my love,
Thou art lost,
Since no sight could ever ease thee.
Phoebe sat
By a fount,
Sitting by a fount I spied her;
Sweet her touch,
Rare her voice;
Touch and voice, what may distain you?
As she sung,
I did sigh,
And my sighs whilst that I tried her,
Oh mine eyes,
You did lose
Her first sight whose want did pain you.
Phoebe's flocks
White as wool,
Yet were Phoebe's locks more whiter.

Phoebe's eyes,
  Dove-like mild,
  Dove-like eyes both mild and cruel,
Montan swears
In your lamps
  He will die for to delight her.
Phoebe yield,
Or I die:
  Shall true hearts be fancy's fuel?
Montanus' Praise of his Fair Pheobe.

Phoebe occurs as a name in *Paul Pry* by Poole, in *The Love Chase* by Sheridan Knowles; and Phoebe Pyncheon is the well-known heroine of *The House of Seven Gables* by Nathaniel Hawthorne.

Just as Phoebe comes from *phao* = to shine, so Selene comes from *ele* = heat or light, which is the same word as the Teutonic hell = bright or light. Selene, like Phoebe and Artemis, was a Greek name for the Goddess of the Moon: the English, when they adopted it as a name for their daughters, committed the folly of latinizing it into Selina: this, two or three generations ago, was a popular name; but is so no longer, though by no means obsolete yet.

A fourth Greek name for the moon-goddess is Cynthia.

The crown majestic Juno wore;
And Cynthia's brow the cresent bore.

wrote Shenstone in his *Attribute of Venus*; and in *Il Penseroso* Milton also alludes to Cynthia as the Goddess of the Moon.

The name is a graceful one, and, at one time much in vogue, is still used, and very popular with the poets. It occurs, for instance, as the name of one of the characters in *The Double Dealer* by Congreve. In America it is frequently met with.

Alexander Pope has a Cynthia in his *Moral Essays*.

Come then, the colours and the ground prepare!
Dip in the rainbow, trick her off in air;
Choose a firm cloud, before it fall, and in it
Catch, ere she change, the Cynthia of this minute.

Lord Brooke, George Wither, Sir Robert Howard, Sir Walter Raleigh, Michael Drayton, Ben Jonson, who wrote a masque called *Cynthia's Revels*; Richard Barnfield, Sir Francis Kyneston, and Anne Radcliffe have all written poems with Cynthia for their burden. William Congreve introduces a Cynthia into his play of *The Double Dealer*, and Mrs. Gaskell has a Cynthia Kirkpatrick in her novel *Wives and Daughters*, whilst William Shenstone writes of her in at least four poems, one being an *Ode to Cynthia*, from which we will quote.

Ah! Cynthia, thy Damon's cries
  Are heard at dead of night;
But they, alas! are doom'd to rise
  Like smoke upon the sight.

. . . . . .

If sleep perhaps my eyelids close,
  'Tis but to dream of you;
Awhile I cease to feel my woes,
  Nay, think I'm happy too.

I think I press with kisses pure,
  Your lovely rosy lips;
And you're my bride, I think I'm sure,
  Till gold the mountain tips.

When waked, aghast I look around,
  And find my charmer flown;
Then bleeds afresh my galling wound,
  While I am left alone.

Take pity, then, O gentlest maid!
  On thy poor Damon's heart:
Remember what I've often said,
  'Tis you can cure my smart.

Finally we will take the Latin name for this same Goddess of the Moon—Diana—from Diva Jana, an old Latin deity, who, in conjunction with Divus Janus, ruled over the day and night = the sun and moon. In the course of ages she became identified with the Greek Artemis, was installed in the temple at Ephesus, exchanged Janus for Apollo, and finally appropriated the silver bow as her symbol. The name first took hold of the French fancy in the Middle Ages, and thence travelled to England, where it became very fashionable amongst the nobility, and is still occasionally met with.

In literature Sir Walter Scott's Diana Vernon in *Rob Roy* is known to us all; and in quite recent years George Meredith's *Diana of the Crossways* has brought the name prominently before us. Shakespeare had a Diana in *All's Well*, and Diana de Lascours comes in Stirling's *Orphan of the Frozen Sea*; Ben Jonson wrote a *Hymn to Diana*, and there is *Diana the Second of Salmantin*, a pastoral romance by Gil Polo; there is also another pastoral romance entitled *Diana of Mont-Major*, and Henry Constable wrote *Diana; or, the excellent conceitful Sonnet*, and Francis and Walter Davison have a sonnet *To Mistress Diana.* We have besides two old ballads, one called *Diana's Darling*, and the other beginning

Diana's a Nymph so chaste and so fair
That Venus herself may not with her compare.

These testify to the popularity of the name. Lord Brooke, too, in his *Dream* speaks of Diana, and William Drummond of Hawthornden has a Madrigal beginning

Fair Dian, from the height
Of heaven's first orb who cheerst this lower place,
Hide now from me thy light,
And, pitying my case,
Spread with a skarf of clouds thy blushing face.

John Chalkhill wrote a poem called *Thealma and Clearchus*, wherein one of the characters is The Priestess of Diana.

"To wear Diana's livery" is to remain unmarried; and footpads are sometimes called "Diana's foresters", because they do their work at night.

Marry, then, sweet wag, when thou art king, let not us that are squires of the night's body "be called *thieves* . . . let us be "Diana's foresters", "Gentlemen of the shade", "Minions of the Moon".

I. Henry IV., Act I. sc. ix (SHAKESPEARE.)

PHYLLIS, an English name according to some authorities, is derived from φυω (*phuo*), the Greek for "I grow", and signifies "verdant", "flourishing", "fruitful", whilst others derive it from Phillyrea, a plant named after Philyra, one of the Oceanides and the mother of Chiron, who, ashamed of having a son half-man, half-horse, besought the gods to change her nature, whereupon she was transformed into a linden tree, these trees being since called by her name amongst the Greeks. Another asserts that the Phillyrea is a kind of willow, and therefore typical of grace; hence Phyllis = a reed, or willow wand. The true Greek word whence these latinized forms have been developed is *phullorroia*, which simply means a falling of leaves.

We first meet the name in the story of the young Thracian Queen, the daughter of either Sithon or Lycurgus, both Kings of Thrace. This royal Phyllis fell in love with Demophoon, the son of Theseus, when he paid a visit to her country. Her affection was returned, and the lover lingered many months, unable to tear himself from her; but at last owing to urgent claims upon him in his own country he set sail for Athens, promising to return before the month was out. For some reason not stated, however, he did not return, and Phyllis, growing weary of life and desperate after long months of watching, determined to put an end to her unhappy existence. Accounts differ as to how she carried out her purpose. One says that she hanged herself, another that she threw herself over a precipice into the sea and was drowned. Her mourning friends raised a tomb to her memory, over the place where her body lay, and thereon there grew up a tree whose leaves at certain seasons of the year suddenly became wet as though weeping for Phyllis. Some days after the tragic death of his love, Demophoon re-appeared, and learning her sad end, rushed to the tree and embraced it, whereupon the tree, though at the time leafless, burst suddenly into bloom. One version of the story has it that upon hanging herself Phyllis was metamorphosed into an almond tree, which is in Greece called Philla. The almond tree, as we all know, blossoms before its leaves appear, and there may be some connection between this natural fact and this version of the story.

Ovid on four occasions refers to the legend: in the *Heroides* 2; *Ars Amatoria* 2, 353; *Tristia* 2, 437; and *Hygin. fab.* 59.

You've gone beyond your time, and ought to give
So kind a wife as Phillis leave to grieve.
You promised me you would no longer stay,
Than till the first full moon should light your way.
(OVID, *Epistles* trans. by Poley.)

Virgil introduces the name as that of a country girl in his 3rd and 5th *Eclogues*, and the nurse of the Emperor Domitian bore the name: the modern bearers of it may therefore feel assured of its antiquity. Of its popularity now in England there can be no question, and in the sixteenth century it was the constant theme of poets, and grew to be the chief pastoral name for a maiden. We have below given a lyric from the pen of Sir Charles Sedley – he wrote several others – and Waller, Spenser, Herrick, Nicholas Breton, John Milton and John Gay, besides many more, wrote verses to "Phillis", to "Phillida" or to "Phillada".

George Wither has a little poem beginning

Amarylis I did woo,
And I courted Phillis too.

Whilst Milton in *L'Allegro* describes how

Where Corydon and Thyrsis met
Are at their savoury dinner set,
Of herbs and other country messes,
Which the neat-handed Phillis dresses.

Sir Charles Sedley addresses a Phillis in the words:

Phillis is my only joy,
Faithless as the winds or seas;
Sometimes coming, sometimes coy,
Yet she never fails to please.
If with a frown
I am cast down,
Phillis smiling
And beguiling,
Makes me happier than before.

Though, alas! too late I find
Nothing can her fancy fix;
Yet the moment she is kind,
I forgive her all her tricks;
Which though I see,
I can't get free;
She deceiving,
I believing,
What can lovers wish for more?

In Spain too the name has its literary representative, for *Phillis* is the name of the drama written by Lupercio Leonardo of Argensola in *Don Quixote* by Cervantes; and in French literature Phillis appears in C. Rivière Dufresny's *La Coquette de Village*, where she asks of Damon "thirty sheep for a kiss" on the first day, on the second promises him "thirty kisses for a sheep", on the third is willing to give "thirty sheep for a kiss", whilst on the fourth day Damon bestows his kisses on her rival Lizette for nothing.

In Addison's *Spectator* Phyllis and Brunetta are rivals, and on one occasion Phyllis procures a wonderul garment of golden brocade, in which to array herself and eclipse Brunetta; but Burnetta, quick to see how she could mortify her rival most, dresses her slave in a like material, and herself appears in simple black.

Amongst so many pastorals, lyrics and sonnets in which a Phyllis appears during the best period of English poetry, it is difficult to make a selection.

Edmund Spenser in *Colin Clout's Come Home Again* speaks of

Phyllis, Charillis, and sweet Amaryllis.
Phyllis the faire is eldest of the three.

. . . . .

Phyllis, the stoure of rare perfection,
Faire spreading forth her leaves with fresh delight,
That, with their beauties amorous reflexion,
Bereave of sence each rash beholder's sight.

Then there is the old ballad which sings of Sir Guy of Warwick, beginning

Was ever knight for ladyes sake
Soe tost in love, as I Sir Guy
For Phelis fayre, that lady bright
As ever man beheld with eye?

There are two pastorals by Nicholas Breton, one called *Phillis and Corydon*, the other

Phillida and Corydon; one called *Phyllis and Damon*, by Wm. Drummond of Hawthornden, who several times uses the name in his poems; another by Edmund Waller *To Phillis*; an "Ancient English Pastoral" called *Harpalus*, preserved by the Earl of Surrey and endorsed with some others "uncertain auctours", which commences:

Phylida was a faire mayde,
As fresh as any flowre.

There is a Phillis in *The Parish Register* by George Crabbe, and a lovely little song by Sir Charles Sedley addressed to *Phillis* and a *Madrigal* unsigned in Davison's collection, to Faustina and Phillida. Herrick asks:

What has the court to do with swains
Where Phyllis is not known?

Whilst John Gay sings of

Phyllida, that loved to dream
In the grove, or by the stream.

And Herrick also has a charming pastoral poem *To Phyllis to Love and Live with him*, commencing:

Live, live with me, and thou shalt see
The pleasures I'll prepare for thee.

John Cleveland celebrates a Phillis in his sonnets and lyrics, and Thomas Lodge also "honoured" a Phillis "*with Pastoral Sonnets, Elegies, and Amorous Delights Whereunto is annexed the Tragycall Complaynt of Elstred*", and Robert Burns wrote a song called *Phillis the*

Fair. Mrs Gaskell entitled one of her graceful novels *Cousin Phillis*. We will close the long list by quoting part of an anonymous lyric written in 1658.

> Oh! what a pain is love;
> How shall I bear it?
> She will unconstant prove,
> I greatly fear it.
> She so torments my mind,
> That my strength faileth,
>
> And wavers with the wind
> As a ship saileth:
> Please her the best I may,
> She loves still to gainsay:
> Alack and well-a-day!
> Phillada flouts me.
>
> At the fair yesterday
> She did pass by me,
> She looked another way
> And would not spy me:
> I woo'd her for to dine
> But could not get her;
>
> Will had her to the wine
> He might intreat her,
> With Daniel she did dance,
> On me she looked askance;
> Oh! thrice unhappy chance;
> Phillada flouts me.
>
> Fair maiden! have a care,
> And in time take me;
> I can have those as fair,
> If you forsake me:
> For Doll the dairy maid
> Laughed at me lately,
> And wanton Winifred
> Favours me greatly.

POLLY: see MARY.

PORTIA: PRISCILLA

PORTIA certainly is derived from the Latin word *porcus*, signifying a pig, though in their anxiety to find a more attractive origin for the loved name, some have endeavoured to trace it back to *porta* signifying a "harbour".

You see me, Lord Bassanio, where I stand,
Such as I am: though for myself alone
I would not be ambitious in my wish,
To wish myself much better: yet, for you
I would be trebled twenty times myself:
A thousand times more fair, ten thousand times
More rich; . . . . . .
but the full sum of me
Is the sum of something, which, to term in gross,
Is an unlesson'd girl, unschool'd, unpractised;
Happy in this, she is not yet so old
But she may learn; happier than this,
She is not bred so dull but she can learn;
Happiest of all is that her gentle spirit
Commits itself to yours to be directed.

Merchant of Venice (SHAKESPEARE.)

Shakespeare's magic wand has made the characters of two women stand out in such fair relief, that no one stops now to ask what the origin of their name was, being content to look upon it as typical of all womanly modesty, truth, courage, and wisdom.

Brutus. Kneel not, gentle Portia.

. . . .

Portia. I grant I am a woman; but withal
A woman that Lord Brutus took to wife:
I grant I am a woman; but withal
A woman well-reputed, Cato's daughter.

. . . .

Brutus. O ye gods,
Render me worthy of this noble wife!

PRISCILLA. The name Prisca, with its diminutive Priscilla, means "ancient", "of ancient birth" =aristocratic, from the Latin word *prisca.* Priscus is the masculine form of the name; and this appears to have originated with the ancient Latin tribe known as the Prisci.

"Truly, Priscilla", he said, "when I see you spinning and spinning,
Never idle a moment, but thrifty and thoughtful of others,
Suddenly you are transformed, are visibly changed in a moment;
You are no longer Priscilla, but Bertha the Beautiful Spinner".
Here the light foot on the treadle grew swifter and swifter; the spindle
Uttered an angry snarl, and the thread snapped short in her fingers;
While the impetuous speaker, not heeding the mischief, continued:
"You are the beautiful Bertha, the Spinner, the queen of Helvetia".
The Courtship of Miles Standish (LONGFELLOW.)

In England, during Puritan times, amongst the decendants of Puritans, and in New England, the name has had some vogue owing to Priscilla having been the name of one of St. Paul's fellow labourers; but it has never been a common name, and the original form of Prisca is rarely met with, though it was the name of a child-martyr under the reign of the Emperor Claudius I. This Prisca was of Consular birth, and at the age of thirteen, having been converted to Christianity, was sentenced by the Emperor to be first flogged and then exposed naked to a lion: the lion crouched at her feet and did her no harm. Then, the legend runs, her tormentors cast the girl into a brazier, but still she remained unhurt; so she was led beyond the city walls and there beheaded.

> Not any kiss
> From Mrs. Priss,
> If that you do
> Persuade and woo.
> Know, pleasure's by extorting fed.
> (WILLIAM CARTWRIGHT.)

In Cartwright's play *The Ordinary* there is a Priscilla.

PRUDENCE, often contracted to PRUE, is one of the many names illustrative of some personal merit, and needs no explanation.

The masculine – Prudentius – was the name of a Latin poet of the fourth century A.D., who was by birth a Christian. Born in Spain, he was trained as an advocate and held some office about the court of the Emperor Honorius, but retired from public life and gave all his time to religious exercises and the writing of poetry. His works are very numerous and enjoyed a wide popularity in the Middle Ages.

> Here, here I live with what my board
> Can with the smallest cost afford.
> Though ne'er so mean the vainds be,
> They well content my Prew and me.
> Or pea, or bean, or wort, or beet,
> Whatever comes, content makes sweet.
> Here we rejoice, because no rent
> We pay for our poor tenement
> Wherein we rest, and never fear
> The landlord or the usurer.
> (ROBERT HERRICK.)

Prudence is oftenest found in parish registers during the time of the Puritans, but it was in use long before then; and Chaucer in his *Tale of*

Melibeus tells us of a Mistress Prudence, who argued so wisely with her husband, Melibee, that when he "hadde herd the wordes of his wyf Prudence, he seyde thus: 'I see wel that the word of Solomon is sooth . . . and, wyf, by-cause of thy sweete wordes, and eek for I have assayed and preved thy grete sapience and thy grete trouthe, I wol governe me by thy conseil in alle thyng' ".

In Ben Jonson's play *The New Inn* a Prudence is one of the characters; and a Prue appears in Wycherley's *The Gentleman's Dancing Master*, and in Congreve's *Love for Love,* whilst Herrick has at least four short poems addressed to Prudence Baldwin, and a Prudence is one of the characters in Lord Lytton's *The Sea-Captain.* Prudence is one of the characters too in Bunyan's *Pilgrim's Progress*; and *Prudence Palfrey* is the title of a story by the American novelist Thomas Bailey Aldrich.

RACHEL is a Hebrew name which signifies a ewe, and its symbolic meaning is gentleness. Dante regarded Rachel as the type of contemplative love.

Behold, Rachel his daughter cometh with the sheep. . . . Rachel came with her father's sheep: for she kept them. . . . And Jacob kissed Rachel, and lifted up his voice and wept. . .

Leah was tender eyed; but Rachel was beautiful and well favoured.

And Jacob loved Rachel; and said, I will serve thee seven years for Rachel thy younger daughter. . . . And Jacob served seven years for Rachel; and they seemed unto him but a few days, for the love he had to her. —*Genesis,* ch. xxix.

RACHEL

The name, though so musical in sound, does not seem to have become particularly popular in England until the early seventeenth century, when it was adopted by the Puritans as one of their favourites; and in the reign of Charles II., glorified by the admiration felt for Rachel, Lady Russell, the daughter of Rachel de Ruvigny and Thomas Wriothesley, Lord Southampton, it became common. Born in 1636, the elder of two sisters, she lost her mother when still an infant. In 1653 she was married to Lord Vaughan, the eldest son of the Earl of Carberry, and though, to use her own words, it was a marriage of "acceptance rather than choosing on either side", she inspired those around her with real affection, and fourteen years passed in the contentment of domestic duties faithfully performed. In 1667 Lord Vaughan died, and Rachel Vaughan went to live with her sister, Lady Elizabeth Noel, at Titchfield.

In 1670 Lady Vaughan became the wife of William Russell, the second son of the Earl of Bedford, a man held in great respect by his friends, but without either title or fortune, though eight years later in 1678, he became Lord Russell, through the death of his elder brother.

The union between Lord William Russell and his wife proved absolutely happy; their devotion to and trust in one another was complete. Eight years after their marriage she wrote to him, "My dearest heart, flesh and blood cannot have a truer and greater sense of their own happiness than your poor but honest wife has".

Lady Russell proved her love for her husband in small things as in great: she entered into his pleasures and into his serious interests, and when matters of state took him from town, she kept him informed by daily letters of all that concerned him in London.

In one letter of overflowing tenderness she stops suddenly in her expressions of love to say "what have I to ask but a continuance, if God see fit, of these present enjoyments? if not, a submission without murmur to His most wise dispensations and unerring providence; having a thankful heart for the years I have been so perfectly contented in. . . . Then let us cheerfully expect to be together to a good old age; if not, let us not doubt but He will support us under what trial He will inflict upon us".

Ten years afterwards she wrote again, saying, "I know nothing new since you went; but I know, as certainly as I live, that I have been for twelve years as passionate a lover as ever woman was, and hope to be so one twelve years more; happy still, and entirely yours".

Scarcely ten months later and all this perfect happiness was overset and Lord Russell a prisoner in the Tower, brought up at the bar of the Old Bailey on a charge of High Treason.

England had slowly outlived the joys and hopes inspired by the Restoration: the vices of the court of Charles II. had made thoughtful people pause and ponder. Old Royalists were dead, new people now stood on the world's stage, and Lord Russell, in the same year that he married Lady Vaughan, had joined the Country party against that of the Court.

By his virtues rapidly advanced to the position of one of its leaders, he had for eleven years defended this party in the House of Commons, and earned for himself the deep love and respect of the great body of the English people.

Too limited in his perceptions to realize the political blunders committed by his party, his wife, with her wider mind, from the first entertained doubts as to the propriety of many of its acts.

When finally the national party insisted that Charles II. should disinherit the Duke of York, Lord Howard intrigued against Russell and obtained his arrest.

Too sure of his own rectitude of purpose to avail himself of the opportunity of escape afforded him, Lord Russell was sent to the Tower.

From that moment Lady Russell devoted herself entirely, and with great intelligence, to her husband's defence, and on the eve of the trial, which began on July 13th, 1683, wrote to him thus:

"Your friends, believing I can do you some service at your trial, I am extremely willing to try; my resolution will hold out, pray let yours. But it may be the court will not let me; however do you let me try".

During the whole trial Lady Russell acted as her husband's secretary and adviser.

Gradually all hope of saving Lord Russell's life faded away.

"I could have wished", said Lord Russell to

Burnet, "that my wife would cease to beat thus among the bushes and to run hither and thither to save me; but when I reflect that it will be one day some mitigation of her sorrow that she left nothing undone that could have given me probable hope, I am resigned".

On the eve of his execution he begged her to "stay and sup with me; let us eat our last earthly food together", and after he had embraced her four or five times and she had left him, he turned to Burnet and said, "Now the bitterness of death is past. What a blessing she has been to me! How miserable I should have been, if, with her tenderness, she had not possessed so much greatness of soul, never to have desired me to do a base thing to save my life! Whereas, what a week I should have passed if she had been crying on me to turn informer and to be a Lord Howard! . . . it was a signal providence of God in giving me such a wife, where there was birth, fortune, great understanding, great religion, and great affection for me! but her carriage in my extremity was beyond all!"

Lady Russell long survived her husband, and she had the satisfaction of knowing that the second act that William of Orange signed on his accession to the throne of England was a bill to abolish the sentence against Lord Russell by declaring it murder. Shortly afterwards the Earl of Bedford was created Duke of Bedford.

More trials were in store for Lady Russell, for her only son, then Duke of Bedford, died of the small-pox, and six months later she was called upon to part with her second daughter, Rachel, Duchess of Rutland; thus of her three children, the eldest, the Duchess of Devonshire, alone remained to her, and profoundly sad, yet calm and patient, she waited quietly for her own end to come.

At the age of eighty-six Rachel Lady Russell died in her daughter's arms on 29th September, 1723, and was buried, by the side of the husband whom she had so devotedly loved, at Chenies, in Buckinghamshire.

Rahel Levin was a Jewess of singular intellectual gifts, and the central figure of a wide circle of men of letters, politicians, and artists. In 1814 she embraced Christianity and married Varnhagen von Ense, a German historian and diplomatist, who owed much to his noble wife. She was as much distinguished by her womanly grace and delicacy, and childlike simplicity, as by the vigour of her intellect and vivacity. In society she was a Queen. Born in 1771, she died in 1833. She left no written work, but her husband published a memoir of her called *Rahel.*

Yet another Rachel remains to be spoken of here, Rachel Eliza Felix, now generally known as Elisa Rachel. She was the daughter of a poor Jewish pedlar, and gained her livelihood at first by singing in the streets. But she so used her great musical gifts as, before her death, to entirely revive the classical school of tragedy in France by her renderings of the chefs-d'œuvre of Racine and Corneille. Her crowning triumph was in 1843 in her representation of *Phèdre.* She died in 1858.

In literature we find Rachel Waverley in *Waverley*, by Sir Walter Scott; Rachel in *The Golden Legend* by Longfellow; Rachael in *Peveril of the Peak*, by Sir Walter Scott; and Rachael, in *Hard Times*, by Dickens.

REBECCA or Rebekah, with their diminutive Becky, comes from the Hebrew word *Ribkâ*, which means a cord with a noose, a snare. The name is still popular amongst Jewish families as having been that of the wife of Isaac and mother of Jacob and Esau, who was noted for her extreme beauty; but it has never gained a strong foothold amongst the English or Irish peoples.

The beautiful Jewess, Rebecca, in Sir Walter Scott's romance *Ivanhoe*, and Rebecca Sharp, better known as Becky Sharp, in Thackeray's *Vanity Fair*, have, however, become household words. In *Guy Mannering* by Sir Walter Scott, there is a Mistress Rebecca, the favourite of Mrs. Bertram, and there is another Rebecca in *The Antiquary* by the same author; and Thackeray wrote "a romance upon romance" called *Rebecca and Rowena*, a skit, purporting to be a continuation of *Ivanhoe*.

> When fair Rebecca set me free
> 'Twas then a golden time for me,
> But soon those pleasures fled:
> For the gracious princess died,
> In her youth and beauty's pride
> And Judith reigned in her stead.
>
> *The Chronicle* (Abraham Cowley.)

ROBINA, Ruby, Robert and Rupert are really direct descendants from the same name,

Hruadperaht, that of an early and very popular Bishop of Worms, its first known owner.

Amongst the Germans, Hruadperaht became Ruprecht; amongst the French, and through them the English, it became Robert. From the days when Robin Goodfellow was implicitly believed in, down to the present, the name has been most popular in England, whilst Scotland has made it pre-eminently her own, and has evolved from it the feminine forms of Robina, Robinia, and Robinetta, with the pet name of Ruby. Robinia and Ruby are constantly met with in the Northern Kingdom, and occasionally in England, whilst Ruperta, though not unknown, has never appealed to the English.

The meaning is "bright fame."

A generation ago one of the most popular drawing-room songs, by J. J. Lonsdale, was called *Ruby* (music by "Virginia Gabriel").

ROSALIE: see Lilian.

ROSE, ROSAMOND, Rosalind, Rhoda, etc.

The most ancient of all these names is Rosamond, and, contrary to the general belief that it means "rose of the world", it has probably nothing whatever to do with the flower at all.

The old Germans had a kind of *dii minores* (minor gods), known as Jotuns, and one of these was Hros, a god shaped like a three-legged horse, and the original form of the name Rosamond was Hrosmond, meaning horse-protection. There was a chieftainess of this name amongst the Gepidae of the Jura, and the name has been a favourite in that district from time immemorial.

To us in England it first became known through the history of Rosamond Clifford and Henry II., as told to us in the old ballad *Fair Rosamond*, and introduced by Sir Walter Scott in his novels of *Woodstock* and *The Talisman.*

Rosamond the fayre daughter of Walter lord Clifford . . (poisoned by queen Elianor, as some thought) dyed at Woodstock [A.D. 1177], were King Henry had made for her a house of wonderful working; so that no man nor women might come to her, but that he was instructed by the king, or such as were right secret with him touching the matter. This house after some was named Labyrinthus, or Dedalus worke, which was wrought like unto a knot in a garden, called a maze . . . When she was dead, she was buried at Godstow in a house of nunnes, beside Oxford.

STOWE'S *Annals.*

The ballad which is far too long to give here in full, after describing "Her crisped lockes like threads of golde", goes on:

Yea Rosamonde, fair Rosamonde,
  Her name was called so,
To whom our queene, dame Ellinor,
  Was known a deadlye foe.

The King therefore, for her defence,
  Against the furious queene,
At Woodstocke builded such a bower,
  The like was never seene.

. . . . .

"My Rosamonde, my only Rose,
  That pleasest best mine eye;
The fairest flower in all the worlde
  To feed my fantasye:

The flower of mine affected heart,
  Whose sweetness doth excelle:
My royal Rose, a thousand times
  I bid thee nowe farewelle!

For I must leave my fairest flower,
  My sweetest Rose, a space,
And cross the seas to famous France,
  Proud rebelles to abase".

. . . . .

And at their parting well they mighte
  In heart be grieved sore;
After that daye faire Rosamonde
  The King did see no more.

In a second ballad called *Queen Eleanor's Confession* she is made to say:

"The next vile thing that ever I did,
  To you I will discover;
I poysoned fair Rosamonde,
  All in fair Woodstocke bower".

There have been many other poems which have treated of this subject—amongst them Samuel Daniel's *The Complaint of Rosamond*; Addison's *Rosamond* an opera; *Henry and Rosamond* by Hawkins; *Fair Rosamond* by Tennyson; *Rosmonda* (in Italian) by Rucellai; and (in Spanish) *Rosmunda* by Gill y Zarate. There are also two operas, one, by Dr. Arne, and the other by Schubert. A well-known character of the name in modern fiction is Rosamond Vincy in *Middlemarch* by "George Eliot".

Rhoda, Rhode, and Rhodocella are Greek names, meaning a rose, and Rhodeia means rosy-cheeked.

Rhoda was the name of the maiden who went to open the door to Peter when he escaped from prison and "came to the house of Mary, the mother of John" (*Acts* xii. 13), and from those days of long ago to the present Rose has been a favourite woman's name in nearly every land, almost all if not all countries having the same sound to represent the flower and the colour. The ancient Romans did not give flower-names to their women-kind, but they had the flower, of course, and from the eighth century to the present day the name may be met with in many an old chronicle or history.

In an unfinished tale called Gondibert, by Sir William Davenant, Rhodalind, daughter of Aribert King of Lombardy, is in love with Duke Gondibert, but Gondibert prefers a young country-girl called Birtha. Whilst the Duke is making love to Birtha, a message comes from the King to say he has proclaimed him his heir, and that he is about to give him his daughter Rhodalind in marriage. The tale breaks off just as Gondibert hastens to obey the King's summons, giving Birtha a ring as pledge of his constancy.

The varieties of the name are almost endless in English alone, for not only has Rhoda been naturalised, but there are Rosa, Rose, Rosie, Rosia, Rosina, Rosetta = rose, Rosalba = white rose, Rosabel or Rosabella = fair rose, Roseclear, = clear-rose, Rosaline, Rosalinda, Rosalind = maiden like a rose, or beautiful and graceful as a serpent. Rosalia or Rosalie, a combination of Rose and Lily, Rosaura = breath of a rose.

From the east to western Ind,
No jewel is like Rosalind.
Her worth, being mounted on the wind,
Through all the world bears Rosalind.

All the pictures, fairest lin'd,
Are but black to Rosalind,
Let no face be kept in mind,
But the fair of Rosalind.

As you like it (SHAKESPEARE.)

Rose is very popular in Ireland, but the true Celtic form is Roscrana.

Rosaura, Röschen, Rosli, Rosi, Rosette and Rosanne are all common on the Continent.

Its popularity needs neither excuse nor explanation.

What flower is that which royal honour craves,
Adjoin the Virgin, and 'tis strewn on graves.

The poet Gay asked this riddle, to which the obvious answer is Rosemary ; but the rose alone was constantly used as an emblem of the Virgin, and prayers appear to have been symbolized as roses, the string of *beads* (from the German word "*beten*", to pray) being called a rosary.

The rose appears not only in sacred pictorial art, but also in Church architecture, the portal of the Cathedral at Upsala in Sweden, for instance, being covered with sculptured roses. Even in heathen days the rose was looked upon as a mystic flower in both Germany and Scandinavia.

Four Saints have honoured the name : firstly, Saint Rosa of Viterbo (1235—1252), to whom Christ is said to have appeared, suspended on His cross, and to whom Saint Rosa cried aloud asking "why He was reduced to so pitiable a state", to whom Jesus answered "'Tis my love, My burning love for man".

Secondly, Saint Rosaline (1263—1329) the

daughter of a Seigneur of Villeneuve: she on being petitioned one day for bread by the poor of the neighbourhood, who had in vain appealed to her father for aid, went secretly to the larder and filled her apron with food to give to them. Her father surprised her in the act, and asked sharply "Rosaline, what have you got in your apron"? "Only roses", said the girl; and, holding out her apron, it appeared full of those flowers. Her father overcome by this proof of God's sanction of her act, commanded his servants that henceforth full liberty was to be given to Rosaline to do whatsoever she might think was right.

Thirdly, Saint Rose of Lima, who, born in 1586 in Lima, the capital of Peru, is distinguished as the first Saint born on American soil. She early dedicated herself to a life of devotion, taking Saint Catharine of Sienna as her model; and having for a long time supported her impoverished parents by her labours, at last enrolled herself in the third Order of St. Dominic, and dwelt in a lonely cell by herself, mortifying the flesh and praying. She died at the age of thirty-one, in 1617.

Saint Rosalia of Palermo is the last. She was, the legend says, carried by angels to a high mountain, and there lived for many years in the cleft of a rock, wearing away the stone with her knees, where she knelt in continual prayer. She is, in Christian art, represented in a cave with a cross and skull, or else in the act of receiving a chaplet of roses from the Virgin Mary.

That grot where olives nod,
Where, darling of each heart and eye,
From all the youths of Sicily,
St. Rosalia retired to God.
Marmion (Sir W. Scott.)

Then there was Rosana, a daughter of the Queen of Armenia, who lent her active aid to the three sons of St. George, when they sallied forth to quench the seven lamps of the Knight of the Black Castle, where her unkind father dwelt; and there was also the Princess Rosetta, with whom St David, the patron Saint of Wales, fell in love; both are mentioned in *The Seven Champions of Christendom.* Lastly there is the Jewish maiden, Rose, beloved by one Hamuel, a low, sottish man: Rose rejected his suit, and he in revenge spread abroad the report that she was demoniac; whereupon she was condemned to be burned to death. But God averted the flames from her, and the stake budded: the maiden stood unharmed under a rose-tree full of white and red roses, then "first seen on earth since Paradise was lost", according to Sir John Maundeville.

In literature we are almost overwhelmed by the number of poems and stories containing the name, from Spenser's "Rosalind",

Indeed (said Lucid) I have often heard
Faire Rosalind of divers fowly blamed
For being to that swaine too cruell hard:
That her bright glorie else hath much defamed
But who can tell what cause had that faire Mayd
To use him so, that used her so well.
Colin Clout's Come Home Again
(Edmund Spenser.)

and Shakespeare's Rosalind in *As You Like it* and his Rosalines in *Romeo and Juliet* and *Love's Labour Lost*, down to *A Riverside Rose* in Mr. C. C. Rhys' *Minora Carmina.* We may mention *Rosa, Rosalynd, and Rosmary,* by Thomas Newton; Rosalind, Spenser's early love, whom he celebrates in *The Shepherd's Calendar* (her real name was Rose Daniel and Rosalind is an anagram of her name); *Rosaline*, a lady sung of by Lodge; *Rosalynde* in Euphues' *Golden Legacy*, "found after his death in his cell at Silexedra"; a romance by Lodge; *Rosalind and Helen*, a poem by Percy Bysshe Shelley; *Rose Aylmer*, a lyric, by Walter Savage Landor; *Rosaura in the City of Politics*, by Crowne; Rose, in *The Recruiting Officer* of Farquhar; *Rose, Blanche, and Violet*, a novel by G. H. Lewes; *Rosaline*, by J. R. Lowell; Rosa Dartle in *David Copperfield*, by Dickens; Rose Bradwardine in *Waverley*, by Sir W. Scott; Rosa Mackenzie in *The Newcomes*, by Thackeray; Rosetta in *Love in a Village*, by Isaac Bickerstaff; Rosetta Belmont in *The Foundling*, by Edward Moore; Rosiclear and Donzel del Phebo in *The Mirror of Knighthood*, a mediæval romance; Rosiphele in Gower's *Confessio Amantis*; Roscrana, daughter of Cornac King of Ireland, "the blue-eyed and white-handed maid, like a spirit of heaven, half folded in the skirt of a cloud", who became the wife of Fingal king of Morven, in *Temora*, by "Ossian"; Rosalina in *The Wild-Goose Chase*, by Beaumont and Fletcher; Rosa in *Bleak House*, by Dickens; Rosabelle, maid to

Geraldine in *The Foundling of the Forest*, by W. Dimond; *Rosabella*, a ballad, by Sir W. Scott; Rosalind in *John Buncle's Song*, by Thomas Amory; Rosalie in *A Serenade of Seville* in *Henrietta Temple*, by Lord Beaconsfield; *My Neighbour Rose*, by Frederick Locker; and some pretty little verses to *A Wild Rose*, by Alfred Austin, the poet-laureate, running

The first wild rose in wayside hedge,
This year I wandering see,
I pluck, and send it as a pledge,
My own Wild Rose, to Thee.

Go, wild rose, to my Wild Rose dear;
Bid her come swift and soon.
O would that She were always here!
It then were always June.

To close we will quote a couple of verses from D. G. Rossetti's beautiful lyric *Rose Mary*.

Mary mine that art Mary's Rose,
Come in to me from the garden-close,
The sun sinks fast with the rising dew,
And we marked not how the faint moon grew,
But the hidden stars are calling you.

. . . .

She breathed the words in an undertone:—
"*None sees here but the pure alone*"
"And oh"! she said, "what rose may be
In Mary's bower more pure to see
Than my own sweet maiden Rose Mary"?

Of notable representatives of the name, the great painter Rosa Bonheur deserves mention here.

ROWENA, or RONWEN, is supposed to have been the daughter of Hengist the Saxon, and she it was for love of whom Gwrtheyrn Gwrtheneu (Vortizern) disclosed the bones of Gwrthevyr the Blessed, and thereby exposed England to invasion. Some think that Ronwen or Rowena and Bronwen, Brengwain or Branwen, the popular heroine of Welsh romance, are one and the same; but, whilst Rowena would seem to have been Saxon, Bronwen = white bosom was Kymrie, and the daughter of Llyr, the King of "the Island of the Mighty" (England), who was "one of the three chief ladies of this Island, and she was the fairest damsel in the world". She was wedded to Matholwch, King of Ireland, a union which, though auspiciously begun, did not in the end redound to the happiness of either bride or bridegroom, and which led to the temporary depopulation of the Emerald Isle. All the marvellous vicissitudes of Bronwen's career are set forth in the second part of the *Mabinogion.*

Her grave is supposed to have been discovered on the Island of Anglesea in 1813, and corresponded to the description in the *Mabinogion*: "a square grave was made for Bronwen, the daughter of Llyr, on the banks of the Alaw, and there she was buried". — *Mabinogion* (translated by Lady Charlotte Guest).

Rowena is the ward of Cedric the Saxon, of Rotherwood in Sir Walter Scott's great novel *Ivanhoe.*

RUTH is of course a name of Hebrew origin: but further than this those who have studied the subject cannot trace it with any degree of certainty. Some authorities interpret it to mean "a vision"; others "beauty"; another combines the two, and thinks it means "vision of beauty" or "vision of brightness"; whilst others again regard it as signifying "trembling", and lastly some take it to mean "to join together".

And she answered, I am Ruth thine handmaid.
The Book of Ruth.

"Orpah kissed her mother-in-law; but Ruth clave unto her.

"And she said, Behold, thy sister-in-law is gone back unto her people, and unto her gods: return thou after thy sister-in-law.

"And Ruth said, Intreat me not to leave thee, or to return from following after thee: for whither thou goest, I will go; and where thou lodgest, I will lodge: thy people shall be my people, and thy God my God:

"Where thou diest, will I die, and there will I be buried: the Lord do so to me, and more also if ought but death part thee and me" . . .

It is this most touching of Bible stories with the gentle, faithful, loving Ruth as its leading character, that has made the name of Ruth so beloved in England; and it is very curious that the same reason has not made the name popular in other European countries: excepting with us the name is almost unknown.

To those who know and love the old Hebrew story, Ruth can now mean only the beauty of self-devotion.

RUTH

The plume-like swaying of the auburn corn,
By soft winds to a dreamy motion fann'd,
Still brings me back thine image—O forlorn,
Yet not forsaken Ruth! I see thee stand
Lone, midst the gladness of the harvest-band—
Lone, as a wood-bird on the ocean's foam
Fall'n in its weariness. Thy fatherland
Smiles far away! Yet to the sense of home—
That finest, purest, which can recognise
Home in affection's glance—for ever true
Beats thy calm heart; and if thy gentle eyes
Gleam tremulous through tears, 'tis not to rue
Those words, immortal in their deep love's tone,
"Thy people and thy God shall be mine own"!

(Mrs. Hemans.)

Perhaps unconsciously taking its tone from Jewish history, the little literature that we have, in which a Ruth figures, is almost all of a somewhat sombre and melancholy cast.

This is especially true of Mrs. Gaskell's pathetic novel *Ruth*, and of Wordsworth's poem of the same name. The poet said that, though written whilst he was in Germany, the subject of his poem had been "suggested" to him by a story which he heard of a poor woman in Somersetshire. The first part of the poem we quote in extract below.

When Ruth was left half desolate,
Her father took another mate;
And Ruth not seven years old,
A slighted child, at her own will
Went wandering over dale and hill,
In thoughtless freedom bold.

. . . .

Beneath her father's roof, alone
She seemed to live; her thoughts her own;

RUTH

Herself her own delight;
Pleased with herself, nor sad, nor gay;
And, passing thus the live-long day,
She grew to woman's height.

There came a Youth from Georgia's shore—
A military casque he wore,
With splendid feathers drest;
He brought them from the Cherokees,
The feathers nodded in the breeze,
And made a gallant crest.

. . . .

Among the Indians he had fought,
And with him many tales he brought
Of pleasure and of fear;
Such tales as told to any maid
By such a Youth, in the green shade,
Were perilous to hear.

. . . .

Sweet Ruth! and could you go with me
My helpmate in the woods to be,
Our shed at night to rear;
Or run, my own adopted bride,
A sylvan huntress at my side,
And drive the flying deer?

"Beloved Ruth"!—No more he said,
The wakeful Ruth at midnight shed
A solitary tear:
She thought again—and did agree
With him to sail across the sea,
And drive the flying deer.

"And now, as fitting is and right,
We in the church our faith will plight,
A husband and a wife."
Even so they did; and I may say
That to sweet Ruth that happy day
Was more than human life.

. . . .

Meanwhile, as thus with him it fared,
They for the voyage were prepared,
And went to the sea-shore,
But, when they thither came the Youth
Deserted his poor Bride, and Ruth
Could never find him more.

God help thee, Ruth !—Such pains she had,
That she in half a year was mad ;
And in a prison housed ;
And there, with many a doleful song
Made of wild words, her cup of wrong
She fearfully caroused.

When Ruth three seasons thus had lain,
There came a respite to her pain ;
She from her prison fled ;
But of the Vagrant none took thought ;
And where it liked her best she sought
Her shelter and her bread.

(WORDSWORTH.)

Quite as sad as this is the true history of another Ruth — Ruth Osborne, who was, in 1751, actually murdered for witchcraft, at Tring in Hertfordshire, when upwards of seventy years of age. It occurred in this wise.

Ruth Osborne asked a farmer named Butterfield for a glass of milk, and, upon her request being roughly declined, the poor old woman muttered something about hoping that the "Pretender's army would loot Butterfield's cattle." Butterfield's cattle were not looted, but they became ill ; and Butterfield was himself also seized with sickness.

The unhappy farmer at once jumped to the conclusion that it was Ruth Osborne's "evil eye" that had worked the mischief; and sent post-haste into Northamptonshire for a certain white witch to counteract the spell. This woman engaged six stout men to guard farmer Butterfield's house and cattle day and night, and armed them moreover with pitchforks; but all to no purpose: neither farmer nor beasts grew better, so the fiat went out by means of the town crier, that old Ruth Osborne and her aged husband should be charged with witchcraft and publicly ducked in the pond on the following Monday.

Hoping to save them from outrage, the overseers placed the poor old couple in the workhouse of Tring, and, on the Saturday preceding the fateful Monday, removed them secretly, for their greater safety, to the Vestry of the Parish Church. On the Monday a mob of some five thousand people assembled outside the workhouse, and clamoured that the Osbornes should be surrendered to them. The master of the workhouse explained that the Osbornes were not there, whereupon, enraged at their escape, the mob attacked the building, looted it, and finally completely destroyed it; and then, seizing the Master, threatened to at once burn him at the stake if he persisted in concealing the whereabouts of the Osbornes. Thus threatened and terrified, the poor man at last gave way and disclosed the secret, whereupon the mob rushed to the church, laid hands upon the persons of their victims, and cruelly maltreated them until both were dead. The ringleader of the mob was afterwards condemned to death.

To close with something a little less lugubrious, we will in conclusion give the opening lines of Tom Hood's pretty poem *Ruth.*

She stood breast high amid the corn
Clasp'd by the golden light of morn,
Like the sweetheart of the sun,
Who many a glowing kiss had won.

SABRINA, or SABRIN, means "the river Severn". According to Geoffrey of Monmouth, in his *Historia Britonum*, which is really only a Latin version of the prophecies of Merlin, Sabrina, or Averne, was daughter of King Locrine and Estrildis, or Astrild, whom he loved in secret. When his queen Guendolen discovered her husband's infidelity, she assembled an army and marched against him. Locrine fell in battle, and then Guendolen pursued her revenge against Estrildis, and caused her and her daughter Sabrina to be cast into the river, which has ever since been known as the Severn. The Bristol Channel is sometimes called the Sabrinian Sea, or the Severn Sea.

Now Sabrine, as a Queen, miraculously fair,
Is absolutely plac'd in her Emperial Chair
Of crystal richly wrought, that gloriously did shine,
Her grace becoming well, a creature so divine:
And as her god-like self, so glorious was her throne,
In which himself to sit great *Neptune* had been known;
Poly-Olbion (DRAYTON.)

Milton refers to the Legend in *Comus*, and Fletcher in *The Faithful Shepherdess.*

SARAH, SARA, SALLY. *Sar* in Hebrew signifies a prince, whence *Sarai* = my princess. The Rabbis say that Jehovah changed this name by taking the last letter of His name and adding it to hers. Surely than this no greater proof of love and regard could be conceived. Are we then to consider that Sarah means a princess of Jehovah?

> The name of Abram's wife was Sarai.
> And God said unto Abraham, as for Sarai thy wife, thou shalt not call her name Sarai, but Sarah shall her name be. And I will bless her.—*Genesis* 11 and 17.

The name has always been a popular one amongst the Jewish people, but amongst the English, at any rate, it did not become a favourite until after the Restoration.

In Ireland its popularity was enhanced by its being taken as the equivalent of three native names Sadhbh (pronounced Soyv) Sorcha = bright, and Saraid = excellent.

Occasionally one meets with Saras, or Sarahs, in reading English histories of the Middle Ages, as for instance the name of Sara Beauchamp in the time of Edward I., but speaking generally the name was not in favour until much later, when Saras, Sarahs, Sadies, and Sallys meet us on every hand.

During the reign of James II. we first hear of Sarah Jennings, a penniless beauty, with a violent and mischievous character, one who had a strange power of winning and retaining love. In about 1680 she became the wife of John Churchill, afterwards Duke of Marlborough, and her husband's "affection for her ran like a thread of gold through the dark web of his career. In the midst of his marches and from the very battlefield he writes to his wife with the same passionate tenderness".

Through the overwhelming influence which her beauty, accomplishment, and imperious temper gained over the weak and lethargic nature of the Princess (afterwards Queen) Anne, Sarah Churchill soon became a power in the state. She it was who induced Anne to forsake her father James II.'s cause, and to take refuge in Danby's camp, and Anne, amidst the intrigues of Court life, clung so tenaciously to her friend, that all restraints of state etiquette were cast aside between them, and they addressed one another as "Mrs. Morley" and "Mrs. Freeman" respectively. Marlborough conscious of his power over Anne turned from plotting against James and plotted instead to drive William of Orange from the throne, but on William's death Anne at once named Marlborough Captain-General of her forces, and he and his wife ruled supreme in the Court. The greed, peculation and treachery of Marlborough, however, proved too much for even Queen Anne's tenacious affections, and her favourites were in 1712 both banished from the Court.

Pope in his *Moral Essays* writes of Sarah, Duchess of Marlborough, under the name of *Atossa*.

The most celebrated of all English actresses was also a Sarah. She was the daughter of Roger Kemble, and began her career as a singer, but soon gave that up in favour of acting.

In her eighteenth year she married Mr. Siddons, who was also an actor, and for some time they acted together at Liverpool.

Two years afterwards Mrs. Siddons made her début in London, in the character of Portia, but was not successful, and she and her husband left

London for the provinces again. There she continued her studies, and when in 1782 she reappeared in London, in the character of Isabella in *The Fatal Marriage*, she took the town by storm, and her success was assured.

Her surpassing intellectual powers, her beauty, the dignity of her carriage, and the purity of her character, commanded the respectful admiration of all who knew her, whether as an actress or a woman.

Sara Coleridge too deserves mention here: she was born in 1803, and was the only daughter of the poet, Samuel Taylor Coleridge. As the authoress of an exquisite fairy tale called *Phantasmion*, and as editress of her father's philosophical and theological works, she gave evidence of high intellectual powers. She died in 1853.

In the first years of the seventeenth century there lived an unfortunate girl called Sara Williams, who was in the service of a Mr. and Mrs. Edmund Peckham. Her mistress charged the poor girl with being "possessed with Maho and all the devils". The proofs of the accusation and the unfortunate girl's defence make very curious reading.

In literature Sarah is not a common name, but there are George Shenstone's "Sal" in a poem *To a Friend*, which begins

> Have you ne'er seen, my gentle Squire,
> The humours of your kitchen fire?

Tom Hood's ballad of *Faithless Sally Brown*, in which it is made manifest that even punning may rise to an art; William Wordsworth's little poems of *George and Sarah Green*, and *Sarah Mackereth*; George Lillo's *Sarah*, and the popular ballad, written by Henry Carey, in the later seventeenth century *Sally in our Alley*, which Palgrave speaks of as "a little masterpiece in a very difficult style".

Of all the girls that are so smart,
There's none like pretty Sally,
She is the darling of my heart,
And she lives in our alley.

There is no lady in the land
Is half so sweet as Sally,
She is the darling of my heart,
And she lives in our alley.

When she is by, I leave my work,
I love her so sincerely,
My master comes like any Turk,
And bangs me most severely;

Her father he makes cabbage-nets,
And through the streets does cry 'em;
Her mother she sells laces long,
To such as please to buy 'em;
But sure such folks could ne'er beget
So sweet a girl as Sally;
She is the darling of my heart,
And she lives in our alley.

Of all the days that's in the week,
I dearly love but one day,
And that's the day that comes betwixt
A Saturday and Monday;
For then I'm drest all in my best,
To walk abroad with Sally;
She is the darling of my heart,
And she lives in our alley.

My master carries me to church,
  And often am I blamed,
Because I leave him in the lurch,
  As soon as text is named;
I leave the church in sermon time
  And slink away to Sally;
She is the darling of my heart,
  And she lives in our alley.

When Christmas comes about again
  Oh! then I shall have money;
I'll hoard it up, and box and all,
  I'll give it to my honey;
I would it were ten thousand pounds,
  I'd give it all to Sally;
She is the darling of my heart,
  And she lives in our alley.

My master and the neighbours all,
  Make game of me and Sally,
And, but for her, I'd better be
  A slave, and row a galley;
But when my seven long years are out,
  Oh! then I'll marry Sally!
And then how happily we'll live,
  But *not* in our alley.

SELINA: see PHOEBE.

SHEILA, SHEELA: see CICELY.

SIBYL, or SYBIL, is either a name of Greek derivation, with a meaning very similar to that of Sophia, namely the Counsel of God, or it comes from *sabius* or *sabus*, an old Italian, not Latin, word, which developing into sibulla signifies a wise old woman.

The first derivation is generally accepted by etymologists as likely to be the correct one.

Accepting, then, the theory of its Greek derivation as right, we shall find Sibylla to be the Latin singular; Sibulla, the Greek, from the Doric *sio-bolla* = *theou-boule*, which means, "the will of God."

The name Sibyllae was given in bygone ages to inspired prophetesses, and especially to those of Apollo. The Sibyllae were generally supposed to be young maidens who dwelt in solitude in caves or hard by some inspired spring or stream, and who were possessed of a power of divination and prophetic utterance in moments of inspiration.

Sometimes described as the priestesses of Apollo they were at other times said to be his favourite wives or daughters. Their number seems to be doubtful, for, whilst Plato in his *Phaedrus* only speaks of one, others set their number down as high even as twelve.

Their dwelling place is also variously stated to have been in the neighbourhood of the Trojan Ida, in Asia Minor, at Erythrae in Ionia, at Samos, at Delphi, and at Cumae, in Italy.

The most renowned was she of Erythrae, known as Herophile, who afterwards, through many wanderings, journeyed to Cumae, where she is said to have lived through long ages in the crypts beneath the temple of Apollo.

Herophile was also called by the names of Amalthaea, Demophile, Daphne, Manto, Phemonoe, and Deiphobe.

It is said that Apollo became enamoured of her, and offered to give her whatever she might ask.

Herophile at once demanded to live as many years as she had grains of sand in her hand, but she forgot to ask for a continuance of health, strength, and beauty. The god granted her request, but she after a time became decrepit and haggard.

Herophile had lived about seven hundred years when Aeneas went to Italy, but she had then still three hundred years longer to live. She gave Aeneas directions how to find his father in the infernal regions, and even led him herself to the entrance of hell.

The Sibyls were in the habit of writing their prophecies on leaves which they placed at the entrance to their caves. It required great care in those who desired to consult them, as to how they picked them up before they were dispersed by the wind, otherwise they became incomprehensible. Later on, the prophetic nymph Albunea was designated a Sibyl.

The *Sibylline books*, so often referred to in Roman history, originated in a collection of oracular utterances written down in Greek hexameters, which dated from the time of Solon and Cyrus.

They were ascribed to the Hellespontic Sibyl, who dwelt beneath the temple of Apollo at Gergis on Mount Ida.

The legend states that this Sibyl offered her nine books of prophecy to Tarquinius Superbus, but that he declined to buy them on account of the exorbitant price demanded for them. The Sibyl in a pet burnt all but three, which the king ultimately purchased, and placed for security in a vault beneath the Capitoline temple of Jupiter, where they fell victims to the flames which destroyed that temple in 83 B.C.

A new collection was made and deposited in the restored temple, whence they were in 12 B.C. transferred to the temple of Apollo on the Palatine, where they remained until A.D. 405.

It was only the rights of expiation prescribed by these books which were communicated to the public, and not the oracles themselves.

These *Sibylline books* must not be confounded with the *Sibylline Oracles* contained in twelve books of Greek hexameters, which were of a much later date. These oracles have come down to us, and contain a medley of pretended prophecies by various authors and of various dates, from the middle of the second century B.C. to the fifth century A.D.

These are the work, partly of Alexandrine Jews, partly of Christians, and written in the interests of their respective religions. Some even refer to events of the later Roman Empire.

> And thou, Alecto, feede me wyth thy foode . . .
> And thou, Sibilla, when thou seest me faynte,
> Address thyselfe the gyde of my complaynte.
>
> (THOMAS SACKVILLE, EARL OF DORSET.)

Sibilla, Sibyl, Sybil, or Sibel early became known as a Christian name, its resemblance in sound to the Gothic *sibja* = peace and friendship, having perhaps something to do with its rapid adoption in Europe. *Sibja* is the same as the Scottish word *sib*, meaning *related*, which reappears in the final syllable of the English word gossip in its old meaning of god-parent.

Robert of Normandy's wife was called Sibila, and one of the Angevin queens was Sibille; the name was, moreover, very popular amongst the Anglo-Normans.

In Ireland and Scotland the name is far more common than in England.

A Sibil occurs in Ben Jonson's *Tale of a Tub;* a Sybil in the poems of Drummond of Hawthornden; Lord Beaconsfield called one of his novels *Sybil, or The Two Nations;* and Sybil Warner is a character in Lord Lytton's romance *The Last of the Barons.*

In *Marmion* Sir W. Scott mentions a well from which Clare fetches water to slake the dying hero's thirst.

Where shall she turn?—Behold her mark
  A little fountain-cell,
Where water, clear as diamond spark,
  In a stone basin fell.
Above, some half-worn letters say,
    Drink-weary-pilgrim-drink-and-pray
    For-the-kind-soul-of-Sybil-Grey,
    Who-built-this-cross-and-well.

SOPHIA, Sophy, is derived from the name of the *Sofh*, or Persian Bible, is said to have derived its name from the Greek *Sophia.* The authorship of the *Sofh* is attributed to Abraham. If this be true, then the Greeks must have taken the word from the East. According to Bochart *Sophi* or *Sofi* means, in the original Persian, one pure in faith, or devoted to God. The books of the Muslim dervishes of the order of the Soofees are called *Ta sow wuf*, which signifies *of spiritual life.* Therefore, though in Greek *Sophia* meant wisdom, in Persian *Sofi* meant purity, whilst the Hebrew word Zophim = seer is said to mean "the secret of Jehovah."

One fundamental idea seems to run through all three forms of the word—namely, that only to the pure in heart should wisdom be given.

Sofian is a name often found amongst old Arabian heroes, the Arabic feminine being Safiyeh. The Turkish feminine name is Sofiyeh and means Chosen.

The name *Sofi* became that of a royal dynasty, and though in some cases so terribly abused by the vices and cruelties of some of the Persian Kings, as to be looked upon as almost synonymous with tyranny, the founder of the line was a man noted for his wisdom.

A race of sheiks who claimed descent, through Ali, from the twelve Saints, had long dwelt in Erdebel, and passed their lives in the study of that sacred book, the *Sofh*. In the fourteenth century lived a member of this family of sheiks, who by his holy living and devotion earned for himself the title of *Sophi-Juneyd-u-Dien* = one pure, or wise, in the faith. From Sophi-Juneyd-u-Dien sprang the race of the Sophis, Sefes, Suffavees, or Sophys, as it is variously spelt. His immediate descendant—a grandson—earned for himself the title of Ismaïl the Cruel, so from the very earliest days the vices as well as the virtues of the race gave evidence of their existence.

The Sophis are still in existence as a religious order, and the reigning Shah of Persia, for the time being, is looked upon as its head.

The Sophists in Greece took their name of course from the word *Sophia*, but by their vain subtleties and false axioms drew down upon themselves the hatred and contempt of the wise, until at last to be a sophist grew to mean that one was a captious or fallacious reasoner.

The English forms of the name are Sophia, Sophy, and Sophie.

> Would Wisdom for herself be wooed,
> And wake the foolish from his dream,
> She must be glad as well as good
> And must not only be, but seem
> Beauty and joy are hers by right.
>
> (Coventry Patmore.)

Amongst the martyrs of the early Christian Church was a Saint Sophia. She suffered for the faith, under the Decian persecution, in the third century, at Firmo in Italy, and her festival is celebrated in the Roman Catholic Church on April the thirtieth. In art, this Saint is represented as Wisdom, wearing a martyr's crown, and encircling with her arms, her three children, Faith, Hope, and Holy Fear.

The magnificent Mosque at Constantinople, first built by Constantine the Great in 325, and afterwards rebuilt by the Emperor Justinian (531), was dedicated to this saint, or to the idea personified in her name, and though for upwards of four hundred years this Church has been used as a Moslem Mosque it has always retained its original name.

By the Emperors of the East Sophia was looked upon as a royal name, and borne by many of their daughters, and as Constantinople was looked upon by the rest of the ancient world as the centre of civilization, the name was rapidly adopted by all countries that held any communication with the great city.

It first passed into Germany and Hungary—a Hungarian princess bore the name in 999—and by the eleventh century instances of Sophia were scattered throughout Europe.

In England it did not become fashionable until the seventeenth century, when it came over with the House of Hanover. King George the First's mother, and his wife were both named Sophia, which was quite enough to cause it to be adopted in fashionable circles : the general public, glad of a fresh name, soon followed suit, and ever since then it has retained its hold on the public favour, though it is not so popular now as it has been.

Hasdrubal, the great Carthaginian general, had a daughter called Sophonisba, whom he had carefully brought up to detest Rome and all things Roman. Her hand was promised to Masinissa, King of Numidia, who joining Hasdrubal in Spain contributed to the support of the Carthaginians.

Owing to the efforts, however, of Scipio, victory finally rested with the Romans, and Masinissa influenced by various reasons transferred his alliance to Rome.

Hasdrubal had in the meantime broken his word and given his beautiful daughter to Syphax, who attacked and conquered Massylia, where Masinissa was now King. Ultimately Masinissa recovered the throne of Massylia, and pursuing Syphax into his own territories captured him, and at once married Sophonisba. The strange story of Sophonisba's life has given rise to more dramas than any other save that of Cleopatra. Amongst French authors who have founded plays upon it are J. Mairet; Pierre Corneille; Lagrange-Chancet; and Voltaire; amongst Italians, Giovanni Trissino, and Vittorio Alfieri; and amongst English, John Marston in his *The Wonder of Women or The Tragedy of Sophonisba*, and James Thomson in his *Sophonisba.*

Whilst Thomson's play was being acted, on the first trial night, all went well, till the unfortunate line which runs

> Oh Sophonisba! Sophonisba oh!

when the whole house was convulsed with laughter, and the unhappy author, who was present, knew that his play was condemned: the line was afterwards parodied by "Oh Jemmy Thomson! Jemmy Thomson oh"!

Sophia has not been a favourite name with lyric poets, but our dramatists have introduced it with considerable frequency. For instance there is Sophia, in *The Bloody Brother*, by Beaumont and Fletcher; Sophia in *The Picture*, by Philip Massinger; Sophia in *The Law of Lombardy*, by Robert Jephson; Sophia in *The Road to Ruin*, by Thomas Holcroft; and Sophia in *The Male Coquette*, by David Garrick.

Fiction yields us two of her very best characters to support the name, namely, Sophia Primrose in *The Vicar of Wakefield*, by Oliver Goldsmith; and Sophia Western, the heroine of Henry Fielding's great novel *Tom Jones*.

For a description of Sophia Primrose we cannot do better than listen to the good Vicar himself—

"Olivia, now about eighteen, had that luxuriancy of beauty with which painters generally draw Hebe; open, sprightly, and commanding, Sophia's features were not so striking at first; but often did more certain execution; for they were soft, modest, and alluring. The one vanquished by a single blow, the other by efforts successfully repeated.

"Olivia wished for many lovers, Sophia to secure one. Olivia was often affected from too great a desire to please. Sophia even repressed excellence from her fears to offend. The one entertained me with her vivacity when I was gay, the other with her sense when I was serious. But these qualities were never carried to excess in either, and I have often seen them exchange characters for a whole day together. A suit of mourning has transformed my coquette into a prude, and a new set of ribands has given her younger sister more than natural vivacity".

And now let us hear what Sophia Western was like.

"Sophia then . . . was a middle-sized woman, but rather inclining to tall. Her shape was not only exact, but extremely delicate; and the nice proportion of her arms promised the truest symmetry in her limbs. Her hair, which was black, was so luxuriant, that it reached her middle, before she cut it, to comply with the modern fashion; and it was now curled so gracefully in her neck, that few would believe it to be her own. . . . Her eye-brows were full, even, and arched beyond the power of art to imitate. Her black eyes had a lustre in them, which all her softness could not extinguish. Her nose was exactly regular, and her mouth, in which were two rows of ivory, exactly answered Sir John Suckling's description in those lines:

Her lips were red, and one was thin,
Compar'd to that was next her chin.
Some bee had stung it newly.

Her cheeks were of the oval kind: and in her right she had a dimple which the least smile discovered. Her chin had certainly its share in forming the beauty of her face; but it was difficult to say it was either large or small, tho' perhaps it was rather of the former kind. Her complexion had rather more of the lily than of the rose; but when exercise, or modesty, increased her natural colour, no vermilion could equal it. Then one might indeed cry out with the celebrated Dr. Donne:

Her pure and eloquent blood
Shone in her cheeks, and so distinctly wrought,
That one might almost say her body thought.

Such was the outside of Sophia; nor was this beautiful frame disgraced by an inhabitant unworthy of it. Her mind was every way equal to her person."

STELLA: see ESTHER.

SUSAN, or SUSANNAH, is derived from *shush* = white lily, compounded with *hannah* = grace, which give *shushannah* or *schuschannah* = graceful white lily.

From this the royal City of Assyria takes its name of Shûshan, which means City among lilies.

Before the City of Shûshan was built, or even thought of, however, an Assyrian princess had been named Sosana or Susana, after the flower.

She was a daughter of King Ninus by a marriage prior to that with Semiramis.

Susannah is therefore an Assyrian name in its origin, and was known in Arabia too as Soosan, and in Greece was familiar under the form of Souson.

To us it has come through the Jews, as a "Bible name". Susanna was the wife of Joacim and very beautiful. Falsely accused of infidelity she was cited before the Sanhedrim and was condemned to death. Through the wisdom of Daniel the false evidence was detected, Susanna saved, and her accusers put to death.

The story of *Susannah and the Elders* occurs in the Apocrypha, in those chapters of the *Book of Daniel* through which St. Jerome thrust his dagger, to shew that he did not consider the story genuine. In spite of this, however, it has always been a popular one in Western Europe, and Susannah's name beloved in England, France and Germany, as is witnessed by the frequency of the names of Susannah, Susanna, Susan, Sukey, Susie, Sue, in England, Susanne, Suzette, Suzon, in France, and Susanne, Suschen, and Suse in Germany.

The name Susanna belonged to one of the

holy women at the Sepulchre, and it occurs in the Calendar of Saints as the name of a Virgin Martyr, who, like so many others, suffered during the Diocletian persecutions.

Susanna is said to have been of noble birth, and a niece of Pope Caius. She laid down her life for her faith early in Diocletian's reign, that is to say, in about the year A.D. 295.

No reliable records exist of her life, but she is commemorated in many ancient martyrologies, and a famous Cistertian church in Rome bears her name.

It is averred that Diocletian wanted Susanna to marry his adopted son Maximian, but that she declined, having determined to consecrate her life to religion. The Emperor thereby discovering that she was a Christian, threatened her with death should she decline to offer up incense to Jupiter.

Susanna was accordingly first scourged and then decapitated.

There was also a Queen Susanna, known as "The Lily of Tiflis" who lost her life at the hands of Mahomedans, for her devotion to Christianity.

In England the story of Susanna seems to have appealed most to the middle and the working classes. The name, with us, has never been a royal one, and though it occurs amongst our aristocracy its representatives must be looked for amongst our quiet country homes and cottages rather than in the houses of the great. Our very literature shews this, for though the name rarely occurs in Drama or Romance, our

Ballad Poetry fairly teems with Susans and Susannahs.

Susan Ferrier, one of our leading novelists at the early part of this century; Susanna Blamire, a poetess at the close of the last century; Susan Coolidge, an American story-writer; and Susan Warner, better known by her pseudonym of Elizabeth Wetherel; all represent the name worthily.

A poem founded upon the Apocryphal narrative, was, in 1622, published by Dr. R. Aylett, entitled *Susanna*, or, *The Arraignment of the Two Elders*, and Laurence Sterne introduces a Susannah in his famous novel *The Life and Opinions of Tristram Shandy, Gentleman.* Moreover, George Crabbe, in his *The Parish Register*, tells us about a worthy farmer's wife named Susan, who

> . . . served the great, and had some pride
> Among the topmost people to preside.

Wordsworth wrote a little poem which he called *The Reverie of Poor Susan*, which was occasioned, according to the poet's own account, by himself being affected by the music of caged birds, as he walked through the streets of London in the stillness of a spring morning.

Nor must we omit Tom Hood's *The Bachelor's Dream*, in which Miss Susan Bates became Mistress Mogg; but save these, and three tiny poems by Robert Herrick to Susanna Southwell, and his sister-in-law Susanna Herrick, we must seek amongst our song writers and ballad writers for the name.

Sweet William and Coy Susan is the title of a

song; so is *Two Loyal Lovers*, which begins:

> Well met my sweet Susan whom I do adore;

a third, called *Love and Loyalty*, begins:

> Susan I this letter send thee;

a fourth, called *The Constancy of Susanna*, begins:

> There dwelt a man in Babylon
> Of reputation great by fame;
> He took to wife a faire woman,
> Susanna she was called by name;

this latter is referred to by Shakespeare in *Twelfth Night*.

One of the Christy Minstrel songs begins:

> O! Susannah don't you cry for me
> I'm going off to Charlestown with a banjo on
> my knee—

Jemmy Duck's song in *The Dog Fiend*, by Captain Marryat, has the refrain at the close of each verse, of

> For Susan on my knee, my boys,
> For Susan on my knee,

and finally, there is the ballad of *William and Susan*, of which we give the first stanza:

> All in the downs the fleet was moor'd,
> The streamers waving in the wind,
> When black-eyed Susan came aboard—
> "O where shall I my true love find?
> Tell me, ye jovial sailors, tell me true
> If my sweet William sails among the crew?"
> (JOHN GAY.)

SYLVIA, or SILVIA, is a name whose history dates back to the days of Roman mythology. Silvanus, or Sylvanus, was an old Italian deity related to Faunus. He was originally god of woods, forests and small plantations. As time went on he came to be looked upon as the protector of fields and gardens, of crops and of husbandmen and their interests in general, as well as of all cattle grazing in meadows, and more especially of those grazing near woods. In course of time, too, the guardianship of the boundaries between meadows was added to his other duties.

Hence it came to pass that the Italian peasantry worshipped him in three distinct capacities; firstly, as *domesticus* or protector of the house and all that appertained thereto; secondly, as *agrestis* or protector of the shepherd and his flocks; and thirdly, as *orientalis* or watcher over boundaries, a more important function perhaps in those days than we in our more law-abiding times are inclined to think. In the last capacity Sylvanus had a grove dedicated to his sole use and situated on the boundary of the different estates he was called upon to protect.

At harvest-festivals farmers and the owners of vineyards, orchards, or forests offered up corn, grapes, fruits and even pigs and rams as votive offerings on rustic altars dedicated to the sylvan god.

The sudden terror which is apt to seize upon people in the profound solitude of a forest used to be attributed to Sylvanus, and it was also firmly believed that there were numerous *silvani* or wood-nymphs attendant upon him. In later times he got confused with Pan. He is often represented as half-man, half-goat, whilst at other times he is depicted as an aged man holding a cypress tree in his hand, because he is said to have become enamoured of a beautiful youth named Cyparissus, who was transformed into a cypress tree.

Sylvia, also called Ilia, is said to have been the name of the mother of Romulus and Remus, the traditional founders of Rome, so that in the feminine form also the name is of long descent.

A Sylvius, fabled to be the son of Aeneas and Lavinia, was the ancestor of all the Kings of Alba, who were called Sylvii.

The name Sylvanus was adopted in Rome some time before the advent of Christianity, and was the name of one of those who took part in the conspiracy against the Emperor Nero; it was also the name of one of Constantius's officers who revolted and had himself proclaimed Emperor, but was afterwards assassinated by one of his own soldiers.

The various forms of the feminine name are Sylvia, Silvia, Silvie; the masculine are far more numerous and include, Silvano, Silvanus, Silvain, Silvestre, Sylvester, Silvestre, Sylvestre, Sylvanus, Silvio, Sylvius, and, contracted, Silas.

This contraction first occurs in the case of St. Paul's friend and companion under persecution, who in the Epistles is called Silvanus; in the Acts, Silas. In 1 Peter v. 12 Peter says, "By Silvanus a faithful brother unto you, as I suppose, I have written briefly". Whilst in Acts xv.

22 it is stated, "Then it seemed good to the apostles and the elders, with the whole church, to choose men out of their company, and send them to Antioch with Paul and Barnabas; namely, Judas called Barsabbas, and Silas, chief men among the brethren".

Enough has been said to shew the antiquity and honourable descent of Sylvia. Owing to its being a "Bible name", Silas was much used in England in the old Puritan days and still lingers in our country villages, whilst the veneration excited by the two Popes Sylvester and Sylvanius or Silverius, as he is more frequently called, has added greatly to the popularity of the name, for both of these Popes were canonized, and both rank as Saints in the Roman Catholic Church Calendar.

Sylvester is very common in Ireland, whilst Sylvia was at one time a pastoral name in England, and is daily growing in popularity with us now, so that there are few of us who do not number at least one or two Sylvias amongst our friends.

Who is Silvia? What is she?
That all our swains commend her?
Holy, fair, and wise is she,
The heav'ns such grace did lend her,
That she might admired be.

Is she kind as she is fair?
For beauty lives with kindness;
Love doth to her eyes repair,
To help him of his blindness:
And, being help'd, inhabits there.

SYLVIA

Then to Sylvia let us sing,
  That Sylvia is excelling ;
She excels each mortal thing
  Upon the dull earth dwelling ;
To her let us garlands bring.

(SHAKESPEARE.)

Pope Sylvester (314), whose occupation of the Papal Chair, owing to the munificence of the Emperor Constantine, marks the commencement of the temporal power of the Papal See, was born in Rome towards the close of the third century. He was a young priest at the time of the Diocletian persecutions, and, whilst they were in progress, Sylvester used to go about trying to impart strength and courage to the sufferers. His own life during these terrible days seemed to be almost miraculously preserved.

In the year 312 a new era set in for the Christian Church, for the Emperor Constantine then declared himself openly to be the protector of the Christians. Just at this turning-point in the history of the Church, it was Sylvester's good fortune to be elected Pope, and he was thus the first Pontiff who ruled the Church in security and peace. He endeavoured to confirm the teachings of the Church and to establish its discipline, and summoned the two great Councils of Arles and Nicæa. St. Sylvester died in 335.

Rather more than 200 years later, a second of the name was elected to the Chair of St. Peter; but instead of his rule, like that of his predecessor, being distinguished by unwonted peace, internal broils and political disasters followed hard upon one another.

Saint Silverius, the son of Pope Hormisdas, who had been married before he entered the priesthood, was called upon to govern the Church at a time when it was divided against itself, and torn in pieces by the factions of two rival Popes.

Silverius did all that in him lay to govern wisely, firmly and according to the Church's laws; but he was ultimately deposed by his enemies, and driven into exile, where he died of starvation; some believed him to have been deliberately murdered.

Others who have borne this name in some form or other, and who should be mentioned here, are, Pope Silvester II., who like St. Silverius, had an uneasy time of it, and who, after being deposed, died at Rome in 1003; Pope Silvester III. also deposed (1044); Silvester IV., Antipope, who was elected in opposition to Pascal II., but driven away, in 1106; and Æneas Sylvius Piccolomini, who ascended St. Peter's Chair in 1458. There were two Roman Consuls named Silvanus and one usurping Emperor. In England we can boast of two quaint poets of the name, Sylvius Bonus, supposed to be Coil the Good, a contemporary of Ausonius and often mentioned by him, and Joshua Sylvester—known as "Silver-tongued Sylvester"—who amongst other works wrote a satire against tobacco entitled *Tobacco Battered and the Pipe Shattered* (1563-1618); and lastly we will name Silvio Pellico the

Piedmontese dramatist and patriot; the victim of Austrian tyranny and a prisoner in Spielberg for ten years. He died, ruined in health, in 1854.

In literature the name Sylvia is chiefly met with in English lyrics of the pastoral romance period, in poets such as Ben Jonson, Shenstone, Waller, Herrick, etc.; but there are other instances of its occurrence, as, for example, Silvia, the daughter of Justice Balance, in *The Recruiting Officer* by Farquhar; Sylvia in *The Picture* by Massinger; Silvia in Shakespeare's *The Two Gentlemen of Verona*; Sylvia in *The Fancies Chaste and Fair* by Ford; *Silvestre* in *Les Fourberies de Scapin* by Molière; *Don Sylvio de Rosalva* a novel by C. M. Wieland. Mrs Gaskell's graceful novel *Sylvia's Lovers*; *Sylvie and Bruno* by "Lewis Carroll"; a poem by George Darley called *Sylvia: or the May Queen*; and Don Silva in *The Spanish Gypsy*, by "George Eliot". In lyrical poetry there is a song by Burns, which he named *Damon and Sylvia*, and another by Waller, *Of Sylvia*, beginning

> Our sighs are heard; just Heav'n declares
> The sense it has of lovers' cares.
> She that so far the rest outshin'd,
> Sylvia, the fair, while she was kind,
> As if her frowns impair'd her brow,
> Seems only not unhandsome now.

Shenstone has at least six poems wherein a Silvia plays a part. One of them contains the pretty verse:

With silent step, and graceful air,
See gentle Sylvia move:
Whilst heedless gazers, unaware,
Resign their soul to love.

And Herrick has innumerable little poems to Silvia.

No more, my Silvia, do I mean to pray
For those good days that ne'er will come away,
I want belief, O gentle Silvia, be
The patient Saint, and send up vows for me.
(HERRICK).

TABITHA: see DORCAS.

THEKLA, or THECLA, meaning "divine fame" or "glory of God", hardly comes within the ranks of English names, though it is occasionally met with in Great Britain. In Germany it is not uncommon, and is found in France, in Italy, and in Russia. It is the name of Schiller's heroine in his tragedy of *Wallenstein*, so successfully translated into our language by S. T. Coleridge.

The name was a Greek one, Θεκλα, probably of heathen origin, though St. Thecla has sanctified the name. She is supposed to have been the "protomartyress" of the Christian Church, and to have been converted to Christianity by the Apostle Paul himself. The book of *The Acts of Paul and Thecla* is, however, apocryphal. St. Thecla was a native of Isauria, or Lycaomia, and was noted for her strength, sweetness, and modesty. She was denounced before the authorities as a Christian, and condemned to be exposed naked in the amphitheatre to wild beasts; but these, forgetting their natural ferocity, laid themselves down at her feet. St. Thecla accompanied St. Paul on more than one of his apostolic journeys, but spent the last years of her life in retirement at Isauria, where she died.

The Cathedral Church at Milan is dedicated to her. Longfellow refers to her in his *Golden Legend.*

Thy voice was in my soul! it call'd me on;
O my lost friend! thy voice was in my soul.
From the cold, faded world whence thou art gone,
To hear no more life's troubled billows roll,
I come! I come!

. . . . .

But I shall come to thee! our soul's deep dreams,
Our young affections, have not gush'd in vain;
Soon in one tide shall blend the sever'd streams,
The worn heart break its bonds, and death and pain
Be with the past!

From *Thekla at her Lover's Grave* (Mrs HEMANS.)

Mrs Hemans has also written a lyric called *Thekla's Song; or, The Voice of a Spirit.*

THEODORA: see DOROTHEA.

THERESA, TERESA, THIRZA, or TIRZAH, with the diminutives Terry and Tracy, means "the reaper". In England the name was hardly known until the sixteenth century, though in Spain it has been popular for many ages, and many examples occur amongst the Spanish nobility in the Middle Ages.

It was the devout St. Theresa, a native of Avila, in Old Castile, who in the sixteenth century made the name popular throughout the Christian world by her life of piety and self-devotion. She attempted to reform the order of the Carmelites, to which she belonged, and was credited with many visions and miracles.

Maria Theresa, Empress of Austria, the mother of the unfortunate Marie Antoinette, also did much towards popularizing the name, for she was personally much beloved, and had many namesakes. It is told of her, though modern historians have done much to discredit the story, that, when her estates were invaded by Frederick the Great and the Elector of Bavaria, and she was obliged to fly to Presburg, she threw herself and her child upon the mercy of her Hungarian subjects, who responded to her appeal by drawing their sabres and shouting, "Moriamur pro rege nostro Maria Theresia".

Garibaldi had a daughter Teresa, and to her Mrs Browning addressed some verses.

Of other literary heroines bearing the name, we may mention Theresa in *Waverley* by Sir W. Scott, and Teresa d'Acunha in his novel *The Antiquary*; Teresa Panza in *Don Quixote*, by Cervantes; Theresa in *Mazeppa*, by Byron; Teresa in *The Painter's Last Work*, by Mrs. Hemans; and Teresa in *Remorse*, by Coleridge, of which we give a short extract below:

There Teresa met me
The morning of the day of my departure.
We were alone: the purple hue of dawn
Fell from the kindling east aslant upon us,
And blending with the blushes on her cheek,
Suffered the tear-drops there with rosy light.
There seemed a glory round us, and Teresa
The angel of the vision! Had'st thou seen
How in each motion her most innocent soul
Beamed forth and brightened, thou thyself would'st tell me
Guilt is a thing impossible in her!

THOMASSINA, Thomassine, and Tamzine, are all feminine forms of Thomas: the generally accepted meaning of this name is "a twin", and it is a traditional belief that the Apostle Thomas had a twin-sister called Lysia.

On the other hand, some have derived the name from the Phœnician synonym of the sun-god—Thammuz—an idol which personified the sunshine, and was greatly beloved of Hebrew women, who worshipped him. The prophet Ezekiel mourned over the idolatry of his countrywomen when he beheld them "weeping for Tammuz". The festival held in honour of this deity took place some time in June, part of that month being named Tamus. It is possible that in their veneration for the god, Hebrew women called their children after him; and that, later on in less idolatrous times, the name was handed down in families without any reference to or thought of its original significance.

THYRA comes from Tyr, the god of strength and victory, who was a son of Odin, the "All-Father" of Norse mythology. Thyra is not a common name anywhere, but is more often met with amongst Scandinavians and Danes than elsewhere. The Princess of Wales' youngest sister, the present Duchess of Cumberland, bears the name.

TIFFANE: see Bertha.

TRYPHAENA, TRYPHOSA.

Salute Tryphæna and Tryphosa, who labour in the Lord.

St. Paul, *Epistle to the Romans*, xvi. 12.

There were two Christian women at Rome,

probably Alexandrian Jewesses, who were noted for their generosity and who materially contributed to the spread of the gospel there. After them the English Puritans named their daughters, in defiance of the meaning of the name, in the case of Tryphæna, which signifies "delicious", "dainty", or "a lover of pleasure".

Tryphosa means "very shining". Mr. Walter Raymond, a Devonshire novelist, has recently published a novel entitled *Tryphæna*.

ULRICA, the feminine of Ulric, Alaric or Aethelric, means "noble ruler", from *adel* = noble, and *ric* = ruler or king. The name both for men and for women is more common in Germany than in England, and was made popular there by being the name of a much-loved Bishop of Ausburg in the tenth century, who was afterwards canonized. St. Ulric won the hearts of the Ausburg people by defending them against the inroads of barbarians from Hungary. A second St. Ulrick was a native of Bristol.

UNA is by many thought to mean "one", and is an expression of matchless perfection. This is an error, for which Edmund Spenser is largely responsible, by giving the name of Una to his allegorical picture of the one true Church. As a matter of fact, the name is purely Irish, and signifies "born in famine". Una in Scott's *Waverley* may be quoted as an example of its use.

A lovely Ladie rode him faire beside,
Upon a lovely Asse more white than snow,
Yet she much whiter; but the same did hide
Under a vele, that wimpled was full low;

URSULA

And over all a blacke stole shee did throw
As one that inly mourned, so was she sad,
And heavie sate upon her palfrey slow;
Seemed in heart some hidden care she had,
And by her, in a line, a milkewhite lambe she had.

The Faerie Queene (SPENSER.)

URSULA = little bear, has for long had votaries in England, and the name of the noble Italian family—Orsini—is also derived from *ours* = bear. It is, however, in no reference to a bear that our English maidens are called Ursula, but because the legend of St. Ursula and the Eleven Thousand Virgins has in some way taken hold of the popular imagination, St. Ursula being reputed of English birth and parentage.

ST. URSULA AND THE ELEVEN THOUSAND VIRGINS.

Ye Britoun martirs, famous in parfitnesse,
Of herte avowyd in your tendir age,
To persevere in virginal clennesse,
Free from the yoke and bond of mariage,
Lyk hooly angelis hevenly of corage
Stable as a stoon grounded on vertu,
Perpetually to your gret avauntage,
Knet to your spouse callid Crist Jhesu.

O ye maidenys of thousandys full hellevene!
Rad in the gospei with five that wer wyse,
Reynyng with Crist above the sterrys serene,
Your launpis lihte for tryumphal emprise,
Upon your hed your stoory doth devise,
For martirdam crownyd with roosys reede,
Medlyd with lilies for conquest in such wise,
Fresshe undiffadid, tokne of your maydenhoode.

Graunt us, Jhesu, of merciful pité
Geyn our trespas gracious indulgence,
Nat lik our meritis peised the qualité,
Disespeyred of our owne offence,

URSULA

Ner that good hoope with thy pacience
With help of Ursula and hir sustris alle,
Shal be meenys to thy magnificence,
Us to socoure, Lord, when we to thee calle.
(LYDGATE.)

The legend tells us that St. Ursula was the only daughter of Nothus, a British prince, and that her hand was sought in marriage by a "ferocious tyrent". Ursula had, however, taken vows of celibacy, and she and her father both feared to break their vows. Ursula, pondering over her unfortunate predicament, bethought her of an expedient for at least deferring her nuptials with the "tyrent". She agreed to his proposals, subject to only one condition, which was, that ten beautiful virgins, of suitable age, should be given to her, and that each should be accompanied by a thousand damsels all vowed to virginity, and that they should all be allowed to sail about in eleven boats for not less than three years, unmolested by any man.

Ursula trusted that these conditions would prove prohibitive, but her ardent suitor succeeded in collecting together all the required maidens, and presented them to her, with eleven beautiful galleys, in which they set forth on their three years' voyage. At the end of three years the wind chanced to carry them up the Rhine to Cologne, and then to Basle; thence they proceeded on foot to Rome on pilgrimage, and, returning to Cologne in the same manner, there fell in with the Huns, and were by those savage hoards slain. A church was built in Cologne, and dedicated to St Ursula; and there, to this day, the curious traveller may have the bones of these eleven thousand devoted virgins pointed out to him.

The Rev. S. Baring-Gould has made exhaustive researches into this legend of St. Ursula, and has carefully traced its gradual growth, and advisedly pronounces it to be "founded on paganism and buttressed with fraud", and he goes on to prove that "Ursula is no other than the Swabian goddess Ursel, or Hörsel, transformed into a Saint of the Christian calendar", and that she was indeed practically identical with the goddess Isis, whom he identifies with "Holda, or the Moon", "the wandering Isis, or Ursula, whom German poets love still to regard as sailing over heaven's deep in her silver boat".[1]

In literature the name has enjoyed some popularity, and instances of its occurrence may be found in *Much Ado About Nothing* by Shakespeare; *Bartholomew Fair* by Ben Jonson; *The Fortunes of Nigel* by Sir W. Scott; *Castle Dangerous* by Scott; *The Padlock* by Isaac Bickerstaff; *The Golden Legend* by Longfellow; and in *John Halifax, Gentleman*, by Miss Muloch.

VENETIA: see Beatrice.

VERA is Slavonic, and a common name in Russia. It signifies "faith". The name, now often given in England, with the variants Verra and Verania, comes from the Latin *vera*, meaning "a true woman".

[1] *Curious Myths of the Middle Ages*, S. Baring-Gould.

VERONICA is a compound name, and means "ideal Saint", or "true image of Christ".

It is a hybrid, being derived from the Latin *verus* = true, and the Greek *eikon* = figure, image, or likeness.

It is a very ancient Christian name, and first found favour with the multitude through a curious and very obscure legend of the Roman Church, which stated that the impress of the Saviour's face was left upon a handkerchief used by a devout attendant to wipe from His brow the drops of agony which fell as He passed along to Mount Calvary bearing His Cross.

From *vera eikonica* has thus come the name Veronica, the image being, as it were, personified in the person of a female saint, who is otherwise quite unknown.

St Veronica of Milan, who lived in the fifteenth century, and who began life as a poor working girl, greatly added to the glory of this name, which has for long enjoyed a considerable measure of popularity.

VICTORIA, Victorine, and Victoriola have been derived from the Latin verb *vinco*, with its past participle *victus*, which has also given us Vincent, Victor, Victorian, in the masculine. It signifies Conqueror, and, applied to the early Christians, was singularly appropriate, as through their faith they withstood and overcame the temptations and horrors of persecution. It was consequently bestowed on many who gave their lives for their religion, both men and women.

The first of these whose name has come down to us was a Roman virgin who suffered martyrdom during the Decian persecution, and two others, since canonized, suffered at about the same time, namely at the beginning (c. 284) of the reign of Decius. These two were St. Victorinus and St. Victor. They suffered in company with five others. Their constancy having first been tried by racks, scourges and other tortures. Decius caused Victorinus to be cast into a great marble mortar, wherein his feet and legs were first pounded up, and finally his head.

The sight of his endurance fired Victor with a like zeal, so that he pointed to the terrible instrument of torture, the mortar, saying "In that is salvation and true felicity prepared for me"; whereupon he was cast into it and pounded to death.

Another who has added to the lustre and popularity of the name was a hermit known as St. Victor de Plancy, who dwelt in solitude at Saturniac in the diocese of Troyes. Of him marvellous things are related by St. Bernard and others. On one occasion, according to his biographer, Victor had sent out some labourers to sow wheat. One of the men yielded to temptation and stole two bushels of the seed. He became straightway possessed of a devil, who caused smoke and fire to issue from his mouth; but St. Victor took pity on the man, and, making the sign of the Cross, drove the devil out.

The man aware of the cause of his calamity,

and grateful to St. Victor for his rescue, repented of and confessed his crime. The hermit's saintly reputation induced Chilperic, King of France, to visit him, and the holy man, welcoming the King with a kiss of peace, offered him hospitality. He had, however, nothing in his cell to offer save a little water, so he fell on his knees and prayed that the vessel which held the water might become filled with heavenly dew, making the sign of the Cross over it as he prayed, and lo! forthwith the pitcher was filled with most excellent wine.

St. Victor was much favoured by visions and ecstacies, and on one occasion beheld the vision which Isaiah had beheld in the year that King Uzziah had died. "I saw the Lord sitting upon a throne, high and lifted up, and his train filled the temple. Above him stood the seraphim: each one had six wings; with twain he covered his face and with twain he covered his feet, and with twain he did fly. And one cried unto another, and said, Holy, holy, holy, is the Lord of hosts: and the whole earth is full of His glory. And the foundations of the thresholds were moved at the voice of him that cried, and the house was filled with smoke".

On another occasion Victor saw the heavens open, and in their midst he beheld a golden cross studded with precious stones more brilliant than stars, and as he gazed he heard a voice saying, "These precious stones which you see set in the cross are the souls of saints, who for the love of Christ have washed their robes and made them white in the blood of the Lamb".

Another martyr, Saint Victor of Damascus, was summoned before the tribunal of Sebastian for being a Christian, and, upon his declining to renounce his faith, was subjected to horrible tortures: his fingers were broken, his skin flayed, and then he was cast into a fiery furnace, wherein he remained for three days without taking any harm. After this, according to the tradition, he was again placed under torture; but felt none of them by reason of his great faith, for which he "was called Victor, for he was victorious over the feebleness of nature, the rage of demons, and the savagery of man".

Saint Victorian, proconsul of Carthage, is yet another who has upheld the glory of this name by suffering martyrdom for the Faith. Of noble birth and a native of Adrumetum, he was for years held in great favour by Huneric, the king of the Vandals, whom he served faithfully; but suddenly Huneric entered upon a crusade against the Christians in his dominions, and Victorian, with many of his co-religionists, was called upon to abjure his faith. This he declined to do, boldly answering "nothing will make me consent to renounce the Catholic Church in which I have been baptised". Furious at his answer, the king ordered that many terrible tortures should be applied, all of which Victorian "suffered with great joy", and under which he died.

The masculine form of Vincent has many representatives in early Church history: St. Vincent de Paul will at once occur to all, but except to allude to it this form of the name hardly concerns us here; and we will therefore pass on to a noble Italian woman and poetess, Vittoria Colonna.

She was born about the year 1490, and was the daughter of Fabrizio Colonna, Grand Constable of Naples, and, on her mother's side, the grand-daughter of the Duke of Urbino. She was therefore of noble birth, and at the age of nineteen married an eminent soldier, Ferdinand, afterwards Marquis of Pescara. Her husband died in 1525. Vittoria and her husband had been quite exceptionally happy together, and upon his death, though still young and very beautiful, Vittoria withdrew to the Island of Ischia, where she led a solitary life, declining all offers of marriage —and she had many—and devoting herself to literature. Her poetry, of which she wrote much, is inspired by her great sorrow and devout religious faith.

The friend of most of the leading spirits of the age, she was especially the friend of Michael Angelo, who alludes to her on several occasions in his sonnets in terms of the highest admiration and affection, and who visited her during her last illness. Vittoria Colonna died at Rome in 1547.

The names of Victor and Vittoria have always been very popular with the reigning houses of Italy; but with us they have not been common in any rank of life until the present century, though there are examples of them in English literature, as, for instance, Victor Amadeus in *King Victor and King Charles Emanuel*, by Robert Browning; Donna Victoria, in *A Bold Stroke for a Husband*, by Mrs. Cowley; and Victorian in *The Spanish Student*, by Henry Wadsworth Longfellow; but during the present age, owing to the devotion felt by the English for their Queen, the feminine form of the name has become very popular. Innumerable little girls, whose fortune it was to be born in the year of Her Majesty's Jubilee 1887, received the name; and their number was increased a hundredfold on the occasion of the Diamond Jubilee in 1897.

Years ago, when she was still Elizabeth Barrett, our greatest modern English poetess wrote the following lines, called forth by the fact that when Queen Victoria first heard of her accession to the throne she wept, overcome by the sense of the responsibilities she was about to assume at an age when most young girls are still free to consult their own ease and pleasure:—

O Maiden! heir of kings!
A king has left his place!
The Majesty of Death has swept
All other from his face!
And thou upon thy mother's breast
No longer lean adown,
But take the glory for the rest,
And rule the land that loves thee best!
She heard and wept,
She wept to wear a crown!

. . . . . .

God bless thee, weeping Queen,
With blessing more divine!
And fill with happier love than earth's
That tender heart of thine!
That when the thrones of earth shall be
As low as graves brought down,
A pierced hand may give to thee
The crown which angels shout to see!
Thou wilt not *weep*
To wear that heavenly crown!

Victoria's Tears (Elizabeth Barrett Browning.)

That is over sixty years ago, and looking back through those long years all will admit that the young girl-Queen's highest aspirations have been nobly fulfilled, and the poet's lines are not empty flattery—

Her court was pure; her life serene;
God gave her peace; her land repose;
A thousand claims to reverence closed
In her as Mother, Wife, and Queen.
(Tennyson.)

But the biographies and records published on the occasion of the Diamond Jubilee are still too fresh in the popular memory to need recapitulation here. At the time of the Queen's Jubilee in 1887, Lord Tennyson, then our Poet Laureate, wrote—

Fifty times the rose has flower'd and faded,
Fifty times the golden harvest fallen,
Since our Queen assumed the globe, the sceptre.

. . . . .

Fifty years of ever-broadening Commerce!
Fifty years of ever-brightening Science!
Fifty years of ever-widening Empire!

and in 1897 England was almost overwhelmed with odes, sonnets, and songs in honour of her who is probably the most widely and sincerely loved Queen the world has ever known.

Wherever sounds the wave or blows the wind,
Thy name is sounded and thy fame is blown,
Queen of the Seas, and Empress of the Ind,
Great and our own.

Yet not for thy vast realm, thy peerless might,
Not for thy length of reign, nor length of days
(Which God increase with honour and delight)
Alone our praise;

But for thy stainless life, the heritage
Of all; the pattern fair, in Court and home,
To every maid and wife, in this thine age
And those to come.
(Cosmo Monkhouse.)

Stand up all! Yes princes, nobles, peoples,
All the mighty Empire—mightier ne'er hath been;
Boom from all your decks and towers, clang from all your steeples
God save Victoria, God save the Queen!
(*Punch.*)

She wrought her people lasting good.
(Tennyson.)

VIOLET, Viola, Violetta, Violante, Yolande, Yelette, and Joletta, are of course all the same, and symbolically mean "modest grace".

The name of the flower which we know as violet is almost universally the same—in Latin *viola*, in Sanskrit *vas*, in Greek *ion*, and the beauty, retiring nature, and above all the exquisite scent of the flower, have made it a universal favourite. Hence its popularity as a girl's name.

In Northern Europe violets were of old employed as one of the flowers necessary to the making up of a bride's bouquet, and the March violet, or Sweet violet, [*viola Martis*] was in Old-Norse called *Tys-fiola* and dedicated to the fighting god of the North, Tyr.

The violet plant is frequently mentioned by Homer and Virgil, besides other classical authors, and an old tradition states that the violet was raised by Diana from the body of Io.

Shakespeare alludes to this belief at the burial of Ophelia, when Laertes says:

> "Lay her i' the earth,
> And from her fair and unpolluted flesh
> May violets spring".

The Greek name for this flower *ἰωνιά* (*ionia*) is said by some to have arisen from the belief that Io fed on violets, when she was by Jupiter transformed into a heifer; whilst others believe that the flower was called after some nymphs of Ionia, who were the first to present the flower to the Father of the Gods.

The violet was the badge of Athens; and orators when they wanted to win favour with the people used to address them as "Athenians crowned with violets"! One of the prizes at the games which took place at the festival dedicated to the goddess Flora, was a Golden Violet.

The Greeks and Romans, and the Hindus, besides other Eastern peoples, were in the habit of dedicating particular flowers to individual gods and goddesses, as for example the poppy to Ceres, the anemone to Venus, the myrtle to Artemis, etc., and in the *History of Sacrifices* attributed to Ovid we are told that "in the old days the knife of the present day had no employment in the sacred rites. The altar used to send forth its smoke contented with Sabine herbs, and the laurel was burned with no crackling noise. If there was anyone who could add violets to the chaplets wrought from the flower of the meadow, he was a rich man".

VIOLET

Though with the Athenians the rose ranked highest, the violet was much beloved by them, and Alcibiades went to Agatho crowned with violets and ivy.

The violet has in France been especially associated with the Buonaparte dynasty, an association which is said to have arisen at the time when the first Napoleon was banished to the Island of Elba.

The story goes that, as he was leaving, he prophesied that he would "return again in the violet season"; thus, during his absence, the violet became the secret badge of his followers, by which they recognized and communicated with one another. His party also wore violet-coloured rings with the motto engraved upon them *Elle reparaîtra au printemps* [it will reappear in the spring], and amongst his followers he was toasted as General or Corporal Violet. Upon his escape from Elba he was, on his return to the Tuileries, greeted with bunches of violets. During the reign of Louis XVIII. it was considered seditious to wear violets; and upon the return to power of the Napoleonic dynasty the violet again came into favour.

Farewell to thee, France! but when Liberty rallies,
  Once more in thy regions remember me then—
The Violet still grows in the depths of thy valleys,
  Though withered, thy tears will unfold it again.
(LORD BYRON.)

The French people loved to draw a parallel between the little flower which grew in obscurity and retained its odour after death, and the great soldier, who, born in obscurity like it, rose to occupy the throne of the Golden Lilies, and still exercised a spell over his fellow-beings after he had himself ceased to live.

The *colour* violet is supposed to indicate "love of truth" and "truth of love"; but in the symbolic language of flowers *all* violets betoken modest grace, yet going into details we find that the blue variety betokens faithfulness, the white innocence, and the wild yellow rural happiness. An old sixteenth-century sonnet runs:

> Violet is for faithfulnesse,
> Which in me shall abide;
> Hoping likewise that from your heart
> You will not let it slide.

Shakespeare, who seems to have had the popular flower-lore of his day at his fingers' ends, must have surely thought of the emblematic meaning of the name, when he bestowed that of Viola upon what is perhaps the sweetest and most retiring of all his group of loveable women —we mean Viola in *Twelfth Night*, who "never told her love".

In speaking, V easily changes into Y, and thus in France out of Violante developed Yolande, a pretty name which is now beginning to be adopted in England: the old-fashioned and rather funny-sounding name of Joletta, met with in old English parish-registers, must have originally come from Violetta.

Scotland is the especial home of Violet, probably because, as a race, the Scots are so fond of flowers, and for centuries Violet has been a popular name there. In England the name was introduced from Italy in 1362, when Lionel, Duke of Clarence, the son of Edward III., married Violante, a daughter of the Duke of Milan. As Lionel made his home in Ireland the name may have been introduced into that country at the same time.

In DRAMA the name occurs often, for besides Viola in *Twelfth Night* mentioned above, Shakespeare has a Violenta in *All's well that ends well*, and there is Donna Violenta in *The Wonder* by Mrs. Centlivre; Violenta in *The Spanish Curate* by Fletcher; Viola in *The Loyal Subject* by Beaumont and Fletcher.

In POETRY Violante in *Don Sebastian* by Dryden; Violante in *The Ring and the Book* by Robert Browning; and *A most lamentable and tragicall Historie, which a Spanishe Gentlewoman named Violenta executed upon her Lover Didaco, because he espoused another, beying first betrothed unto her*: newly translated into English meter by T[homas] A[cheley] (1576); and D. G. Rossetti has a poem called *Albertuccio della Viola*, beginning:

> Among the dancers I beheld her dance,
> Her who alone is my heart's sustenance.

In FICTION Sir W. Scott introduces a Violente into his novel *Count Robert of Paris*; Lord Lytton has a Violet in *The Sea Captain*, and a Violente in *My Novel*; and one of Black's best novels is *Madcap Violet*; there is a Violenta, too, in the fairy-tale of *The White Cat* by the Comtesse D'Aulnoy (1682).

We will close by quoting from J. R. Lowell's poem:

Violet! sweet violet!
Thine eyes are full of tears;
Are they wet
Even yet
With the thought of other years?
Or with gladness are they full,
For the night so beautiful,
And longing for those far-off spheres?

Loved one of my youth thou wast,
Of my merry youth,
And I see,
Tearfully,
All the fair and sunny past,
All its openness and truth,
Ever fresh and green in thee
As the moss is in the sea.

Thy little heart, that hath with love
Grown coloured like the sky above,
On which thou lookest ever,—
Can it know
All the woe
Of hope for what returneth never,
All the sorrow and the longing
To these hearts of ours belonging?

Out on it! no foolish pining
For the sky
Dims thine eye,
Or for the stars so calmly shining;
Like thee let this soul of mine
Take hue from that wherefor I long,
Self-stayed and high, serene and strong,
Not satisfied with hoping—but divine.

Violet! dear violet!
Thy blue eyes are only wet
With joy and love of Him who sent thee,
And for the fulfilling sense
Of that glad obedience
Which made thee all that Nature meant thee!

VIRGINIA. Many assume that the name Virginia, or Virginie, is derived from the Latin *virgo*, a virgin ; whereas its origin really is the Latin *ver*, spring ; and the name should be interpreted as "flourishing" : its original spelling was Verginia, and it was a common enough name in ancient Rome, where it belonged to a plebeian *gens*.

Over the Alban mountains the light of morning broke ;
From all the roofs of the Seven Hills curled the thin wreaths of smoke ;
And blithely young Virginia came smiling from her home :
Ah ! woe for young Virginia, the sweetest maid in Rome !
With her small tablets in her hand, and her satchel on her arm,
Forth she went bounding to the school, nor dreamed of shame or harm.
She crossed the Forum shining with stalls in alleys gay,
And just had reached the very spot whereon I stand this day,
When up the varlet Marcus came ; . . . .
He came with lowering forehead, swollen features, and clenched fist,
And strode across Virginia's path, and caught her by the wrist.

Virginia (MACAULAY.)

We all know the story of Appius Claudius and young Virginia, upon which so many tragedies have been founded in England, France, and Germany. Of these the English are *Appius and Virginia* by Webster, *Virginia, a tragedy* by Frances Brooke, and *Virginius* by J. Sheridan Knowles.

Bernardin de St. Pierre's romance *Paul et Virginie*, which has been dramatised in English by Cobb, made the name popular in France.

VIVIEN, VIVIAN, VYVYAN, VYVIAN. This name comes from the Latin *viva* = alive (feminine), and is used for both men and women alike.

Four Christians, two women and two men —St. Vivia Perpetua, St. Bibiana or Viviana, St. Vitalis, and St. Vitus—have shed glory upon the name by suffering martyrdom for the truth, whilst a fifth, a Scot by birth, became a bishop, and was afterwards canonized and known as St. Bibianus. The disease known as St. Vitus's dance is called after the saint, on account of the power he was supposed to possess over nervous ailments. His name and that of St. Vitalis is connected with the Latin *vita* = life, itself from the same root as *viva.*

In early romance we all know of Vivien, the beguiler of the magician Merlin, who

> once had told her of a charm,
> The which if any wrought on anyone
> With woven paces and with waving arms,
> The man so wrought on ever seem'd to lie
> Closed in the four walls of a hollow tower,
> From which was no escape for evermore;
>
> . . . . . .
>
> And Vivien even sought to work the charm
> Upon the great Enchanter of the Time.
>
> *Merlin and Vivien* (TENNYSON.)

The name has of late years become fashionable, perhaps through Tennyson's *Idylls*, though the wily Vivien of Arthur's court seems to be a curious prototype to select for any child, whether boy or girl.

Vivian Grey, a novel by Lord Beaconsfield,

enjoyed an immense popularity at one time, and is still read on account of its supposed autobiographical incidents. A Viviana is the heroine in *Guy Fawkes* by Harrison Ainsworth.

WILHELMINA is a common name for women in Germany, and has been introduced thence with some success into England. Wilmett is the true English feminine of William, but though more musical in sound and less clumsy than Wilhelmina, it has almost died out amongst us. The English diminutives are Minnie and Mina, and very occasionally Minella.

The name means either "helmet of resolution", "helm of resolution", "helmet of many", or "helm of many", according to various derivations.

The Icelandic word *hialmr* means "helmet", the Saxon *helma* means "helm", a word that to this day bears the same meaning in Germany and in England, that is, the upper part of a rudder. According to Mr Skeat and other good authorities, *wil* = will or resolution, whilst older but now partially discredited authorities derive it from the German *viel* = many.

In any case the bearers of the name should fit themselves to be the defenders or the guides of others.

WINIFRED: see Gwendolen.
YOLANDE: see Violet.
ZOE: see Eva.